DIVERSITY and
LEADERSHIP

Jean Lau Chin
Adelphi University

Joseph E. Trimble
Western Washington University

Los Angeles | London | New Delhi
Singapore | Washington DC

Los Angeles | London | New Delhi
Singapore | Washington DC

FOR INFORMATION:

SAGE Publications, Inc.

2455 Teller Road

Thousand Oaks, California 91320

E-mail: order@sagepub.com

SAGE Publications Ltd.

1 Oliver's Yard

55 City Road

London, EC1Y 1SP

United Kingdom

SAGE Publications India Pvt. Ltd.

B 1/I 1 Mohan Cooperative Industrial Area

Mathura Road, New Delhi 110 044

India

SAGE Publications Asia-Pacific Pte. Ltd.

3 Church Street

#10–04 Samsung Hub

Singapore 049483

Printed in the United States of America

Library of Congress Cataloging-in-Publication Data

Chin, Jean Lau.

Diversity and leadership / Jean Lau Chin, Adelphi University, Joseph E. Trimble, Western Washington University.

pages cm

Includes bibliographical references and index.

ISBN 978-1-4522-5789-1 (pbk. : alk. paper)

1. Leadership. 2. Leadership—Cross-cultural studies.
3. Minorities. I. Trimble, Joseph E. II. Title.

HM1261.C455 2015

658.4′092—dc23

2014009868

This book is printed on acid-free paper.

Acquisitions Editor: Maggie Stanley

Editorial Assistant: Georgia McLaughlin

Production Editor: Stephanie Palermini

Copy Editor: Kimberly Hill

Typesetter: Hurix Systems Pvt. Ltd.

Proofreader: Dennis Webb

Indexer: Maria Sosnowski

Cover Designer: Anupama Krishnan

Marketing Manager: Liz Thornton

MIX
Paper from
responsible sources
FSC
www.fsc.org FSC® C014174

14 15 16 17 18 10 9 8 7 6 5 4 3 2 1

DIVERSITY and
LEADERSHIP

Brief Contents

Detailed Contents

Preface

Many talk of the business case for diversity to justify the importance of promoting diversity in an organization. It is simply good business to be responsive to diverse customers and diverse staff. As the population becomes increasingly diverse in many countries and institutions worldwide, it is also socially responsible for organizations and leaders to attend to diversity. This includes the theories and practices that we use to understand, exercise, and appraise leadership, especially when enacted by diverse leaders not typically in the ranks of leadership. The purpose of this book is to

- Expand the existing perspectives on leadership to be inclusive of diversity that is currently largely based on North American and Euro American male norms.
- Introduce other perspectives from international and minority groups in which different worldviews and cultural orientation values may prevail.
- Expect diverse responses. Leaders and potential leaders with privileged social identities may express surprise and hopefully be open to different perspectives and values as ways to expand their own exercise of leadership. Leaders and potential leaders with less privileged social identities may feel an affirmation for leadership styles and behaviors that do not fit that of the "prototypic" leader.

Together, new paradigms for diversity leadership will emerge, which will be relevant to a diverse and global society. While we underscore repeatedly the importance of context in this book, the focus is on how leaders lead, what influences the enactment of leadership and the interaction or exchange that occurs between members and leader. We hope to challenge the teaching/learning of leadership by addressing difference and the cultural competence of leaders, members, and organizations in the exercise of leadership. We recognize that there can be a dark side to leadership. In offering new perspectives, we offer them not as examples of ideal leadership; rather, we offer them as paradigms that recognize the changing demographics within organizations and societies and the increasing demand on leaders to lead a diverse workforce (both locally and internationally) as well as the increasing entry of racial/ethnic minority groups and women into leadership roles.

This book is intended for leaders and potential leaders, graduate and undergraduate-level students in courses on diversity, leadership, management, and multiculturalism; and those interested in leadership and how it influences the lives of organizations. It is intended for those in fields of business, psychology, gender studies, and sociology to understand the role of leadership in advancing social and organizational outcomes.

The structure of the book is organized around introducing concepts of diversity and multiculturalism into the study of leadership. The first three chapters contextualize this goal as important to 21st century leadership and define the relevance of diversity concepts to leadership. We feel this is missing in the literature today. The next four chapters address leader identity, leadership style, societal, and organizational contexts as to how they shape the exercise of leadership and of leaders themselves. The last two chapters address the importance of leadership training and the need for new and alternative paradigms of leadership to be relevant to the 21st century.

The scope of the book focuses on diverse leaders and leadership within diverse contexts. It differs from diversity books that focus on promoting diversity as an organizational goal or those that focus on leadership without attention to issues of diversity. While we recognize there are many dimensions of diversity, this book is limited to race, ethnicity, gender, and sexual orientation largely because these are visible dimensions that are salient in society according of privilege to one or more of its statuses. While religion, socioeconomic status (SES), and disability have also influenced our perceptions of leadership, there is little study of these dimensions vis-à-vis leadership. While we hope this diversity perspective will promote dialogue and organizational and societal change to incorporate diversity as a goal, the intent of the book is to promote awareness, skill development, and training of diverse leaders to effectively lead in the 21st century. We do this by identifying cross-cultural and cross-group differences in leadership styles and in understanding the importance of multiple and intersecting social identities on the exercise of leadership. We draw on empirical research where it exists but are mindful of using a grounded theory approach to identify phenomena that may not be found in existing theories.

Acknowledgments

There are many contributors to the production of this book who need to be acknowledged. My graduate students have contributed dauntless hours to the interviewing of leaders, collecting and analysis of data, and transcription of tapes. I thank Joshua Dietz, Monica Pal, Wen Li, Sunia Choudry, Hui Mei Nan, Vanessa Li, and Lauren Moy for their assistance. Joseph Trimble extends his gratitude to his students for their thoughtful assistance: Lanen Vaughn, Lisa Greene, and Maggie Montgomery.

In using a grounded theory approach, the leaders themselves, as participants, have contributed significantly with their time, their expertise, and their lived experiences in helping build the paradigm for Diversity Leadership. These include the past presidents of Division 45: The Society for the Psychological Study of Race, Ethnicity, and Culture; the leaders, observers, and committee participants of the Diversity Leadership Summit held January 2013 in Houston, TX, especially Lyne Desormeaux, Pam Remer, and Katina Sawyer; and the many leaders who were surveyed and interviewed for the studies.

We would also like to thank the following reviewers for their valuable feedback:

Marilyn Y. Byrd, University of Mary Hardin-Baylor; Richard Cooper, Lindenwood University; Charles Flemming, McKendree College; Kimberly Hunley, Northern Arizona State; Jason Kanov, Western Washington University; Henry Lawrence, California State University, Long Beach; Carmela R. Nanton, MacArthur School of Leadership, Palm Beach Atlantic University; Denise T. Ogden; Penn State—Lehigh Valley; June Schmieder, Pepperdine University; Chaunda L. Scott, Oakland University; Leslie Shore, Metropolitan State University; Jean Gabriel Starika-Jolivet, Ashford University; and Al Zainea, Central Michigan University, Global Campus.

The cover design was recommended by Molly E. Trimble and modified by Stephanie Friesen. We extend our deepest gratitude to them for their creative suggestions and thoughtfulness.

—Jean Lau Chin

Leadership for the 21st Century

Notable Quote: On 21st Century Leadership

"Leadership is an influence relationship among leaders and followers who intend real changes that reflect their mutual purposes" (Rost, 1991, p. 102).

"Besides practical needs, there are important reasons to examine the impact of culture on leadership" (House, Javidan, Hanges, & Dorfman, 2002, p. 3).

Vignette on "How to Become a Great Leader"

. . . But today's crises never completely mirror yesterday's, and it would be better in the first place to build leaders who can prevent crises before they arise. In my view, a great leader is inspiring, uplifting, a uniter of differences, and someone who brings out the best in human aspirations. I named this model "the soul of leadership" and set out to see if leaders with a soul could be trained. Knowing that business, politics, and the military are not spiritual enterprises, I didn't formulate the training along "soft" or idealistic lines. Instead, I used a "hard" criterion: what groups actually need. If you aspire to be a great leader, the first requirement is that you look and listen so that you can find out the true needs that a situation demands to be fulfilled. (Chopra, 2013, p. 1)

Leadership today is more important than ever as the 21st century brings about rapid and significant change in society and our institutions and challenges the way in which we do business and function in organizational settings. Our future will be different from what our reality is today. Our skills and how we practice them in the future are likely to be unknown to us today. We need to prepare our citizens to serve as leaders during times of uncertainty and equip them with skills that we may not even know exist if they are to be relevant and effective as leaders. What kind of leaders do we prepare and train our citizens to become? The psychology of leadership should add to our understanding of who become our leaders, what the process of communication and exchange is between leaders and their members, how leaders and members develop shared outcomes, and what the nature of the organizations in which leadership occurs is. Answers to these questions will, in turn, have implications for how we select our leaders, how leaders access leadership roles, and how leaders exercise leadership once in these roles.

Schwartz (2010) talks about how humanity has entered three great transformations. The first occurred when human beings moved from a survival strategy of hunting and gathering to a state of civilization based on agriculture. The second began with the Industrial Revolution of the mid-20th century. We are now on the cusp of the third Great Transformation—the revolutionary advance of science and technology. This has also been coined the Digital Age, a time in which the world about us is changing rapidly because of advances in technology, communication, and mobility. Schwartz summarizes how we are seeing dramatic increases in life, new patterns of human migration, a consortium of nations bound together by their common need for lawful collaboration as well as groups able to unleash terror and disruption to the rest of the world.

Changing Population Demographics: Multicultural Perspectives

While nations were presumably homogenous in the racial and ethnic make-up of their populations during the 20th century, researchers could construct profiles of national character and identity. The United States has been no different in creating the image of an American; although uniquely known as a "land of immigrants," it led the movement toward diversity. It is ironic that its main symbol of the "American dream" as a "land of equal opportunity" ignores its history of having nearly obliterated its indigenous population, the American Indians, enslaved the Black American population, and promoted a melting pot myth based on the expectation of conformity by new immigrants to a White and Westernized image of being American. During the 19th century, the United States saw the end to slavery but not to segregation based on race and gender. Following WWII in the 20th century, the look inward within the United States promoted racial and gender equality in the workforce. With a growing non-White racial and ethnic minority population, demands for attention to diversity escalated. Predictions were that by the year 2050, shifting population demographics would result in non-White racial/ethnic groups becoming 50% of the U.S. population (U.S. Census Bureau, 2013). Hence, an attention to diversity was considered good business, quality services, and ethical practice. Questions of equity and representation, typified by the Civil Rights and Women's movements of the 1960s, framed the debate.

Now in the 21st century, diversity has given way to globalism. The growth of multinational organizations mirrors the increasing diversity of the U.S. population and communities—challenging our notions of effective management strategies while diverse individuals also seek and gain access to leadership roles. We now see our world, our institutions, our communities, and countries throughout the world facing changing population demographics and becoming increasingly more global and diverse. Many countries globally are now more heterogeneous due to ease of migration, changing economic conditions, and the growth of multinational organizations. Ethnic minority groups in the United States and globally share a common experience of oppression and discrimination; they increasingly demand equality and access to society's resources. Women dare to challenge the masculinized social norm in countries such as Saudi Arabia and Iran. Although many societies have evolved to promote greater gender equality, gender access to "simple" things, such as an education or what a woman wears, still gives rise to violence against women.

Malala Yousafzai, a 15-year-old Pakistani schoolgirl, was shot in the head and neck in an assassination attempt by a Taliban gunman while on a school bus in October 2012 because she was campaigning for girls' education (Ellis, 2013). Since the age of 11, using a pseudonym, she had been writing a blog for the BBC. She has been hailed as an inspiration for her bravery, and will receive the Tipperary International Peace Award. Other women have been gang raped, burned with acid, or beaten for daring to drive in the 21st century. The world now responds with indignation, unlike earlier centuries where women were burned at the stake like Joan of Arc for heresy at the age of 19 and the "witches" of Salem where no one dared to protest. In these contexts, cultural norms and beliefs are so strong about gender role expectations they have led to discrimination and violence.

Countries face intergroup conflicts because of the historical dominance of one or more groups. Civil wars, intergroup tension, and violence arise because of religious, ethnic, or racial differences. Power and privilege are associated with those from dominant groups while prevailing culture norms and beliefs often render these inequities invisible. In the United States, skin color and race dividing Black versus White has been the predominant divider while religion has divided Muslims between Shiite versus Sunni in the Middle East. The Indian caste system, a traditional organization of South Asian, particularly Hindu, society divides people into a hierarchy of hereditary groups called castes, which were traditionally associated with an occupational monopoly such as weaving or barbering. The caste system, currently banned, was increasingly criticized as a discriminatory and unjust system of social stratification in the early 20th century especially in regard to the impoverished untouchables—hence a socioeconomic status (SES) division.

The Indian government has, for decades, implemented affirmative action programs, education, and job reservations for people previously considered untouchables and in lowest castes (now known as the *Dalits*, or "crushed people").

Changing Demographics and Ethnic Distributions

The U.S. Census Bureau predicts that by 2050, the U.S. population will reach more than 600 million, about 47% larger than in the year 2010 (U.S. Census Bureau, 2013). The primary ethnic minority groups—namely, Latinas and Latinos, African Americans, Asian Americans, American Indians, Alaska Natives, Native Hawaiians, and Pacific Islanders—will constitute over 50% of the population. About 57% of the population younger than age 18 and 34% older than age 65 will be ethnic minorities (U.S. Census Bureau, 2013). The demographic profile based on the 2010 census indicates that during the past decade (2000), the growth rate of Latinos was eight times faster than that of Whites. Asian Americans and Pacific Islanders also had a rapid growth rate in part because of immigration from Southeast Asia and China. For Latinos, increased immigration and high birth rates explain the population increase. Projections for the year 2020 suggest that Latinos will be the largest ethnic group, second only to White Americans, and followed by African Americans.

Currently, Latinos and Latinas number 51 million persons, about 16% of the U.S. population (U.S. Census Bureau, 2013), and comprise a diversity of races and countries of origin (e.g., Mexico, Puerto Rico, Cuba, Colombia, Argentina). The largest groups of Latinos and Latinas are Mexican Americans (63%); next are Puerto Ricans (9%), followed by Cubans (4%). Collective countries from Central America (8%) and South Americans (6%) represent higher percentages than Puerto Rico and Cuba though.

The estimates indicate that African Americans number about 35 million people (U.S. Census Bureau, 2013). Among them are notable group differences in terms of socioeconomic levels, urban or rural areas, and within-group cultural variation. Much of the psychological treatment of African Americans has focused on the relation of social conditions, such as poverty and unemployment, to adverse health and mental health outcomes (Rodríguez, Allen, Frongillo, & Chandra, 1999). However, a growing number of African American scholars have demonstrated the need for more examination of cultural strengths such as communalism (Mattis & Jagers, 2001), spirituality, and an interpersonal orientation (emphasis on group over individual) (Randolph & Banks, 1993).

Asian Americans number 14,674,252 and Pacific Islanders and Native Hawaiians number 540,013 in the United States (U.S. Census Bureau, 2013). There are 32 different cultural groups with distinct ethnic or national identities and different religions, histories, languages, and traditions that are included within the category of Asian American. The most numerous Asian groups in the United States are Filipinos, Chinese, Koreans, Japanese, Vietnamese, and Asian Indians. As with other immigrants, Asian immigrants have migrated to the United States for political and economic reasons and face the stresses of acculturation, racism, and language barriers.

On the basis of the 2010 census, the U.S. Census Bureau (2013) declared that 2,932,248 citizens are American Indians and Alaska Natives—an 18% difference from the 2000 census, when the figure was 2,475,956. The 2010 count represents less than one tenth of 1% of the total U.S. population of 308,745,538. On the basis of the 1960 census, the Census Bureau reported that 552,000 residents of the United States were American Indians (in 1960, the Census Bureau did not include an Alaska Native category, so this figure may be an undercount). Thus, between 1960 and 2010, the American Indian population apparently grew by over 400%. This rapid population increase is staggering and strains credulity, because such rates of increase are almost unheard of in the field of demography. One explanation for the increase may be that many more individuals chose to identify with their American Indian heritage in 2010 than did so in 1960 and 2010 (U.S. Census Bureau, 2013).

Considering the increasing ethnic and cultural diversity occurring in the United States, attention should be given to the growing Muslim population. According to a recent survey, Muslims represent about 2% of the U.S. populations. A 2011 study conducted by the Pew Foundation found that the majority of Muslims are African Americans, Arabs, and Asians and that overall Muslims come from 77 different countries (Pew Research Center, 2011). The U.S. Census Bureau does not collect information on one's religious affiliation or preferences; hence, the census tallies on the Muslim populations are estimates. Muslims are immigrant populations and thus their cultural backgrounds contribute to the growing diversity in the United States.

Although there is overlap with the Muslim population, there are also growing numbers of immigrants from Arab speaking countries. According to the Arab American Institute (AAI), countries of origin for Arab Americans include 21 different groups with distinct ethnic or national identities, histories, languages, and traditions; these include the following: Egypt, Iraq, Jordan, Kuwait, Lebanon, Morocco, Palestine, Saudi Arabia, Somalia, Sudan, and Syria. In 2008, there were 3,500,000 Arab Americans, accounting for 1.14% of the American population. The largest subgroup is by far the Lebanese Americans, with 501,907, nearly a third of the Arab American population, followed by Egyptians and Syrians.

In the 2000 and 2010 census, individuals had the option of marking more than one "race" category and so were able to declare identification with more than one group. For example, whereas less than 3% of the total U.S. population chose to do so, more than 5,220,579 individuals who chose to mark multiple categories marked "American Indian and Alaska Native" along with one or more others. The "race alone or in combination" count is much higher than the "race alone" counts of 2,932,248 (U.S. Census Bureau, 2013). The discrepancy raises the question about which count is more accurate or representative of the "true" Indian population, 2,932,248 or 5,220,579.

Native Hawaiians and other Pacific Islanders listed more "race alone or in combination" (55.9%) than any other race group. American Indians and Alaska Natives followed with 43.8%, Asian were 15.3%, Black or African American were at 74%, and White was at 3.2% (U.S. Census Bureau, 2013).

People with mixed ethnic backgrounds present interesting ethnic identity cases because they have at least two ethnic groups from which to claim and negotiate an ethnic declaration. Based on extensive interviews with people of mixed ethnic background, the clinical psychologist Maria P. Root (1992) identified four basic reasons why a multiethnic person would choose to identify with a particular group regardless of how others may view them. Root maintains that: "(1) One enhances his or her sense of security by understanding a distinct part of his or her ethnic heritage; (2) parental influences stimulated by the encouragement of grandparents promote identity, thereby granting permission to the offspring to make a choice; (3) racism and prejudice associated with certain groups lead to sharing experiences with family, thereby assisting the individual to develop psychological skills and defenses to protect himself or herself (the shared experiences help build self-confidence and create the sense that one can cope with the negative elements often associated with the group); and (4) gender alignment between parents and children may exert influence on ethnic and racial socialization particularly when they have good relationships and are mutually held in esteem" (p. 15). Use of the new multiracial item created contentious debates and problems for all who relied on census outcomes to tabulate and report problems for health care professions, economists, demographers, and social and behavioral scientists (Perlmann & Waters, 2002). Prewitt (2002) believed that the addition of multiracial category represented a "turning point in the measurement of race . . . and that the arrival of a multiple-race option in the census classification will so blur racial distinctions in the political and legal spheres and in the public consciousness that race classification will gradually disappear" (p. 360). This is unlikely because minority groups will continue to remain and be visible and distinguish themselves from dominant groups because of dimensions of diversity associated with power and privilege.

As more and more people from various countries immigrate to the United States, the complexity and richness of the cultural landscape will change considerably. Immigration is happening elsewhere, and thus, the cultural landscapes are changing there too. On this point, Graeme Hugo (2005) maintains that "Global international migration is increasing exponentially not only in scale but also in the types of mobility and the cultural diversity of groups involved in that movement. As a result, more nations and communities will have to cope with increased levels of social and cultural diversity. Moreover, the nature of the migration itself is changing so that the lessons of the past with respect to coping with that diversity may no longer be appropriate. Experience in some parts of the world suggest that it may be difficult to reconcile the increasing diversity with social harmony and social cohesion" (p. 1).

The changing demographic context, both locally and globally, calls into question the relevance of leadership models that historically have not been inclusive of ethnic and racial groups and fostered a research agenda that was ethnocentric and bound by time and place. How well prepared will leaders be in leading a diverse workforce and providing products and services to a diverse clientele? What will we teach our future leaders as they become increasingly diverse? How will leadership models build a knowledge base that can be generalized to the population as a whole? New priorities for research, teaching, and practice must be developed so that the body of knowledge about leadership will hold greater relevance and applicability. The changing demographics will inevitably move the field toward the full consideration of diversity in ways that are inclusive and reflect the diversity of our changing demographic context. The question is, how soon and with what tools?

The Challenge of Understanding and Defining Identity

Definitions of ethnic identity vary according to the underlying theory embraced by researchers' and scholars' intent on resolving its conceptual meanings. The fact that there is no widely agreed upon definition of ethnic identity is indicative of the confusion surrounding the topic. Typically, ethnic identity is an affiliate construct, where an individual is viewed by themselves and by others as belonging to a particular ethnic or cultural group. An individual can choose to associate with a group especially if other choices are available (i.e., the person is of mixed ethnic or racial heritage). Affiliation can be influenced by racial, natal, symbolic, and cultural factors (Cheung, 1993). Racial factors involve the use of physiognomic and physical characteristics, natal factors refer to "homeland" (ancestral home) or origins of individuals, their parents and kin, and symbolic factors include those factors that typify or exemplify an ethnic group (e.g., holidays, foods, clothing, artifacts). Symbolic ethnic identity usually implies that individuals choose their identity; however, to some extent the cultural elements of the ethnic or racial group have a modest influence on their behavior (Kivisto & Nefzger, 1993).

Understanding the meaning of race, ethnicity, and the minority experience is a challenge that requires conceptual and methodological tools. Despite the findings of the Human Genome Project that race does not appear to have a biological basis, race and ethnicity are constructs or categories that continue to be an integral aspect of our social fabric. Racial and ethnic categories are used to establish political and social structures, and these categories in turn are the result of social, historical, and political processes that continue to influence and define the experience of ethnic minority populations as well as nonethnic minority populations and leadership. It is often difficult to separate ethnicity and race from socioeconomic status, the experience of migration, acculturation, and discrimination. At times, the issue of race and ethnicity may serve as a proxy for other variables (e.g., socioeconomic status [SES], ethnic identity, acculturation, acculturative stress, racism, discrimination). On this point, Fearon (2003) makes an excellent point when he pointed out that, "There are often multiple plausible ways of partitioning 'ethnic groups' of a country. For example, the 11 largest groups listed for United States by the *Atlas Narodov Mira* are 'Americans (including Blacks), Jews, Germans, Italians, Mexicans, Poles, Irish, Swedes, Austrians, Puerto Ricans, and Anglo-Canadians'" (p. 214). This rendering of the United States' ethnic groups may be plausible, but is quite different from the White, Black, Hispanic, and Asians categories used in the census and by the social identities embraced by many in the United States. Changes in the terminology and designation of ethnic groups are underway where definitive attention is being given to the specificities of each designation. For example, in a large-scale study on patterns of ethnic and cultural diversity, James Fearon (2003) identified 822 "ethnoreligious" groups in 60 countries. He states that the concept of an *ethnic group* is inherently slippery.

The challenge in defining identity is to move away from simplistic categories of race and ethnicity and toward the development of constructs that reflect the true complexity of culture and ethnicity and its relationship to organizational psychology and leadership phenomena. Another challenge rests on focusing efforts on the study of leadership development and the influence and remediation of the consequences of racism, oppression, and discrimination. In doing so, we can understand how these lived experiences contribute to shaping and categorizing ethnic and cultural identities. Those who share minority status in their social identities may also share positions of marginality and experience perceptions and expectations based on these social categories.

Despite a growing and compelling body of work in the multicultural literature that argues against a universal approach to the study of human behavior, too many leadership scholars and researchers carry out their affairs as though a universal approach remains appropriate. Perhaps one reason for this pattern is the absence of a comprehensive resource about the critical issues of diversity and difference that need to be considered about leadership among diverse individuals. The myth of uniformity among ethnic minority groups is nearly dead, although researchers continue to use an *ethnic gloss*. "An ethnic gloss is an overgeneralization or simplistic categorical label used to refer to ethno-cultural groups such as American Indians, Asian Americans, Hispanics, African Americans, and other nationalistic or indigenous groups where unique cultural and ethnic differences found among group members are ignored" (Trimble & Bhadra, 2013, p. 500; Trimble, 1991, 1995). Throughout the book, we challenge the false notion that all ethnic minority groups are alike or that all leaders are alike; we highlight differences among racial and ethnic minority groups to illustrate the relevance of cultural variation to the exercise of leadership.

In the 21st century, leaders and members will increasingly find themselves in heterogeneous contexts within institutions and communities. This societal shift demands that our theories and models of leadership be responsive to demographic differences and rapid change. Leaders need to be prepared to lead a diverse workforce, confront complex situations that are influenced by diverse communities, and lead in ways that are culturally responsive and competent. Leadership theories and research need to be more inclusive and robust if they are to remain relevant to the concerns of contemporary society—which are marked by change, innovation, and diversity.

Underrepresentation of Diverse Leaders

Despite growing population diversity in the U.S. population, disparities exist in corporations, higher education institutions, sciences, and political sectors on the representation of women and racial/ethnic minorities in the ranks of leadership. Using the number of CEOs and corporate director-ships on Fortune 500 companies as a measure, Zweigenhaft and Domhoff (2006) reported a steady increase in the number of women and members of non-White racial and ethnic groups becoming part of the power elite in the United States. The number of Fortune 500 companies having at least one woman holding a corporate directorship grew from 0.16% in 1978 to 89.2% in 2003; however, only 7.9% of those holding the top title in these companies were women.

Data on racial and ethnic minorities' numbers in the power elite are more complex because they are not regularly or consistently collected. In 2004, 8.1% of board seats on Fortune 500 companies were held by Blacks, although this could have meant that a company had more than one Black person holding a seat or that a single individual was holding more than one seat in different companies. In 2001, there were 7 Black CEOs of Fortune 1000 companies, all men. In 2005, the number of Hispanic directors on Fortune 500 boards was 69, or 1.4%; there were 6 Latino CEOs of Fortune 500 companies, all men. For Asians, 96 men and women held 127 seats at S&P 1500 companies, representing less than 1% of the total. Despite their ostensibly higher levels of education and success, Asians accounted for less than 1% of the total number of executives, officers, and directors listed by Standard & Poor's during 2004. Moreover, Asians in CEO positions were primarily ones who started their own companies, such as Jerry Yang of Yahoo or Charles Wang of Computer Associates.

Leaders in the United States mirror our dominant population majority of White, heterosexual, Protestant males. Zweigenhaft and Domhoff (2006) demonstrated that even as more women and minorities enter leadership positions, the *power elite* in the United States—that is, those who own and manage our banks and corporations, finance the political campaigns, and serve in government as appointed legislative and military leaders—still remain quite homogeneous. The *power elite* continues to be dominated by a prototypical leader defined by White, social masculine norms.

While underrepresented in leadership roles, what happens when women and racial/ethnic minorities attain positions of leadership? Diverse leaders coming into these ranks often must learn the rules of the game and play by them. Entering the power elite often shapes the identities and leadership behaviors to conform to the dominant culture. These new and diverse lead-ers often become more like those already in the power elite. Zweigenhaft and Domhoff's (2006) findings suggest that the power elite continues to remain homogenous and "high social origins continue to be the most important factor in making it to the top. While common values and a subjective sense of hard-earned and richly deserved class privilege characterizes the new diversity within the power elite, it seems that these newcomers have found ways to signal that they are willing to join the game as it has always been played, assuring the old guard that will call for no more than relatively minor adjustments" (p. 7). Zweigenhaft and Domhoff suggest that higher social class origins, elite educations, a lighter skin color, and the ability to make oneself acceptable to established members of the power elite, which they call "identity management" are the factors that explain why some people come to be included. This raises some interesting questions. Is there room for diverse forms of leadership or are diverse leaders constrained to what already exists? Do diverse leaders coming into these ranks learn the rules of the game and play by them, thereby shaping their identities and leadership behaviors to conform to the dominant culture? Or do they bring something different from their experiences and social identities that result in differences in how they exercise leadership? Do they have a different leadership experience? By shifting our focus to diversity leadership, we suggest that we ask new questions to challenge the status quo of institutions, offer new paradigms to explain new or unexplored phenomena of leadership, and identify new dimensions based on dimensions of diversity and difference.

Omission of Diversity in the Leadership Literature

While we generally acknowledge the importance of diversity in the lives, communities, and workplace environments of today's global and multicultural societies, this has not infused our understanding of leadership. Theories and research on leadership have neglected the influence of diversity on access to leadership positions and the exercise of leadership. Some of the major leadership theories, including trait theories (Bass, 1990; Lord, 1986), contingency theories (Fiedler, 1993), leader-member exchange theories (Graen & Uhl-Bien, 1995), and leadership styles (Bass & Avolio, 1994; Burns, 1978), have largely sought universal dimensions to characterize leader behaviors and attributes. Examination of contexts in these theories has largely been confined to the organizations in which leadership is exercised.

A search of keywords in the leadership literature relating diversity and leadership (e.g., diversity and leadership, leadership and access, leadership and diversity, leadership and race, leadership and ethnicity, leadership and women) yielded a few 100 publications. Most of these were dissertation abstracts rather than published studies. Much of the work involved the underrepresentation of women or racial/ethnic minorities in formal positions of leadership. While research on women and leadership has been more robust (e.g., Ayman & Korabik, 2010; Eagly & Carli, 2007; Fletcher, 2003; Heilman, 2001; Kellerman, 2004), this is often treated as a special topic and not viewed as substantive to general models of leadership.

Omission of diversity in the literature about who leaders are and how diversity influences the exercise of leadership has been noteworthy. Textbooks on leadership typically discuss models of leadership as universal phenomena without reference to diversity. When women or racial/ethnic minorities are mentioned, they are usually treated as exceptions or special populations—a phenomenon that is mirrored in the popular media (i.e., *Fortune* and *Time* magazines). In essence, current leadership theories show a White (Euro-American), North American, heterosexual, male bias (Den Hartog & Dickson, 2004) and omit dimensions of diversity in understanding how leadership is exercised or who our leaders are.

With changing population demographics and communities becoming more diverse, the historic "prototypic" community member will become less visible and in the minority. As diverse individuals other than the prototypic community members ascend to positions of leadership in these societies and make up growing numbers of a country's population, countries throughout the world will need to grapple with the question of who best can lead them. Must the prototypic leader look like and share the same beliefs and values as the dominant group? How will this shift the power dynamics of the leader-member exchange? Is there a difference in the leadership styles of diverse leaders and what they bring to their leadership? Will there be more latitude for different styles of leadership?

Hence, a paradigm for diversity leadership is important and a focus of this book. While definitions of diversity include dimensions of race, ethnicity, gender, sexual orientation, disability, religion, age, socioeconomic status, as well as those of theoretical persuasion, philosophy, life experience, and so forth, we confine our focus to dimensions of race, ethnicity, and gender in this book.

Changing Contexts: From an Industrial to Global Perspective

Before the 21st century, world political leaders were primarily men. Few women emerged as heads of state. When they did, they were generally viewed as exceptions in history. Several examples illustrate how their leadership was viewed in history. Empress Dowager Cixi from China was a powerful and charismatic figure who became the *de facto* ruler of the Manchu Qing Dynasty and ruled over China for 47 years from 1861 to her death in 1908. She rose from being a concubine to empress and exercised almost total control over the court under the nominal rule of her son the TongZhi Emperor and her nephew the GuangXu Emperor, both of whom attempted to rule unsuccessfully in their own right. Many historians consider her reign despotism and attribute the fall of the Qing Dynasty, and therefore Imperial China, as a result of Cixi's rule.

Cleopatra VII's reign in Egypt marked the end of the Hellenistic Era and the beginning of the Roman Era in the eastern Mediterranean. She was the last Pharaoh of Ancient Egypt and a descendant of Alexander the Great nearly 300 years before. Her patron goddess was Isis, and thus during her reign, it was believed that she was the reincarnation and embodiment of the goddess of wisdom. Cleopatra's story has fascinated scores of writers and artists through the centuries. While she was a powerful political figure in her own right, it is likely that much of her appeal lay in her legend as a great seductress who was able to ally herself with two of the most powerful men (Julius Caesar and Mark Antony) of her time.

Joan of Arc was a 15th century national heroine of France. She was tried and executed for heresy when she was only 19 years old; this judgment was broken by the Pope and she was declared innocent and a martyr 24 years later. Her valour on the battlefield was renown in her attempt to recapture Paris and leading the troops to victory.

All three women leaders were noted for their uncharacteristic leadership. As women leaders, both Cleopatra and Empress Dowager Cixi emerged as leaders by seizing power, ascended to power through their seduction of men, and reigned because of their alliance with the men of their times; their route to power and leadership are generally viewed as invalid, tyrannical, and exercised in a masculinized context. Joan of Arc, on the other hand, was victim to charges of heresy and executed; she was not unlike the victims of the Salem witch hunts in the United States, in which women were feared for their mysterious powers and executed in a world ruled and dominated by men. Today, women leaders are often described by their clothing fashion in the media as if this were material to their leadership, for example, Hillary Clinton, former U.S. Secretary of State, by her choice of pantsuits, U.S. first lady Michelle Obama by her bare arms and sense of style.

Although the United States is a relatively new country, its reputation as a world power in the 20th century is noteworthy. It has yet to elect a woman president despite its stature as one of the first democracies in the world. Few first ladies were known for championing substantive issues with the exception of Eleanor Roosevelt and Hillary Clinton. Within the corporate sector, of the 50 most powerful women in business in Fortune 500 companies ranked by Fortune magazine in 2006, 36% either resigned or were fired 5 years later; of the 25 most powerful men in 2007, only 12% had resigned 5 years later.

During the 20th century and prior, global political leadership was characterized by a conqueror-colonial mentality. Western countries colonized the countries they conquered; members of their group became the country's new power elite. The 20th century was characterized by such events as the Arms Race and the race to the moon—a competitive streak to determine who was the first and most powerful. Post World War II, the threat of world destruction caused world governments to seek peace and nuclear disarmament; command and control models of leadership gave way to studies of democratic versus autocratic models of leadership. The 1960s gave rise to the Women's Movement and Civil Rights Movement within the United States, giving way to empowerment and shared leadership models.

The Industrial Revolution brought about efficiencies in the mass production of goods and manufacturing during the 20th century that changed our way of living. Leisure time became a commodity and affluent material consumption a goal. The postindustrial revolution of the information society or Digital Age is changing that; we are now a society shifting from the production of goods to the delivery of services and information. Innovation and change marks the 21st century. Does this demand different kinds of leadership?

Why Does It Matter?

These changing contexts of the 21st century signal the importance of our attention to diversity in the ranks of leadership. Events of the 20th century shaped our emphasis on values in the exercise of leadership. These include emphasis on ethical concerns of our leaders and how they lead posed by the Enron scandal, on social justice values fueled by the movements of the 1960s, on collaborative leadership given our growing recognition of our interdependence in a global society, the need for transformational change based on our vision for the future, and last on diversity as being inclusive and valuing of differences across groups.

Redefining Leadership: Global and Diverse

The 21st century is witnessing the emergence of "third world countries" as new world powers demand their liberation from colonial "masters."

China, Japan, Africa, and Latin America, where the United States and other Western countries went for cheap labor, are now resource rich, seeking liberation and self-governance. Productivity in these "underdeveloped countries" now far outpaces that of "advanced" Western nations. We are in a postindustrial era where multinational corporations are the new "conquerors" throughout the world in the global market. Nuclear power is generated not for war but to harness power used for energy. Fear of terrorism and creating sustainable environments are global concerns. This global consciousness in the midst of rapid change, advanced technology, and growing population diversity make us interdependent if we are to achieve world peace and promote economic and social well-being for all citizens of the world.

These changing social contexts now challenge past notions of American homogeneity and U.S. ethnocentrism. Global leaders of countries and corporations will need new paradigms of leadership if they are to be responsive to the diversity among their followers and within their institutions. Management practices and organizational cultures will need to be redefined if diverse followers are to feel empowered and diverse leaders are to be effective.

Leadership theorists are beginning to redefine criteria for effective leadership in the 21st century to include flexibility in thinking and responsiveness to a changing world. Although many definitions of leadership exist, virtually all definitions include the following components as central to the phenomenon of leadership: Leadership is a process, involves influence, occurs within a group context, and involves goal attainment. Using these components, Northouse (2004, p. 3) defined leadership as "a process whereby an individual influences a group of individuals to achieve a common goal." Rost (1991, p. 102) contributed a postindustrial concept of leadership for the 21st century, which he defined as "an influence relationship among leaders and followers who intend real changes that reflect their mutual purposes." This contemporary definition is composed of four basic components, each of which is essential and must be present if a particular relationship is to be called leadership: (1) The relationship is based on influence. This influence is multidirectional, meaning that influence can go any which way (not necessarily top-down), and the influence attempts must not be coercive. Therefore, the relationship is not based on authority but rather persuasion. (2) Leaders and members are the people in this relationship. If leadership is defined as a relationship, then both leaders and followers are doing leadership. Rost does not say that all players in this relationship are equal but does say all active players practice influence. This emphasis expands the study of leadership traits to a focus on the exchange that occurs between leaders and members (Graen & Uhl-Bien, 1995). It shifts the focus on individual leaders to a focus on teams as central to leadership training—that is, on kinds of teams, dynamics and processes of teams, and member diversity of teams (Rodrigues, 2001). In particular, it differs from the emphasis on charismatic leaders common during the 20th century (Heames & Harvey, 2006).

McCall and Hollenbeck (2002), in an empirically based, qualitative study, conducted interviews with 101 global executives (92 men and 9 women) stationed throughout the world, highlight the importance of context in examining leadership today. Their extensive interviews of seasoned leaders led to the following list of competencies for the global executive: (1) open-minded and flexible in thought and tactics; (2) cultural interest and sensitivity; (3) able to deal with complexity; (4) resilient, resourceful, optimistic, and energetic; (5) honest and authentic; (6) possess stable personal life; and (7) value-added technical or business skills.

Harvey and Buckley (2002) offer a comparison of the Management Environments Transitions between the 20th and 21st century as shown in Table 1.1.

Table 1.1   Management Environment Transitions From the 20th Century to the 21st Century

20th Century	21st Century
1. High percentage of manufacturing industries	1. High percentage of service industries
2. Emphasis on functional expertise	2. Emphasis on management processes
3. Domestic market	3. Foreign markets & cultures
4. Legitimate authority in hierarchical organizational structure	4. Virtual team & network organizational structures
5. Clearly defined operating procedures	5. Fluid & reactive operating procedures
6. Well-defined industry boundaries	6. Ill-defined industry boundaries
7. Fairly constant market	7. Turbulent market
8. Bricks & mortar	8. Virtual offices
9. Communication slow & unreliable	9. Communication instantaneous & continuous
10. Technology growth emerging	10. Technology growth exponential
11. Many employees with similar responsibilities & skills	11. Many employees with unique responsibilities & skills

Source. From Harvey, M.G., & Buckley, M.R. (2002). Assessing the "conventional wisdoms" of management for the 21st century organization. *Organizational Dynamics, 33*, 368–378.

As both studies show, leadership for the 21st century means an ability to lead in an increasing global and diverse society; amidst rapid scientific and social change, in a sustainable environment given climate change, population growth and migration and natural resources; and within a digital age of rapid information dissemination. Leaders must address increased diversity in their institutions and communities, increasing change, complexity, and interdependence. Leaders will need to be flexible, continuous and lifelong learners, and recognize differences in the values and assumptions held among diverse groups. They will need to be collaborative, share leadership, and learn collective styles of leadership. They will need to be critical thinkers, global leaders, and adaptive in their leadership styles. While this is new in many Western countries, it has been noted to be indigenous in many "developing countries" or non-Western countries.

There is a need for leadership and organizational theories that transcend cultures to understand what works and what does not work in different cultural settings (Triandis, 1993). Furthermore, a focus on cross-cultural issues can help researchers uncover new relationships by forcing investigators to include a much broader range of variables often not considered in contemporary leadership theories, such as the importance of religion, ethnic background, history, and political systems (Dorfman, 1996).

The importance of context in the 21st century leads us to reexamine our concepts of leadership. We need to ask new questions, create new paradigms, and identify new dimensions to expand our thinking about how leadership is perceived, enacted, and appraised. Paradigms need to be inclusive and diverse to consider the perspectives of those not typically in the positions of leadership, or defining the theories of leadership, and of all members who participate, shape, and influence the enactment of leadership within the broader social and organizational contexts in which leadership is embedded. Diversity leadership puts our focus on "who our leaders are" and "what they bring" from their lived experiences and dimensions of identity to the exercise of leadership.

We see global and diverse as related, but not interchangeable, terms. Diverse leadership is defined as different and varied, including the social identities of leaders as well as the types of leadership related to group differences of citizens within countries. Its use in psychology has often been associated with issues of disparate power, privilege, and equity among different groups within a country or culture. Subgroups within a country or culture with less privilege and power, who are often in the minority, share the common experience of oppression and inequity as well as a common affinity as members of a social group different from the mainstream or dominant group. Hence, a diverse perspective involves looking at differences between these social groups.

Global leadership, on the other hand, is defined as worldwide, international, and intercultural; it includes cross-cultural differences between societies and countries. While power, privilege, and equity may apply, its use has been associated with an examination of differences based on economic, political, and cultural forces worldwide and across governmental entities. A global perspective involves looking beyond geographic boundaries of one's country.

We move from defining leadership to examining the purpose of leadership. Allen et al. (2010) define it to be as follows: (1) Create a supportive environment where people can thrive, grow, and live in peace with one another; (2) promote harmony with nature and thereby provide sustainability for future generations; (3) create communities of reciprocal care and shared responsibility—one where every person matters and each person's welfare and dignity is respected and supported; the senior author adds: (4) use a difference paradigm to promote inclusiveness.

Summary

Leadership today is more important than ever as the 21st century brings about rapid and significant change in society and our institutions and challenges the way in which we do business and function in organizational settings. Changing population demographics, both locally and globally, suggest that our models of leadership and cadre of leaders need to be less ethnocentric and more diverse if we are to be successful in responding to these rapid changes and leadership needs. And yet, researchers of leadership and their resultant models seldom incorporate diversity into their formulations. Moreover, the ranks of leadership remain narrow; despite the growing numbers of women and racial and ethnic minority groups in the workforce, they remain significantly underrepresented in the ranks of leadership throughout most industry sectors. As we witness global changes in world leadership and a shift to a digital age that is postindustrial, redefining leadership to be global and diverse is essential. This should lead the way to identifying competencies and new paradigms for diversity leadership.

Discussion Questions: Context and Change—From Whence We Came to Where We Are Headed

1. Discuss the difference between global and diverse leadership.

2. Discuss factors that might contribute to the underrepresentation of ethnic minority groups in leadership roles.

3. Discuss how definitions of leadership might change as a result of changing population demographics and rapid social change.

4. Compare the management environments discussed in Table 1.1 and discuss the challenges that leaders face in the 21st century.

5. Rost (1991, p. 102) defined leadership as "an influence relationship among leaders and followers who intend real changes that reflect their mutual purposes." Identify some of the problems that might occur if the leader and organizational members disagree on the nature of the relationship.

6. By 2020, 50% of the U.S. workforce will be composed of the current 2014 ethnic minority populations, dominated by Hispanics and followed by African and Asian Americans. Identify some cultural characteristics of the groups that the corporate world will have to factor into the management of employees.

2

Dimensions of Diversity

Notable Quote: On Being Extraordinary!

As one Asian American female leader who is an Army colonel said, "As a minority, you have to do extraordinary things to get to where you are; White men just have to be ordinary."

On Being Female!

"As Deputy Commissioner and a lawyer, I worked with the mob. You had to be tough. As a woman, if I was soft, I was seen as weak; if I was tough, then I was a bitch. Men get away with it." (Asian American female leader)

Vignette: On Microaggression and Privilege

I was talking with a "prominent" White male at a cocktail reception. We were joined by a second White male who interrupts us, ignoring me to begin a conversation of his own. Recognizing this slight, the "prominent" White male introduces us. I soon leave this conversation to join another group. The second White male again joins my conversation and is asked by the other parties if he knows me. His response was: "Of course I do, she knows [1st prominent White male]." I gained instant credibility by my association with the first "prominent" White male although I was totally marginalized by his interruption and making me invisible in the first encounter. (Senior author, Asian American female leader)

Chapter 1 examined the changing contexts of today's leadership and our need to redefine leadership amidst the global and diverse environment of the 21st century. The inclusion of diversity into our understanding of leadership is central to this book using a difference framework. In this chapter, we merge the concepts and the literature in diversity and leadership. Attention to diversity is about valuing differences and inclusion of all groups. Attention to diversity, however, is not simply about representation of diverse leaders in the ranks of leadership. It is not simply about underrepresentation or affirmative action. Attention to diversity means paradigm shifts in our theories of leadership to be inclusive of all who may lead; it means incorporating how dimensions of diversity shape our understanding of leadership. It means attention to the perception and expectations of diverse leaders by members and to the interactive and reciprocal process between leaders and members who shape access, exercise, and appraisal of leadership.

Ultimately, diversity leadership is about what diverse leaders contribute to the exercise of leadership and about the diversity of contexts and members in which their leadership is embedded. Although leadership theories have evolved and reflect changing social contexts, they remain silent on issues of equity, diversity, and social justice. Diversity leadership is about how differences and inclusion are reflected in the paradigms used to define leadership and evaluate its effectiveness.

Culture and Ethnicity in Leadership

Having a paradigm of diversity leadership enables leaders to develop culturally competent models for 21st century leadership that are characterized by new social contexts, rapid technological change, emerging global concerns, and changing population demographics. Many studies have pointed to the centrality of culture in affecting leader and follower behavior (Gertsner & Day, 1994; Hofstede, 2001; House, Hanges, Javidan, Dorfman, & Gupta, 2004; Triandis, 1995; Trompenaars & Hampden-Turner, 1998); most of these studies examine cross-cultural differences and variation across national origin and cultures. There is often a presumption of cultural homogeneity within countries and among its leaders and members. Many leadership and cross-cultural studies are designed to eliminate heterogeneity.

The study of cultural values (Hofstede, 2001) and cultural variation in worldviews (Sowell, 1994; Sue, 1978) can provide insight into the challenges leaders face in new and changing contexts of contemporary times. This is what remains stable across contexts and carries over into leadership contexts. Worldviews are the overall perspectives from which one sees and interprets the world. They include a collection of beliefs or value orientations about life and the universe and give meaning to life's purposes. Cultures have been found to vary in the patterns of relationships that are valued, encouraged, and appropriated to construct daily social interactions (Triandis, 1995). Five dimensions of worldviews, as described below, have been identified to define much of human activity, and in turn, what leaders do:

- Human Nature—Are people basically evil or are they basically good? Are they born with a Tabula Rasa or a mixture of good and evil? This influences how leaders view what they must do to lead. Do they need to prohibit or prevent the dark side from emerging or do they simply need to guide it?
- Relationship of People to the Environment—Are people subject to the forces of nature? Are life's goals to be in harmony with nature or to overcome the forces of nature? This influences social rules and organization structures that define such things as land ownership, property rights. What does progress mean? Do leaders approach change with a "conquer and destroy" mentality, or do they work on being in harmony with nature?
- Nature of Human Activity—Is human activity defined by one's Being or Doing? This will influence how leaders motivate their members? Do leaders base their solutions on who people are or what people must do? Or is human activity focused on where people are headed, such as Being-in-Becoming?
- Nature of Interpersonal Relationships—Are our social and leadership relationships lineal (hierarchical) or collateral (egalitarian) based? Are they individual or collective based? This will influence whether leaders emphasize the individual or group in defining incentives and whether they come from a position of authority or peer in their communications.
- Time Sense—Do people run their lives based on the past, present, or future? Do they respect history, live for the moment, or worry about the future? Is their sense of time fluid or fixed? This can influence how leaders schedule meetings, whether they emphasize being on time for meetings, and how planning occurs.

Different cultures and societies show different profiles in their worldviews with distinct profiles between Western and Eastern societies typically emerging; however, diversity remains among subgroups and individuals. In particular, the dimension of Individualism versus Collectivism has often aligned with Democratic versus Communist political regimes and with Western versus Eastern countries, respectively. Becoming versus Doing has also distinguished Eastern versus Western views of human activity; the notion of being includes that of "staying with" or being attuned to oneself. An emphasis on *Being* as a worldview is reflected as: "It's enough to just 'be.'" It's not necessary to accomplish great things in life to feel your life has been worthwhile. An emphasis on *Becoming* as a worldview is reflected as follows: "The main purpose for being placed on this earth is for one's own inner development." An emphasis on *Doing* as a worldview is reflected as follows: "If people work hard and apply themselves fully, their efforts will be rewarded. What a person accomplishes is a measure of his or her worth." The Asian learner is internal with a worldview emphasis on "to be" but is external in his or her learning outcomes to be altruistic. This contrasts with the Western learner who is external with a worldview emphasis on "to do," but is internal in his or her learning outcome to gain knowledge. Do leaders base their solutions on who people are or what people must do? Or is human activity focused on where people are headed, such as Being-in-Becoming.

Eastern views tend to be associated with lineal (hierarchical) relationships over collateral (egalitarian) ones. Following WWII, leadership theorists began to study effectiveness of democratic versus autocratic versus laissez-faire styles of leadership; this interest correlated with the autocratic leadership styles of political dictatorships of the times. As we progress in the 21st century, leadership theorists [in Western countries] now focus on the need to shift from democratic versus autocratic styles (studied post WWII) toward democratic versus collective styles of leadership (Allen et al., 2010), while those in Eastern countries ironically have found the need to move toward democratic styles of leadership. These cultural values and worldviews, in turn, have been associated with aspirational goals of leadership. While often viewed as opposites and dichotomous, we need to view them as continuous and differently. This shift from a good-bad dichotomy shifts to a difference perspective, and there is a regression to the mean by all parties.

Cultural Values and Beliefs

Cultural values and worldviews underlie the framework for the GLOBE studies (House et al., 2004), which are a set of comprehensive studies that examine culture and leadership. They draw on three theories—Implicit Leadership theory, which posits that implicit beliefs and assumptions distinguish effective leaders from ineffective leaders (Lord & Maher, 1991); Value Belief theory of culture, in which values and beliefs held by members of a culture influence the degree to which the behaviors of individuals, groups, and institutions within that culture are enacted (Hofstede, 2001; Triandis, 1995); and Implicit Motivation theory (McClelland, 1985), which suggests that the mix of motivational needs for achievement, authority and power, and affiliation characterize a leader's style.

The GLOBE studies found cultural variation in the leadership dimensions endorsed by leaders across 62 countries via a survey of 17,000 middle managers from 951 organizations in the food processing, finance, and telecommunications industries. The studies empirically established culturally based shared conceptions of leadership referred to as Culturally Endorsed

Implicit Leadership Theory (CLT) dimensions of leadership that both facilitate and inhibit outstanding leadership; these were consolidated into six global leadership dimensions that contribute to outstanding leadership. These are implicit assumptions about leadership that drive both perception and behaviors of what is effective leadership. These dimensions, in turn, correlated with nine Cultural Orientation Value (COV) dimensions reflecting the association of organizational cultures and leadership styles with societal cultural values and practices.

Regional cluster CLT profiles were empirically derived to represent the content of a leadership belief system shared within a culture and prototypical leader behaviors and attributes endorsed by members within a culture. Cultural orientation values (COV) were found to meaningfully relate to the centrality of leadership attributes in these belief systems.

Cultural Variation: Implicit Leadership Theories

While four of the six leadership dimensions on the Global Leadership and Organizational Behavior Effectiveness (GLOBE) studies were generally perceived as associated with effective leadership and two as impeding outstanding leadership, there was cultural variation in endorsing these leadership dimensions. Different countries have different profiles. The six CLT leadership dimensions representing classes of leader behavior (House et al., 2004, p. 46–48) include the following:

- Charismatic/Value-Based—include visionary, inspirational, self-sacrificing, integrity, decisive, performance oriented behaviors, and was universally endorsed (perceived) as leading to effective leadership. This dimension is complex and multidimensional, including transformational, charismatic, authentic, and humanistic elements found in many leadership theories.
- Team-Oriented—include collaborative, team integration, diplomatic, not malevolent, and administratively competent behaviors. This dimension was strongly correlated with charismatic/value-based leadership and also universally endorsed. It also reflects dimensions cited by Rost (1991) about 21st century leadership skills.
- Participative—include not autocratic, and participative behaviors. This and humane-oriented dimensions are generally viewed positively but show significant variability across cultures.
- Autonomous—include individualistic, independent, autonomous, and unique behaviors. This and the self-protective dimension are generally viewed as neutral or negative but show significant variability across cultures. It characterizes collectivistic elements.
- Humane—modesty, compassionate, and humane oriented. It is associated with many Eastern societies and religions.
- Self-Protective Leadership—include self-centered, status conscious, conflict inducer, face saver, and procedural behavior. Leaders on this dimension were

perceived as loners, asocial, noncooperative, and irritable and were universally perceived as negatively associated with effective leadership.

CLT leadership ratings on the GLOBE studies aligned with national indices of economic health and achievement as measures of effectiveness. This macro level analysis of leadership dimensions reinforces the importance of national character correlating with leadership styles.

The nine COV dimensions reflecting societal cultural values and practices showed cultural variation across countries and regional clusters in the degree to which these cultural value dimensions contribute toward each CLT dimension (House et al., 2004, p. 30). In general, COV values but not practices were related to CLT leadership dimensions. This suggests that members perceive and expect of their leaders behaviors that align with their cultural values, not with what they do. The nine COV dimensions include the following:

- Performance Orientation—degree to which a collective encourages and rewards group members for performance improvement and excellence.
- Assertiveness—degree to which individuals are assertive, confrontational, and aggressive in their relationships with others.
- Future Orientation—extent to which individuals engage in future oriented behaviors such as delaying gratification, planning, and investing in the future.
- Humane Orientation—degree to which a collective encourages and rewards individuals for being fair, altruistic, generous, caring, and kind to others.
- Institutional Collectivism—degree to which organizational and societal institutional practices encourage and reward collective distribution of resources and collective action.
- In-Group Collectivism—degree to which individuals express pride, loyalty, and cohesiveness in their organizations or families.
- Gender Egalitarianism—degree to which a collective minimizes gender inequality.
- Power Distance—degree to which members of a collective expect power to be distributed equally (CEO of Mattel met with employees in the cafeteria to decrease power distance; this would not work in Malaysia where expectations of a leader prototype is high power distance).
- Uncertainty Avoidance—extent to which a society, organization, or group relies on social norms, rules, and procedures to alleviate unpredictability of future events.

Cross-Cultural Versus Diverse

While culturally based conceptions of leadership are important to diversity and leadership, we need to differentiate between cross-cultural studies and diversity studies. There are several limitations from a diversity perspective. The GLOBE studies do not measure leader behavior. While the GLOBE studies are valuable as cross-cultural studies demonstrating cultural variation, they do not examine subgroup profiles within countries, such as diversity, and do not distinguish how differences among subgroups affect perception and expectations of leaders when they are not prototypic.

In fact, the methodology minimize diversity and within country variability by excluding multinational organizations from the samples and sampling only leaders from the dominant subculture "in order to predict national level behaviors." The GLOBE studies were silent on demographics of race, ethnicity, age, and educational levels of the leaders; racial/ethnic composition of the organizations that they lead; or demographics of the researchers collecting the data. Items that showed semantic variation across countries were deleted from the final survey. In short, while examining cross-cultural variation of leadership and the cultural values and beliefs that correlate with leadership dimensions and effectiveness at a macro level on leadership styles of organizations and countries, the GLOBE studies do not address diversity or its influence on individual leadership behavior.

Cross-cultural studies compare differences between societies and countries while diversity often compares differences within countries. The latter includes issues of power, privilege, and equity important to diverse groups within a country or culture. Often, those subgroups with less privilege, which are in the minority, who share struggles from oppression have a sense of commonality and affinity among its members. These differences could be based on race, ethnicity, gender, and so forth. For example, Hickman (2010) observes resistance often expressed by Whites when differences and multiculturalism are discussed presumably on the basis of perceived differences. He suggests reframing a cooking project to promote diversity within a corporation. Instead of asking for "ethnic recipes to reflect your heritage" that might raise resistance among Whites, he suggests asking for "family recipes from all employees" to make Whites feel included. What is missed in this suggestion is the mistaken assumption that Whites do not have an ethnicity or culture. In a society that privileges Whites over non-Whites, this suggestion minimizes the expectation of difference and fails to recognize that non-White or ethnic minorities may perceive "family recipes" as reflecting "only mainstream recipes" and feel excluded. It's like saying "all American" while excluding those who do "not look all American."

Diversity and Leadership

In addition to the centrality of culture and ethnicity in leadership as demonstrated by the GLOBE studies, we also focus on the centrality of diversity in leadership given the changing demographics both locally and globally. This focus is based on evidence within the multicultural literature organized around reflecting principles of diversity and include: inclusiveness, cultural competence, and difference.

Inclusiveness

The changing North American demographic context calls into question the relevance of leadership research that have not been inclusive of ethnic and racial groups. For example, the American Psychological Association (APA) maintains that the purpose of the association shall be to advance psychology as a science and profession and as a means of promoting health and human welfare. Until about 40 years ago, the mission appeared to be limited to a White population as references to African Americans, Asian Americans, American Indians and Alaska Natives, Hispanics, Pacific Islanders, and Puerto Ricans were almost absent from the psychological literature; in fact, the words *culture* and *ethnic* were rarely used in psychological textbooks. About 40 years ago, ethnic minority and international psychologists began questioning what APA meant about *human* and to whom the vast body of psychological knowledge was applied. America's ethnic minority psychologists, and those from other countries as well as a small handful of North American psychologists, argued that American psychology was not inclusive of what constitutes the world's population; they claimed that then current findings were biased, limited to studies involving college and university students and laboratory animals, and therefore not generalizable to all humans.

Similarly, leadership research fostered a research agenda that was ethnocentric and bound by time and place of White, middle class, and North American perspectives (Cassell & Jacobs, 1987). How well prepared will leaders be to lead organizations with a diverse workforce serving a diverse population? How will these leaders culturally resonant with the lifeways and thoughtways of culturally unique populations? Changing demographics will press the field toward the full consideration of diversity in ways that are inclusive (Trimble, 2013).

All groups within an organization and society ought to have a voice and be included in the decision making of the organization, although not necessarily to the same degree. At the same time, diverse leaders from all dimensions should have the potential to access positions of leadership and to exercise their leadership without bias that derives from stereotypic expectations based on their social identities. Inclusiveness is an affirmation and respect for all, which presumes that leaders and organizations will become culturally competent to deal with all groups fairly and be responsive to their needs as part of the goals of the organization.

Cultural Competence and Sensitivity

What does it take for a leader to be culturally competent and sensitive? How can diversity leadership research and practice be culturally competent and sensitive? Connerley and Pedersen (2005) use a Knowledge-Skills-Awareness model of learning to examine leadership in a diverse and multicultural environment. The model emphasizes that (1) *Knowledge* implies that one's thoughts and behaviors can be inconsistent and people may be unaware of their inconsistencies; (2) *Skills* mean that one should be prepared to practice the skills necessary to attain cultural sensitivity and competence; and (3) *Awareness* means that leaders should be conscious of their reactions to people who are culturally different from them. They make the case for diversity in business and industry, including the need for multicultural skills, and the importance of the journey, to develop these competencies to become culturally competent and sensitive. All three components of awareness, knowledge, and skill are required for a balanced perspective of competence; emphasizing one over the other can dilute the overall competency goal. It is consistent with diversity training in the development of an organization's workforce.

Moritsugu (1999) offers a more general definition where he maintains that it is "the knowledge and understanding of a specific culture that enables an individual to effectively communicate and function within that culture. This usually entails knowledge of language and meta-language, values, and customs, and symbols and worldviews" [of a specific culture] (p. 62). The emphasis here is on *knowledge* and *understanding*. Emphasizing *skills* and *knowledge* in the context of leadership and diversity acknowledges that multiculturalism is generic to a genuine and realistic understanding of human behavior in all [contexts] and communication. Culturally informed practices can be likened to a bridge that helps transcend the gulf or the chasm of differences in practices, expectations, and modes of communication that separate persons whose backgrounds and outlooks have been molded by their respective cultures.

There are numerous definitions and explanations of the terms cultural competence and cultural sensitivity. At a general level, competence is a state where one is psychologically and physically adequate and has sufficient knowledge, judgment, skills, or strengths. Sensitivity is the capacity of a person to respond psychologically and attend to changes in his or her interpersonal or social relationships. When *cultural* is added to these terms, it addresses a gap when differences between individuals or groups are present. Orlandi (1992) defines cultural competence as "a set of academic and interpersonal skills that allow individuals to increase their understanding and appreciation of cultural differences and similarities within, among, and between groups" (p. vi). He continues by drawing attention to one's "willingness and ability to draw on community-based values, traditions, and customs and to work with knowledgeable persons of and from the community in developing focused interventions, communications, and other supports" (p. vi). The key words in his definition are *skills, understanding, appreciation, willingness,* and *ability;* the most salient of these is *willingness,* for without a conscious intent and desire the achievement and realization of *cultural competence* is not likely to occur.

A few definitions expand the construct to include stages of competence development and may define stages a leader or an organization goes through to achieve multicultural competence. Paz (2003) described six stages (originally defined by Cross, Bazron, Dennis, & Isaacs, 1989) that include the following: (1) *Cultural destructiveness.* This is the most negative end of the continuum and is represented by attitudes, policies, and practices that are destructive to cultures and to individuals within cultures; (2) *Cultural incapacity.* This stage represents systems or individuals with extreme biases, who believe in racial superiority of the dominant group and assume a paternalistic posture toward the *lesser* groups; (3) *Cultural blindness.* This stage represents beliefs that color or culture makes no difference and that all people are the same. Values and behaviors of the dominant culture are presumed to be universally applicable and beneficial. It is also assumed that members of the nondominant culture do not meet the dominant group's cultural expectations because of some cultural deficiency or lack of desire to achieve rather than the fact that the system works only for the most assimilated; (4) *Cultural precompetence.* This stage occurs when there is an awareness of one's limitations in cross-cultural communication and outreach. However, there is a desire to provide fair and equitable treatment with appropriate cultural sensitivity. There may be a level of frustration because the person does not know exactly what is possible or how to proceed; (5) *Cultural competence.* This is the stage represented by the acceptance and respect for differences, continuing self-assessment regarding culture, careful attention to the dynamics of differences, continuous expansion of cultural knowledge and resources, and a variety of adaptations to belief systems, policies and practices; and (6) *Cultural proficiency.* This stage occurs when one holds culture in high esteem and seeks to add to their own knowledge by reading, studying, conducting research, and developing new approaches for culturally competent practice. Thus, a sensitive person can progress from a cultural destructiveness stage to a proficient stage of competence by actively engaging in the study and expression of respect for others regardless of their cultural or ethnic background. Achieving true cultural competence and cultural sensitivity is complex and daunting (Constantine & Ladany, 2001; Pope-Davis & Coleman, 1997). Putting these constructs into the enactment of leadership or construction of leadership research compounds the complexities.

Multiculturalism

In recent years within the diversity multicultural literature, the term, *multiculturalism,* has replaced the term *competence* although the terms often are used synonymously. While the core meanings of *competence* and *sensitivity* are retained, *multiculturalism* is a more inclusive construct as its embraces multiple aspects and facets of what it means to value cultural pluralism. Because of the additive nature of the construct, definitions of *multiculturalism* are multiple and lengthy. Sue et al. (1998) define multiculturalism that encourages the exploration, study, and internalization of cultural pluralism. Multiculturalism and cultural competence are used here to examine all facets of diversity leadership, including its assumptions, research methodology, leader-member-organization exchange, and access to the ranks of leadership.

Multicultural Incompetence

Culture and all that it implies is explicit and implicit to multiculturalism (Trimble, 2013). Instead of asking whether or not one is culturally competent, which has been typical, perhaps it would be better to ask if one is *multiculturally competent* as this captures the direction of society becoming increasingly diverse and global. The leadership literature is just beginning to catch up with this trend. Connerley and Pedersen (2005) emphasizes that *multiculturalism* is "a new perspective in mainstream psychology complementing the three other major theoretical orientations in psychology: psychodynamic theory, existential-humanistic theory, and cognitive-behavioral theory addressing the needs of culturally diverse client populations" (p. 113).

While there is a great deal of disagreement about definitions of *multicultural competency*, there is much more agreement about recognizing instances of *multicultural incompetence*. The fallout and the untoward consequences of cultural incompetence are unprecedented in the annals of the history of our planet; the emotional, psychological, physical, ecological, and economic costs are extraordinary and often beyond comprehension. Leaders who use terms without recognizing differences in their local meaning and leaders who fail to participate in or reciprocate cultural rituals are examples of such cultural insensitivity. Advocating and encouraging cultural competency in all aspects of life, including leadership, will reduce the sociological, psychological, organizational, and financial costs of multicultural incompetence.

The costs of cultural incompetence go far beyond the costs to leaders and members and their communities. The costs weigh in heavily on leaders and researchers who aspire to work closely and collaboratively with ethnocultural communities and to lead within diverse and multinational organizations. Increasingly, leaders will have to devote considerable time forging close long-term relationships with members in communities and organizations that they lead. Trickett and Espino (2004) summarized the extensive literature on participatory community research approaches and commented that, "It is time to place the collaboration concept in the center of inquiry and work out its importance for community research and intervention. Although some would see it as merely a tool or strategy to getting the 'real' work done, our strong preference is to view the research relationship [between researcher and participant] . . . as a critical part of the 'real' work itself" (p. 62); such collaboration through establishing mutually beneficial partnerships is a necessary part of the process.

For culturally sensitive leadership research to occur, it is essential to foster and encourage ethical decision making that is inclusive of differences across all ethnocultural populations and to examine leadership styles that reflect the unique sociocultural realities of diverse ethnic and racial leaders. Research that marginalizes those leaders who do not reflect majority social identities is both irresponsible and multiculturally incompetent. There are three ethical dimensions of multiculturally sensitive research: (1) applying a cultural perspective to the evaluation of research risk and benefits, (2) developing and implementing culturally respectful informed consent procedures and culturally appropriate confidentiality and disclosure policies, and (3) engaging in community and participant consultation with a standard of "principled cultural sensitivity" (Trickett, Kelly, & Vincent, 1985). The need to identify multicultural incompetence and its link with ethics emerges from the increasing distrust among diverse leaders and their communities about research that is not inclusive of multiple perspectives.

Given the paucity of diversity leadership research, it is imperative to use grounded research methods to draw on collaboration with diverse leaders to develop new dimensions, study relevant questions to those with different life experiences, and challenge the assumptions of existing paradigms of leadership (Bengsten, Grigsby, Corry, & Hruby, 1977; Burhansstipanov,

Christopher, & Schumacher, 2005; Fisher & Ball, 2002). Researchers must also be aware of scientific, social, and political factors governing definitions of race, ethnicity, and culture; understand within-group differences; and become familiar with skills in constructing culturally valid and reliable assessment instruments (Trimble, 2010; Trimble & Fisher, 2005). Interest in multicultural competence is not uniform and consistent. Some critics see the domain as an example of "political correctness," while others see it is a passing fancy that will dwindle in influence over time. Still others challenge the use of grounded research as being "unscientific" because it is qualitative and does not draw on existing leadership theories.

Moodian (2009) talks of competencies for global and diverse leaders with a focus on the changing global environment that differs from how leadership has been historically exercised in more homogeneous settings. Developing and acquiring multicultural competence is an extraordinarily complicated and engaging but necessary process. The range of differences between and within groups includes those from diverse cultural backgrounds, different levels of acculturation, complexities of culture, lived experiences, cultural values, and modes of coping. It is a process that includes the acquisition of competency skills and knowledge through didactic approaches; however, this is incomplete without the awareness and experience of cultures in its moods and settings. This does not imply that leaders discard the contributions of the past and present; the challenge is to recognize that the human condition cannot be fully understood without viewing it in context from a diverse multicultural perspective. A diversity leadership paradigm involves learning to reframe knowledge from the past, and testing assumptions and hypotheses with a new set of approaches and procedures in contexts not considered in the past. We may find that specific thoughtways and lifeways of certain ethnocultural groups may have some extraordinary value for the exercise of leadership as a whole and vice versa.

Difference

Valuing differences is a core aspiration and principle of diversity. As we look to inclusiveness, cultural competence, and multiculturalism, the issue of difference is central to diversity. Groups often look for commonalities since it leads to affinity bonds among groups within an organization and between a leader and members; these commonalities promote cooperation leading to increased productivity toward the goals of an organization. These differences also raise conflict and tension but can be facilitative in bringing new perspectives, innovation, and creativity if they are valued and respected. The valuing of differences aligns with feminist principles and multiculturalism to be inclusive of all differences and a commitment to a collaborative process that empowers and give voice to all groups and individuals.

Diversity and Cross-Cultural

In examining diversity and leadership, we see it as complementary with cross-cultural leadership. Chin (2013) examined within-country differences among diverse leaders across five racial/ethnic groups in the United States (White, Black, Hispanic, Asian, Native American Indians) on the CLT leadership dimensions; she found important variation across diversity dimensions of race, ethnicity, and gender. While commonalities across all groups were consistent with GLOBE findings that there are universal dimensions associated with endorsement of effective leadership, the variation across these diverse racial/ethnic groups was noteworthy. In particular, there was divergence between White and diverse leaders of color as well as between women and men in their perceptions of leadership—variables that were not studied in the GLOBE studies. Chin attributed these differences to the common lived experience of minority status in the United States and of marginality and oppression among diverse leaders of color that differed from that of White males in the study.

The leader profiles showed higher endorsement of Humane and Collectivism orientation values compared with the U.S./Anglo GLOBE profile. While this was consistent with the cultural orientation values of the diverse leaders of color, their profiles did not match the regional/country cluster GLOBE profile from which they immigrated. Whether this reflects acculturation changes associated with immigration or minority status experiences in the United States or differences between the samples in both studies is unclear and needs further investigation.

While all five racial/ethnic groups showed no differences in their endorsement of leadership dimensions, diverse leaders of color and women leaders strongly identified with their social identities of race/ethnic or gender and felt it was influential in their exercise of leadership; White men leaders did not. It is noteworthy that diverse leaders of color and women felt their minority group status influenced negative perceptions, expectations and appraisals of their leadership roles compared with White men leaders; these lived experiences appeared to explain their greater need to be self-protective and their tendency toward social justice in their leadership goals. At the same time, these lived experiences were perceived to be strengths in their exercise of leadership suggesting their use of an affirmative paradigm in framing their experiences. This study illuminates some of the discrepancies associated with national profiles that often do not characterize the subgroups within a country.

Dominant-Minority Relations

Since its founding, the United States rested on the core principle of equality and freedom from religion oppression, which was the rationale for the Pilgrims immigrating to the "new world." Racial/ethnic heterogeneity was largely invisible while driving the nature of race relations. While the U.S. Declaration of Independence declares "that all men are created equal," the United States has been contradictory in its actions supporting slavery and denial of suffrage for women. Dominant-minority status defined by race has largely characterized this dichotomy and has generally been ignored as influencing the exercise of leadership as they have in intergroup and social relationships.

Different worldviews and lived experiences having to do with such issues as acculturation, discrimination, socioeconomic status, race, biculturalism, religion, sexual orientation, and gender have greatly influenced ascriptions of power, privilege, and status associated with such differences between groups. Privilege has extended to Whites over non-Whites, heterosexuals over homosexuals, and Christians over non-Christians. Groups in the majority are typically ascribed dominant status and afforded greater access and opportunities. These differences have been the basis of ongoing political strife, war and civil unrest, and social separation in the United States and globally. In some instances, a group retains dominant status even when their numbers do not make up a majority. Race, for example, has often been the discriminator in many colonized and third world nations where the colonizer (usually White men) maintained leadership and power even though they were minority by their numbers.

Differences in dominant and minority status often result in social separation and conflict in intergroup and social relationships. And yet, there has been little study of the influence of social group membership and differences in lived experiences among diverse leaders on the exercise of leadership and leadership styles. Studies have suggested that leaders and members hold views of what a "typical leader" or leader prototype is; often, these leader prototypes are based on social identities holding dominant status in their respective societies (van Knippenberg & Hogg, 2007; Zweigenhaft & Domhoff, 2006); see Chapter 4 for a full discussion of this issue.

Privilege and Marginal Statuses

Dominant status creates privilege. Being White and being male often result in the privileges of access, acceptance, and advantage within society. This privilege is often invisible to those who have it; they see their benefits as "normal" even when they acknowledge the disadvantages held by minority status members. Privilege often creates insider-outsider status between dominant and minority group members especially when dimensions such as race and ethnicity are made invisible on the belief that it "makes no difference." Without acknowledging dimensions of privilege and dominant social statuses as important, leadership studies often eliminate such differences to get a "typical sample" of leaders. In so doing, minority group leaders are viewed as exceptions, and we miss how issues of marginalization, oppression, racism, sexism, and other social factors influence intergroup relations and communication that, in turn, influence leadership style, leader behaviors, and perceptions of leader potential and effectiveness.

Power and Empowerment

McClelland (1985) discussed how power and achievement motivation affected leadership style and behaviors; his theory was incorporated into the GLOBE leadership dimensions. However, there has not been an understanding of how power dynamics between the dominant and minority status of leaders interplay with the power inherent in their leadership roles. Moreover, power dynamics between social identities associated with dominant and minority status of both leaders and followers are not well understood.

Power related to a leader's position versus power related to a leader's dominant-minority status may not be aligned when the leader's social identity is one of minority group status. Contemporary theories of leadership tend to minimize power in leadership, probably in reaction to "bad" leadership associated with the dictatorships of Hitler and Mussolini and their abuse of power during WWII and to the emphasis on empowerment associated social justice and equity goals during the Civil Rights and Women's Movements of the 1960s. This needs reexamination in looking at diversity leadership.

Ethnocentric Bias in Current Theories of Leadership

Current leaders in the United States largely mirror its dominant majority population of White (Euro-American), heterosexual, Protestant males. Entering the power elite often shapes the identities and leadership behaviors to conform to that dominant culture (Zweigenhaft & Domhoff, 2006). This will begin to shift as more women and racial/ethnic minorities enter leadership positions. However, this leadership prototype still influences our understanding of leadership.

Most of the leadership research during the past half-century was conducted in the United States, Canada, and Western Europe (Yukl, 2010). As a result, current theories of leadership show a North American bias

(Den Hartog & Dickson, 2004) and generally reflect the structures and cultures of North American organizations run by Euro-American, heterosexual men. In fact, what are described as universal theories of leadership are, in fact, quite culture specific, and thus ethnocentric. Many theories reflect a Eurocentric colonial mentality of dominance and power, which has led to attempts to redefine leadership. Contemporary theories have shifted to empowerment, shared power, and servant leadership (Greenleaf, 1977) as models of ideal leadership. For leadership theories to be truly inclusive, we cannot ignore the "who" part of the equation in our leaders to ensure that the experiences of diverse leaders are included.

Northouse (2004) provides a summary of the major approaches to leadership and will not be repeated here except as they relate to diversity leadership. Trait approaches are rooted in identifying a universal set of traits or personality characteristics believed to differentiate leaders and non-leaders, for example, intelligence, self-confidence, determination, integrity, and sociability. While intuitively appealing, it is largely based on measures of those already in positions of leadership and does not take into consideration different semantic meanings, equivalence of traits across cultures, or how they may exclude those with potential but not in positions of leadership—they are ethnocentric. A presumption of universal traits that characterizes effective leadership has been largely unsuccessful since the research has been based on a subset of leaders without taking into consideration cultural variation and situational contexts. Moreover, studies using an emic approach have identified traits that are simply not measured, thereby challenging the universality of the array of traits that have been identified in "mainstream studies" (Ayman, 2004; Cheung, Van de Vijver, & Leong, 2011).

The focus on situational approaches to leadership stress the directive and supportive dimensions of leadership that need to be applied to situations and how leaders need to be flexible and adaptive to meet the changing needs of their subordinates and different situations (Yukl, 2010). It has been used extensively in leadership training and development. However, there has been little empirical research supporting the theoretical underpinnings. The types of situational variables used in the early contingency theories include task characteristics (e.g., complexity, stress), subordinate characteristics (e.g., skills, experience, motivation), and leader-subordinate relations (e.g., shared goals, mutual trust) (see Northouse, 2004). Most of the research on the early contingency theories of leadership used survey methods with subordinates' ratings of how often their leader used each type of behavior. The dependent variables were usually ratings of subordinate satisfaction or ratings of leadership effectiveness by superiors of the leader. This stream of research has several implications for improving flexible and adaptive leadership, which include the following: (1) Learn to diagnose the situation and use relevant contingency theories to identify appropriate types of leadership behavior for each type of situation; (2) increase flexibility by learning how to use a wide range of relevant behaviors; methods found to be useful for improving behavior include multisource feedback, behavioral modeling, role playing, and executive coaching; and (3) proactively influence aspects of the situation to create substitutes for leadership; for example, improve the selection of competent subordinates to reduce the need for close supervision and direction (Yukl & Mahsud, 2010). While adaptability is important to the skills for diverse leaders, these studies did not distinguish different outcomes for different types of leaders.

Of several contingency theories to leadership, Fiedler's (1993) approach is the most widely recognized. This is a leader-match theory as to how well the leader's style fits the context (i.e., style to situation). Style dimensions often differentiate between task-motivated and relationship-motivated leadership styles in which the former are concerned primarily with reaching a goal while the latter are concerned with developing close interpersonal relationships. To measure these styles, Fiedler developed the Least Preferred Coworker Measure to measure and match leadership style with the demands of a situation in this theory. Situations are characterized in terms of three factors: leader-member relations (where positive group atmosphere and trust support good leadership), task structure (where clarity of the task and structure gives control and influence to the leader), and position power (amount of authority a leader has to reward or punish followers). While empirically useful in discriminating effective leadership, the theory is potentially harmful in not attending to unconscious biases associated with race, ethnicity, and gender in ratings of Least Preferred Coworker Measure. The measure has also been criticized for having low face validity.

Leadership style approaches focus on what leaders do rather than who they are as in trait theories. One of the more common approaches differentiate task versus relationship behaviors and expanded the study of leadership to include the actions of leaders in various contexts; however, it has not yet identified a universal set of leadership behaviors that result in effective leadership. Transformational leadership style (Bass & Avolio, 1994; Burns, 1978), with its focus on vision, change, and charismatic influence, has become favored as the leadership style important for leaders of the 21st century. This began in the 1980s when leadership researchers became more interested in transformational leadership as many U.S. companies began to acknowledge the need to make changes in their leadership in order to survive amidst increasing economic competition from non-U.S. companies. In examining the endorsement of leadership styles among diverse U.S. leaders of color, however, Chin (2013) found that many felt compelled to embrace a transformational leadership but actually preferred a more collaborative leadership style consistent with cultural values of collectivism and consensus building. These findings reinforce the influence of social trends influencing the exercise and perception of leadership.

Leadership-Member Exchange (LMX) approaches address leadership as a process centered on the interactions between leaders and followers; the focus here is on developing high quality exchanges and how leaders use some subordinates (in-group members) more than others (out-group members) (Graen & Uhl-Bien, 1995). Leaders build relationships with members. Because members often form subgroups with special interests and personalities, leaders are urged to have special relationships with an inner circle or in-group. In-group members are favored, given greater responsibility and influence, and have greater access to resources. LMX approaches have been criticized for running counter to our principles of fairness and justice. The emphasis on building exchanges with in-group members would appear to potentially disadvantage minority and oppressed group members as historical out-groups. Moreover, the research focuses on the dyadic level with little theorizing at the group level whereby subordinates may evaluate and be influenced by concerns about what is fair within the context of the organization (Hogg, Martin, & Weeden, 2003); see Chapter 5 for a full discussion of leadership styles.

Reframing Current Theories to Include Diversity

A special issue on Leadership in the *American Psychologist* (Sternberg, 2007) reviewed the state of the art updating trait-based and situational leadership models. Although the issue promoted integrative strategies to incorporate contexts, cognitive processes, and organizational culture, it has been criticized for its omission of diversity and inattention to contexts of leadership. Hackman & Wageman (2007) suggest it did not go far enough to include different questions about the incorporation of contexts and the inclusion of both leaders and followers in our understanding of leadership. Graen (2007) suggests that it needed to include questions that consider broader contexts over time that are more inclusive of how the leadership process emerges. Wielkiewicz (2007) pointed out that all the articles were written from an "industrial" perspective placing primary emphasis on positional leaders and their actions, whereas an ecological perspective placing emphasis on contexts and processes of leadership deserved more consideration. Chin & Sanchez-Hucles (2007) cited the omission of dimensions of diversity and how it intersects with leadership. For leadership theories to be robust, they should be able to address complexity and not to treat diversity as simply a matter of different groups for whom leadership may be relevant.

In general, theories of leadership have neglected how diversity influences access to leadership positions and the exercise of leadership by diverse leaders. Although leadership theories have evolved to reflect changing social contexts, those derived from traditional paradigms remain silent on issues of equity, diversity, and social justice. Models of leadership derived from traditional paradigms do not strive toward inclusiveness or the removal of barriers for those historically precluded from these roles (Eagly & Chin, 2010). Merging concepts from the diversity and leadership literatures will yield more robust and inclusive paradigms that consider who leaders are, the composition of members they lead, and what effective leadership is in a diverse and changing social environment. The rapid changing contexts and growing population diversity warrant more dynamic and complex leadership models.

The attention to issues of identity, acculturation, assimilation, and discrimination in the diversity literature can be illuminating in reflecting the "who" part of the equation in leadership. The diversity research has found that issues such as resiliency, self-efficacy, and locus of control are correlated with good coping and adjustment strategies for racial/ethnic minority groups in response to social barriers and discrimination; it is likely that diverse leaders of color can resort to these strategies to be more effective leaders.

See Table 2.1 for a summary of reframing current theories of leadership.

Table 2.1   Reframing Current Theories of Leadership

Theory	Dilemma	Reframing for Diversity Leadership
Trait	Focuses on who leaders are. Has failed to identify a universal set of traits that distinguishes leaders.	Shift to leader identity intersecting with dimensions of social identities
	Ethnocentric; not inclusive; traits are based on those already in positions of leadership and may be biased against those groups who have had poor access to leadership roles.	
Situational	Focuses on where leaders do it. Application of directive and supportive dimensions across different contexts/situations.	Adaptability of leaders across diverse contexts; bicultural and cognitive flexibility as a function of acculturation
	Fiedler's leader-match contingency theory uses the Least Preferred Coworker Measure, is potentially harmful in not attending to unconscious biases associated with dimensions of diversity, for example, race.	

Table 2.1   (Continued)

Theory	Dilemma	Reframing for Diversity Leadership
Leadership Style	Focuses on what leaders do. Transformational leadership has become favored in the 21st century; however, varying definitions that include charisma as a trait favor more Western and masculinized notions of leadership.	Expand these notions of what leaders do to include non-Western perspectives
Leader-Member Exchange (LMX)	Focus on the interaction between leaders and members. Leadership is cocreated in groups. Runs counter to principles of fairness and justice because it emphasizes building exchanges with in-group members as those who would most contribute to the organization's goal. Principles would exclude and disadvantage minority and historically oppressed members as out-groups; privileges the in-group and viewed as unfair and discriminatory by out-groups.	Build a DLMOX framework that includes diverse leaders and members interacting within the context of their organizations and lived experiences

A paradigm for Diversity Leadership should be set in a context of 21st century postindustrial society. It should refer to culture as a central focus and include subgroup variation with attention to how dimensions of diversity influence access, exercise, and the appraisal of leadership. These dimensions include the social identities of leaders and members and lived experiences associated with dominant-minority status and privileged-marginal status within society. While modifying existing theories and drawing on alternative dimensions, diversity leadership is a framework that incorporates difference and contexts along with culture.

Identifying the Gap in Diversity and Leadership

A special issue in the *American Psychologist* (Chin, 2010) on diversity and leadership attempts to address this gap and to identify how race, ethnicity, gender, and sexual orientation influence access to positions of leadership and the exercise of leadership. Some of the big questions posed were as follows: What are the access barriers to leadership roles for diverse racial/ethnic individuals? How is the exercise of leadership among diverse leaders different from existing paradigms? The issue illuminated new dimensions and the potential for new paradigms for understanding leadership. Several issues emerged.

- Affirmative paradigm—Fassinger, Shullman, and Stevenson (2010) discussed the significance of identity associated with LGBT individuals and how the use of an affirmative paradigm enhances their exercise of leadership. This is an experience shared by other marginalized groups who face a persistent challenge of having to prove one's competence.
- Intersection of dimensions of diversity—(Ayman & Korabik, 2010) discussed intrapsychic and interpsychic dimensions and worldviews as important factors related to gender and ethnicity in influencing the exercise of leadership. Increasingly, we find that the intersectionality of social identities is important to consider in how they influence leadership behaviors.
- Social and ecological contexts—Eagly and Chin (2010) discussed the social construction of gender and how this results in biased perceptions about how women can and do lead.
- Intergroup communication—Pittinsky (2010) discussed intergroup exchange and the creation of in-groups and out-groups as contextual factors, which influence the exercise of leadership.

Contexts of Leadership

Reframing current leadership theories means an attention to context—to the interaction and process between leader and members. Leaders need to be change agents in promoting affirmative paradigms, recognize how implicit leader assumptions shape leadership behaviors, and how the exercise of leadership is influenced by social identities and contexts, which vary over time and place, and across cultural values.

Research findings consistently point to the inattention to contexts of leadership or a narrow definition of contexts especially when considering diversity leadership. Lived experiences of leaders shaped by societal as well as organizational contexts influence what leaders bring to their leadership and shape the interaction between leader and members. Perceptions and expectations of leaders associated with social identities and leader prototypes held by members will also shape that exchange. These exchanges will differ, depending on whether or not social identities of leaders and members are aligned and the heterogeneity of the organization. See Chapter 7 for a full discussion of this issue.

The Culture of Organizations

Yukl (2010) talks of leaders influencing organizational culture. Leadership becomes a matter of accepting things as they are or changing the organizational culture to be what it ought to be. Expanding our examination of leadership to the social and cultural contexts in which it is embedded is essential and goes beyond an emphasis on organizational culture. Schein (2004) was among the first to define organizational culture and argues that culture and leadership are two sides of the same coin. This will be discussed in Chapter 6.

Diverse Leader-Member-Organizational Exchange Paradigm (DLMOX)

Hickman (2010) offers a Leading Organizations Framework, which is holistic and useful for understanding and analyzing the role of leadership in a postindustrial society of new era organizations. Globalization is one of the major components of a complex dynamic environment that organizational participants must recognize and factor into their planning and actions. Hickman frames the environment of new era organizations as the exchange between leaders and organizational participants (employees), which results in the following: Shared responsibility for leadership, vision, ethics/values, culture, inclusion, change, capacity building, and social responsibility. As a result of this exchange, leadership is a matter of assessing and adapting the organization to external changes. It is also implementing the organization mission and adapting its structure to generate organizational contributions to society. According to Hickman, leaders and participants in new era organizations must innovate and create value beyond the organization's usual boundaries.

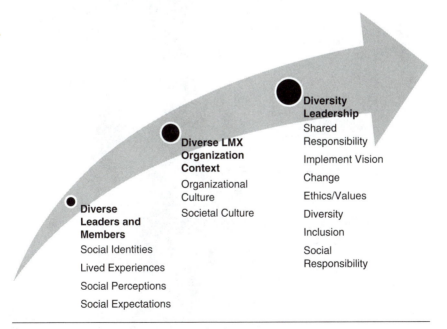

Figure 2.1   Goals of Diversity Leadership

   Diversity Leadership is a result of this exchange between diverse leaders and members within diverse organizational and societal contexts (see Figure 2.1 for Goals of Diversity Leadership). Hence, we modify Hickman's framework to a Diverse Leader-Member-Organizational Exchange Paradigm (DLMOX) to highlight the diverse composition of leaders and members and define the organizational and external environment as both diverse and global (see Figure 2.2). The environment of new era organizations is inclusive of the social identities and lived experiences of diverse leaders and members, the perceptions and social expectations which shape the leader-member exchange, which in turn, influence how an organization implements its mission and adapts it structure to external change. This diverse organizational framework goes from an individual/dyadic perspective to a group/social perspective, from an organizational to societal and ecological perspective, and from a situational to systemic leadership perspective. It will serve as a framework for the book and will be discussed further in Chapter 6.

Figure 2.2   Diverse Leader-Member-Organizational Exchange (DLMOX) Paradigm

Redefining Leadership: Inclusive of Social Contexts and Systems

Our inclusion of diversity and culture in this chapter helps redefine leadership to include changing social contexts and examination of systems in which leadership is embedded. Marshall Goldsmith discusses the "changing role of leadership . . . increasing importance of partnerships both inside and outside the organization" (2003, p. 3–8). In his interviews of high-potential leaders globally, he posits that leaders of the future will need to work with their managers in a team approach that combines the leader's knowledge of the unit operation with their managers' understanding of the larger needs of the organization. Such a relationship requires taking responsibility, sharing information, and striving to see both the micro- and macro-perspective. While partnering with management can be much more complex than "taking orders," it is becoming a requirement, not an option. When direct reports know more than their managers, they have to learn how to influence "up" as well as "down" and "across."

Several significant events at the beginning of the 21st century in the United States further influenced the emphasis on creating new forms of leadership. The Enron scandal, revealed in October 2001, eventually led to the bankruptcy of the Enron Corporation, an American energy company based in Houston, Texas, and the de facto dissolution of Arthur Andersen, which was one of the five largest audit and accountancy partnerships in the world. In addition to being the largest bankruptcy reorganization in American history at that time, Enron was also considered as the biggest audit failure. By the use of accounting loopholes, special purpose entities, and poor financial reporting, Enron was able to hide billions of dollars in debt from failed deals and projects. Chief Financial Officer Andrew Fastow and other executives not only misled Enron's board of directors and audit committee on high-risk accounting practices but also pressured Andersen to ignore the issues. Many executives at Enron were indicted for a variety of charges and were later sentenced to prison. As a consequence of the scandal, new regulations and legislation were enacted to expand the accuracy of financial reporting for public companies. One piece of legislation, the Sarbanes-Oxley Act, increased consequences for destroying, altering, or fabricating records in federal investigations, or for attempting to defraud shareholders. The act also increased the accountability of auditing companies to remain unbiased and independent of their clients. The Enron scandal led to calls for ethical leadership.

The economic meltdown and crisis in the mortgage and finance industries in the United States had global ramifications; it also raised calls for integrity and authenticity in leadership, and a reexamination of basic principles of leadership. Perhaps we need different kinds of leaders in the 21st century:

public and world leaders to govern our nations, thought leaders to plan our future, ethical and authentic leaders in our corporations, and global leaders in higher education to prepare us for a new future. We are a different and rapidly changing world, placing an emphasis on transformational and collaborative leadership styles over transactional and individual styles are important to be effective for the 21st century.

Salience of Culture and Diversity in New Forms of Leadership

The salience of sociocultural events has fueled an emphasis on different forms of leadership. These include the following:

- Value-based leadership resulting from a social justice perspective fueled by the Civil Rights and women's movements of the 1960s.
- Collaborative leadership, also called team or participatory leadership, became prominent as we saw more women in the workforce, and advances in technology led to a reduced need for physical strength in the labor force.
- Transformational leadership emphasized promoting change with a shared vision in attempts to respond to a society undergoing rapid change.
- Ethics-based leadership emerging from failures of leadership to uphold moral principles as reflected in the Enron scandal.
- Ecological leadership recognizing the complexity and intersection of broader sociocultural contexts in which leadership is embedded.

Race relations in the United States remain prominent while changing population demographics demand an attention to diversity in our ranks of leadership; this trend is now parallel in other countries globally. This calls for new forms of leadership, including an examination of the diversity of leader and member characteristics associated with social identities and their lived experiences in our understanding of leadership, and the exchange that occurs between them. Diversity leadership gives voice to inclusiveness and difference to capture the complexity and benefits of a diverse leader/member society.

Differences in Worldviews

In redefining leadership to be inclusive of global and diverse perspectives, and of contexts and systems, we offer some emerging perspectives among diverse leaders who are not typical of the power elite in most mainstream U.S. institutions. Several emerging themes of cultural variation in worldviews and their effects on leadership are noteworthy. Differences between Western and Eastern views on the nature of interpersonal relationships have been consistently found; individualism versus collectivism have been reflected in political forms of government, and in social forms of organizations and societies. While seemingly influential, they have not been studied in leadership styles or organizational contexts in which leadership occurs. Second, while societal differences between independent versus interdependent self-construals and personal versus relational self-concepts have consistently been observed, limited attention has been given to their importance to leader identity.

Chin (2013) identified some leadership dimensions endorsed by diverse leaders of color that differ from those commonly associated with being "leaderful." Drawing from qualitative semistructured interviews and focus group panels, diverse leaders of color discussed factors influencing their exercise of leadership. Diverse leaders of color and women leaders appeared to prefer a collaborative leadership style over a transformational one consistent with cultural values and implicit assumptions about leadership.

Qualitative analyses of subgroup differences were illuminating. Asian American leaders chose to be assertive through indirect means in order to maintain harmony in interpersonal relationships consistent with their cultural orientation values. Native American Indian leaders eschewed collectivism and showed less concern for rules and order; analysis of these responses suggests that they were responding from the position of their out-group status from the mainstream culture rather than the importance of these values within the Native American Indian community. These results suggest that terms used to measure leadership may not be semantically equivalent across diverse groups, and leadership behavior will reflect the social context in which it is embedded.

The endorsement of a collaborative style in their aspirational ratings together with a low endorsement of a charismatic orientation among these leaders may reflect the growing importance of cultural values associated with collaboration endorsed by racial/ethnic minorities and women in the United States as well as growth in their numbers within ranks of leadership in contemporary society. Asian Americans differed significantly from other racial/ethnic groups in their emphasis on egalitarianism, individualism, and collectivism. They endorsed an emphasis on social order, benevolence, loyalty to the group, and social and interpersonal communication using indirect means—all consistent with Confucian Asian values. At the same time, they endorsed planning, individual accomplishment, and rewarding individual effort and eschewed emphasis on some collectivist dimensions. Their endorsement of assertiveness defined as emphasizing cooperation and social relationships using indirect means of communication suggests that these dimensions may carry different semantic meanings. Native American Indians distinguished themselves on cultural orientation value dimensions with a more collectivistic and humane orientation, emphasizing group pride and accomplishments as well as benevolence and compassion. They were more likely to endorse multiple choice items on a survey of "being confrontational and direct in getting things done" while minimizing being indirect in their social relationships, or "expecting subordinates to obey orders and respect lines of authority and respecting hierarchy." This may reflect their adapting to mainstream leadership contexts by both conforming to the "rules of the game" while also maintaining their group pride and cultural values. Given their cultural history in the United States and their greater experience as leaders in the sample, their lesser concern with rules and order or competition may reflect their "refusal to buy into mainstream U.S." rules and culture.

Diverse leaders of color identified a greater need to be self-protective on a quantitative survey, although this was moderated by participation in voluntary leadership roles. While this is typically a dimension eschewed as aligned with outstanding leadership (on the GLOBE studies), this need for greater self-protection among U.S. diverse leaders of color might be associated with their shared lived experiences associated with oppression and minority status. In fact, qualitative comments among these diverse leaders included consensus that they "needed to work twice as hard to get half as far," or as one minority female leader said, "as a minority, you have to do extraordinary things to get to where you are; White men just have to be ordinary." In the face of persistent challenges about one's competence because of race and ethnic social identities, racial/ethnic minority leaders can develop an "affirmative armor" to assert their competence and protect their sense of self as a strength.

Collaboration as a Leadership Style

These results were corroborated from a focus group panel of 14 diverse leaders from African American, Latino(a) American, Asian American, and Native American Indian groups (Moritsugu, Arellano, Boelk, Pfeninger, & Chin, in progress). Each leader was interviewed and produced an excerpt of what was seen to be his or her leadership style. What emerged were some striking commonalities in endorsement of leadership styles. Virtually all favored collaboration and consensus as their preferred leadership style. Most eschewed an authoritative leadership style, which they viewed as more common among Anglo males, although necessary for them to adopt if they are to be effective in some contexts. Harmony, cooperation, collectivism, and community were adjectives used to describe elements of a collaborative leadership style. The emphasis on cooperation over competition was illustrated in an example by one leader during her run for president of a national association. She shared how she helped an opponent before the election, an atypical behavior in a competitive race, but a value that was part of her upbringing in the Mexican culture. Only two of the leaders supported a transformational style as characteristic of their leadership style in their excerpts. During the focus group, these leaders agreed that transformation happens when there is consensus and when people support the initiatives that the president helps facilitate.

Results from two qualitative studies (Chin, 2013) confirm that diverse leaders of color generally feel their exercise of leadership is influenced by their ethnicity, culture and minority status, or lived experiences associated with gender and race. What emerged in the focus group were some unique expressions of leadership styles characterized by their different ethnicities and shaped by their cultural values, philosophies, and worldviews. While all preferred a collaborative or consensus leadership style, they expressed it differently. This may have been reflected in choice of language and/or explication of meaning associated with specific terms.

Native American Indian leaders viewed effective leadership as not being visible but to push others forward. The Asian American leaders viewed leadership as inclusive of modesty and harmony interpersonally and as explaining their collaborative style of leadership. The Latino/a American leaders viewed cultural values of *familismo* and *personalismo* as central and preexisting conditions for leadership; the importance of establishing a relationship before proceeding to lead was stressed.

The emphasis on community and interpersonal relationships emerged as a strong preference and precondition for effective leadership. This was reflected in the concern for members as a dimension of leadership and in embracing the mottoes that 'it takes a village" and "standing on the shoulders of those before you" to enable all members to get ahead. These diverse leaders believed that effective leadership means stepping back and allowing the strengths of others to emerge, and that facilitating growth and change means creating a community where people feel they can have a voice and express their opinions. One Native American Indian leader articulated this as a "silent leadership" style consistent with Native American Indian values. The salience of these implicit leadership assumptions among diverse leaders of color is important because these phenomena are often not considered as important factors in the leadership literature, most likely because most leadership studies do not include the voices of diverse leaders of color. These findings suggest new dimensions and different perspectives to be considered in understanding leadership if we are inclusive of diversity.

Leader Identity

Differences between private and public self-descriptions of leadership were evident in differences between survey results and focus group results on leadership (Chin, 2013). While diverse leaders identified themselves as leaders on an anonymous survey, they were reluctant to publicly label themselves as leaders. Five out the 14 diverse leaders interviewed identified their "reluctance" to label themselves as leaders; virtually all but one identified themselves as "reluctant" to self-label as leader or to assume leadership roles without encouragement from mentors or past leaders. "Having to be asked" or urged to seek leadership positions was a consistent theme that many associated as consistent with cultural values of modesty.

While the leadership literature often uses case studies and case examples of models of effective leaders, these are typically those of White, heterosexual men. The need for expanding such case examples, not as exceptions but as different styles of effective leadership shaped by different cultural assumptions and values, is essential. If we are to focus on diversity leadership, we need to understand the experiences of leaders who make up this cadre. Often, people will refer to White men leaders as leaders but will add qualifiers to those who do not fit in this prototypic category—for example, women leaders, Black leaders, gay leaders, and so forth. Examples and quotes from diverse leaders (defined as those not typically viewed as simply leaders) are informative in understanding how diversity and leadership interact. The overriding conclusion by diverse racial/ethnic leaders about perceptions of themselves and of their leadership is that "It is a different experience!"

From Exception to Inclusive

The goal of this book is to move these exceptional cases to be inclusive within a diverse leadership paradigm. Bennett (1998) suggests a shift from an ethnocentric to an ethnorelative worldview, which recognizes the existence of multiple perspectives. Those who remain "culturally constrained" have not moved beyond the limits of their own cultural lens versus "cultural transcenders" who have committed to exploring the complexities of diversity (Moodian, 2009, p. 21). The remaining chapters reflect the application of this perspective to leadership.

Summary

Culture and ethnicity are central to how leaders exercise their leadership and to how members perceive and what they expect of effective leaders. Cultural value orientations and worldviews, which frame the GLOBE studies examining culture and leadership, showed significant cultural variation in leadership profiles across 62 different countries throughout the world.

Cross-cultural research on leadership, however, does not address diversity, which is about the subgroups and subcultures within an organization, society, or country. Principles of diversity, which emphasize inclusion and difference, contexts and multiculturalism, privilege and marginality, are important to reframe current theories so that they are inclusive and relevant today. Redefining leadership to be inclusive of all groups and considering organizational and social contexts are essential if we are to nurture the development of culturally competent leaders able to navigate the complexities and diversity of 21st century organizations and societies.

Discussion Questions: Valuing Differences— Diverse and Global Leadership

1. Discuss the differences between the terms cross-cultural and diverse. What implications does it have for leadership?

2. Identify instances of multicultural incompetence that you may have observed in the leadership within different organizations.

3. Using the principles of diversity identified in the chapter, how can a leader be responsive and competent if his or her experiences are vastly different from that of the organization or its group members?

4. Identify some contemporary sociocultural events that led to an emphasis on new forms of leadership; for example, why did the Enron scandal lead to calls for ethical leadership?

5. Identify an organizational outcome. Using the DLMOX paradigm, what are some processes that a leader might use to achieve that outcome?

6. Culture has been a difficult construct to define with over 100 different definitions. Discuss why is this is the case. In your discussion, consider how various dimensions of culture would be important to leadership characteristics.

7. Cultural groups are not static; lifeways and thoughtways are in continuous change as members of a group relocate to different cultural contexts or face new life challenges. Discuss how a leader with a culturally specific leadership style might be responsive to this dynamic sociocultural change process. What are some characteristics that enable a leader to be culturally competent and sensitive?

3

Paradigms for Diversity Leadership

Notable Quotes: "Other" Views of Leadership

Lao Tzu, Confucian scholar on leadership: "A leader is most effective when people barely know he exists. When his work is done, his aim fulfilled, his troops will feel they did it themselves."

Native American Indian male leader about his leadership: ". . . And so I always believe the doors will open where I am supposed to be, in the path that the creator set for me."

Native Hawaiian female leader on our direction for leadership: "As we connect with our ancestors to make change for future generations, our past is before us!"

Black woman leader on her being outspoken: "I'm too outspoken, I'm too loud, I'm too Black, and that's not how we do things here . . . the fact that I don't use a formal top down hierarchical kind of style; I've actually been told that's inappropriate."

Asian woman leader on integrity and leadership: "Know who you are. . . . *Yan mo ko, bang chi gon.* It means you are not looking for anybody [to give you anything], then you can act in the way your conscience tells you."

Vignette: Images of Leaders: Have Times Changed?

While the image of a leader as the tall, White, charismatic leader operating from a command and control position of power is changing, leaders in the United States today still mirror our dominant majority. Maintaining this image, President Franklin D. Roosevelt made sure never to show his physical disability in public pictures. Yet President Barack Obama, while not a descendant of slaves or running his presidential campaign on race, was forced to confront the issue of race early on in his campaign. As our first non-White president, it is difficult to discern if the overt criticism directed toward his credibility as a leader is, in fact, covert criticism of his race. Donald Trump, leading the charge to demand that President Obama produce his birth certificate, demonstrates this incredibility that someone non-White could be a legitimate leader of the United States. The charges levied against President Obama of being in cahoots with terrorists give the message that someone non-White simply cannot be trusted.

We suggest reframing leadership to be inclusive of diversity, to be responsive to broad social contexts and systems, and to be relevant to rapid changes occurring in the 21st century. The inclusion of culture and diversity into our understanding of leadership frames how we think about our leaders, the members of and organizations in which they lead, and the exchange that occurs between leader and members. In attending to cultural variation, we can examine biases and ethnocentric viewpoints and privilege versus marginal statuses, which interact with the power, influence, and effectiveness of leaders. All these points are important because leaders are increasingly expected to manage an increasingly diverse workforce and to be responsive to the needs of a diverse customer base.

Chin (2009) suggested a new look at diversity "in our minds and in our actions"; How do leaders think about diversity among their followers and in themselves? What leadership styles or dimensions of social identities are elicited or displayed in what contexts? How do lived experiences associated with privilege and marginalized status influence access to and the exercise of leadership? How do we challenge existing notions of leadership to move toward a postindustrial, postcolonial, diverse, and global view of society and its institutions? How do we advance our approaches to leadership to be inclusive, multidimensional, and complex to ensure their relevance in a rapidly changing and diverse global society? We offer some principles of diversity to frame our attention to the values, beliefs, and biases that underlie how we perceive and shape the behaviors of leaders and recognize our tendencies toward ethnocentric bias.

New Paradigms of Leadership: DLMOX

Based on these diversity principles, we need to examine leaders, members, and the exchange that occurs between them as well as the contexts in which leadership occurs. This leads us to redefine Leader-Member Exchange theory (LMX), which is inclusive of all groups and attuned to the organizational and social contexts in which leadership occurs. Diversity by its very definition of inclusivity and difference necessitates flexibility and the ability to adapt what leaders do given the unique composition of an organization's members, differing organizational contexts and their cultures, and the match between leader and member social identities.

These diversity principles also guide the development of leadership research. Too often, leadership theories are static rather than dynamic and interactive as if we might find stand-alone traits associated with good leadership or can identify a finite number of contexts in leadership. To be inclusive of diversity, perception and expectations of members and the exchange that occurs with leaders are as important. The interactive and reciprocal process between leaders and their followers shapes both the exercise and appraisal of effective leadership.

Leadership does not happen in isolation. Contexts of leadership matter. It is an interpersonal and a group process that is cocreated between leader and members. Social identities and lived experiences of leaders and members provide the contexts of leadership along with organization's mission and goals. This interacts with the culture in which organizations are embedded in both time and place. These principles lead us to a new definition of Diverse Leader-Member-Organization Exchange (DLMOX) as the broad context of leadership to be discussed in Chapter 6.

Diversity Leadership Paradigms

New paradigms of diversity leadership must be parsimonious but also be multidimensional and complex and promote social justice and equity as outcomes.

Cultural Values

Attempts to arrive at universal dimensions of leadership often fail to be inclusive of indigenous values and worldviews designed outside the cultural orientation values of their creators. As suggested by implicit leadership theories, these cultural orientation values shape and are shaped by the views of their creators and need to be factored into diversity leadership paradigms. Kao, Sinha, and Wilpert (1999) discuss the indigenization of organizations in Asia, which began as an outgrowth of the overwhelming dependence on Western approaches to studying and explaining human behavior to a shift that cherishes the unique social and cultural factors influencing human behavior and their application for leadership models. This has resulted in the emergence of characteristic patterns of management and organizations that are both distinct and reflective of cultural values and philosophies.

Multidimensional and Complex

While single dimensions of leadership are parsimonious and appealing, they are often simplistic and fail to capture the complex and multiple dimensions influencing the exercise of leadership. Cultural variations contribute to that complexity and must allow for bidirectionality in these dimensions. Often use of single dimensions results in placing those dimensions on a unidimensional scale, which favors or privileges the dominant groups represented.

Social Justice Orientation

Promoting a diversity leadership paradigm implicitly values being a change agent, promoting equity, and valuing differences. This is inherently a social justice orientation to eliminate injustice and unfairness and is reflected in virtuous leadership approaches (Kilburg, 2012) or a humane orientation (House et al., 2004). We need to ask the questions: Are any groups precluded from leadership roles by virtue of their race, ethnicity, sexual orientation, religion, and so forth? Do organizational goals and policies seek to promote an environment that is inclusive and relevant to all groups and are socially responsible to greater needs of society?

Intersecting Ethical Principles and Diverse Leadership

Emphasis on ethics and integrity in our leaders has grown exponentially given events of the 21st century such as the Enron scandal. There is a growing awareness of how different cultural values influence work ethic, business practices, and leadership style leading to an emphasis on ethics as a growing dimension of leadership. Gannon (1997, cited in Pedersen, 1999) identifies differences in work principles and how they influenced different views on ethical behavior. Whereas farming was indigenous to work in both China and the United States, work in China based on rice farming as early as the 7th century was established on principles of survival leading to the need to work toward the common good of the village. In contrast, work in the American culture was established on principles of individual rights influenced by the availability of plentiful resources. Often, these principles are developed based on values and beliefs, as opposed to actual behaviors and decisions and the emergence of moral and ethical codes based in the philosophies and ideals of the culture. Different emphases and interpretation in different cultures result in different practices and rules of engagement, which influence work principles, cultures within organizations, and leadership behaviors.

The intersection of ethical principles with diversity principles also influence the nature of how research is conducted. This has meant the inclusion of diverse perspectives in the development of a diversity leadership paradigm and the inclusion of not only leaders from a community but also the community itself. Joseph Trimble and Celia Fisher (2005) note that this is often absent in research on ethnic communities. The absence of diverse ethnic perspectives in current leadership theories can be considered both culturally insensitive and unethical in posing decreasing access to leadership among minority groups. Linda Smith (1999, p. 1) talks about how such research "is inextricably linked to European imperialism and colonialism. . . . And remains a powerful remembered history for many of the world's colonized peoples" (Smith, 1999, p. 1). Consequently, leadership research that favors or limits its focus on White, male middle class North American leaders can be potentially harmful in marginalizing the leadership behaviors of other groups; that is, their unique culturally embedded style could be construed as ineffective, weak, and limited. It is of particular concern in the global and diverse context of 21st century leadership.

Hence, grounded research methods are more useful to align researchers with leaders and to examine their leadership behaviors and styles across both their own communities and within mainstream communities. From the multicultural literature, there remains the need for ethnic minority communities to heal from the effects of past research that have disempowered them and misinterpreted their culturally unique worldviews of communities. For some researchers, this is premised on research ethical guidelines that emphasize the importance of establishing firm collaborative relationships with community leaders (Fisher & Ball, 2002; Jason, Keys, Suarez-Balcazar, & Davis, 2004; Mohatt, 1989). In developing a diversity leadership paradigm, the inclusion of the societal context also demands an attention to how research results and the conduct of research serve to maintain the existing status quo, which may be biased against promoting inclusion of diverse perspectives about the exercise of leadership. Research that contains errors in protocol, violations of cultural norms, beliefs, and values because researchers misrepresent or misunderstand the intent of their participants, or research that pushes a research agenda onto a community to advance a universal model are disrespectful and intolerable. Moreover, it continues the legacy of oppression and exploitation historically experienced by diverse leaders from minority communities.

As Smith (1999) so eloquently points out, "Self-determination becomes a goal of social justice, which is expressed through and across a wide range of psychological, social, cultural and economic terrains" (p. 199). No matter what approach one adopts, a collaborative relationship is essential for the research to occur in a culturally congruent and resonant manner. In essence, the researcher and community representatives forge a long-term relationship that is maintained and sustained in all phases of the research venture. Ethical planning for scientific inquiry requires flexibility and sensitivity to the contextual challenges and concerns of each ethnic group and research problem (Trimble & Fisher, 2005). This means the responsibility of researchers to collaborate with communities, share results that have practical value, and accept conditions imposed by the community in gaining access to research participants. *Relational methodology* means that one takes the time to nurture relationships not merely for the sake of expediting the research and gaining acceptance and trust but because one should care about the welfare and dignity of all people (Trimble & Mohatt, 2005).

Grounded Research Theory—Emic Approaches

Much of the gold standard of research is to start from existing theoretical models and test the hypothesis. This has raised and reinforced the ethnocentric nature of our leadership research. We might begin to ask: Are we doing research by the lamppost because that is where the light is? In conducting diversity research, we need to ask about that which we do not see, and may not exist, in our current theories. Grounded theory research is a phenomenological method that can be used to generate a theory of leadership that is inclusive of dimensions of diversity rather than testing any existing theory when we are uncertain as to whether or not existing theories are suited for the population under investigation (Corbin & Strauss, 2007; Lester, 1999). In examining leader experiences and perceptions, common themes associating leadership with social identities and lived experiences, Chin (2013) used grounded theory research to identify dimensions from the leaders' perspectives in order not to privilege certain types of scientific knowledge or marginalize other viewpoints. The lived experiences or social situations formed the unit of analysis using grounded theory research as a method to emphasize diverse local worlds, multiple realities, and their complexities. It is an emphasis on the views, values, beliefs, feelings, assumptions, and ideologies of individuals rather than the methods of research (Creswell, 2013). Hence, it is appropriate as a tool to study leadership among diverse racial/ethnic minority leaders in the United States rather than drawing on theories that favor White males who are both dominant in U.S. leadership positions and reflected in existing leadership theories.

Given the ethnocentric nature of extant research, several new dimensions of leadership emerged from this method of using interviews and focus groups with participants engaging in and generating concepts of leadership; these would not have emerged if we were testing existing theoretical paradigms. For example, in our qualitative research with a diverse panel of leaders representing Black, Latino, Asian, and Native American Indian ethnicities, the concept of "invisible leadership" emerged as one favored by Native American Indians and of "reluctant leadership" among Asian Americans in accordance with cultural values embraced during leadership.

In developing a paradigm of diversity leadership, the use of grounded theory research as a method is to expand our view rather than restrict it. Rather than starting with or from an established theory, our intent is to generate theory as a dynamic process that is informed and continually revised by input from diverse leaders, whose perspectives may not be present in existing paradigms of leadership. It is a focus on leaders and leadership in context that changes as leadership is exercised and as societal trends evolve. It is a process of mutual exchange.

Cultural Measurement Equivalence

In constructing and using assessment tools in cross-cultural or cultural-sensitive research in leadership, serious attention must be given to cultural equivalence of the constructs, concepts, terminology, and lexicons. In effect, an instrument's content, format, and metric style must be congruent with and comparable across the cultural groups from which study participants come. Researchers must provide hard evidence that the components of the measurement process meet the standards of functional, conceptual, metric, linguistic, and stimulus equivalence. Otherwise, cultural variations in leadership styles may be confounded by the lack of cultural measurement equivalence; "comparing elements from differing societies leads to inadmissible distortions of reality" (Kobben, 1970, p. 584).

Cultural equivalence refers "to the problem of whether, on the basis of measurements and observations, inferences . . . can be made in different groups of subjects" (Poortinga, 1983, p. 238; Trimble, 2010; Trimble & Vaughn, 2013). However, cultural measurement equivalence is complex in that it can include the following: functional equivalence, conceptual equivalence, stimulus equivalence, linguistic equivalence, and metric equivalence. Johnson (1998) pointed out "(that) in no other field of inquiry . . . has this seemingly elementary concept (equivalence) been assigned as many alternative meanings and disaggregated into as many components as in the field of cross-cultural research" (p. 2). Conceptual and stimulus equivalence exists when the meaning of stimuli, constructs, or concepts is similar or identical for culturally different respondents. Linguistic equivalence is similar, although the emphasis is placed on the linguistic accuracy of item translations. Metric equivalence or scale equivalence (Poortinga, 1975), probably the most technical and the most difficult to evaluate, "exists when the psychometric properties of two (or more) sets of data from two (or more) cultural groups exhibit essentially the same coherence or structure" (Berry, 1980, p. 10). For example, use of forced choice scale alternatives laid out in a linear manner may not fit with the cognitive and evaluative preferences of certain cultural groups; a Likert-type format may work for one group but not for another. Subject bias also pulls for social desirability. Depending on whether responses are collected publicly or privately, the influence of social context and social norms on responses is possible.

Use of conventional scaling procedures in cultural comparative research has introduced a number of methodological problems, especially in the use of a structured response format (Johnson, 1998). Mounting ethnographic evidence points to the following problems. First, researchers tacitly, and perhaps incorrectly, assume that the numeric intervals between choice alternatives on the continuum are equal and can be assigned an integer value. Second, the number of choice alternatives are presumed, perhaps also incorrectly, to represent the full range of categories that an individual would use to evaluate an item. Third, the dimensions of the scale items may not truly be comparable between cultural groups. Finally, the effects and the outcomes of the categorization process, difficult to define in any group, may be confounded by the possibility that not all cultural groups respond to stimuli in a linear manner. For example, Harzing (2006) found consistent cross-cultural differences in acquiescence and extremity across 26 countries. Several points emerge: (1) Not all cultural groups judge, evaluate, and assess stimuli in a linear manner; (2) the number of salient choice options can vary from individual to individual both within and between societal groups; (3) responses are difficult for some because they do not yet understand what the collective will accept; (4) the conventional psychometric format common to paper and pencil tests and instruments may not work in all cultural and ethnic groups; and (5) the need to capture information through a paper and pencil approach may be inconsistent and unrelated to *emic* styles of information sharing (Trimble, Lonner, & Boucher, 1984).

Etic-Emic Approaches to Measurement

Whereas personality traits are often viewed as leadership traits, Cheung, Van de Vijver, and Leong (2011) summarize several approaches to cross-cultural measurement of personality. The goal of many cross-cultural studies is to address the universality of established Western models of personality by examining the level of cross-cultural invariance of the personality structure. This etic approach was found to be biased against non-Western cultures and minority groups within a culture leading to looking at personality and culture through in-depth analyses of personality in a specific cultural context, often called *emic* approaches. There is an increasing appreciation that culture exerts effects on different levels (McAdams & Pals, 2006), including display rules, characteristic adaptations, and life meanings, and on different aspects of assessment. In leadership research, when those unfamiliar with the cultural values and behaviors of a leader are the ones assessing his or her leadership behaviors, they might make attributions about leader behavior from an ethnocentric perspective and fail to reflect the intent or values of the leader that may be different.

In particular, Cheung et al. (2011) identified *openness* as a concept of personality that was found not to be equivalent between Asian and Western cultures using factor analysis. While *openness* is one of the "Big Five" personality traits often thought to be universal, it did not load on any of the Chinese Personality Assessment Inventory (CPAI) factors, an indigenous measure of Chinese personality. Hence, it is suggested that *openness* is more relevant to Western cultures. While *openness* was recognized in implicit theory of personality in the Chinese culture, it coexisted with other traits or was embedded in other factors on the CPAI. In conducting further indigenous measures of Chinese personality, Cheung further identified an *interpersonal relatedness* factor consisting of more indigenously derived scales such as harmony and *Ren-Qing* or reciprocity in interpersonal relationships. These will be discussed later as cultural specific dimensions important to leadership that do not have their equivalence on Western measures of personality. Yang (2006) noted in individualist cultures, personal-oriented personality traits are more developed, differentiated, and influential [in leadership], whereas in collectivist cultures, social-oriented personality traits are more developed, differentiated, and influential. Cheung et al. (2011) concludes with the need for a combined etic-emic approach in which Western models of personality structure may provide a comprehensive picture of the intra-individual aspects of personality but should be complemented by non-Western models of personality that focus more on the social and relational aspects of personality.

The concept equivalence of transformational leadership has also been tested across cultures. While found to be valid as a concept in most cultures (Judge & Piccolo, 2004), the behaviors defining them are not found to be the same (e.g., Den Hartog, Van Muijen, & Koopman, 1997 in a Dutch sample). This too will be discussed later. These examples of leadership concepts that have not been equivalent across culture raise the generalizability of leadership research conducted that is not inclusive and the need for additional models. Ayman and Korabik (2010) view gender and culture as the social context for the interaction between leaders and their followers and propose an integrative model of leadership examining differences among cross-cultural and cross-national groups.

Back Translation

Translated tests can be problematic and not equivalent. For example, "out of sight, out of mind" has been back translated as "blind and insane." The achievement of cultural equivalence through use of item linguistic translation procedures is central to understanding the cultural equivalences of measures. Typically, researchers interested in using a measure with more than one ethnic or cultural group will use a *translation-back translation* (TBT) technique. The TBT technique is straightforward as a researcher first asks a bilingual person to translate the items into the language of the intended research population then asks another linguist to translate the items back into the original language of the measure; items from the translated versions are compared and adjustments are made accordingly. The procedure is repeated until the versions match one another conceptually and functionally (Marin & Marin, 1991). Use of the conventional TBT technique is flawed and unreliable, thus it is not recommended (McGorry, 2000; Van de Vijver, 2000).

Several interesting and plausible alternatives for assuring item and scale equivalence using translations have been proposed and empirically tested. Erkut, Alarcon, Coll, Tropp, and Garcia (1999) developed a dual-focus method that relies more on concept translations than straightforward word-for-word translations. Indigenous researchers are invited to join the full research team and together they work through the meanings of concepts intended for use in the measures. Similarly, Geisinger (1994) recommends use of an editorial board consisting of bilingual translators who have credentials similar to those of the translator; both collaborate on the translation of items. Finally, Johnson (1998) identified some other interesting approaches to item and scale translations, including decentered translation, use of independent bilingual translators who develop alternative versions of the target measure, rank ordering of alternative versions of the measure in the source language, use of cognitive "think-aloud" protocols, and facet analysis.

Creating New Paradigms

When researchers used existing dimensions to study leadership cross-culturally, they have found universal dimensions. For example, the GLOBE studies identified six cultural endorsed leadership dimensions; personality researchers identified the "Big Five," which has been applied to leadership traits. However, this has been limiting in restricting leadership dimensions to known and existing ones. The growing trend toward drawing concepts from indigenous non-Western cultures has led to identifying new dimensions, for example, Cheung et al., 2011 in the concept of *Ren-Qing*, and Markus and Kitayama (1991) in identifying dimensions of self-identity (discussed in Chapter 4). These reflect attempts to address the incongruity between existing leadership models for non-Western, non-White (Euro-American) leaders and organizations that often hold differing worldviews about relationships and social protocol in business and leadership. Some alternative views for creating new paradigms in response to the inadequacy of existing leadership theories follow. See Table 3.1 for a summary.

Table 3.1   Creating New Paradigms

Dimension	Concept	Origin	Proposed
Diversity leadership	Focus on the inclusion of all groups in leadership, and the infusion of diversity principles into leadership and organizations	Cultural competence	Chin (2010)
Theory Z	Alternative to theory X and Y, theory Z focused on increasing employee loyalty to company	Japanese management	Ouchi (1981)
Servant leadership	Leader serves the people he/she leads as an end rather than the means	Civil Rights movement	Greenleaf (1977)
Daoist leadership	Dao is "actionless." Like water, a Daoist leadership style is altruistic, modest, adaptable and flexible, clear and transparent, soft but strong—an Asian version of the Big Five personality traits common in Western theories.	Eastern perspective	Lee (2004)
Feminist leadership	Bias toward women and inequity in social status and roles making the role to leadership a "labyrinth."	Feminist perspective	Eagly & Carli (2007) Chin, Lott, Rice, & Sanchez-Hucles (2007)
Invisible leadership	"Leading from behind" reflects the belief that good leadership means stepping back and allowing the strengths of others to emerge	Native American perspectives	Chin (2013)
Reluctant leader	Refers to the reluctance of leaders to step forward without the endorsement and encouragement of their peers and elders; it is syntonic with cultural values of modesty and community support	Ethnic minority perspectives	Chin (2013)
Relationships:	Central role of reciprocity in systems of social exchange within Asian cultures	Asian cultural values	Cheung et al. (2001)
Ren-Qing	Ren-qing involves the moral obligation to maintain a relationship important to the leader-member exchange.		
QuanXi	QuanXi describes the basic dynamic in a personalized network of influence.		

(Continued)

Table 3.1   (Continued)

Dimension	Concept	Origin	Proposed
Performance-maintenance	Performance function includes strict observance of regulations and pressure for production as well as concern for planning and processing of work. Maintenance function is directed at group maintenance and preservation. The performance leadership function involves forming and reaching group goals, while the "maintenance" function involves preserving group social stability or relationships.	Related to task versus relationship orientation based on differences between Western and Eastern perspectives	Misumi & Peterson (1985)
Hierarchy: benevolent paternalism	Leaders exercise their leadership authoritatively but with beneficence. Noted in collectivistic cultures with high power distance.	Asian, African, and Russian cultures	Ayman & Chemers (1983)
Prophetic-caliphal leaders	The caliphal model depends on coercion and the application of authoritarian inducements. The prophetic model depends on love and free submission with a minimum use of coercion. The prophetic-caliphal model is based on two assumptions: behavioral continuity of traditional forms of behavior in Arab society that are cultural rather than hereditary, and can be modified.	Arab cultures Khadra (1990)	
Implicit leadership	Social cognition similar to implicit leadership theories where leader effectiveness and influence is largely dependent on presenting an image consistent with followers' expectations of a leader.	Cross-cultural and cultural values GLOBE studies	Dorfman (1996) Yukl (2010) House et al. (2004)
Humanistic-altruistic leadership	Has been exemplified more by religious leaders such as the Dalai Lama, Nelson Mandela, or Mother Teresa	Eastern perspectives	
Collectivistic versus individualistic leadership	Characterized by consensus and collaboration, collectivism has been associated with collaborative leadership styles.	Dimensions of worldviews Hofstede (2001)	

Egalitarianism versus hierarchical orientation	Emphasis on equality between leaders and members compared to a hierarchical orientation aligned with power distance between leader and member	Dimension of worldviews	
Work-family interface	A new paradigm that operates in a gender friendly culture responsive to the family demands of women	Feminist perspective	Erkut (2001) Cheung & Halpern (2010)
Interpersonal versus task orientation	Typically dichotomized as masculine and feminine and associated with a doing versus feeling orientation	Leadership style	
Cooperative versus competitive leadership	Leadership is often viewed as a competitive process based on Greco traditions compared to the Chinese traditions of leadership based on harmony and cooperation.	Greek versus Confucian philosophy Li (2013)	
Shared power and empowerment	Leadership is responsive to members and associated with social justice and equity goals that shift the base of power to members	Civil Rights movement	
Affirmative paradigms	Aversive racism Stereotyped threat	Racism Dovidio & Gaertner (2004); Steele (1995)	
Ethical leadership	Morality and integrity of the leader together with pursuing social justice goals	Moral judgment Kilburg (2012)	
Authentic leadership	Maintaining authenticity of leader identity	Leader identity	
Global leadership	21st century post-industrial emphasis on innovation, technology, and rapid change	Globalism	
Global teams	Emphasis on designing and maintaining effective teams that are diverse	Globalism	
Asian versus Western	Asian emphasis on a holistic view, harmony and balance, valuing cooperation, collectivism, hierarchy of roles, and altruism Western emphasis on a detailed view, valuing competition, individualism, egalitarianism, and assertiveness	Eastern versus Western perspectives	

Theory Z: From Ethnocentric to Global

Theory X maintained a cynical mistrust of the worker, while Theory Y maintained an idealistic trust of the worker proposed by McGregor (1985); these American-based theories suggested that a participative style of leadership is more effective than an authoritarian style. It was popular in the 1970s until the outsourcing of business internationally found that it did not apply to Japanese management or corporations outside the United States. This discrepancy appeared related to the greater degree of power distance (i.e., emphasis on hierarchy between manager and worker) inherent between Japanese managers and their workforce (Hofstede, 1980, cited in Pedersen, 1999). In the United States and Denmark, low power distance countries, there was a preference for a participative leadership style while high power distance countries, for example, France, Spain, and Mexico, expect and respond better to authoritative leadership style (Rodrigues, 2001, cited in Pedersen, 1999).

Ouchi (1981) proposed Theory Z, the so-called "Japanese Management" style popularized during the Asian economic boom of the 1980s, in reaction to McGregor's Theory X and Theory Y. In contrast to Theory X, which stated that workers inherently dislike and avoid work and must be driven to it, and Theory Y, which stated that work is natural and can be a source of satisfaction when aimed at higher order human psychological needs, Theory Z focused on increasing employee loyalty to the company by providing a job for life with a strong focus on the well-being of the employee, both on and off the job; it was proposed that this management style tends to promote stable employment, high productivity, and high employee morale and satisfaction. Theory Z, as proposed by Ouchi, combines the best parts of both Japanese and American firms by focusing on sharing, collaboration, trust, teamwork, and inclusive decision making, which is in line with Daoistic principles of leadership.

Servant Leadership: From Privilege to Inclusive

Servant leadership is one of the more popular leadership models today. Developed by Robert K. Greenleaf (1977), the servant leader serves the people he or she leads; this implies that they (the people's needs) are an end in themselves rather than a means to an organizational purpose or bottom line. Servant-oriented leadership was made popular with the late Dr. Martin Luther King Jr. during the Civil Rights era by giving priority attention to the needs of their colleagues and those they serve as humble stewards of their organization's resources (human, financial, and physical). Servant leadership has been described as one of the ways in which President Obama is representative of the modern ethnic minority leader. His work as a community organizer embraced this leadership style early in his career; he used the community and a sense of purpose beyond himself to organize one of the most inclusive and expansive presidential campaigns in the history of the United States of America. His repeated message was about the people and his trying to reach goals for the collective good.

Servant leadership models derived from racial and ethnic minority group leaders who often held marginal status in society and organizations dominated by leaders with privilege. Getting a place at the table was a challenge, and issues of equity a goal. Dictatorial use of power in governments throughout the world especially following WWII made power bad. The 1960s Civil Rights movement followed by the Women's Movement, Peace Movement, and Gay Pride Movement led to a push for the sharing of power and empowerment and inclusion of communities as the goal of leadership.

Daoist Leadership: Promoting Different Worldviews and Cultural Values

The Daoist model of *wu-wei,* often translated as "nonaction" or "actionlessness" approach, can be perceived to some extent as based on Theory Z. The leader observes and encourages a participative form leaving the essentials of the task to those who are in charge supporting the autonomy of the task results (E. Li, personal communication, July 2013). Daoist leadership model, introduced by Y.-T. Lee (2004), is based on Daoism philosophy as a way to understand human existence and the meaning of the universe in relation to human existence. Using water as a metaphor for leadership, a Daoist leadership style is deemed distinctive but useful. Like water, Lee posits that a Daoist leadership style is altruistic, modest, adaptable and flexible, clear and transparent, soft but strong—an Asian version of the "Big Five." Using Asian metaphors, Lee describes leadership as like water—flexible, molds itself to the shape of its container, adaptable, humble because it is always on bottom, and powerful because it can mold mountains as it flows.

The emphasis on Daoist principles speaks most directly to a leader's use of power and position and calls for leaders (1) to follow natural laws and the way things are and (2) to be very humanistic or humanitarian by following human laws. These emphases on humans being in harmony with nature and in harmony with each other, respectively, are the backbone of Daoism. There is an emphasis on hierarchy or a clear order of human beings (*ren* or human beings), earth (*di* or land), heaven (*tian* or sky), and nature (*zi ran*) (Fei, 1984). It is a clear reaction to the command and control theories of an earlier era.

Individuals who follow the Dao (including those who are leaders) according to Lee (2004): (a) exert minimal influence on the lives of followers; (b) encourage followers to take ownership of tasks; (c) employ "soft tactics," such as persuasion, empowerment, modeling, teamwork, collaboration, service; (d) reject the use of violence; (e) demonstrate creativity and flexibility; (f) promote harmony with nature and others; (g) live simply and humbly; (h) reject the trappings of status and promote equality; (i) recognize the underlying spiritual dimension of reality; and (j) give to and serve others. These principles appear to provide an ethical framework for many of the latest trends in the literature: empowerment, teamwork, collaboration, servant leadership, spirituality in the workplace, and rapid innovation. The more one serves, the more one leads.

Leadership first means follower-ship or service-ship just like water. Second, leadership means nonintrusiveness or noninterference (by practicing *wu wei,* i.e., following natural laws or Dao), and it also refers to change, as discussed at length below. Daoism can also be used to build a harmonious relationship between a leader and a follower (i.e., conflict resolution). For example, Robert Rosen made a cogent case that 21st century success will belong to CEOs who develop a "global mindset" that goes beyond the limits of any single country's culture or approach. Daoism may challenge people to go beyond "either-or" dichotomous thinking to achieve "both-and" integrative thinking.

Recent studies by Richard Nisbett and his colleagues (Nisbett & Masuda, 2003) showed that the East Asian view of causality is holistic, marked by a tendency to attend to the entire field when making causal attributions. This way of viewing causality has been labeled dialectical reasoning or *yin-yang* thinking (Lee, 2001). It includes the principles of change, contradiction, and interrelation based on Chinese Daoism or traditional culture. For example, an unpleasant situation can become a peaceful one (i.e., change), a conflict can be viewed as something positive (i.e., contradiction), and any problem or dilemma involves two parties (i.e., interrelation). Most of the research on Daoist leadership has been theoretical; however, some empirical research suggests that leaders who display self-sacrificial altruistic behavior (a yin quality) lead their followers more effectively than those without self-sacrificial altruism consistent with Daoist leadership principles. Based on the *Zhouyi or The Book of Changes,* the core text of Daoism, the yin (smooth and supportive) and yang (the constructive and firm) are in dynamic flux of change. Daoism and Confucianism, two Asian philosophies fundamental to the Chinese tradition, are complementary; the former is perceived to have more of the yin quality and the latter perceived to have more of the yang quality (Li, 2013).

Feminist Leadership: Does Difference Make a Difference?

The literature on women and leadership dating back to the 1970s has implications for the exercise of leadership among diverse leaders within the United States. They bring in dimensions of equity, differences in leadership style, incongruity of roles, and bias toward women that are related to our stereotypes of social identities and roles of women in society (see Chin et al., 2007; Eagly & Carli, 2007; Heilman, 2001). In particular, Eagly and Carli replaces the "glass ceiling" with the "labyrinth" metaphor to reflect that there is a path, but it is difficult to navigate.

According to the research, women tend to be more transformative and collaborative in their leadership styles. However, both men and women perform similarly in actual positions of leadership. The absence of gender differences among men and women leaders in the field contrasts with differences when leading in empirically created or laboratory situations; this has been interpreted to reflect the influence of priming for social stereotypic behavior. Sanchez-Hucles and Sanchez (2007) speak to the intersection of gender and ethnicity in our understanding of women and leadership and the use of feminist principles when women lead. Preliminary findings suggest that there is an interaction of social group membership with the exercise of leadership. Organizations with a diverse workforce often require frequent interaction among people from different cultural or social groups; in such settings, social and cultural identities as well as assumptions and perceptions about those who are different often get evoked (e.g., women vs. men, White vs. African, Latino, or Asian), resulting in in-group/out-group dynamics which impact the leadership experience (Ayman, 2004).

Invisible and Reluctant Leadership: Promoting Ethnic Minority Perspectives

Some preliminary results emerged using a grounded theory approach to understand the leadership styles of past-presidents of the Society for the Study of Race, Ethnicity and Culture of the American Psychological Association (Moritsugu, Arellano, Boelk, Pfeninger, & Chin, in progress). A consistent theme emerged among the panel of ethnic minority leaders about their concern for members as a dimension of leadership. The society's motto of "it takes a village" and "standing on the shoulders of those before you" reflected the belief that good leadership means stepping back and allowing the strengths of others to emerge; facilitating growth and change was an aspect of leadership that meant creating a community where people feel they can have a voice and express their opinions. The Native American

Indian and Asian American leaders preferred less confrontational styles of "invisible" and "reluctant" leadership.

One female leader articulated this "silent leadership" style and "pushing from behind" as consistent with her Native American Indian values; she described her style as one of encouraging group members to express themselves and listening to the opinions of all before making decisions, even if it means not sticking to the clock. She indicated that she might go behind the scenes to talk with individual members to get things done rather than to be visibly out front. She saw this as a way of delegating and supporting others in their leadership by "pushing them from behind."

The "reluctant leader" was another style that emerged. While preliminary survey results showed that these ethnic minority leaders identified themselves as leaders, they were reluctant to publicly label themselves as leaders in a leadership panel (Moritsugu et al., in progress). While 5 out the 14 leaders referred to their reluctance to self-label as leaders in their interview excerpts, virtually all but one during the public panel discussion identified themselves as reluctant to assume leadership roles without encouragement from mentors or past leaders. Having to be asked or urged to seek leadership positions was a consistent theme. It was identified by one Asian American leader as consistent with cultural values of being "given face" by one's peers and community. In fact, some of the panelists demonstrated this reluctance as they deferred to other panelists in taking the microphone and waiting for it to be passed. This dynamic played out in the exchange among the panelists as all respectfully ensured that each would have his or her turn; they self-regulated in sticking to the time constraints as they shared their stories or words of wisdom. The nonverbal negotiation and deference to one another was also evidenced and especially noted among the Asian American leaders. Described as consistent with Asian values, this was identified by one Asian American leader as consistent with the emphasis on modesty and reflected in a difficulty with talking about oneself because it calls attention to oneself.

While this "invisible" and "reluctant" style are syntonic with cultural values emphasizing connectedness and relationships, it was also noted that these styles may not be adaptive in leadership contexts where cultural values differ, for example, in dominant or mainstream contexts where there is an emphasis on competition.

Incorporating Non-Western Perspectives in Leadership

In examining cross-cultural management, Thomas (2008) identifies some non-Western theories of leadership. While there is no generally accepted definition of leadership (Bass, 1990), descriptions of great leaders abound in such diverse writings as Homer's Iliad, the Bible, and the writings of Confucius. Thomas suggests that the meaning and importance of leadership may vary across cultures and over time. Western theories of leadership have progressed through four periods in which each had a dominant theoretical approach. In the early 1900s, trait theories, or the so called "Great Man" theories, were unable to consistently identify traits necessary and sufficient for leadership success because they focused on leader-centric traits without attention to followers and differing situations. This led to a more behavioral approach, which shifted the focus from "what leaders are" to "what leaders do." Theories and leadership research emphasized task versus relationship oriented behaviors and, in fact, showed both gender differences and cultural variation. Relationship-oriented leaders often were found to increase subordinate satisfaction (Aycan, 2006), but the influence of task-oriented leaders was more complex across cultures. A strong task orientation among North American leaders and Western European leaders has been found, whereas a strong relationship orientation has been found among leaders in African, Arab, and Latin American countries (Cellich, 1997, cited in Pedersen, 1999). A third period was reflected in contingency theories, which began with Fiedler's (1967) basic idea that the situation moderates the relationship between the leader's style and effectiveness. Cross-cultural studies found that high performing Filipino managers were more task oriented, and high performing Chinese managers were more relationship oriented (Bennett, 1977). This was interpreted to reflect the moderating effect of culture on leader behavior and outcomes (Triandis, 1993).

A fourth period shifted to leadership styles. Post WWII, leadership studies examined democratic-autocratic-laissez-faire leadership styles as ways to compare the effectiveness of political governments. This shifted toward favoring democratic leadership styles, which became transactional styles of leadership. Burns (1978) proposed transformational leadership—that is, visionary, change oriented, and nonconservative—in response to rapid social change and sociopolitical issues of its times. Transformational leadership as described by Thomas (2008) challenges the role of the global manager and reflects a shift from the days of sending corporate troubleshooters or seasoned expatriate managers in. In today's society of multinational corporations, all business is global business and can benefit from transformational styles of leadership. As we examine global leadership, there is a shift from the dominance of U.S. based and Western theories of leadership to include Eastern theories especially as we see countries such as China, India, and Russia dominating the world scene.

Along with implicit theories of leadership, this fourth period defined leadership as a process that includes member perceptions of the leader (Lord &

Maher, 1991, cited in Thomas, 2008). Accordingly, followers develop mental representations or prototypes of leaders through exposure to social situations and interactions with them resulting in both universal and cultural specific expectations of leadership. This was found to be especially true of charismatic or transformational leaders, which connotes vision and change where followers must attribute extraordinary leadership abilities to those leaders who exhibit certain behaviors. House (1977) described charismatic leadership as the ability of a leader to elicit emotional attachment from followers, to instill confidence, and to enhance follower commitment to the mission set forth by the leader. By mirroring follower value orientations, and follower intrinsic motives, charismatic leadership gives meaningfulness to follower activities by providing a sense of moral purpose and commitment. Leader behavior then deals with symbolic acts, visionary messages, intellectual stimulation, and displays of confidence in self and followers. Charismatic leaders are often viewed as demonstrating great personal sacrifice, and performing beyond normal requirements. Definitions of *charisma*, however, may vary across cultures and gender. Charisma, according to the GLOBE studies (House et al., 2004), is said to be "the power to inspire devotion and commitment for the group's goals" (p. 500) and to "produce power through infectious qualities of leadership and influence, involving a leader's aura, dynamism, and persuasiveness" (p. 515). Masculine definitions are associated with tall, powerful carriage and presence connoting influence and strength that may be at odds with social stereotypes of different racial/ethnic groups and women. For example, a Chinese woman leader described as charismatic by many responded with "It's an advantage to be a woman. Not that I took advantage. I have a reputation of always being approachable (a yin factor). I always have this big smile on my face, which makes a lot of people very happy. . . . Lots of women look up to me because they think that I'm a very good role model." Hence, this quote captures the essence of yin, feminine, and modeling characteristics as key to her leadership and of a different view of charisma. Modeling characteristics are, in fact, a key in Chinese leadership (Li, 2013).

Relationships: Quanxi and Ren-Qing in Leadership

Quanxi and *Ren-Qing* were identified as indigenous personality traits that are culturally specific to Asian cultures (Cheung, Van de Vijver, & Leong, 2011). While both constructs can be translated as "connections" and "relationships," these terms do not sufficiently reflect the wide deeper cultural implications of the constructs. It is very much related to the construct of "face," or *miànzi* in Asian cultures, a more well-known construct meaning social status, propriety, prestige, or more realistically a combination of all three, as it governs the nature of interpersonal and business relationships and leadership.

Ren-Qing is the expression behavior within relationships based on the "five constant virtues," *wu-lun,* which derive from culturally embedded rituals or *li* in Asian cultures. *Li* is the foundation of Confucian interpersonal process, originated during the Zhou Dynasty, and may be perceived as a form of law where family or court deviation from such principles are punishable. *Ren-Qing* is a lighter form of social law, which encourages the balance between harmony, benevolence, and justice. The actual display of *ren-qing* with appropriate equity and fairness is an essential guiding factor for a successful leadership structure where the leader is an exemplary model (E. Li, personal communication, July 2013). *Ren-Qing* is a construct in Asian cultures where reciprocity has a central role in systems of social exchange; it is defined as the personal and interpersonal relationship that regulates behavior in social life, business matters, and leadership. It involves the moral obligation to maintain the relationship and governs social protocol in giving, receiving, and returning gifts and favors in the long run (Yan, 1996). As such, Asian businesses often rely on the *Ren-Qing* of those with whom they do business to execute successful negotiations. Inattention to *Ren-Qing* in business is often considered an insult and can result in negotiation failures.

Quanxi, a related construct, describes the basic dynamic of personalized networks of influence. It can be translated as relatedness fundamental to the Chinese tradition. All in the universe is related to everything else as the season and time changes the myriad of things follows in the cosmos, nature, and everyday life. Unlike the common usage of this term only based on human relations, the derivation of this term is from the *Book of Changes*, a core text of Daoism. At the most basic level, the *Quanxi* of the male and female is represented by the yin and yang for the creative aspects of reproduction. This *Quanxi* leads to the creative solution of problem solving when there are situations that are in conflict. The degree of *Ren-Qing* that has been accumulated and used in this process will be a mark of leadership effectiveness (E. Li, personal communication, July 2013; Li, 2013).

Quanxi describes a personal connection between two people in which one is able to prevail upon another to perform a favor or service or be prevailed upon. The two people need not be of equal social status. *Quanxi* can also be used to describe a network of contacts, which an individual can call on when something needs to be done, and through which he or she can exert influence on behalf of another.

The value of *Quanxi* has a major influence on the management of businesses based in China and also those owned by overseas Chinese in Southeast Asia, sometimes known as the bamboo network. In East Asian societies, the boundary between business and social lives can sometimes be ambiguous as people tend to rely heavily on their closer relations and friends. It can result in nepotism in the workforce since it is common for leaders to draw from family and close ties to fill employment opportunities instead of assessing talent and suitability as is common in Western societies.

These constructs are important in how non-Western perspectives are missing from the extant literature in leadership. The existence of these constructs challenge the emphasis on the "Big Five" factors of personality from Western culture that carried over into leadership studies as attempts to confirm universal traits that could be measured across cultures. Cheung et al. (2001) challenged this etic approach as failing to include emic dimensions not measured by the "Big Five" as discussed earlier. In a revolutionary study, she identified additional factors, including *Ren-Qing*, that correlated with behavior and personality in Asian cultures but did not exist in Western cultures.

Performance-Maintenance Theory

Misumi and Peterson (1985) proposed a performance-maintenance theory of leadership directed toward achieving group goals. It is presented here as an example of how leadership dimensions cannot simply be applied cross-culturally without taking into consideration more complex social contexts, cultural value orientations, and meaning of the sociopolitical zeitgeist following WWII. The performance function includes strict observance of regulations and pressure for production as well as concern for planning and processing of work while the maintenance function is directed at group maintenance and preservation. The performance leadership function involves forming and reaching group goals, while the maintenance function involves preserving group social stability or relationships. Concrete leadership behaviors tend to reflect some degree of emphasis on each function.

These two functions are analogous to the task versus relationship orientation found in U.S. based leadership research. The empirically based, factor analytic studies were conducted during a period in Japan where democratic, autocratic, and laissez-faire concepts of leadership style were both very difficult to represent operationally and very difficult to communicate in a nonemotional manner; the concepts were heavily value-laden and politically meaningful at a time when Japan was adapting to a democracy being imposed on the country by foreign influences. Autocratic leadership was naively reflected by primarily P-oriented behavior and counter-M-oriented behavior while democratic leadership was naively reflected by primarily M-oriented behavior and by behavior involving a combined P and M emphasis. Japanese leadership was assumed to be P-oriented or autocratic in nature.

The performance-maintenance studies maintained an emphasis on the interaction of these two basic functions unlike parallel research in the United States that tended to place these two functions in opposition, at the extremes of a single dimension. According to Misumi, this approach to leadership precludes any explicit test of the interaction of P and M functions; he attributes this to the greater emphasis of U.S. researchers on inductive rather than deductive reasoning used in the P-M research and to cultural differences between the United States and Japan that affect leadership as a culturally contingent phenomenon. The P-M theory was developed during a time of tremendous growth and change in Japan with leadership researchers grappling with issues of leadership and democracy and their implications for Japan's future growth.

"Unexpectedly," the typical finding of these P-M studies in Japan was that the highest levels of performance and the most positive work attitudes are found under P-M type leadership (which combined interaction of P and M), followed by M-type, P-type, and finally P-M-type leadership (which were laissez-faire), in that order. These studies support the interactive perspective of P-M and that P-oriented leadership without the M function can be counterproductive. Misumi and Peterson (1985) hypothesized that the "implicit leadership theories" maintained by people in Japan may associate the two leadership functions as a unidimensional "leader exchange" of the two functions.

In general, M-type leadership may be preferred in situations with highly anxious subordinates and in which physiological arousal needs to be minimized while P-type leadership may be desired in situations where subordinates with little investment or low achievement orientation are used to accomplish a task that requires quick work but little quality. The fact that M-type leadership was consistently superior over P-type leadership was attributable to the typically long-term groups and the typical value placed on good quality, accurate work in Japanese organizations. Over time and across situations, in the typical long-term relationship between a Japanese supervisor and subordinate group, the P-M type of leadership is generally desirable.

Hierarchy: Benevolent Paternalism

Ayman and Chemers (1983) found evidence for a benevolent paternalistic leadership dimension in Iran (before the Islamic revolution) in which leaders exercised their leadership authoritatively but with beneficence. While defined a bit differently in different cultures, this same dimension has shown up in many Asian countries, such as India (Kao, Sinha, & Wilpert, 1999) and China (Cheng, Chou, Wu, Huang, & Farh, 2004).

Paternalistic leadership involving a hierarchical relationship between leader and followers has been noted in collectivistic cultures with high power distance. The leader is like a parent based in traditional values of *familism*, Confucian ideology, and feudalism dating back to 5th century BC (Aycan, 2006). Paternalistic leadership has been noted in Pacific Asian societies, Africa, and Russia and has been associated with positive employee attitudes. This type of leadership involves elements of individualism—that is, making decisions without considering opinions of others—and *personalism—that is,* viewing one's relationship to others from an egocentric perspective. Therefore, there is tendency for the great man or prophetic leader to emerge who would garner feelings of love, unity of purpose, and voluntary submission to authority by followers (analogous to the charismatic leader) as opposed to the caliphal leader who must use coercion and fear to maintain his status (Thomas, 2008, p. 160).

Prophetic-Caliphal Leadership

Leadership in Arab societies is strongly influenced by Islamic religion and tribal tradition as well as contact with Western culture (Ali, 1990). Leaders are expected to behave like fathers—that is, to be authoritarian and patriarchal. These sheikocracies have created a duality in Arab leaders who both maintain tradition and are influenced by Western management practices (Al-Kubaisy, 1985).

The prophetic-caliphal model of leadership is an abstraction of the dynamics of Arab leadership, another non-Western perspective. It consists of four elements or dimensions and two submodels. The four elements are personalism, individualism, lack of institutionalization, and the importance of the great man. The two submodels are the "prophetic model" and the "caliphal model." These elements and submodels are highly interdependent and tied together in a comprehensive, dynamic system of leadership relationships (Khadra, 1990, pp. 37–39). *Personalism* is defined as a subjective, egocentric view of the relationships of the individual to other people and things. It implies a low degree of objectivity along with a strong emotional commitment. It contrasts with *individualism*, which is defined as the tendency to make decisions regardless of the opinions of the group, or in spite of such opinions. Therefore, personalism and individualism are two sides of the same coin, complementing and reinforcing each other. The combined effect of the two elements is the lack of institutionalization. A logical consequence of the interaction of the three previous elements is a strong predisposition toward expecting the great man and accepting his role—that is, the fourth element in the model.

The caliphal model depends on coercion and the application of authoritarian inducements, probably because of the feeling of equality among the competitors and the lack of feeling of inferiority on the part of challengers' vis-à-vis the incumbent leader. The prophetic model, on the other hand, depends on love and free submission with a minimum use of coercion. Members in these contexts are free to express their opinions as the leader is always expected to show interest in diverse ideas (Jasim, 1987). Finally, the prophetic-caliphal model is based on two assumptions regarding leadership. First, the dimensions of the model represent a sort of behavioral continuity of traditional forms of behavior in Arab society. This continuity is cultural rather than hereditary and can be modified by applying the appropriate means (Hamady, 1960; Rikabi, 1964; Sayegh, 1965). Second, leadership (especially in the political context) is interrelated with the other subsystems of society—that is, the political, social, economic, and ideological subsystems.

Implicit Leadership Theories: Cross-Cultural Perspectives

Dorfman (1996) and Yukl (2010) offer a cross-cultural model of leadership emphasizing social cognition similar to implicit leadership theories where leader effectiveness and influence are largely dependent on presenting an image consistent with followers' expectations of a leader. This model highlights the need to manage the interaction between leaders and managers who are culturally different. Although there is little research on this model, Ah Chong and Thomas (1997) found that followers are likely to have expectations based on leader's culture, but it is more complex. For example, U.S. subordinates of Japanese managers expect them to be task oriented as expected in Western cultures. However, if leaders adapt their behaviors to characterize the followers' culture (i.e., if Japanese managers become more task oriented as in U.S. culture), it is effective only if perceived as genuine by followers (Thomas & Ravlin, 1995). This presents a challenge for how diverse leaders can be both authentic and effective.

Contrasting Western Versus Eastern Worldviews

As the aforementioned perspectives demonstrate, cultural variation consistently emerges in the cultural orientation values and the implicit leadership dimensions, which may shape the exercise of leadership. Differences between Western and Eastern worldviews have consistently been identified. Several identified below are known to shape differences in leader identity, in leadership style, and leader behaviors. Although they may be presented as dichotomous dimensions, they are, in fact, continuous. Moreover, they may be dual dimensions.

Collectivism Versus Individualism

While this dimension captures some of the political and government differences between countries, it has also been reflected in differences in the cultural values held by members of different cultural groups. Collectivism has been associated with collaborative leadership styles and is increasingly being viewed as the type of leadership needed for the 21st century. While viewed as new to forms of leadership, these values and means of group process have been indigenous to racial and ethnic minority communities in the United States, to many Asian and non-Western countries, and to women for centuries. The fact that it has only now made its way into the leadership literature probably reflects the Westernized and masculine views that have dominated leadership theories.

Humanistic-Altruistic Orientation

While leaders are and have been praised for their charitable behaviors, humanistic and altruistic leadership has been exemplified more by religious leaders such as the Dalai Lama or Mother Teresa than by corporations or governments although Nelson Mandela of South Africa is a good example. All were recipients of the Nobel Peace Prize. The institution of the Dalai Lama has become, over the centuries, a central focus of Tibetan cultural identity, "a symbolic embodiment of the Tibetan national character." Today, the Dalai Lama and the office of the Dalai Lama have become focal points in their struggle toward independence and, more urgently, cultural survival. In that role, the Dalai Lama has chosen to use peace and compassion in his treatment of his own people and his oppressors. His Holiness has three main commitments in life: (1) On the level of a human being, his first commitment is the promotion of human values such as compassion, forgiveness, tolerance, contentment, and self-discipline; (2) on the level of a religious practitioner, his second commitment is the promotion of religious harmony and understanding among the world's major religious traditions . . . all major world religions have the same potential to create good human beings; (3) his third commitment is to work to preserve Tibet's Buddhist culture, a culture of peace and nonviolence (Dalai Lama, n.d.).

Mother Teresa was known for her charitable work for the poorest of the poor as a Catholic nun in India. By the time of her death in 1997, she had established Missionaries of Charity in 123 countries in the world and became known as "mother to the poor," a symbol of compassion to the world and a living witness to the thirsting love of God (Mother Teresa, n.d.).

Nelson Mandela, former and first Black president of South Africa between 1994 and 1999, was imprisoned for his antiapartheid revolutionary activities for 27 years before becoming president. He was credited for dismantling the legacy of apartheid in South Africa, a freedom fighter, prisoner, president, and Nobel laureate who led South Africa out of apartheid, and who steered the country from White-minority rule to multiracial democracy. As president, determined to forge racial reconciliation in South Africa, he hired Afrikaner staff, embraced rugby and even invited one of the prosecutors who had him imprisoned, Percy Yutan, to lunch to demonstrate his support for peace and absence of revenge.

Qualitative research findings about the leadership styles among diverse racial/ethnic minority leaders in the United States demonstrated a concern and value for equity and fairness in the exercise of leadership (Chin, 2013). This social justice orientation appears related to benevolence and altruism as reflected in the humanistic cultural value orientation in the GLOBE studies and not unlike the humanistic qualities embodied in Mother Teresa, the Dalai Lama, and Nelson Mandela. For ethnic minority leaders, women, and LGBT individuals, their lived experiences, associated with a common experience of marginalization, discrimination, and oppression, explains the presence of this orientation and its association with leadership.

Conflict Management and Negotiation Across Cultures

While the Chinese are noted for valuing harmony, good relationships, respect, and being cooperative, foreign negotiators arriving in China are often unexpectedly met with fierce, adversarial bargaining (Blackman, cited in Pedersen, 1999); Chinese negotiators have also been defined as "inscrutable, skillful, tough, shrewd, and tenacious" (Fang, cited in Pedersen, 1999, p. 46). This preying on the foreigner's ignorance of the Chinese bureaucratic system provides an interesting contrast with the stereotypic image of the Chinese as passive and unassertive or as acting on harmony and good relationships. In drawing the boundary between those who are part of the "family" when principles of *ren-qing* and *quanxi* come into play, Chinese negotiators can justify their different leadership styles with "foreign negotiators" as necessary and appropriate in doing business.

The important factor to note here is the high context culture of China where inscrutability is almost always the result of the lack of cultural guidance where a relationship has not been built or transferred from someone that has already built it. To transform the skillfulness into harmonious cooperation with mutual respect, extensive homework to mutually learn the appropriate *li* or rules of the culture in preparing for the meeting and forming relationships based on *quanxi* where they can invoke the other's *ren-qing* as part of the ritual would be helpful (Li, 2013).

Another difference between cultures in negotiating styles is related to the expectation of a long-term relationship (Connerley & Pedersen, 2005, p. 160). Chinese negotiators often spend time on the relationship and will give concessions for the short term because of their expectation for a long-term relationship. At the same time, they are less likely to be emotionally expressive so as not to give away their intent. Russian negotiators, on the other hand, do not expect to develop long-term relationships with their bargaining partners, and therefore do not spend time on relationship building, and therefore will make few concessions. Arab cultures use emotional appeals because they use subjective feelings and are willing to make concessions. Latin American negotiators are often more emotionally expressive and passionate in their negotiations. The differences in these negotiating styles reflect the cross-cultural and diversity in negotiating styles or solutions to leadership dilemmas. The differences in process between American and Chinese negotiators have been characterized by the statements: "It's not personal; it's business" versus "It is a matter of *Quanxi.*"

Expanding Current Theories to Include Diversity

As leadership research expands to be inclusive and diverse of those who are studied, existing assumptions about leadership dimensions are being challenged. Increasingly, dimensions that are value driven are beginning to shape our understanding of leadership. As demonstrated above, these dimensions become fraught with value-laden judgments; dimensions quickly become polar opposites and associated with value judgments (e.g., good vs. bad, strong vs. weak). Ethnocentric bias results in valuing one's own perspective; for example, early studies of leadership focused on democratic forms of leadership prominent in North American countries and invariably viewed them as ideal styles. Their failure to incorporate non-Western views of leadership led to negative criticisms because of inherent bias toward capitalism, competition, and aggressiveness. See Table 3.2 for a summary of Dilemmas of Diversity Leadership. These are discussed below.

Table 3.2   Dilemmas of Diversity Leadership

Dimension	Dilemma	Challenge
Difference and Diversity	Between-group differences are small but significant.	Avoid stereotyping of differences
	Focus on universals tends to ignore differences.	
Lived Experiences	Leadership influenced by cultural values, lived experience, and social identity. These include acculturation, oppression, discrimination, and privilege.	Managing and valuing differences in lived experiences
Social and Member Perceptions	Perceptions create both illogical and biased expectations of leaders. Aversive racism and sexism	Promote images of credible leaders
		Avoid poor performance appraisals based on social identities rather than leadership performance
Social Identities	In-groups versus out-groups	Intergroup (mis)communication
Organizations	Heterogeneous versus homogeneous	Address structural and functional purposes of organizations
	Majority versus minority	

Egalitarianism Versus Hierarchical Orientations

The image of leadership has been evolving over time. A masculine leadership prototype of task orientation has prevailed (Heilman, 2001; Schein, 2004). Lately, there has been growing recognition of the importance of people skills for leaders and the increased prominence of the transformational leadership and leader-member exchange paradigms in the leadership literature (e.g., Eagly & Carli, 2007; Rudman & Glick, 2001). As more women and racial/ethnic minorities enter the workplace and leadership positions, more androgynous conceptions of leadership emerge that emphasize both task and people skills. Because of negative associations about feminine and racial/ethnic minority styles as being weak, many will emphasize an androgynous style to counteract these stereotypic perceptions.

Globalization has also led to the greater influence of Asian management styles, which have been noted to be more relationship focused (Triandis, 1993). It may be that this more androgynous conception of leadership will open up more opportunities for women and minorities to be considered as leaders and assist them in negotiating their way through the labyrinth (Eagly & Carli, 2007).

Work-Family Interface

Kolb and Williams (2000) argue for a fundamental change in organizational cultures, away from masculinized contexts toward gender equitable work environments. In an analysis of 60 prominent women leaders, Erkut (2001) found that obstacles remained in their leadership experiences, although they have diminished but have definitely not disappeared. The identification of "mothering" metaphors for leadership among these women leaders was an unexpected finding. These obstacles are embedded in how work environments are organized that were designed neither with women nor the support of a family structure in mind. Cheung and Halpern (2010) found concerns about the work-family interface for women in top executive and professional roles in China, Hong Kong, and the United States. They found the interplay of personal attributes, processes, and environments as factors associated with successful leadership and propose an alternative model of leadership that operates in the context of a "culture of gender" that defines expectations for women leaders. Work-family interface is not typically addressed in traditional leadership paradigms. Although the image of a family man is a positive one for male leaders, the challenges of managing a household or being mothers are not included as it is for women leaders.

With the growth of women in the workforce, work-family interface has been identified as central to the leadership experiences of women leaders in China, Hong Kong, and the United States (Cheung & Halpern, 2010). They propose an alternative leadership model that operates in the context of a "culture of gender" that defines expectations for women leaders. The social contexts in these three settings are different. In Hong Kong, women in the workforce often can afford maids, while women in China often have grandparents heavily involved in caretaking of their children. Both these contexts differ from that in the United States where child care is often through day care for their children. Therefore, concerns and solutions for work-family interface will vary.

It raises new considerations for the design of our workplace institutions that demands long hours and commitment that "neglect" family responsibilities. Women leaders have been questioned about their commitment to their careers as the existing paradigms have upheld the family man ideal who also made a "full commitment" to their jobs, which was possible only when he had a wife at home to take care of household duties and childrearing. Today, as more women enter the workplace and rise to positions of leadership, these assumptions are changing. Japan, in contrast, has also held leader expectations of loyalty to the company as a lifelong commitment, although that too is changing.

Interpersonal Relationships Versus Task Orientations

Studies of this dimension have identified differences between men and women in the strength of whether their orientation and leadership style are based on interpersonal relationships or a task orientation. Cultural variation has emphasized the importance of interpersonal relationships among Asian leaders based on cultural orientation dimensions of *Quanxi* and *Ren-Qing* discussed earlier. As 21st century leadership begins to show a greater emphasis on relationships, this dimension is an area in which to combine etic and emic approaches to leadership. As Chin (2013) found, Asian American leaders preferred to use indirect methods of communication over confrontational ones in order to preserve harmony and the interpersonal relationship. This can be explained and defined as related to their embracing of indigenous constructs of *Quanxi* and *Ren-Qing* but also redefining the definition of assertiveness as it is commonly used in Western cultures. An interpersonal and relationship dimension is embedded in their definition consistent with Cheung's concept of a combined emic-etic approach.

Cooperation Versus Competition

Access to and the attainment of leadership roles is often viewed as a competitive process based on Greco traditions compared to the Chinese traditions based on harmony and cooperation (Li, 2013). The demands of an election process to vote for the best candidate is viewed on the one hand as ensuring a representative and democratic process. On the other hand, it is viewed as a process fraught with self-promotion and aggressive confrontation and conflict. For many, it encourages attack and assault as in negative campaign images of one's opponent, finding one's opponent's vulnerability to gain an edge. And yet, the winner is expected to be gracious while the loser concedes. Is there a different way?

Power to Empowerment

Emphasis on empowerment associated social justice and equity goals emerged during the Civil Rights and Women's Movements of the 1960s following the disenchantment with the abusive use of power exemplified in the dictatorships of Mussolini and Hitler during WWII. Decrying the coercive use of power has led to the avoidance and denial of power in leadership described by McClelland (1985) and resulted in promoting servant leadership models and feminist goals in leadership where vertical lines of power from the top down is shifting toward shared power that is horizontal.

It also involves a shift from authoritative leadership as bad to the recognition of the abusive use of power and authority as bad.

Summary

As we examine existing paradigms and theories of leadership, we make ways for new paradigms of leadership that would be inclusive of all perspectives and incorporate principles of diversity into its formulation. We incorporate cultural values, multidimensional and complex dimensions; promote social justice and equity; and consider social contexts and philosophies of ethics and integrity to arrive at a Diversity Leader-Member-Organization Exchange paradigm. To enable such paradigms to be less ethnocentric, we suggest that grounded theory research, using qualitative methods and developing cultural measurement equivalences, are necessary. Past theories of leadership presumed to be universal but, in fact were cultural specific, Eurocentric, and individualistic. Incorporating non-Western perspectives might consider collectivism in leadership. Incorporating variation in cultural value dimensions and worldviews raises new possibilities for how a diversity leadership paradigm can be inclusive and culturally competent. These could include such dimensions as Daoist leadership, feminist leadership, benevolent paternalism found in Asian leadership, and prophetic-caliphal leadership found in Arab countries. As we move toward a global and diverse society, expanding current theories to include dimensions of work-family interface, egalitarianism and hierarchies, interpersonal relationships, harmony and cooperation, and empowerment will enable these paradigms to be relevant and contemporary for 21st century leadership.

Discussion Questions: Reframing Leadership Theories—Research to Evolve New Paradigms

1. Take an existing theory of leadership (e.g., transformational leadership). Identify its principles and dimensions. Critique and reframe that theory to be more inclusive and culturally competent.

2. How do race, ethnicity, and gender of a leader influence the exercise of leadership? Discuss some examples of how a leader has or has not addressed this in his or her leadership.

3. Identify and discuss the linguistic interpretation problems associated with item translation and administration of an instrument measuring leadership. For example, does the construct "trust" or "charisma" translate equivalently across all cultural and social identity groups?

4. Identify a culture or group that is collectivistic or individualistic. Identify some of cultural characteristics and behaviors that might embody its orientation. Are there aspects of that group that might also embrace characteristics of the opposite orientation? How might these characteristics emerge in the leadership of someone from that group?

5. Distinguish between paternalistic and maternalistic styles of leadership. What cultural factors would have to be in place for one or the other styles to work effectively?

6. Discuss the prophetic-caliphal model of leadership. What lifeways and thoughtways factors would have to be in place for the model to be effective in a cultural group other than the Middle East?

7. Etic approaches of identifying universal dimensions versus emic approaches of identifying indigenous dimensions have been used extensively in the cross-cultural literature; some have argued that these are artificially polarized. Discuss if and how there can be a mediating position in its application to leadership. Discuss whether or not there are any truly universal principles that can be applied to any cultural group about their leadership.

4

Leader Identity

Notable Quotes: On Racial/Ethnic Identity

"I'm Cablasian!" said Tiger Woods, who attained rapid fame for his exceptional golf skills especially as one of the first non-Whites to play in a White man's game. As Caucasian-Black-Asian, he declined to allow himself to be categorized into predetermined racial categories.

On Gender Perceptions

"I think that was a pretty good job for a girl!" told to a high-powered Asian woman leader by her male superior.

On Ethnic Minority Leaders

"We're viewed differently and I think minorities are still not as comfortable in the nonminority environments. On the one hand, I can wave my credentials, but on the other hand, there are settings in which the credentials don't mask the fact that I'm different. . . . I experience the imposter syndrome." (Asian American male leader)

"I'm a very spiritual person and sometimes I think that creates problems for my colleagues who tend to be very scientifically oriented." (Native American Indian male leader)

Vignette: Passing for White

"One Drop": My Father's Hidden Life—A Story of Race and Family Secrets (Broyard, 2007) is the story of literary critic Anatole Broyard, a light-skinned Creole, who chose to pass as White to enable his family to benefit from

White privilege. He kept this choice secret from his children until his death. His daughter, Bliss Broyard, found close relatives that her father had hidden from her because they were visibly African American. In the memoir, "[s]he uncovers the 250-year history of her family in America and chronicles her own evolution from a privileged WASP to a woman of mixed-race ancestry" (back cover). The Broyard family's story is extreme but not unprecedented in which individuals live in multiple dimensions simultaneously. Intergroup relations and intragroup relations are therefore very complex across all dimensions of diversity.

Shift From Leader Traits to Leader Identity

Presumably, this leads to selection of those most suited for leadership roles. At a time when leaders were typically White, Anglo males (Euro-American), this approach appeared to reflect the goal of selecting the "best candidates." When attention was directed to dimensions of diversity, including gender, race, and class, it results in outcomes that, in effect, exclude women and ethnic minorities. As attention to women and leadership emerged, identifying leader traits shifted to identifying differences between men and women leaders and a tendency to dichotomize traits that mirror differences between feminine and masculine styles.

How do race, ethnicity, and other dimensions of diversity in a leader influence the exercise of leadership? Trait theories of leadership largely focused on leadership traits that were presumably "universal," failing to note cultural variation and/or gender variation in these traits. While social contexts, social constructed roles, and cultural values are known to influence the display of gender-related traits, decades of research on trait theories could not come up with a common consensus of traits associated with good and effective leadership.

A shift from leader traits to leader identity is important to the examination of diversity leadership. It moves away from traits that may be culturally specific and/or reflective of the dominant group already in positions of leadership. Leader identity, moreover, is self-defined and can be varied and complex. It is about "who leaders are." It includes a developmental process of developing leader identity that shapes leader behavior and the perceptions and expectations of followers about their leadership. It is important to note how increased awareness enables both leader and followers to understand biases, often unconscious, and to promote behaviors that improve organizational outcomes and leader effectiveness exclusive of these biases.

The focus on leader identity as a dimension includes not only the incorporation of traits and characteristics of the leader but also an examination of who the leader is. What do leaders bring? What is the essence of the self of leaders? This includes dimensions of identity, which are multiple and intersecting and reflect a leader's authenticity. It applies the principles of diversity discussed in Chapter 3.

There is a growing body of literature on leader authenticity and on social identities that shapes our understanding of leadership that has relevance for the examination of diversity leadership. The emphasis of authenticity is on integrity and notions of self-construals that distinguish good versus bad leaders, manipulative versus truthful leaders. However, these social identities may be more fluid across contexts among those coming from social categories whose social identities are marginalized or viewed as out-groups. Those viewed and identifying as foreigners, women, racial/ethnic minorities, LGBT, and so forth are challenged by perceptions and expectations to behave in one voice across all contexts.

Self: Who Leaders Are

How does identity development and lived experiences shape leader identity? What do leaders bring to their leadership? Is it part of one's character or a trait? Is there a difference in the identities among diverse leaders? It is not uncommon to label men leaders as "simply leaders" versus those are "women leaders," "Black leaders," "gay leaders," and so forth. Does difference make a difference? Does this bring advantages or disadvantages?

These questions boil down to our definitions of "self." How are our definitions about "who we are" influenced by worldviews and cultural values? How does this play out in the identities of "who leaders are"?

Independent Versus Interdependent Self-Construals

Markus and Kitayama (1991) identified dimensions of self-identity reflecting the extent to which a person is engaged or disengaged from an interpersonal relationship that has shown to reflect differences between Western and Eastern leadership styles of communication. While one's view of self is often defined as universal, Markus and Kitayama (1991) have questioned such a unitary self-construal. From a worldview perspective, they have defined independent versus interdependent self-construals where one's definition of oneself is internal and independent of others versus a definition where one's definition of oneself can only be vis-à-vis one's relationships with others; for example, I am my mother's daughter. While one's schema of the body is anchored in time and space (philosophy), the exact content and structure of inner self may differ considerably with culture;

there may be a public versus private self (Triandis, 1995). There may be an individual versus relationship as functional unit of conscious reflection (i.e., leadership).

In Western cultures, there is faith in the inherent separateness of distinct persons; this is egocentric in nature where others are important as standards of reflected appraisal, or sources that can verify and affirm the inner core of the self. There is no intersection between self and other although boundaries may be closer or further. This contrasts with Eastern or non-Western cultures; there is faith in the foundational connectedness of human beings to each other; individual behavior is organized by how one perceives to be the thoughts, feelings, and actions of others in the relationship. The goal of interpersonal relationships is to fit in with relevant others, to fulfill and create obligations; while internal attributes exist, they are viewed as situation specific and self is not a bounded whole because it changes with the nature of the social context. This difference has been defined as independent versus interdependent self-construal. The Chinese synthesize this self-construal into an integrated or harmonious whole with an emphasis on Confucian interrelatedness and kindness (*jen*—Hsu as a Chinese virtue) as a cornerstone of interpersonal relationships. Hispanics have a similar concept of *simpatico*. The Thai emphasize the need to avoid disturbing others, self-effacement, and humility while Japanese have the concept of *wa*, which is not to disturb the harmonious ebb and flow of interpersonal relations. Tatara (personal communication, July, 2008) describes the Japanese self and identity as characterized in its language with multiple forms of *I* to denote the different relationships between speaker and listener. This differs from the English language where there is only a single form of *I*. As a result, interdependent self-construal includes amorphous as opposed to solid boundaries and diffuse as opposed to integrated sense of self.

Self-definition or self-construal in the relationship (Markus & Kitayama, 1991) influences the personal versus social self. In collectivist cultures, the relational and collective level of self-representation tends to be more salient than in individualistic cultures. The shift from personal to relational level is accompanied by increased concern with relational considerations such as fostering interpersonal harmony (e.g., Asian). It influences use of tactics with the tendency to use fewer hard tactics because it is likely to strain the relationship. It includes a preference for soft over hard targets when trying to influence in-group targets.

This has important implications for leadership that can be characterized as a relationship between the leader and members. Members have a working self-concept that involves their self-construal views, current goals, and possible selves. Leaders can affect motivation by influencing these aspects of identity. For example, independent (individual) self-construal versus interdependent (relational and collective) self-construal will dictate how the leader defines the dyadic relationship and the relative emphasis placed on such aspects as negotiation, communication, and influence.

Racial and Ethnic Identity

Identity has been a significant and influential domain of study in the multicultural literature (Phinney, 2000). One of the early pioneers in the field, Jean Phinney (1990), developed an ethnic identity development model about how non-White individuals develop a sense of their ethnicity. At about the same time, Cross (1991) put forth what he called the Nigrescence model of identity, which describes "a process of becoming Black" for racial identity development among Blacks while Helms (1993) developed a White identity development model about how Blacks and Whites develop their racial identity. While trait theory is prominent in the leadership literature, leader identity has been generally omitted in our theories and measures of leadership. The interaction of leader identity with racial, ethnic, and gender identity has the potential for theories being more inclusive of diversity; hence, we propose a shift from leadership traits to leader identity and its intersection with multiple identities embraced by diverse individuals in their exercise of leadership.

The assessment and measurement of racial and ethnic identity is complicated and filled with many problems owing in part to the fact that human beings have multiple, intertwined identities that influence one another in ways that are not fully understood. Multiple identities come in many forms. No one is solely a member of a distinct racial or ethnic group, just as no one is solely a man or a woman. All persons are members of particular age groups and have particular sexual orientations. They may have disabilities. In addition, they may follow vocations that provide them with unique role identities. The enactment and nature of an individual's multiple identities can be influenced by an individual's *lifeways* and *thoughtways,* which may be at variance with conventional expectations and proscriptions. A person's multiple identities, as well as the sociocultural contexts in which these identities are enacted, must be factored into the measurement of an identity construct. However, most of the research on the measurement of identity has been limited to the abstraction of race and ethnicity at a social and psychological level of analysis; other dimensions of one's identity are given less attention in the behavioral and social science literature (Cheung, 1991; Trimble, 2005).

Patrick Moynihan (1993) argued that identity is "a process located in the core of the individual and yet, also, in the case of his communal culture" (p. 64). It's a powerful phenomenon that strongly influences personality, one's sense of belonging, one's sense of sameness, and one's quality of life. To further an understanding of identity, most social and psychological theorists must contend with the concept of self. And to approach an understanding of the self-concept, one is obliged to provide plausible if not substantial explanations for the following domains: physical traits and characteristics, personal experiences and their memory, personal behaviors, "what belongs to me and what I belong to," "the person I believe myself to be," and "who and what others tell me I am" (Gans, 1979, p. 195; Cirese, 1985). Explanations for these domains consume volumes.

The definitions and interpretations of *identity*, *ethnicity*, and *race* can be summarized to mean, at a minimum, the sameness of a band or nation of people who share common customs and traditions. Certain bands or nations may share common experiences born from oppression, domination, and colonialism. At one level of interpretation, the combined definition is sufficient to capture the manner in which the identity is generally conceptualized and used to measure ethnocultural influences on its formation and development (Trimble & Dickson, 2005). The psychologist Jean Phinney (1990) notes that there are "widely discrepant definitions and measures of ethnic identity, which makes generalizations and comparisons across studies difficult and ambiguous" (p. 500). Currently, the most widely used definition of the construct in psychology is the one developed by Phinney (1990, 2000, 2003). She maintains, that, "ethnic identity is a dynamic, multidimensional construct that refers to one's identity, or sense of self as a member of an ethnic group" (2003, p. 63). From her perspective, one claims an identity within the context of a subgroup that claims a common ancestry and shares at least a similar culture, race, religion, language, kinship, or place of origin. She goes on to add that, "Ethnic identity is not a fixed categorization but rather is a fluid and dynamic understanding of self and ethnic background. Ethnic identity is constructed and modified as individuals become aware of their ethnicity, within the large (sociocultural) setting" (2003, p. 63). At another level, the term *identity* is almost synonymous with the term *ethnicity*, prompting some sociologists, such as Herbert Gans (2003), to suggest that identity is no longer a useful term.

Ethnicity and race are the principal cultural constructs used to measure identification, identity development, and identity formation, the three areas that subsume most of the literature in the field. The ethnic construct dominates literature themes while race is limited to a few measures of the overarching identity construct. A few researchers argue for replacing the term *race* with ethnicity and still others prefer to use the term *culture* to refer to the identity process ostensibly lodged in one's ethnocultural orientation and ancestral history. As psychosocial constructs, ethnic identity and ethnic self-identification are not without controversy because there are varied views on their salience, relevance, stability, characteristics, and influences. Add to the discussion and debate that identity, whatever form it takes, is rarely static and immutable. To emphasize this point, Fitzgerald (1993) maintains that it is a mistake to think of identity as an unchanging entity as "it is the illusion of unity that is still quite real with most people" (p 32). Social categories and people are protean, and this suggests that they do not present an orderly structure that lends itself to measurement and comprehension.

Identity is complicated and filled with many problems owing in part to the fact that human beings have multiple, intertwined identities that influence one another in ways that are not fully understood. The problems are compounded by the growing popularity of identity and the effect it has on its meaning. "As identity became more and more a cliché," maintains Philip Gleason (1983), "its meaning grew progressively more diffuse, thereby encouraging increasingly loose and irresponsible usage" (p. 931). The tone is consistent with Peter Weinreich's contention that "a person's appraisal of the social world and its significance is an expression of his or her identity." Consequently one can have multiple intertwined identities that shift according to a number of circumstances and situations (Weinreich & Saunderson, 2003, p. xix).

To approach the inquiry, the origins of the meanings of identity, ethnicity, and race are provided. When the derivations and meanings of the three constructs are combined, a loose definition emerges to indicate the sameness of a band or nation of people who share common customs and traditions; certain bands or nations may share common experiences born from oppression, domination, and colonialism. The essential element in this conversation focuses primarily on how social and behavioral scientists attempt to measure *sameness*.

Although there are several compelling definitions of the construct, ethnicity is not without controversy. Most scholars agree that the construct is a social construction. Some view it as an invention, a synonym for identity, symbolic, political, fictional, imagined, and pseudo or contrived. Ethnicity and race are linked to identity; however, the linkage is not straightforward because there are varying opinions on what is more salient and in need of emphasis to understand identity formation and development—ethnic identity or racial identity. Several scholars insist that the concept of the self must be factored into the discussions and theory building. Many have been influenced by the seminal work on social identity initiated by the social psychologist Henri Tajfel (1982), who viewed the self as the core of the identity process and those who attempt to capture one's multiple ethnic and racial identities.

Several important conclusions emerge from a review of the literature on ethnic and racial identity. First, valid and reliable measures of ethnic and racial identity must be grounded in theory or, at a minimum, on several fundamental propositions. Cheung (1991) reminds us that typically "ethnicity has been treated as no more than a self-evident, *ascriptive* quality, as have been sex and age. Operationally, ethnicity was always measured by one or a combination of a few objective indicators such as color, place of birth, and language, neglecting the subjective aspect of ethnicity" (p. 575). Relying on a deconstructive perspective, the cultural anthropologist Dwight Heath (1991) argued that many of the assumptions and uses of ethnicity are garbled "and confused in a markedly inconsistent manner [and are] unlikely to yield further insights that are theoretically or conceptually helpful in terms of understanding how alcohol interacts with the human animal" (p. 610). Although both Cheung and Heath are highly critical of the measurement tendencies, they are quick to point out that some positive contributions have been made to the field of ethnicity, especially in the way the ethnic variable has been viewed in some studies.

Second, we must acknowledge the conclusion that the measurement of ethnicity is no small task, especially given the debate surrounding its theoretical foundations and its usefulness. Researchers must consider the "various cultural and structural dimensions of ethnicity" (Cheung, 1991, p. 575) and "distinguish between general aspects of ethnic identity that apply across groups and specific aspects that distinguish groups" (Phinney, 1990, p. 508). To accomplish this, we must move away from viewing ethnic groups as homogeneous entities; in fact, there may be more heterogeneity within certain ethnic and racial groups than for the dominant groups in North American society (Cheung, 1993; Trimble, 1991).

What emerges from a careful review of the literature is uncertainty and ambiguity—uncertainty about the meanings of identity, ethnicity, and race; uncertainty about their usefulness in describing the census of the U.S. population; uncertainty about a person's "appraisal of the social world and its significance as an expression of self-identity (Weinreich & Saunderson, 2003, p. xix);" uncertainty about what theory best explains their psychosocial dynamics, components, and processes; uncertainty about the cultural equivalence of measures and how best to control for cultural bias; uncertainty as to why ethnicity and race are given so much prominence in North American and in other parts of the world; and uncertainty about the applicability of the findings generated by the incongruent and inconsistent measures. Apart from accounting for demographic distributions, there are uncertainties about the causal relationship between ethnic and racial identity outcomes; most empirical studies using ethnic and racial identity as a moderating or independent variable fail to predict anything of psychosocial importance.

The inconsistencies and incongruities suggest that the field of ethnic and racial identity is in a condition of disorder and confusion. Weinreich and

Saunderson (2003) summarized the confusion best when they asserted that it is "a kaleidoscope set of conceptualizations (where) methods of assessment of parameters of identity, deriving from disparate conceptualizations of self and identity, are often unrelated" (p. 361). A good starting point for a probing inquiry is the emergence of a multiracial or multiethnic classification category. In the cultural and ethnic comparative research realm, researchers typically rely on monoethnic or monoracial categories to test hypotheses about the contribution of one's cultural *lifeways* and *thoughtways* to some outcome variable or variable domain; in our case, it is leadership.

There is yet another challenge that most assuredly will press the wit, vigor, and intellect of those bent on advancing an inquiry into ethnic and racial identity. The number of ethnic and racial groups in North America is increasing, not declining; the pot is not melting, and the populace does not appear to be assimilating at the rate many demographers and sociologists predict. All over the world geopolitical boundaries are changing as a result of political turmoil, colonialism, and globalization; consequently, individuals are changing their ethnic allegiances and identities as they move from one environment to another or their boundaries are rearranged (Arnett, 2002). Indigenous groups are asserting sovereign rights and demanding recognition and access to their ancestral lands. Once suppressed, voices are demanding their right for recognition. Consequently, the number of ethnic groups worldwide are increasing prominently and becoming more independent and visible; this presents new challenges for the field of ethnic and racial identity. Clifford Geertz (2000), the esteemed cultural anthropologist stated, "As the world becomes more thoroughly interconnected, economically and politically, as people move about in unforeseen, only partially controllable, and increasingly massive, ways, and new lines are drawn and old ones end". . . "The catalogue of available identifications expands, contracts, changes shape, ramifies, involutes, and develops" (p. 225). Accordingly, the only principled way we can meet the challenge posed by the enlarging catalogue is to engage in a thorough inquiry, all the while realizing that the world is constantly changing. Salience for these racial and ethnic identities has grown in importance as leaders and members become more diverse in organizations throughout the world.

Gender Identity

"Traditionally, men have been seen as better leaders because they have more authority, focus and drive, and because they more readily take tough, but necessary decisions such as downsizing, or firing people. But Alice Eagly shows that this masculine stereotype is outdated." Today's transformational leaders are required to have more teacher- or coach-like qualities; to be motivational rather than threatening; inspirational embodiments of the corporate values rather than autocratic enforcers. These qualities match women's leadership style well. Eagly's research on women and leadership show that women tend to be collaborative; they take colleagues' opinions into consideration; they tend to seek what's best in the broader context rather than competing for the 'top dog' position".... "This is not to say that men do not have these qualities too," says Professor Eagly. "However, women tend to be more transformational in their leadership style than men. Women now are more likely to be prepared for leadership challenges; they are more educated. Women in the United States account for 57% of bachelor's degrees, 60% of master's, and 52% of PhDs. They increasingly are contributing to household finances; 38% of wives in U.S. married couple families are employed; often the woman earns more than the man. From a broader social perspective, women advocate for more supportive societal contributions to make it possible for them to enjoy fulfilling careers—more child care facilities, more parental leave for fathers and mothers, fewer work hours—without having to miss out on opportunities for higher executive roles" (Hayes, 2012).

Eagly, Makhjani, and Klonsky (1992) found that when women leaders directly asserted their authority by acting in a directive, autocratic style, they were particularly likely to be devalued compared to male leaders. Ridgeway (2007) notes that this is status based rather than a consequence of stereotypes. Status beliefs legitimatize leadership for those from advantaged social categories; if you are male, you already have an advantage as a leader because you have status. Eagly defines this as role incongruity between being female and being a leader that produces prejudice and maintains the glass ceiling. Eagly acknowledges bias against female leaders related to the fact that there is greater overlap between attributes possessed by typical men and leaders than between typical women and leaders. Therefore, women are less likely to emerge as leaders in small groups. Positive constraints against women leaders are attributed to gender role incongruities by Eagly and Chin (2010), to differential attributions of status to gender by Ridgeway (2007), to different leadership categorization by Lord and Hall (2007); all result in women not emerging as experienced and wise while this association for men has been activated together over time leading to their categorization as leaders.

Other Dimensions of Diversity

Dimensions such as sexual orientation, religion, and disability all play a role into what constitutes part of one's identity and who leaders are.

However, there is little in the literature about other dimensions of diversity and the exercise of leadership. Several overarching principles are important in framing these dimensions from a diversity leadership perspective. One is the notion of moving away from single prototypes of leadership marked by membership in a privileged or dominant social group. Second is the issue of visible and nonvisible dimensions of identity and diversity. Third is the element of self-disclosure. Last is the degree of stigma or marginalization associated with social group membership associated with these dimensions.

Sexual orientation differs from race, ethnic, and gender identities because it is not always a visible dimension of one's identity; consequently, it raises the issue of leader self-disclosure as an important dimension. While newer notions of leadership are less tied to proscriptive expectations of how a leader is "supposed" to look, act, or bring about change, Fassinger, Shullman, and Stevenson (2010) propose an affirmative paradigm for LGBT leadership to create more room for different types of leaders with varying styles and perspectives. With the contemporary emphasis on inclusion, collaboration, and diversity in the workplace, they suggest that identity status dimensions of LGBT leadership bring forth the effects of marginalization on leadership enactment. Stigma associated with homosexuality addresses the denigration, disrespect, and disempowering of sexual minority individuals and groups and intersects with leader identity and member perceptions of their leadership. The absence of literature in this area suggests that sexual minority people may bring different sensibilities, values, skills, and experiences to the task of leadership, thereby offering a richer perspective than when it is limited to that of more privileged groups. While self-disclosure of sexual orientation or "coming out" is a major issue for LGBT communities, there is no coverage of this in the leadership literature. Does it change perceptions of leader effectiveness? Fassinger and colleagues propose a model in which sexual orientation (particularly as captured in identity disclosure) interacts with gender orientation (including gender) and with the situation (especially group composition) to affect both the leader and the followers in a complex and dynamic process of leadership enactment. This process occurs within a context of stigma and marginalization that is relatively unique to sexual minorities, involving (a) a concealable stigma (with all the attendant complexities of perceived handling of that concealment); (b) beliefs about control over the stigmatizing characteristic; (c) oppression and discrimination that receive considerable social sanction and public approval; and (d) the fact that the stigmatized characteristic may not be known to the individual possessing it, because of the process of recognizing and accepting discredited status that occurs in the lives of most LGBT people. The model helps advance further investigation such as: Does self-disclosure influence the perception of authenticity in the leader?

Disability has also received scant attention in the leadership literature. Usually associated with weakness, it is often treated as a taboo topic for media coverage or disclosure by leaders. This reflects the underlying tendency, often unconscious, to overgeneralize the specific disability to deficits of intellect and leadership competence. President Franklin Delano Roosevelt is a good example; he went to great lengths to never be seen in public in a wheelchair because of his paralysis from polio. He usually appeared in public standing upright, while being supported on one side by an aide, one of his sons, or propping himself up using a solid lectern.

Religion and leadership has also been scant in the literature. One's religious affiliation has generally been covert in the U.S. presidencies, presumably because there has been little diversity in the religious affiliations of U.S. presidents; almost all identify as Christian belonging to one of the Protestant denominations. The few exceptions were duly noted, with President John F. Kennedy as the only Catholic president and Governor Mitt Romney of Massachusetts as a Mormon, and have received considerable media attention. Attention to religion in the literature has generally addressed the broader concept of spirituality and values (Dent, Higgins, & Wharff, 2005). Research on religion and leadership is in its infancy with a focus on defining and discovering essential factors and conditions for promoting a theory of spiritual leadership within the context of the workplace.

Multiple and Intersecting Identities

Research on identity has generally concentrated on single dimensions of identity; we now know that individuals often embrace multiple and intersecting dimensions of identity related to race, ethnicity, gender, religion, sexual orientation, and disability (Chin, 2009; Chin & Sanchez-Hucles, 2007; Comas-Diaz & Greene, 1994; Greene, 2010). How these intersect with leader identity is an important consideration. Sanchez-Hucles and Davis (2010) examine the multiple and intersecting dimensions of identity and their effects on leadership; they focus on the access barriers faced by women and minorities associated with stereotyped evaluations of leader performance that influence leader effectiveness.

As studies of ethnic identity from the diversity literature show, racial and ethnic groups often develop and maintain unique identities distinct from the national, mainstream, or organizational identity (Helms, 1993; Phinney, 1990). Moreover, positive ethnic identity is correlated with high self-efficacy. For example, based on Albert Bandura's concept of self-efficacy (Bandura, 1977), Teresa LaFromboise and her colleagues put forth the concept of *bicultural self-efficacy* that refers to domain-specific estimates of people's confidence in their ability to negotiate and cope with perceived interactions and incompatibilities in language (e.g., translation), social interaction (e.g., understanding nuances social norms), and value (e.g., weighing the merits of individualistic versus collectivistic ways of viewing the world) domains between their culture of origin and a second culture (LaFromboise, Coleman, & Gorton, 1993). Conceptually, bicultural self-efficacy is important because it impacts (a) the choices that a person makes in regard to engaging in both cultures, (b) the effort an individual puts forth in engaging in both cultures, (c) how long an individual persists in engaging in both cultures in the face of obstacles, and (d) how an individual feels about engaging in both cultures. In addition, bicultural self-efficacy is important because it has the potential to reduce one's susceptibility to stress and depression in pressing situations and strengthens resiliency to adversity. Ultimately, bicultural self-efficacy might serve to buffer the negative impact of acculturative stress on mental health.

However, these social identities may receive attributions of lesser power and status, whereas leader identities often communicate power and influence. Hence, the incongruence between social identities and prototypic leader images of the dominant group may well influence the credibility and influence a leader is likely to have; that is, Black and Asian leaders may automatically be viewed as less credible than White leaders. Moreover, we might question whether diverse leaders with strong, positive ethnic identities are likely to be more effective or hindered because they are less willing to modify their behaviors to be more like the prototypic leader. The intersection between social identities and leader identity is an important avenue for further investigation. Eagly and Carli (2007) suggest that the greater difference there is between these identities and those of the prototypic leader, the more it makes a difference. Must diverse leaders conform to the dominant prototype to attain status and credibility as a leader? How might we argue for a more affirmative paradigm to value the differences brought by multiple social identities? Does the salience of social identities vary over time and context?

Aversive Racism

Aversive racism, termed by Dovidio and Gaertner (2004), reflects unintentional or unconscious discriminatory evaluations of racial/ethnic minority individuals because of underlying anxiety about race and ethnicity. Such social perceptions and expectations also apply to women. These biases and stereotypes associated with gender and race often result in more exacting standards for women and racial/ethnic minority leaders; they also negatively influence their performance as leaders. When members hold these perceptions and act on them in their selection and expectations of leaders, they are likely to result in poorer performance appraisals or create situations of stereotyped threat. Steele (1995) found that diverse individuals might underperform in situations where they are evaluated on a domain in which they are regarded, on the basis of stereotypes, as inferior, which he termed *stereotyped threat*. Specifically, presenting participants with gender stereotypical portrayals of women prior to a group task caused women (but not men) to be less interested in being the group leader and more interested in being a follower (Davies, Spencer, & Steele, 2005). Aversive racism and stereotyped threat both demonstrate the adverse impact of racism as part of lived experiences. Helms (1993) notes its relationship to power, which has been downplayed in recent leadership research.

Social Identities and Leadership

Leadership is inextricably tied to social group membership (van Knippenberg & Hogg, 2007). Leadership is informed by the social identities that a leader brings and is informed by social categorizations that highlight individuals' social identities as group members. These social identities and social categorizations play a role in the processes that shape perceptions and expectations about leaders. They, in turn, shape leader behaviors and leader identities.

Identity and self-concept have begun to assume center stage in behavioral research on leadership (Lord, Brown, & Freiberg, 1999), especially as we find growing diversity in our ranks of leadership. The emphasis on a single leader prototype defining who is a good leader is diminishing.

Leader Prototypes: Based on Narrow Gender and Racial Stereotypes

Lord and Hall (2007, pp. 48–64) describe underlying scripts that guide leader behavior and leader prototypes that guide perceptions of leadership. These scripts enable people to form judgments and to categorize people and groups. Scripts of leader prototypes have developed based on leader qualities such as trust, fairness, influence, and charisma. Often, these qualities are inferred from visible characteristics such as age, race, gender, and so forth, which have constrained and excluded those in these social categories for leadership. As such, these leader prototypes have resulted in stereotypes about whether or not certain social categories are fit as leaders when, in fact, the characteristics (e.g., gender) may have little to do with leadership. Lord and Hall (2007) call for flexibility in these prototypes to allow for a more diverse image of leader prototypes.

While these cognitive scripts or prototypes serve as a shorthand way of identifying categories, their application to social categories has led to stereotypes and bias. These categories are often defined by central features (i.e., visible qualities), not by critical features (i.e., leadership qualities) that produce clear distinctions between in and out group members. For example, images of influence associated with Whiteness may preclude persons of color from being viewed as influential and, therefore, potentially effective as a leader. The role of leadership training is to enable leaders to know and expect such stereotypes. Members are perceivers who actively contribute to the leadership perception process rather than passive responders to leader characteristics. Hence, trait theories are insufficient because they do not factor in member perceptions that shape the development of leader prototypes.

Leadership categorization theory (Lord & Hall, 2007) suggests that leadership is recognized in an individual when the pattern of traits or behaviors associated with a potential leader matches a salient prototype used by perceiver; hence, it is a good fit. Leadership is often inferred from events and outcomes that result in causal attributions to potential leaders. For example, being a tall, White male is recognized and inferred by the perceiver as determining who is seen as a leader. Implicit leadership theories are often based on this category prototype matching. It is so strong that once the perceiver makes the category, category consistent information is often believed to be seen when it is not. For example, if someone fits the prototype, what they do can be erroneously attributed to have occurred. If someone is tall and White, his behaviors may be attributed to have been influential and effective when it is not.

LMX Leadership Theories Favor Dominant In-Groups

Individuals emerge as leaders because they fit with a group identity that develops over time (Hogg, 2001). As group identity becomes stronger, the group prototype plays a stronger role in determining leadership. Social identity analysis of leadership argues that leadership effectiveness depends on the psychological salience of the group to its member. This would tend to favor dominant social identities as in-groups.

In fact, research on LMX leadership theories have distinguished between personalized versus depersonalized groups. "When there is high group solidarity and members identify strongly with the group, a depersonalized style works better because the leader can treat all members as equals, and does not isolate anyone" (Hogg, Martin, & Weeden, 2003, p. 18–33). LMX leadership theories emphasize working with a subgroup of subordinates to achieve organizational goals as indicative of leader effectiveness; members of these in-groups are afforded privileges while others are marginalized and excluded. In favoring the in-group, this approach would be problematic with diversity leadership as a goal; intergroup behavior based on in-group favoritism and ethnocentrism would be dichotomized against out-group denigration and exclusion.

Leadership Identity and Social Power

According to Lord and Hall (2007), leadership, identity, and social power are dynamically intertwined in a process that unfolds as leaders and members interact and establish a status structure. Leadership perceptions and perceived social power occur through a flexible, dynamic, cognitive social process. Unlike LMX theories where prescriptions focus on preferred groups that result in unintended bias toward social out-groups, leadership categorization theory is an implicit social perception process and often operates outside of conscious awareness. The scripts and prototypes that people used to evaluate leadership and power reflect implicit sense making and offer guides to social situations; they are flexible and constructed to meet specific contextual demands. Using this approach, biases against female leaders could be explained in part by the fact that there is much greater overlap between the attributes thought to be possessed by typical men and leaders, than between typical women and leaders (Heilman, Block, Martell, & Simon, 1989).

The contexts influencing the development of identity as a leader include such issues as ethnic identity and lived experiences related to oppression, cultural differences, and acculturation. In addition to the attribution of power on the basis of one's leadership position, these social categories and contexts also shape the identities of leaders and the power to which they are accorded.

Salience of Social Identities Among Leaders

The salience of social identities among leaders will vary depending on whether or not they are members of dominant or major social groups. There are often several phenomena at play. The ascendance of those considered to be "one of us" to leadership is often conveyed with pride; this results in a reciprocal obligation for the leader to favor or accede to the needs of all groups. The question arises, as for example, with Barack Obama, the first biracial president of the United States. The salience of his skin color made it more difficult for some to claim "he is one of us" or to heighten expectations because "he is one of us." Black members often felt that he was not responsive enough to their needs while White members feared that he was giving in too much in favoring Blacks.

By the same token, leaders whose social identities are from more marginalized groups in society often feel their social identities to be a more salient part of their leader identity. This includes being made conscious of these identities by others as well as having these identities influence how they enact their leadership. White male leaders in the United States, as you might expect, do not feel their identities of being male or White have much to do with their leadership.

Cognitive Flexibility

For those from marginalized or minority groups, their differences in social identities have contributed to a sense of cognitive flexibility—that is, being able to see different perspectives, to shift between groups, and translate between groups. This has implications for workgroup teams—a mechanism of leadership in a complex, digital age where technology and knowledge is more complex. Leaders need to assemble good working teams to be effective; this contrasts with the charismatic leadership, who by sheer force of personality, can be persuasive in mobilizing a group to act.

Leaders with bicultural racial/ethnic identities are likely to demonstrate more cognitive flexibility while also likely to be constrained by social role perceptions and expectations associated with these identities. They develop flexibility in thinking in response to a changing world (Rost, 1991); diverse individuals facing adjustment to a bicultural environment and/or racism are more likely to develop more cognitive flexibility in negotiating their world.

Leadership Qualities and Social Categorization

Social categorization is how members and followers perceive leader qualities. Four leadership qualities of influence, trust, fairness, and charisma have been consistently identified as traits associated with good leadership. Image management is how one can infer these traits from the behaviors of leaders. It has been suggested that these can be developed in leaders through coaching.

Based on social categorization theories of leadership, in-group members are more likely to be influential. Hence, when women and racial/ethnic minorities feel unheard or have their comments ignored (an outcome identified in the qualitative interviews conducted by the senior author), they have to be part of the in-group to have a voice. In-group members are also more likely to be trusted. Trust works well for team performance. During Barack Obama's campaign as the first biracial candidate to run for president, Whites feared that they could not trust Obama since he was not part of the in-group. Judgment of a leader's fairness is also more likely to vary with whether he or she is part of the in-group or out-group. Leader who are part of the in-group are more likely to be judged more fairly. For leaders who are part of the out-group, judgments of their getting less fair treatment is deemed to be OK.

Many years of research on task versus relationship orientations suggest that it is a complex and interactive process rather than a dichotomous one. For example, when the task is clear, then a directive task oriented leadership approach works; when task is dynamic and complex, then a relationship oriented leadership approach works better. Misumi and Peterson (1985), in looking at non-Western forms of leadership, maintain that a leader who is both demanding and personally caring is most effective regardless of the task or population. This contrasts with the U.S. leadership literature, where leadership effectiveness is viewed as dependent on the interaction of leader and follower characteristics and the nature of the task (i.e., Fiedler's contingency theory). According to Misumi, the personal attachment to the leader and obligation to the leader is what mostly motivate people to do their work. This was empirically supported in a study where 80% of Japanese workers preferred a manager with a father-like character (Hayashi, cited in Markus & Kitayama, 1991). This raises the question of how extant leader prototypes are culturally based.

Leadership as an Outcome of Social Categorization Process

Leadership categorization theory (Lord, Foti, & DeVader, 1984; Lord & Maher, 1991) focuses on the social cognitive processes that underlie leadership perceptions. The social identity process of a leader is often influenced by the organizational contexts in which leadership is exercised. When people identify strongly with a group (i.e., high salience), leadership effectiveness is significantly influenced by how prototypical of the group the leader is perceived to be by the members. Therefore, if a diverse leader is not prototypical of the group, can he or she lead the group? Or will he or she be viewed as ineffective when members strongly identify with the prototype. When the group is more compact and cohesive, then group prototypically becomes important if a leader is to be effective. In summary, a leader must be what members expect.

Leadership can also be viewed as an outcome of self-categorization. The process takes the form of perceiver readiness and cognitive fit; it is both comparative and normative in that once a category becomes cognitively salient and self-defining for an individual, it leads to outcomes that could include in-group favoritism, prejudice and discrimination, and stereotyping.

As the group becomes more salient among the members (as members feel they belong and are cohesive), members will be more likely to relate to the leader based on the prototype rather than as unique individuals; therefore, leader-member relations become depersonalized.

When a leader can be group serving, favor the in-group, show group commitment, and be fair, he or she is viewed as a leader. Hence, for leaders who fit the prototype, their credentials are not in question, whereas for leaders who do not fit the prototype, their credentials need confirmation. This was found in the qualitative interviews among women, racial/ethnic, and sexual orientation minorities conducted by Chin (2013) where there was consensus in their experience of "always having to prove themselves."

High in-group prototypic leaders are often viewed as more charismatic. The salience of these prototypes paves the way for constructing a charismatic leadership personality who reflects the members' image of themselves, facilitates the leader to member alliance; that is, the leader "becomes one of us" and attains status and credibility.

Content of Leadership Categories

Lord identified 27 characteristics that were highly prototypical of leaders. The top 10 include the following: (1) dedicated, (2) goal oriented, (3) informed, (4) charismatic, (5) decisive, (6) responsible, (7) intelligent, (8) determined, (9) organized, and (10) verbally skilled. Others include the following: masculinity, adjustment, extroversion, dominance, flexibility, experience, and social influence. They reflect characteristics that must be inferred from one's behaviors and actions. As such, they have been associated with images of White males who have been dominant as leaders in today's existing social and organizational structures.

Social Power and Leadership Power

Identity and social power are dynamically intertwined as group members interact and establish a status structure. The effect of group identities on leadership perception and social power is often a priori, but the direction of relationship can be reversed. While social identities that leaders bring influence how they exercise their leadership, those embraced by members and followers similarly shape perceptions and expectations of leaders and their behaviors. Moreover, they interact with the conferring of leadership power by members.

When one is perceived as a leader, bases of social power are enhanced (Lord & Hall, 2007). Leader perception and perceived social power emerges as a dynamic process that involves target, perceiver, task, and organizational context. It operates like many other implicit social perception processes; for example, spontaneous trait inference, which guides social actions but often operate outside of conscious awareness. For example, Hugo Chávez, former president of Venezuela, was a good example of how he used his social categorization as "a leader of the people" to emerge and maintain his leadership. Coming from a childhood of poverty, Chávez used this to shape his "anti-imperialist" policies and alliance with the people of Venezuela. He was a prominent adversary of the U.S. foreign policy as well as a vocal critic of U.S.-supported capitalism. Following *Chavismo*, his own political ideology, he focused on implementing socialist reforms in the country as a part of a social project known as the Bolivarian Revolution. His promises of widespread social and economic reforms won the trust and favor of a primarily poor and working class following. Much of his support came from his "strong man" populist image and charismatic appeal. Although he publicly used strong revolutionary rhetoric from the beginning of his presidency, the Chávez government's initial policies were moderate, capitalist, and center-left. He was not known for holding his tongue. For example, on the discovery of the new world, he said, "Christopher Columbus was the spearhead of the biggest invasion and genocide ever seen in the history of humanity" (Ghosh, 2013). On the issue of poverty, he described the world as: "An infernal machine that produces every minute an impressive amount of poor, 26 million poor in 10 years are 2.6 million per year of new poor, this is the road, well, the road to hell" (Chavez, n.d.).

Status Characteristics and Emergence of Leadership

There are cultural presumptions about competence with higher performance expectations for those advantaged by the characteristics than for those disadvantaged by it (e.g. women, non-White) (Ridgeway, 2007). The status of the social category to which one belongs is often generalized to presumed competence among its members. Status characteristics becomes effectively salient whenever it differentiates among those in the situation (e.g., race and gender), and when it is culturally linked to the group goal, task, or setting (e.g., gender for a gender type task as in associating male and sports).

An effective leader must act flexibly and modify behavior to match task and social requirements; when there is a mismatch, for example, women and minorities, the status characteristics of their social identities result in their not automatically perceived as leaders. The nature of the task also influences status and perception of leadership. In gender-neutral tasks, men displayed moderately higher verbal and nonverbal power and prestige behaviors (e.g., speech initiations, time talking, and visual dominance). This became more exaggerated on masculine tasks. The reverse is true on female tasks.

Double Standards: Influence of Social Categories on Expectations of Leaders

Leaders starting with a disadvantaged status must produce objectively better performance than those with advantaged status leading to the common observation that "minority leaders need to work twice as hard to get half as far." On focus groups with diverse leaders (Chin, 2013), a woman leader in the military proclaimed, "You have be extraordinary while men just have to be ordinary to become leaders."

What does this double standard do to self-esteem and confidence over time? Double standards play a significant role in advantaging those from higher status social categories in the attainment of leadership positions. Often, simply "being there" is an advantage. The question then is how to support access for those not at the table? One is to give them the role. For those from status disadvantaged groups, simply being granted the role of chair or manager brings a presumption of competence that enhances expectations for new leader and supports legitimacy; for example, title adds to image of competence.

When a person from a salient but status-disadvantaged category becomes leader (e.g., women, racial minorities), it violates the central, hierarchical structure of group members' status beliefs about the category. It leads group members to resist a status-disadvantaged person in the role. It undercuts the legitimacy of the leader and reduces his or her power compared to the deference often afforded to a status-advantaged leader. The resistance is greater when the status-disadvantaged leader tries to wield more coercive and directive power. For example, Obama's presidency faced unprecedented obstacles and resistance as he pushed his Affordable Care Act in his second term; yet he also met with resistance in his first term with various forms of disrespect not typically accorded to the office of the president, for example, when Representative Joe Wilson of South Carolina shouted "You lie" during President Obama's address to Congress in 2012 after Obama said that illegal immigrants would not benefit from his health care reform plan.

Procedural Fairness

Tyler (1997) discusses procedural fairness and relational models of justice that influence leadership and identity based on a relational model of legitimacy. People consider the resources supplied to a group but also importance of a group in defining its self-worth. Tyler (1997) uses the psychology of justice perceptions to explain psychological factors influencing group members' willingness to voluntarily follow rules set down by authorities. They will trade acknowledgment of their status within group for their deference to the authority of the leader.

As an example, Native American Indians used their assessment of the fairness of authority, which influenced their willingness to restrain water use during a shortage (Moore, 1989). Both respect and pride (i.e., identification with organization) were influenced most by procedural fairness; these identity aspects were important in determining organizational oriented behavior (i.e., following the rules and staying within the group). On a survey of diverse leaders (Chin, 2013), Native American Indian leaders did not feel respect and pride from White mainstream groups; therefore, they did not endorse following rules despite the emphasis of doing so within cultural values. For those with high interdependent self-construal, they cooperated more when given a voice because they felt more included but would not if they did not feel their voice was included.

Influence and Individual-Centric Versus Collective-Centric Identity

Yukl (2010) discusses how relational and collective identity affects the use of influence tactics such as rational persuasion, inspirational appeals, consultation, ingratiation, personal appeal, exchange, legitimating, pressure or assertiveness, hard versus soft. Cultural differences have been noted among collective-centric identity; for example, the use of gifts, coalition tactics, and upward appeals as influence tactics were more effective among Chinese managers than American ones.

In *Theories of Educational Leadership and Management,* Tony Bush (2011) maintains that power may be regarded as the ability to determine the behavior of others or to decide the outcomes of conflict. Bush supports a move from individual-centered to collective-centered leadership. He notes that where there is disagreement, it is likely to be resolved according to the relative resources of power available to the participants. He gives as an example that principals may have the capacity to determine many institutional decisions and to affect the behavior of their colleagues, but they do not have absolute power because their power and influence to exert and maintain control flows from an individual-centric model of leadership.

Citing Bacharach and Lawler (1980, p. 44), Bush distinguishes between power and influence. Power is "authority [that] flows downward, and is unidirectional; on the other hand, influence is multidirectional and can flow upward, downward, or horizontally." Wielding individual power paves the way for the leader to create a multidimensional influential style that can permeate and flow through the constituency in a relational manner. However, it is the leader who is always in control and who provides constraints on the fluidity and potency of the influence. In an individual-centric leadership style, control rests totally with the leader, who serves as a filter for how much an influence can tilt and sway an organization's direction.

In an individual-centric leadership style, power and influence are not oriented toward the collective well-being and tangibles of the group, society, organization, or institution. Instead they focus on their basic needs for success, advancement, and status of the leader. It may run counter to group centeredness where the overarching goal centers more on the directives of the leader rather than the consensual interests of the collective. Using a collective-centered approach, leaders set the prevailing goal of achieving consensus on all decision-making activities. The goal is achieved through a process-oriented mode of communication where opinions and the voices of the group are valued above the individual.

For individual-centric leaders, many indicated they were interested in promoting a personal agenda stemming from intrinsically motivated values and status mobility. In an ongoing survey conducted by the senior author of this book, many of her respondents of diverse leaders of color indicated they were not interested in competing with their constituents for resources and resource allocations. For many collective-oriented leaders, a high respect for humility, dignity, lack of vanity, deference to the group's welfare, and functioning from a self-effacing demeanor in a gracious, respectful, and polite manner was more important. Almost to a person, those who expressed and endorsed these styles did not see their styles as weaknesses or in any way influencing their persuasiveness, potency, and effectiveness. They did not see themselves as megalomaniacs consumed with a high need for achievement, power, influence, and the domination of others. They maintained their high respect for and expression of humility; they tended to be modest, unassuming, selfless, feign engaging in self-pride, and most important avoided passions for greatness, control and power, and micropolitics. In decision-making ventures, many of our respondents showed careful thought in wading through tough decisions. All their activities were intended to cause no harm that would damage the overall welfare of the group through inconveniences and lack of respect. All these characteristics and values run counter to an individual-centered approach to leadership where the leader is at the center of group; in this context, a high value is often placed on rugged individualism where individual achievement is the primary goal. Culturally diverse approaches tend to value the rugged individual, too, but the centers of power and influence are not centralized and emphasized solely at the leader's discretion.

Group centeredness can take on other features and characteristics. In the business world, leaders may be focused on the welfare of the institution and company. While their needs for success advancement are essential, the welfare of the institution is paramount; the success of the institution dominates individual needs for power and success. Yet it is possible for one to place the needs of the institution first and at the same time nurture one's needs for advancement, influence, and power.

Changing Images of Leaders

We often perceive traits associated with leaders that may not have much to do with effective leadership; these characteristics are often embraced by leaders themselves. Terms such as "he looks like a leader," "he is presidential, charismatic, or a visionary" are all terms used to describe leaders. They often capture what followers want in their leaders—which, in turn, are influenced by social constructions of leadership that do impact leadership styles. The image of leadership has been evolving over time. A masculine leadership prototype has prevailed that has been more task oriented (Heilman, 2001; Schein, 2004). Lately, there has been growing recognition of the importance of people skills for leaders and the increased prominence of the transformational leadership and leader-member exchange paradigms in the leadership literature (e.g., Eagly & Carli, 2007; Rudman & Glick, 2001). As more women and racial/ethnic minorities enter the workplace and leadership positions, more androgynous conceptions of leadership emerge that emphasize both task and people skills. Globalization has also led to the influence of Asian management styles, which have been noted to be more relationship focused (Triandis, 1993). It may be that this more androgynous conception of leadership will open up more opportunities for women and racial minorities to be considered as leaders and assist them in negotiating their way through the labyrinth (Eagly & Carli, 2007).

Image Management

Image management has implications for the training of leaders because, as we have noted, perceptions of social identities often intersect with perceptions about whether or not one is a leader. Leadership has been described as an outcome of self-categorization processes. Studies in these social categories of leadership include forms of in-group favoritism. While this promotes cooperation and group cohesiveness among in-group members, it often results in prejudice, discrimination, and stereotyping against those categorized as out-group members.

From a diversity leadership perspective, it is important to diminish social constraints that preclude those who do not fit a prototypic image from leadership roles. Given our discussion of social identities and categorization, it is incumbent on insiders to recognize this bias. In drawing on Zweigenhaft and Domhoff's (2006) work about how entering the power elite often shapes the identities and leadership behaviors of leaders resulting in their conforming to prototypes of the dominant culture, we need to be proactive about the limitations of such conformity. On the other hand, some have described the importance of impression management if one is to project an image of credible leadership. This then is the challenge for leaders whose social identities do not fit the dominant culture. Conscious attention to the following behaviors is important:

- Dressing not just to project expected leadership images (e.g., a navy blue suit) but also to prevent distractions from stereotypic perceptions (e.g., being too feminine or too ethnic).
- Communication styles of not just projecting one's voice and presenting with a confident demeanor but also to avoid being ignored and not yielding the floor. This often occurs with women and racial/ethnic minorities whose voices are minimized by those in the dominant group because of their privilege.

For the global leader, cross-cultural leadership is image management. The identities of leaders across borders become more pronounced as leaders are often compelled to present the image of their country as part of most initial rituals in cross-cultural encounters. As we grapple with between-group and in-group differences, the leader in multinational corporations must consider the importance of culture and diversity; at times, the privilege associated with one's leader status may be at odds with dimensions of his or her social statuses, which may be marginalized. In these situations, leaders must tend to the fine balance between conforming, embracing the culture of an organization's members, versus remaining authentic to one's own.

Status and Legitimacy

Social cognitive factors affect perceptions of leadership in which observers or members possess implicit theories about what a good leader is as indicated in the GLOBE studies. However, these can and do give rise to a set of stereotypical traits and behaviors, which leaders are expected to exhibit—for example, military, political, and religious leaders (Lord & Maher, 1991). They also influence perceptions of who are leaders and granting of status and legitimacy to leaders. The question is how these social cognitive factors interact with perceptions of leadership among those belonging to out-groups or nondominant social and cultural groups.

Therefore, can women or Asians make good leaders since they do not typically demonstrate stereotypic traits and behaviors associated with implicit theories of good leadership?

As one woman leader described her behind the scenes efforts to build a new center for her university, she found the need to get credit for her efforts as well as to commend and share the glory with others if she were to be successful as a leader. Hogg (2001) describes prototypicality as the normative attitudes and behaviors of in-group members; hence, prototypic leaders are those who embrace or project those behaviors perceived and expected by group members as associated with good leadership. By being prototypical, the leader becomes socially attractive. This may become associated with such things as competency and trustworthiness, but from a social identity theory of leadership, it is less important than the status accorded to the leader.

Challenges and Dilemmas

We end this chapter on leader identity with several overarching principles. In recognizing the diversity that leaders bring about who they are and how it influences their exercise of leadership, we suggest a shift from identifying traits to recognizing the importance of cultural value orientations and the implicit leadership theories held by leaders and members about leadership that will shape leader behaviors. This brings some challenges and dilemmas. How do we avoid the ethnocentrism so common in our thinking and reflected in our theories? How do we avoid dichotomizing those leaders coming from dominant social groups and largely reflect the current contexts of corporations in a society from those coming from minority social groups? Are their aims and lived experiences different? How do we use these differences within an affirmative paradigm rather than fall prey to in-group versus out-group categorizations.

Leaders with social identities reflective of dominant social groups are less likely to see the privilege associated with their in-group social status. The challenge for members and an organization is how to avoid stereotypic leader prototypes and social categories that favor in-groups. Leaders with social identities reflective of marginalized or minority groups are likely to face a different experience; they face the additional challenge as to whether and how to conform to the power elite and in-group. Do we simply say, "It is what it is"? Or do we act according to principles of diversity leadership and look to say, "What can it be?" based on a system of fairness and inclusiveness, social justice, and equity values. How do we enable diverse leaders to develop the self-monitoring skills and to use race [and other dimensions of diversity] as a resource instead of a deficit or weakness as Ospina and Foldy (2009) suggest.

Two characteristics of leaders whose social identities are from marginalized or minority groups are worth noting. While the GLOBE studies identified self-protection as a leadership dimension with low endorsement, Chin (2013) found that diverse leaders often felt the need for developing mechanisms of self-protection in response to the frequent barrage about needing to prove their competence often associated to perceptions about their social identities rather than their performance. Diverse leaders also face the challenge of being "authentic" and yet leading two lives in their communities of origin and the mainstream community and of the need to conform to fit the prototypic image of a leader. They felt there was a constant need to justify and prove themselves; hence, the use of an affirmative paradigm promotes their ability to lead and wear their multiple and intersecting identities with pride.

Summary

The complexity of social identities reflects what leaders bring to their leadership and contributes to redefining leadership. In shifting from leadership traits to leader identity in our understanding of leadership, the focus is on the self, or "who leaders are," and their authenticity. These identities are multiple and intersecting; they often define in-group preferences and out-group exclusion and play out in the exchange between leaders and members. They result in social and leadership power, which may result in incongruence between a leader's identity and the social identities that he or she holds. Unlike traits, these identities are developmental and evolving and often shape leader behavior and the perceptions and expectations of members. The degree of mismatch between a leader's identities and that of members of an organization might also result in double standards in appraising leadership behavior and different applications of how members may be willing to follow leaders. Whether a leader exercises an individual-centric or collective-centric approach to leadership reflects cultural values and orientation of the leader as well as that of the organizational members. These identity characteristics influence social constructions of leadership and images of ideal leadership prototypes, which tend to favor the social identities of the dominant social group in the organization and society. Hence, leaders coming from nondominant groups may need to learn to manage their image to establish their status and legitimacy as a leader.

Discussion Questions: Developing Self-Awareness— From Leadership Traits to Identity

1. What is leader identity and how does it interface with our other social identities?

2. Identify some ways in which the leadership experiences of women, non-White, or homosexual leaders are different from that of heterosexual White men?

3. How does a leader remain authentic, or true to himself or herself, but fluid as demands for different dimensions of identity need to be brought forward? Does this defy notions of the integrated self? Explain.

4. Is leader authenticity a matter of integrity? Does one's *moral compass* remain constant, dictating that leader behave similarly across different contexts and situational demands?

5. Identify and discuss some unconscious beliefs and stereotypes that people have about an effective and successful leader. How do these beliefs drive perceptions and expectations of leaders? Are these harmful or advantageous?

6. In thinking about different leadership styles, what psychosocial factors influence identity formation among existing and prospective leaders? How might that self-identity process unfold?

7. Some leaders walk a fine line between being openly visible and quietly invisible about their identities. Discuss the question: "Do you bring all of yourself to work?" Discuss why or why not.

8. Discuss the similarities and differences between an individual-centric versus collective-centric identity and how it relates to leadership styles.

5

Leadership Style

Notable Quotes

"Leadership style flows from the personal values, and the personal values come from my culture." (Latino-American male leader)

"If you can believe that you're imperfect and come to accept that and that you have to improve yourself then I think you can become a better leader." (Asian-American male leader)

"I can remember [being told] that 'you wear these flowery dresses and you're so sweet to the point that nobody anticipates that you're going to say something harsh. So it comes as a bigger surprise; that's why you're having this problem posing as authority. Your voice . . . you sound like a little girl. You don't sound like an authority figure.'" (Told to a White female leader)

Vignette: Invisible Leadership—"Pushing From Behind"

"What I've learned about leadership from my culture is that your role as a leader isn't so much to be out in front and visible as much as to be the person behind pushing people to be the best that they can. My tribe is matriarchal so it's natural for women to take a leadership role from the perspective of my tribe. Women are the ones who have always made decisions and have been the leaders. Although the women make the decisions, they also decide which man to put in a leadership role and would advise that man." (Native American Indian woman leader)

Leadership Styles

Leadership style is a focus on "what leaders do" compared with leader identity, which is a focus on "who leaders are." As leadership theories shifted from an examination of leader traits or leadership in situations to an emphasis on leadership style, research emphasized the behaviors of leaders and expanded the study of leadership to include how leaders behave toward subordinates in various contexts. The emphasis on leadership style was responsive to the rapidly changing environment of the 20th century and the need for leaders to be fluid and dynamic in response to these changes. It was an attempt to identify not a fixed set of leader traits or situations in which leadership occurs but rather to examine styles of behaving or processes of interaction in which leaders engage with their subordinates.

During the 20th century, interest in democratic versus autocratic versus laissez-faire styles of leadership grew post-World War II in response to the military dictatorships of Hitler in Germany and Mussolini in Italy compared to democracy in the United States—and the fear of nuclear war. These were charismatic leaders irrespective of their destructive power. Military images of command-and-control types of leadership prevailed embodied in the election of General Dwight Eisenhower as president of the United States. In the 1980s, leadership researchers became interested in charismatic and transformational leadership as many U.S. companies began to acknowledge the need to make changes in their leadership in order to survive amidst increasing economic competition from non-U.S. companies. Other leadership styles also emerged, often in response to the contexts and social zeitgeist of the times. Coined by Matthew Arnold in the 19th century, social zeitgeist refers to the spirit of social change and uncertainty that marks the thought or feeling of a period or age; the zeitgeist is much more than the prevailing worldview at a given time in history. It's a force that influences events. For example, an emphasis on dimensions, such as authenticity and integrity, emerged in response to the scandals of Enron and Penn State and the economic downturns in the real estate and banking industries at the end of the 20th century. A review of some leadership styles relevant to diversity leadership follows.

Value Dimensions in Leadership Styles

The emphasis on leadership styles often resulted in dichotomous dimensions such as transformational versus transactional leadership. Instead of posing these dimensions as alternatives, value judgments often emerged deeming one dimension as better. The focus on singular dimensions also implied the opposite as undesirable. Hence, the introduction of value judgments is inherent in the evolution of transformational leadership, servant or shared leadership, humane or virtuous leadership, leader authenticity and integrity. In developing our understanding of diversity leadership, we need to recognize the influence of values that shape our formulation of leadership theories and to examine our premises to ensure that our theories remain inclusive of diverse viewpoints and representative of all voices. Instead of asking which style is best, we might begin to ask questions about which styles are best for which situations and in which contexts.

Are Differences in Leadership Style Related to Gender, Race, or Ethnicity?

Another question to be asking is whether differences in leadership style are related to gender, race, or ethnicity. Eagly and Johnson (1990) found that men and women leaders behave more alike than different when occupying the same positions. As women and men rise to meet the challenges of their leadership positions, they tend to behave more similarly with one another when in similar position, presumably in response to the situational demands of the position. In contrast, the emergence of leadership in laboratory experiments tend to evoke social perceptions, expectations, and stereotypes; consequently, men and women leaders who emerge in laboratory experiments tend to conform to more stereotypic gender roles.

Zweigenhaft and Domhoff (2006) found that racial/ethnic minority leaders tend to conform to behaviors of the power elite once they reach these ranks of leadership. Similarly, cross-cultural studies (Dorfman, Den Hartog, & Mitchelson, 2003; House, Hanges, Javidan, Dorfman, & Gupta, 2004) suggest there are universal leadership dimensions together with cultural variation in the pattern of these dimensions.

Task Versus Relationship Leadership Styles

Much research was conducted post World War II on task versus relationship leadership styles. These styles have alternately been called agentic versus communal styles, task motivated versus relationship motivated leadership styles, task versus interpersonal, or task versus expressive styles of leadership. In general, gender differences have emerged with women leaders being more relationship oriented and men leaders being more task oriented. The strength of these differences correlate with social perception and stereotypic expectations of men and women to behave accordingly with a tendency to dichotomize task versus relationship styles of leadership as mutually exclusive. Women are more likely to be perceived as communal and interpersonal, possessing traits of warmth and gentleness that appear more tailored for subordinate and service roles (Kite, Deaux, & Haines, 2008). Men are more likely to be perceived as task oriented and associated with traits of decisiveness that appear more tailored for leadership roles. While these perceptions may have a basis in actual behaviors, their stereotypic portrayal of men and women tends to be constraining while the association of communal traits with weakness is disadvantageous for women. It can result in men and women leaders having different types of social interactions with their men and women supervisors and subordinates and influence the outcomes experienced by each party (Ayman, 1993).

A meta-analysis of leader stereotypes (Koenig, Eagly, Mitchell, & Ristikari, 2011) demonstrated that stereotypes of leaders are culturally masculine, with greater agency than communion traits although this masculine construal of leadership is decreasing over time. Several studies (e.g., Bass & Avolio, 1994) found women to be more attentive than men to "the human side of enterprise" (McGregor, 1985), suggesting that female leaders tend to base judgments more on intuition and emotions than on rational calculation of the relationships between means and ends, more toward social stereotypes of being more interpersonal, selfless, and concerned with others. This can also be viewed as an advantage.

In a meta-analysis of gender and leadership style (Eagly & Johnson, 1990), gender differences did not emerge in organizational studies between interpersonal versus task-oriented style. However, stereotypic gender differences did emerge in laboratory experiments and assessment studies—that is, studies when participants were not selected for holding a leadership position. Social perceptions and expectations apparently influence the leadership styles of women being more relationship based when in situations of self-assessment or when appointed to leadership roles in laboratory studies. Men conformed more toward the social stereotypes of being more task oriented, self-assertive, and motivated to master their environment while women conformed more toward social stereotypes of being more interpersonal, self-less, and concerned with others.

It is important to note that leadership measurement scales often force a dichotomy when these dimensions are measured as two ends of a continuum; they might be better measured as two separate dimensions where one may be high on both. This would make for a more dynamic process to understand the interaction between leader, follower, and context and measure it as a multidimensional and bidirectional dimension. It also makes clear the need to avoid stereotypic bias and value-driven assignments associated with the task versus relationship leadership styles.

Cross-cultural differences have emerged and are consistent with findings that the emphasis on relationships over the task is more central among

Asian, Arab, and non-Western leaders. This plays out negotiation and decision making by leaders whereby these leaders use the negotiation process to evaluate the quality of the relationship; they believe in the long-term gain and that an initial negotiation is one to confirm belongingness as opposed to confirming authority and dominance as might be in the case of negotiation among Westerners. Hence, when non-Westerners "give in," this can be misconstrued by Westerners as "losing" while it is viewed by non-Western leaders as serving the long-term relationship.

Assertiveness

Assertiveness has been defined as another dimension often associated with effective leadership; it is often juxtaposed with passivity. It is often characterized by confidence and affirming one's rights or point of view without threatening or submissively permitting another to ignore or deny one's rights. It is a characteristic more associated with a task-oriented approach of getting things done and of men. While women are often said to benefit from assertiveness training, men are said to benefit from sensitivity training.

As discussed in Chapter 3, Asian American leaders defined assertiveness to include using indirect means of communication in order to maintain harmony in interpersonal relationships consistent with cultural orientation values. While Westerners may label this as passivity by Westerners, it demonstrates the difference in concept equivalence of assertiveness across cultural groups based on differences in worldviews. Inherent in the dichotomy between task versus relationship oriented leadership styles are the concepts of *Ren-Qing* and *Quanxi* discussed in Chapter 3, which are based on relationships, interpersonal and social obligation, and loyalty. They played a prominent role in business negotiations and leadership styles.

Transformational Leadership Style

Transformational leadership is when leaders and followers engage in a mutual process of "raising one another to higher levels of morality and motivation." Transformational leaders raise the bar by appealing to higher ideals and values of followers. In doing so, they may model the values themselves and use charismatic methods to attract people to the values and to themselves as leaders (Burns, 1978). Kouzes and Posner (2002) developed their model of transformational leadership based on more than 1,300 interviews across private and public sector organizations to consist of five fundamental practices that enable leaders to get extraordinary things accomplished. These include the following: (1) Model the way (2) inspire a shared vision, (3) challenge the process (4) enable others to act, and (5) encourage the heart.

Rost (1991, p. 102) defines leadership as "an influence relationship among leaders and followers who intend real changes that reflect their mutual purposes." To be called leadership, the relationship must be based on influence; this influence is multidirectional, and attempts must not be coercive. Therefore, the relationship is not based on authority but rather persuasion. Influence is often defined as an important component of transformational leadership.

Transformational Versus Transactional

Initially, research compared transactional with transformational styles of leadership where transactional leaders emphasized the operations, organization, and decision-making processes while transformational leaders emphasized vision, change, and innovation. This evolved to favor transformational styles of leadership starting in the 1980s as U.S. corporations began to experience rapid change with the growth of multinational corporations and international business. Vision, change, and innovation associated as core components of transformational leadership came to be viewed as necessary for leaders in the 21st century to be prepared for rapid changes following a shift from an industrial to a digital age and global society where technology has ushered in rapid and dramatic change.

Charisma

House (1977) proposed a theory for charismatic leadership. It involves attitudes and perceptions of followers about the leader and specifies those traits that increase the likelihood of being perceived as charismatic. These include the following traits: strong need for power, high self-confidence, and strong convictions; impression management and articulation of an appealing vision also increase the likelihood of appearing charismatic. Along with vision, change, and innovation, the charisma of a leader who can unite and inspire the group toward a mutual purpose has been cited as one dimension of transformational leadership (see Burns, 1978). Charismatic leadership has been defined as those leaders with a special magnetic charm or appeal arousing special popular loyalty or enthusiasm for a public figure (as a political leader). Gardner and Avolio (1998) suggest that charismatic leadership is an impression management process enacted theatrically in acts of *framing, scripting, staging,* and *performing.*

Examples of such charismatic leadership have generally involved dominant male figures, such as General Douglas MacArthur, Reverend Martin Luther King Jr., Mahatma Gandhi, Winston Churchill, and Franklin D. Roosevelt. The questions to ask are: Is there a difference between women and men on the dimension of charisma? Does charisma vary across cultures? While charismatic leaders generally convey a commanding presence consistent with masculinized images, this tends to be true of Western leaders. It is interesting to note that non-Western charismatic leaders typically communicate more humanistic and altruistic features of compassion, modesty, and benevolence. Witness the images of Mahatma Gandhi, Nelson Mandela, and the Dalai Lama, who are noted for their compassion and endurance amidst adversity. Their quotes reflect their different styles of leadership. Mahatma Gandhi, preeminent leader of Indian nationalism, was known for his pacifist stance while in India: "Always aim at complete harmony of thought and word and deed. Always aim at purifying your thoughts and everything will be well" (Gandhi, n.d.). Nelson Mandela was imprisoned for 27 years for his antiapartheid political activity in South Africa and later the first African president from 1994 to 1999. "It is better to lead from behind and to put others in front, especially when you celebrate victory when nice things occur. You take the front line when there is danger. Then people will appreciate your leadership" (Mandela, n.d.). The Dalai Lama, in exile since 1959 in India following the failed Tibetan uprising, is known as leader of the Tibetans. "The topic of compassion is not at all religious business; it is important to know it is human business, it is a question of human survival" (Dalai Lama XIV, n.d.).

We have some qualitative evidence that charismatic women leaders do not present with a loud and commanding presence as men. Mother Teresa, known for her humility and servitude, has been a model to many worldwide. Rather, charismatic women might be more distinguished by their nurturing and smiles. The examples below illustrate this point. When Nancy Pelosi was elected as House Minority leader in 2002, she became the first woman ever to head a party in either chamber of the U.S. legislature. McGrory (2002) wrote, "He is called the Hammer. She's a velvet hammer. He is Tom DeLay, the newly elected House majority leader, who is all coercion and threat. She is Nancy Pelosi of California, who is all persuasion and smiles." This description reflects the gender bias and differential language used to describe women leaders in masculinized contexts. Though pointing to Nancy Pelosi's collaborative and interpersonal strengths, the description reflects the tendency to "feminize" women leaders to suggest weakness or incredulity when women behave as decisive and effective leaders. Anson Chan, former Secretary of State in Hong Kong, is someone about whom there is uniform consensus about her charisma. When asked about charisma in men and women, she said: "I actually think it's an advantage to be a woman. Not that I took advantage. I have a reputation of always being approachable. I always have this big smile on my face, which makes a lot of people very happy. People feel that I'm approachable, that I'm a good listener, and that I'm prepared to listen to what they say. But at the same time, lots of women look up to me because they think that I'm a very good role model" (Chin, 2013). What is emphasized as charisma in both of these women leaders is their persuasion and smiles.

Related images about strong women include Nancy Pelosi and Hillary Clinton's leadership described as a "Velvet Glove with an Iron Fist." The image reflects the mystique of women—for strong women, their guise of softness, and the ambivalence about strong women. Consider the mixed images about Hillary Clinton, former U.S. Secretary of State, who brought disdain because of her strong and commanding style; she was viewed as cold and unfeeling—that is, "unfeminine." She was "redeemed" during her run for president after she cried, showing emotion "befitting of women."

Again, the issue of concept equivalence plays a role in defining charisma. It may be defined differently across gender and cultural groups. Whether or not the definition of transformational leadership includes charisma conveys masculine versus feminine images of transformational leadership. Those definitions, which include charisma as a commanding presence, are more aligned with masculine definitions. Those definitions that stress vision and change suggest that transformational leadership is more of the exchange between leaders and followers and are more aligned with feminine definitions of relationships. In those empirical studies using the latter definition of transformational leadership, women emerge as being more transformational and having an advantage.

Charismatic leadership, as defined by some, is how leaders communicate that they truly care about the group's welfare and are willing to go the extra mile. These examples of charismatic leadership are based on the relationship between leader and follower, not solely on the personality of the leader. William Clinton, former U.S. president, was noted for how he could communicate "I can feel your pain and I'm willing to do something about it." Central to Mother Teresa and the Dalai Lama's appeal was their appeal to members' motives and aspirations; they motivated followers to go beyond self-interest; their dedication to the cause and willingness to engage in personal sacrifice and danger was lauded. This element of self-sacrifice, associated with religious and Eastern philosophies, tends to characterize their charisma in contrast with the commanding and influential presence of General George S. Patton who said, "No bastard ever won a war by dying for his country. He won it by making the other poor dumb bastard die for his country (Patton, n.d.)" and of Winston Churchill who said, "We shall defend our island, whatever the cost may be, we shall fight on the beaches, we shall fight on the landing grounds, we shall fight in the fields and in the streets, we shall fight in the hills; we shall never surrender" (Churchill, 1940).

Cultural Variation

A meta-analysis of transformational, transactional, and laissez-faire leadership styles among women (Eagly, Johannesen-Schmidt, & van Engen, 2003) found that female leaders were more transformational than male leaders and also engaged in more of the contingent reward behaviors that are a component of transactional leadership. Male leaders were generally more likely to manifest the other aspects of transactional leadership (active and passive management by exception) and laissez-faire leadership. The small but significant differences are consistent with feminist principles of inclusion, collaboration, and social advocacy. Despite stereotype-based suspicions that women might not be effective leaders, these differences displayed by women leaders are generally associated with good managerial practices in current-day organizations (e.g., Judge & Piccolo, 2004).

Women leaders have been found to be more transformational compared with men leaders although the differences are small but significant. We might attribute this to the "feminine" features associated with images of competent men leaders as transactional or task oriented. Or we might attribute this to feminist leaders "challenging the status quo" of male privilege and their marginal status in the ranks of leadership aligned with equity goals. Hence, they are more likely to promote change and innovation.

The measurement equivalence of transformational leadership has been tested across cultures. In most cultures, three styles of laissez-faire, transactional, and transformational leadership have been found, but the behaviors defining them are not the same (e.g., Den Hartog, Van Muijen, & Koopman, 1997). Bass (1990) provides an example that boasting about one's competence is inspirational and builds confidence in subordinates in Indonesia, but doing so in Japan is considered to be unseemly. On the whole, many cross-cultural studies have demonstrated the validity of transformational leadership (Judge & Piccolo, 2004). However, Chin (2013) found that diverse leaders of color in the United States endorsed transformational leadership as a preferred leadership style on a quantitative survey; however, follow-up individual interviews and focus groups showed that they preferred collaborative leadership models but felt they needed to aspire to transformational leadership styles (because they are in vogue).

Collaborative Leadership Style

As the women's movement and civil rights movement of the 1960s raised our consciousness about gender and racial/ethnic inequities and oppression, collaborative leadership styles emerged. Central to this style are values of collaboration and empowerment with concepts of "shared power" and "servant leader" emerging as models of leadership. This was a shift from power to empowerment in response to experiences of oppression in the United States and the emergence of social responsibility gaining prominence as a concern of leadership.

Hank Rubin (2009) described "a collaboration [as] a purposeful relationship in which all parties strategically choose to cooperate in order to accomplish a shared outcome." He says: "You are a collaborative leader once you have accepted responsibility for building, or helping ensure the success of, a heterogeneous team to accomplish a shared purpose. Your tools are (1) the purposeful exercise of your behavior, communication, and organizational resources in order to affect the perspective, beliefs, and behaviors of another person (generally a collaborative partner) to influence that person's relationship with you and your collaborative enterprise and (2) the structure and climate of an environment that supports the collaborative relationship" (p. 17).

Collaborative leadership styles have become increasingly popular with growing recognition of the diverse and global environment in which we live. This leadership style is viewed as enabling leaders to be at the forefront of change, and for leaders to be able to work across groups together in a global environment. It has led to growing recognition of the importance of flexibility and adaptability for effective leadership in the 21st century.

Today's most pressing challenges in society include issues such as managing resource constraints, controlling health care costs, training the 21st century workforce, developing and implementing new technologies, and stabilizing financial systems to foster sustainable economic growth. The future of collaborative leadership depends on the ability of leaders to engage and collaborate with the business, government, and social sectors. Nick Lovegrove and Matthew Thomas (cofounders of The InterSector Project) writing for the *Harvard Business Review* (2013), interviewed over 100 leaders who have demonstrated their ability to engage and collaborate across these three sectors and found six distinguishing characteristics:

- Balanced motivations. A desire to create public value no matter where they work, combining their motivations to wield influence (often in government), have social impact (often in nonprofits), and generate wealth (often in business)
- Transferable skills. A set of distinctive skills valued across sectors, such as quantitative analytics, strategic planning, and stakeholder management

- Contextual intelligence. A deep empathy of the differences within and between sectors, especially those of language, culture, and key performance indicators
- Integrated networks. A set of relationships across sectors to draw on when advancing their careers, building top teams, or convening decision makers on a particular issue
- Prepared mind. A willingness to pursue an unconventional career that zigzags across sectors and the financial readiness to take potential pay cuts from time to time
- Intellectual thread. Holistic subject matter expertise on a particular intersector issue by understanding it from the perspective of each sector

For collaboration to be effective there must be mutual respect of the cultures and identities that each member brings. This has not been common in more traditional organizations and institutions where an emphasis on hierarchy occurs. Managers are typically expected to manage a team of people with a set of resources; success, power, and influence are defined by having more people and more resources to control. In contrast, effective collaboration is contingent on managing people and resources outside one's control. Collaborative leadership also reflects cultural value orientations and the negotiation that occurs across diverse social and task-oriented groups.

Women and Collaboration

Research has demonstrated that women have a somewhat more democratic and participative style than men (Trinidad & Normore, 2005), perhaps because people resist women who take charge in a particularly assertive manner. In meta-analyses of studies on leadership styles of women and men, female leaders are somewhat more transformational than male leaders, especially in mentoring and developing workplace colleagues. They tend to adopt a positive managerial approach that trades on rewards rather than a negative approach that trades on reprimands (Eagly, Johannesen-Schmidt, & van Engen, 2003; Eagly & Johnson, 1990). This evidence supports the tendency for women to adopt a more collaborative, cooperative, or democratic leadership style and for men to adopt a more directive, competitive, or autocratic style, which has emerged in all types of studies. What is striking is that women seem to be intentionally different and more collaborative based on differences in personality and social interpersonal skills.

Collectivism

Collective leadership, simply stated, is leading together as partners according to Petra Künkel, who defines it as "the capacity of a group of leaders to deliver a contribution in service of the common good through assuming joint and flexible leadership, according to what is perceived and required." Each coleader feels no need to personally stand out or impose his or her views but cultivates the ability to know or sense what needs doing. In many non-Western cultures, leadership is considered a collective rather than an individual capacity; leadership is defined then as a relationship or a process, not a person, which contrasts with Western cultures that often emphasize who the leader is.

Unlike individual heroic leadership, coleadership embraces the diversity of people and perspectives and frees up self-initiative and collective intelligence. When practiced across sectors, it creates the conditions for societal learning and innovation through an increased sense of interdependence and a deeper trust in self-organization.

The distinguishing feature of a collaborative leadership style is working with members, using a team approach, and acknowledging their input, while a transformational leadership style is distinguished by the influence a leader has on the members. Collectivistic dimensions underlie this style and are consistent with many Eastern cultures and racial/ethnic minority groups in the United States. In fact, a collaborative style of leadership was preferred over a transformational style of leadership among racial/ethnic minority group leaders studied by Chin (2013). In endorsing a collaborative leadership style, these diverse leaders of color saw it as more central to a consensus-building process, ensuring that all voices are heard and engaging members and the community in the process of leadership. This style better reflected their collectivistic view over an individualistic view of society and their cultural orientation values.

In recognition of the difference between collectivist and individualist societies, Gauthier (2011) proposes the following model of collective leadership that integrates three new areas of leadership theory:

- Shared/distributed/rotating/collective leadership (lateral or peer influence, concertive action)
- Complexity leadership (entanglement between top-down, bottom-up, circular)
- Leadership as a relational process (interpersonal influence, dialogue, mutuality)

There is mutual adjustment among and between members and leaders— a shared sense making and collective learning. DAC leadership outcomes include the following: (1) Direction: understanding and assenting to the value of the collective's goals; (2) Alignment: organizing and coordinating knowledge and work; and (3) Commitment: members subsuming their own efforts and benefits within the collective effort and benefit.

Team Leadership

Related to collaborative leadership is team leadership that focuses on groups working together to achieve a specified outcome. Groups that bring together diverse individuals have been shown to outperform more homogeneous groups because they ordinarily include members with differing ways of representing and solving problems; however, this can depend on the individual consideration given by leaders to its members (Homan & Greer, 2013). While diversity in teams can initiate subgroup categorizations of creating "us-them" distinctions and reduce interpersonal liking, low trust, and high levels of conflict that impedes team outcomes of performance and satisfaction, diversity can also initiate the exchange and processing of different perspectives and ideas, which can enhance team performance and satisfaction. Diversity in composition of group members brings advantages because the best solutions to complex problems generally result from teams that apply differing tools and skills.

The challenge for organizations is to leverage this potential by promoting diversity in groups and its leaders while working to lessen the conflict, communication barriers, and lack of mutual respect that can develop between in-group and out-group members (e.g., Polzer, Milton, & Swann, 2002; see review by van Knippenberg & Schippers, 2007). Considerate leaders "show concern and respect for followers, look out for their welfare, and express appreciation and support" (Judge, Piccolo, & Ilies, 2004, p. 36). Leaders who are themselves from groups traditionally excluded from leadership may be more likely to have the consideration attending to relationships and individual need and the multicultural competence to manage the challenges of a diverse workgroup and to reap its advantages.

Servant Leadership

Also related to collaborative leadership is servant leadership, which reflects attempts to transform leader-member relationships to be more egalitarian by redefining the relationship to be one of servant leaders responding to the needs of followers. Servant leadership was first developed by Robert K. Greenleaf (1977) and became one of the popular leadership models in reaction to concerns about the abuse of power among leaders. Servant leaders achieve results for their organizations by giving priority attention to the needs of members and those they serve. They are humble stewards of their organization's resources (human, financial, and physical). Servant leadership was made popular with the late Dr. Martin Luther King Jr. and has been described as one of the ways in which President Obama is representative of the modern ethnic minority leader, demonstrated by his early career as a community organizer. He used the community and a sense of purpose beyond himself as he orchestrated one of the most inclusive and expansive presidential campaigns in the history of the United States of America; his message was about the people and the goals he was trying to reach and solve for the collective good.

In most contexts today, top-down, command-and-control leaders no longer provide the most effective or admired type of leadership (Eagly & Carli, 2007). In response to these changes, scholars of leadership have increasingly emphasized that effective leadership emerges from inspiring, motivating, and mentoring followers. Such leadership is embedded in inter-personal exchanges and dialogues in organizations in which leadership is distributed throughout the organization as both followers and leaders take responsibility for adapting to challenges (e.g., Graen & Uhl-Bien, 1995; Spillane, 2006)—often described as shared leadership. Collaborative leader-ship styles are essentially a focus on the issues of power in the exercise of leadership; who holds the power and how it is distributed.

Ethical Leadership

Recent research has tried to understand moral behavior in the workplace mainly from an intrapersonal perspective, blaming ethical failures on the person's moral character, moral development or moral identity, or on iso-lated aspects of the situation. In doing so, little attention has been paid to the interplay between the person and the interpersonal context in which this behavior takes place. An emphasis on ethical leadership addresses the question studied by Zimbardo (2007) on how good people do bad things. In describing the dark side of leadership and power, he uses it to mobilize change in the concept that everyone can be a hero by making one small change.

Scandals involving leaders at the beginning of the 21st century such as Enron and Penn State (see Chapter 2) seem to have resulted in an increased emphasis on virtue and ethics as a goal for redefining leadership. Is there a need for leaders to act with virtue?

Virtuous Leadership

According to Kilburg (2012), five virtues espoused by Plato and Confucius have endured the test of time. These virtues frame the three essential components of effective leadership: strategy, character, and influ-ence. Strategy involves setting the direction for where to go while influence is the ability to create meaningful relationships with others through which work of the organization is accomplished. Character is the continuous exercise of virtuous behavior.

According to Kilburg, leaders must be virtuous human beings. Using a philosophical model to understand the "what and how" of effective leadership, he frames this as an exercise in answering two important questions: What are we to do? What are executives to do to lead their organizations? How do leaders determine identity (character) of an organization and strategic direction it will pursue and influence how it will go about achieving its organizational goals?

To be virtuous means having the five Socratic virtues or character strengths: wisdom, courage, temperance, justice, and reverence, which are essential to leadership competence. Good leadership occurs when the process of discerning, decision making and action involving these virtues is followed. Kilburg distinguishes corrupt leadership and derailment of leadership when leaders deviate from these virtues. He conceptualizes where leadership goes awry in terms of psychodynamic conflict and identifies the seven deadly leadership errors tied to failures to follow these virtues. These virtues mirror some of the traits currently emphasized in the leadership literature: Wisdom is cognitive strength in acquiring and using knowledge, courage is emotional strength and the will to accomplish goals in the midst of opposition, temperance is the exercise of moderation, justice is ethical behavior and doing what is right, and reverence is an adherence to order and hierarchy. Using a competency approach, Kilburg delineates the virtues into skills that can be learned, ties them to behavioral principles, and uses case examples to support the success of his model.

Kilburg integrates a global context with the organizational context of leadership, of comparing and contrasting historical 20th century leadership with 21st century leadership. The context for global leadership is placed amidst a comparison of the change in society 2010 from a century ago in 1910. None of the developments today were foreseen by leaders of nations and businesses a century ago. There has been a radical transformation in the geopolitical and economic systems of the world with a movement from imperialism to an unraveling of the empires of the 19th century toward the growth of democracies as a predominant form of government. Population growth has climbed dramatically. Science and technology today, influencing our speed of communication, information exchange, and global output of goods and services, outruns the imagination of those from a century ago.

Li (2012) draws on philosophy to compare differences between Asian versus Western learners and draws implications for virtuous leadership as well. The Asian learner is internal with a worldview emphasis on "to be" but is external in his or her learning outcomes to be altruistic. This contrasts with the Western learner who is external with a worldview emphasis on "to do" but is internal in his or her learning outcome to gain knowledge.

Failure of Leadership

Penn State University's firing of its President, Graham B. Spanier, and head football Coach, Joe Paterno, was a historic moment in 2011. It was a sanction against the failure of leaders to act and to uphold their ethical responsibility to protect those in their charge. What was being challenged was that leaders cannot allow the politics of athletics and the power of money to win over their judgment and ethical responsibility to act. In this public and profound action, college athletics and higher education will never be the same. The message was that cultures of silence that enable sexual abuse in the interest of the sport and the high money stakes will not be tolerated. Expectations of leadership will be held to a higher standard.

Former assistant coach of Penn State University, Jerry Sandusky, was charged with sexually assaulting eight boys before and after his retirement in 1999. Even after reports alleging sexual abuse, Sandusky was allowed continued access to young boys. University officials from the coach to the president were held responsible by its board of trustees, a first given that President Spanier and Coach Paterno were not the perpetrators. In holding leadership to a higher standard, the burden of responsibility did not stop with Coach Paterno reporting the alleged sexual abuse; he needed to ensure that action was taken. It elevates the ethical responsibility of our leaders to act and holds them to a higher standard of reporting.

From this incident, we must question how the values of a masculinized context of athletics and college football could have allowed this sexual abuse to go on for 20 years. No longer is it a man's world and privilege to engage in such behavior while other men looked the other way and blamed the victim. The Penn State scandal signals and symbolizes a sea change in our society in which leaders have the burden of responsibility to act, protect, and stop it.

Fairness: Procedurally Fair

De Cremer and van Knippenberg (2002) bring in the dimension of procedurally fair leaders who do not need to be charismatic to engender cooperation and vice versa. Instead of leadership based on the personality of the leader to influence and motivate followers as in transformational leadership styles, humane and ethical leadership is based on principles of fairness, integrity, and ethics. This concept of fairness and distributive justice has been found to weigh in judgments of effective leadership. More importantly, these judgments of fairness are influenced by the social identities of the leaders.

Humane Leadership

Humane leadership is growing in importance within the leadership literature. Described as one of the leadership dimensions in the GLOBE studies, endorsement of humane leadership was also found to be important among diverse leaders of color (Chin, 2013). Similarly, it has characterized the leadership styles of many Eastern leaders, including the Dalai Lama and Mahatma Gandhi as described in Chapter 4. Ayman (2004) similarly described it as a dimension of benevolent paternalism as described in Chapter 2. An important underlying principle is that of compassion found in many Eastern cultures. It leads to a social justice orientation or sense of social responsibility as a goal and outcome of leadership.

Confucian Leadership

Lao Tzu, a Chinese philosopher, in his "Moral Principles" quoted in Tsui, Wang, Xin, Zhang, and Fu (2004, p. 18) says: "As for the leader at the very top, it is best if people barely know he exists. Because he says very little, his words have more value. And when the work is done, the people are pleased because they think they did it all by themselves." This opening quotation from the writings of the Chinese philosopher Lao Tzu speaks to a unique cultural specific leadership style steeped in Chinese traditions and values. Although there are a variety of leadership styles in present-day China, many of the leadership styles are grounded in Confucian and Daoist principles and teachings, Communist tenets, and selected influences from the Western world of business management and organization styles (Liu, 2013; Tsui et al., 2004). Humanistic orientations are at the core of Confucianism beliefs, where an emphasis is placed on a family's welfare, the belief that all people are teachable, and that the improvement of one's life can be attained through a group orientation; the achievement and maintenance of social harmony through relationships is the utmost goal of Confucianism. In effect, a leader first devotes time and thought to self-reflection in an effort to achieve communal balance in relationships with others and at the same time minimize influences on the actions of others.

Therefore, according to Jeong-Kyu Lee (2001) "Confucian leadership is based on two main themes: personal order and sociopolitical order. Both themes emphasize reciprocal interpersonal relationships between superiors and subordinates—that is, hierarchically authoritative leadership, as well as reciprocal humanitarian leadership" (p. 9). In some ways, the person who follows these principles and guidelines might be referred to as an "invisible leader," who accordingly shares such characteristics as modesty, respect, generosity, avoidance of the limelight, and acknowledgement of the value and work of others (Tsui et al., 2004). In many ways, the profile of the invisible leader is one who closely follows Confucianism beliefs and thus could be described as a one who advocates benevolent paternalism in their approach to leadership. It differs from the prophetic-caliphal leader described in Chapter 3 although there is shared emphasis on hierarchy.

Li (2013) draws on the concept of virtue ethics by Chinese philosopher Zhang Zai as one of great importance to leadership as the essence of inner character. It involves the vital energy behind emotions, which can become creative; the goal is self-completion (*chengxing* 成性) through development and cultivation (*gongfu* 功夫). Zhang Zai advocates the change of the quality of the vital energy as a way (*dao* 道) toward becoming a scholar (*xuezhe* 学者), the nobleman (*daren* 大人), or a sage (*shengren* 圣人). These three levels of development are based on the fundamental Confucian conception of the "Inner Sageliness and Outer Kingliness" (*neishengwaiwang* 内圣外王), the ancient model of leadership. It is central to the applications of leadership benevolent paternalism and differs from the more pejorative connotations of paternalism as developed in the West.

Benevolent Paternalism

A benevolent paternalistic leadership style has its origins in the way early tribes and civilizations organized themselves and how order, direction, function, and structure were maintained and delegated among community and tribal members. Basically such styles could be arranged according to paternalistic and maternalistic lines of authority; there are and were societies that were egalitarian, where leadership responsibilities were shared among the tribal and community members. Basically a paternalistic form of leadership is one where a father or a male elder governs the community or organization often without given them many responsibilities, duties, and civil or individual rights; it often has negative implications in as much as the father-leader treats the community or organizational members as his children. Maternalistic leadership is one where the woman orders and guides the direction of the community and organization with an emphasis on benevolence expressed through nurturance with a moral emphasis on the care and welfare of children and women.

A paternalistic leadership style is one that is usually employed by dominant males where their style and power are used to control and protect staff; in turn, employees or organizational members are expected to be compliant, devoted, and obedient. In some ways, the dominance of the male discourages creative thinking and innovative ideas. Based on the observations and conclusions of Farh and Cheng (2000), certain components of paternalism stem from a Confucian ideology that forms the cultural expectations that leaders should act as parents with strong authority and display fatherly benevolence and morality to their followers in order to maintain control over employees and company wealth. According to Westwood and Chan (1992) paternalism is a father-like leadership style in which strong authority is combined with concern and with a great care not to cause or create inconveniences. Moreover, Westwood (1997) suggests that paternalistic leadership is effective in many Chinese business contexts in part because the style follows the principles of compliance and harmony. Pellegrini and Scandura (2008), through a careful and thoughtful review of the literature on paternalistic leadership, conclude that, "The growing interest in paternalistic leadership research has led to a recent proliferation of diverse definitions and perspectives, as well as a limited number of empirical studies. [In this nascent stage], the diversity of perspectives has resulted in conceptual ambiguities, as well as contradictory empirical findings" (p. 566).

Pellegrini and Scandura (2008) are correct in their conclusions and observations; definitions of the leadership style vary accordingly to include culturally different variations influenced by a country's specific lifeways and thoughtways. For example, in a comprehensive 10-country study on paternalistic leadership preferences, Aycan et al. (2000) found that samples of American employees reported higher paternalistic values compared with employees from Canada, Germany, and Israel and maintenance of positive relationships consisting of benevolence/morality associated with positive relationships. Similarly, in a recent empirical study, Pellegrini, Scandura, and Jayaraman (2007) found that paternalistic leadership approaches significantly and positively influenced employees' organizational commitment in a North American context. In another cultural comparative study on paternal leadership style preferences, Pellegrini, Scandura, and Jayaraman (2010) compared employee attitudes toward paternalistic leadership and its correlates. They found that paternalism had a significant positive effect on job satisfaction in India; the relationship was not significant among employee samples in the United States. Additionally, the researchers found that paternalistic leadership was positively related to leader-member exchange and organizational commitment. The authors conclude that, "The current results suggest that, for too long, negative perceptions of paternalism may have limited theory and research, which may have limited the potential that paternalistic leadership may hold to better understand the full spectrum of leadership" (p. 414).

In an effort to clearly illustrate and describe distinct leadership styles Aycan (2006) constructed a matrix describing four distinct styles from the perspective of their specific behaviors and basic fundamentals. The styles she identified included benevolent paternalism, exploitative paternalism, authoritarian approach, and an authoritative approach. In essence, benevolent paternalism is a leadership style where the emphasis is placed on kindness, compassion, empathy, and openhandedness. As suggested by Farh and Cheng (2000), forms of paternalism have their origins in Confucian ideology, which emphasizes positive social relations; what can emerge is "benevolent leader with loyal minister" and "kind father with filial son." These principles form the cultural expectations that a leader should be benevolent to his or her followers. Combined with definitions of paternalism, the leader blends elements of benevolence so that employees or organizational members are expected to be compliant and devoted and yet are treated with respect, kindness, gratitude, and generosity. In classic form of paternalistic leadership styles, power and influence are individual-centric and not necessarily oriented to collective well-being and tangibles of the group. In effect, authority flows downward. In collectivistic oriented societies, benevolent paternal styles can be more effective and accommodating of their lifeways and thoughtways. Relationships do matter under such circumstances. Control-centrism, for example, runs counter to group centeredness of collectivist organizations. In those settings, the benevolent leader's goal is consensus achieved through a process-oriented mode of communication and decision making. Achievement of the laudable goal tends to generate employee or member loyalty. Constituents learn that their benevolent leaders are not interested in competing with them for resources and resource allocations. They note that their leader does not promote a personal agenda stemming from intrinsically motivated values and status mobility.

Constituents, employees, and group members also observe and recognize that benevolent paternalistic leaders respect humility, lack vanity, and often defer to the group's welfare. Most important, they do not perceive the characteristics and expression of benevolent style as weaknesses or lack of influence in generating positive outcomes; and in this context, such leaders are viewed as strong and quietly persuasive. They are not perceived as megalomaniacs consumed with a high need for achievement, power and influence, and domination of others. In addition to their respect and expression of humility, they tend to be modest, unassuming, selfless, feign engaging in self-pride, and avoid passions for greatness, control, and power and micropolitics. Moreover, they tend to show their careful thought by being accommodating, patient, and helpful. Most important, they operate on principles of "do no harm" and do not inconvenience others; socio-psychological toxic environments are unacceptable for them and thus are avoided at great costs.

In a comprehensive study of different paternalistic leadership styles utilized by Chinese leaders and managers in small and medium-sized enterprises, Liu (2013) explored four types of organizational culture identified by a competing values framework. The research was based on 12 formulated hypotheses concerning the impact of group, developmental, hierarchical, and rational culture on benevolent, moral, and authoritarian leadership. Liu collected data from 515 cases in 23 Chinese enterprises. Specifically, Liu conducted the study to explore the relationships between hierarchical culture, benevolent leadership, moral leadership, and authoritarian leadership. Also relationships were explored with group culture, developmental culture, and rational culture. Findings show that four culture types are positively associated with benevolent leadership. In addition, hierarchical culture positively impacted moral leadership, but it was not significantly related to authoritarian leadership. The impact of group, developmental, and rational culture on moral and authoritarian leadership is not statistically significant in Chinese managers of the sampled enterprises.

The prominent cross-cultural psychologist Michael Bond recently stated that, "We need multicultural studies testing models linking constructs to any outcome of interest, like well-being. How well that model performs should be tested on a culture-by-culture basis, the power of its constructs assessed and its power to predict an individual's well-being calculated. That culture-specific formula constitutes the indigenous signature endorsing the culture general model" (Bond, 2013, p. 161). The literature on the paternalistic and benevolent paternalistic leadership is extensive; however, there are few empirical studies attesting to its influence on institutional and organizations structures, and thus, more cultural sensitive research should be conducted on the construct to better understand its effectiveness. On this note, Pellegrini et al. (2010) conclude that, "When paternalistic leadership is studied jointly with other leadership constructs, it may provide a more complete picture of leadership dynamics both in the domestic U.S. context as well as in other cultures" (p. 414).

Authentic Leadership

A great deal of theoretical discussion exists in the literature regarding authenticity in leadership. Authentic leaders are individuals in positions of responsibility who are trustworthy, genuine, believable, and reliable. These leaders "conform to fact" or are speakers of the truth. Contemporary theories of leadership have begun to consider leader identity by endorsing the importance of authenticity in today's leaders—"in knowing who they are, what they believe and value" (Avolio, Gardner, Walumbwa, Luthans, & May, 2004, p. 803). Avolio (2007) defined authentic leadership development as considering the dynamic interplay between leaders and followers, taking into account the prior, current, and emerging contexts in explaining what actually improves or develops leadership. Avolio et al. (2004) defined authentic leaders as "those individuals who are deeply aware of how they think and behave and are perceived by others as being aware of their own and others' values/moral perspective, knowledge, and strengths, aware of the context in which they operate, and who are confident, hopeful, optimistic, resilient, and high on moral character" (p. 4). An example of authentic leadership is leaders demonstrating passion for the vocation of an organization by describing the vocation and encouraging employees to mutually live the vocation. Employees can then understand the passion and purpose and consequently model the behaviors encouraged by the leader. By engaging employees psychologically, authentic leaders can create a healthy work environment. This is because engaged employees bring positive attitudes, emotions, and behaviors to the workplace, thereby creating a sustainable healthy workplace characterized by positive financial, people, and quality outcomes (Shirey, 2006).

Authentic leadership theory suggests attributions of self-awareness and understanding, empathy for others, building trust, and an affinity for building affiliation and supporting the community all lead to authenticity in leadership. Authentic leaders possess commitment to self-core enhancement by being in tune with and true to self (Bhindi & Duignan, 1997; Starratt, 2007). However, authenticity concerns more than self-reflection and self-focus (Cohen, Taylor, Zonta, & Vestal, 2007; Ferrara, 1998). Therefore, developing authentic capacity in others is also an attribution of authentic leaders (Goffee & Jones, 2000; Helland & Winston, 2005; Jensen & Luthans, 2006; Walumbwa, Avolio, Gardner, Wernsing, & Peterson, 2008) by removing privilege barriers (Goffee & Jones, 2000) and demonstrating interest in the talents of followers (Starratt, 2007; Woods, 2007). Authentic leaders reach beyond self and followers by recognizing community and culture customs, histories, and traditions; thus, authentic leaders tend to create responsive social structures leading to self, follower, community, and organizational success (Boerner, Eisenbeiss, & Griesser, 2007; Goffee & Jones, 2000; Helland & Winston, 2005; Spreier, Fontaine, & Malloy, 2006).

Authenticity and Bicultural Leaders

With emerging calls for new leadership models, authentic leadership is growing in importance with an emphasis on leaders to be transparent, to be real in who they are, and to act with integrity. In examining the cross-cultural application of this theory to Chinese leadership, Whitehead and Brown (2011) identified its complexity and the need to expand its Western-based definition. We might similarly examine its applicability to diverse racial and ethnic groups within the United States. While it appears reasonable to have leaders be trustworthy and authentic, the model fails to consider the realities of diverse leaders whose multiple and intersecting dimensions of identity include race and ethnicities that are not part of the dominant social groups.

Within such bicultural environments, the salience of different racial and ethnic identities will depend on the contexts in which leaders find themselves. The tendency to code switch has been noted among bicultural individuals as they navigate between family, ethnic communities, and the mainstream environments. Might then a leader be deemed lacking in authenticity as these identities shift as he or she navigates across different social contexts—for example, a Latina leader speaking to a largely Latino/a audience versus a primarily White audience? A further challenge is for leaders of color whose social identities are less privileged than that of their leadership positions. This is a double-edged sword (Thomas & Ravlin, 1995; Thomas, 2008); while leaders can be more effective in conforming to the culture of their followers, they might also be questioned as to their authenticity (e.g., forgetting where they came from, trying to be White).

Feminist Leadership

Female leaders might well face this same challenge about their authenticity as they negotiate different gender compositions in the audiences that they face. We see this in the frequent dilemma faced by female leaders to be feminine as defined by their gender or leaderful as defined by their position; hence, we need to realize that achieving authenticity can be a more difficult matter for female than male leaders. According to Hayes (2012), "traditionally, men have been seen as better leaders because they have more authority, focus, and drive, and because they more readily take tough but necessary decisions such as downsizing, or firing people." Alice Eagly suggests that this stereotype is now outdated (Eagly & Carli, 2007). Modern transformational leadership takes a different approach; leaders today are required to be more teacher-like or coach-like: motivating rather than threatening; inspiring embodiments of the corporate values rather than autocratic enforcers. These are qualities that match women's leadership style very well. As women tend to be collaborative and take colleagues' opinions into consideration, they tend to seek what's best in the broader context rather than competing for the "top dog" position. They tend to be more democratic, more universalistic. . . . "This is not to say that men don't have these qualities too, [according to Professor Eagly]. . . . And from a broader perspective, women advocate more supportive societal contributions to make it possible for them to enjoy fulfilling careers—more childcare facilities, more parental leave for fathers and mothers, fewer hours—without having to miss out on opportunities for higher executive roles" (Hayes, 2012).

Global and Multiethnic Focus

In expanding perspectives of leadership with a global, multiethnic, and multinational focus, we need to recognize that it is quite a different experience for Black leaders in the United States than in a country in Africa or in a multiracial corporation. Moreover, the leadership styles of diverse racial and ethnic groups in the United States may differ depending on the context in which they are exercised. The invisible leadership, discussed earlier among Asian Americans, can also be found among today's Native American Indian leaders in their origins from that of traditional American Indians. An example follows.

Authenticity and Chinese Leadership

While cultural differences exist between Eastern and Western notions of leadership, Whitehead and Brown (2011) finds evidence supporting the theory of authentic leadership as a part of the Chinese view of leadership. Chinese leadership patterns align with a collectivist culture (Wong, 2001), which respects cooperation, affiliation, and subordination (Ping Ping, Hau-siu Chow, & Yuli, 2001). In fact, Chinese people rank high in willingness to subordinate personal objectives to a group purpose (Rawwas, 2003). The importance of understanding a Chinese-authenticity connection can enhance cross-cultural communication and avoid the premature return of expatriate managers from U.S. firms because of their inability to discern the subtleties of foreign business environments (Katz & Seifer, 1996; Rawwas, 2003).

Chinese leadership is paradoxical, from a Western vantage point, in that both authoritarian and benevolent attributes are observable in the same leader. This may be cause for misunderstanding and oversimplified labeling when Westerners only focus on the condition of subordinating to the collective greater good and believe that Chinese leaders are only autocratic. Ping Ping et al. (2001) provided strong evidence for a people-oriented leadership style correlating with high worker satisfaction. The best Chinese leaders seem to be high in both people and task orientation; authoritarian and participatory methods coexist, representing the complexity of the collectivist environment. The Chinese collectivist model represents an interesting balance in both authoritarian rule and participatory leadership, thus satisfying the needs of both people and organizations and resulting in both paradox and harmony.

Wenquan, Chia, and Liluo (2000) developed and validated a leadership indicator scale specifically for Chinese that was compared against Western measures; the study found certain elements of Chinese leadership and American leadership to enjoy common ground. Both cultures seek leaders who are responsive, receptive, embracing, and participatory but who also know how to take charge and accomplish difficult group-oriented tasks. Chinese value faithfulness, morality, loyalty, and service, while paying strong attention to effort and education (Wong, 2001). Such traits align with authentic theories, which consider the social order to be at least as important as the individual (Cohen et al., 2007). On the other hand, American authenticity may be demonstrated by the degree to which individual voice and true-to-self constructs are manifest. While both capture the essence of authenticity, if the definition of authenticity has a scope that includes both a social orientation as well as a true-to-self orientation.

The Chinese are able to embrace multiple philosophies without a sense of conflict, which is an uncomfortable paradox for Westerners. Wong (2001) stated Chinese may be completely comfortable with Catholicism, Protestantism, Buddhism, and so forth, all at the same time. They see all truth pointing toward the inward growth of the individual. Seeming conflicts are reconcilable because Confucian and Buddhist influences in the Chinese culture teach truth is often irrational, paradoxical, and illogical.

Leadership Styles of Traditional Native American Indians

The typical leadership styles of traditional American Indians provide a good illustration of the differences that existed between conventional forms of leadership style that prevailed in the Western world. Although we may never know how traditional Indian leadership practices and styles existed pre-European contact, there is enough information available that enables us to list the essential and important elements (American Indian Research and Policy Institute, 2005; Warner & Grint, 2006). Linda Sue Warner and Keith Grint (2006) point out that, "indigenous leadership styles encompassed a continuum of styles that defy any simple reduction" (p. 232).

The core value for the leadership style is a strong belief in connectedness; that is, everything is connected to everything else. A firm and unquestioned commitment to spirituality, the sacredness of all life, and respect for all that exists and existed sets in and around the leader. American Indians did not view spirit and spirituality as objects to be set apart from life; they believed that spirituality and the sacred are inclusive of all that is and can be. Those who demonstrated strong leadership skills and talents usually were thought to have a stronger sense and respect for the spirit and the sacred than others.

The selection or appointment of an Indian leader was determined by the needs of the tribe and community. Selection was not necessarily based on popularity but rather on the characteristics and traits of the individual and the perception that, whatever the problems or needs were, the person could assist in bringing about a solution. In essence, the ability to respond to a need or crisis determined the choice; hence, the decision was situation or context based. If the crisis or need was resolved, then another leader was chosen to meet yet another circumstance of importance. One's term was not marked by a definitive period of time but rather on the degree to which a need was met or an obligation fulfilled.

With a few exceptions, Indian leaders of the past did not seek the distinction or appointment; they did not campaign or pursue community support. In some instances, leaders emerged because of their hereditary lineage; however, the leader may have been reluctant to assume full and complete responsibility. Leaders typically embraced strong positive values such as generosity, respectfulness, kindness, integrity, and trustworthiness. When some leadership responsibility and direction was requested of them, they acknowledged their responsibility; they tacitly knew that they had to set a strong positive example for others to observe and follow. Firmly developed positive values were essential in honoring the connectedness and relationships in the community or village.

Traditional leaders made it a point to engage the community and village in all the discussions, especially the ones that needed serious attention. Many leaders would spend their time visiting with families and elders often spending a great deal of time with them. In effect, they saw their appointment as "a sphere of influence that must be contextualized" (Warner & Grint, 2006, p. 231); most did not believe their role was a formal, coveted, delegated position. Moreover, they tended to see their role primarily as a facilitator and promoter of community values, traditions, beliefs, and interests (Badwound & Tierney, 1988).

Gathering information from community and village members was a key element in reaching decisions and resolving conflicts and issues, especially those that needed serious attention. Reaching those decisions, though, was not always guided by fixed time constraints. Traditional leaders generally considered everyone's opinions that often were gathered in collective settings. Information gathering tended to be group centered rather than individual centered. Decisions were not reached until all the opinions and voices were heard. Traditional leaders placed a high premium on respect and that carried over in the discussion and deliberation process. The leader's goal was to achieve consensus; achieving that laudable goal was tedious and time consuming. The process represented the leader's deep respect for connectedness. In honoring the connectedness of all things, the leader recognized that a decision could never be ordered or imposed on the community and village. Most often, the decision and outcome was respected by the elders and community and village members in large part because all voices were thought to be heard, valued, and considered.

There are some data to substantiate the various points and observations described in the previous paragraphs. In an interview survey with 21 tribal members from the Winnebago Reservation in Nebraska, Jeff Hart (2006) found the following to be the key words for describing a tribal leader with effective leadership characteristics: education, role, vision, respect, teach, spiritual, protect, caring, serving, battle, follower, choose, true leadership, responsibility, traditional, trust, listen, earned, and veteran. The respondents also told him that "wise councils, spiritual leaders, and elders were essential to the organization of a tribe," that "clanship and families were found to be high on the list as descriptors for traditional leadership," and "being a role model and having vision ranked high" (p. 5). On this point, Linda Sue Warner and Keith Grint (2006) maintain that "role models rely on actions more than the spoken word or the written word, though both the latter are used in support of and to perpetuate behavior" (p. 238.) The respondents also indicated that the following characteristics and attributes were significant: knowledge and the process of knowing; willingness to share; patience; willingness to spend time with the community to share information; hopefulness; and a strong appreciation and respect for "shared leadership."

In a careful and thoughtful review of literature on the leadership characteristics and practices, Tracy Becker (1997) compared the typical Native American Indian leaders with the typical leadership style in U.S. governance (see Table 1, p. 8). She concluded that, for Native American Indians in general, leaders were chosen for their knowledge, experience, and contributions and remained in the position for as long as the tribe needed them; they had no power over others, respected the strong value of tribal customs and traditions, and thus strived to uphold and maintain them. Consensus guided decision-making processes; the maintenance of relationships was essential in conflict resolution matters. Spirituality was at the center of all activities and matters of importance and significance to the tribe. She contrasted these descriptors with the typical form of leadership styles in the U.S. government. Following the order of points made previously, the list includes the following: "leadership is a position; leaders seek leadership positions either through elections or employment; they can create laws and have them enforced. The rights of the individual are salient in most relationships; the majority of the group, community, or populace decides an outcome; judicial matters are governed by restitutions; and reason not 'spirituality' influences most decisions and deliberations" (Becker, 1997, p. 8).

Challenges and Dilemmas

Leading Change

As Pollyanna Pixton, President of Evolutionary Systems, Partner at Accelinnova (n.d.) claims, "It's no longer enough to respond to change—organizations must lead change or be left behind. How responsive is your organization to the new ideas that will improve operations as well as develop breakthrough product lines and services? And how do you foster innovation and creativity in your company to increase productivity and profits"?

The answers your organization needs in order to succeed are very likely to be found within the people who work with you. Those on the front lines know best how to lead change with subtle product improvements, bold new directions, and improved services that strengthen your position in the marketplace."

Value Judgments

The unfortunate emphasis is how these leadership styles quickly devolve into judgments of good versus bad, strong versus weak, and male versus female, resulting in images of weak and ineffectual feminized leadership. From a multicultural and diversity perspective, this has great implications for marginalizing leadership styles that differ from the dominant prototypic leaders. Eagly and Chin (2010) notes, for example, that collaborative leadership styles may be more syntonic with women but may not be accepted in masculinized contexts.

Summary

Leadership style is a focus on "what leaders do" compared with leader identity, which is a focus on "who leaders are." Different leadership styles have become more salient and favored in response to changing environmental trends and social forces, such as WWII and the rise of the digital age. These styles often are laden with value judgments and unresponsive to differences because of dimensions of diversity. In examining leadership styles, we need to recognize the influences of gender on task versus relationship leadership styles, the influences of cultural values and orientation on collaborative leadership styles, or of the favoring of transformational leadership styles during times of change. Ethical and humane leadership styles arise both in response to cultural and philosophical orientations and worldviews favoring fairness and trust. Ethical models of leadership style also resulted from the rising concern over failures of leadership and leader integrity in such events as the Enron scandal during the 20th century. Finally, an emphasis on authentic leadership styles makes way for a attention to difference rather than narrow definitions of leadership style. Expanding perspectives of leadership within a global and diverse society also paves the way for new paradigms of leadership style responsive to dimensions of diversity. Confucian leadership styles and benevolent paternalism in leadership draw on cultural values and orientations of Eastern cultures, which favor harmony and respect for authority in relationships. Feminist leadership styles draw on principles of inclusion and collaboration central to feminist theory. Invisible leadership draws on the strong belief in interconnectedness apparent in Asian and American Indian cultures. Attending to these value dimensions of leadership can help leaders lead change and avoid value judgment, which marginalizes leadership styles that differ from the dominant leader prototype. It is a dynamic process between leader, member, and context; its measurement can be multidimensional and bidirectional, challenging us to broaden our perspective of effective leadership styles.

Discussion Questions: Multidimensional Leadership Styles Amidst Diverse and Global Contexts

1. Pick one of the leadership dilemmas from Table 3.2. Identify additional issues posed by the dilemma. Describe some challenges a leader might face in attempting to address them.

2. What do diverse leaders bring? Discuss the benefits and costs of lived experiences associated with sexism and racism faced by women and racial/ethnic minority leaders. How might this influence their exercise of leadership?

3. Is there a feminine advantage? Do women leaders have innate abilities to connect that give them an advantage in transformational and collaborative leadership styles?

4. Are diverse leaders, who have had to adjust to a bicultural environment and/or racism, more likely to develop greater cognitive flexibility, giving them an advantage in exercising innovative leadership?

5. Pick one of the leadership styles discussed in the chapter. How might one or more dimensions of worldviews influence how a leader might exercise his or her leadership using that style?

6. What are the similarities and differences between a benevolent paternalistic leader and a benevolent maternalistic leader? Might this change if benevolence was replaced with a tightfistedness style of leadership?

7. Discuss if and how charismatic leadership might be different across different cultures and gender. Give some examples as to how this might be manifested.

8. Discuss ethical leadership and the context of leadership. Would any of the scandals or failures of leadership have been different in a different context and social zeitgeist? Is ethical leadership related to social context or to one's core philosophy of ethical behavior?

6

Organizational Contexts

With Contributions by Beauregard Stubblefield-Tave

Notable Quotes: *On Self-Disclosure*

"Do you bring all of you to work?" asked by Richard Lui, MSNBC daytime anchor, to raise consciousness about disclosure of sexual orientation, of illegal immigrant status, and other less visible dimensions of diversity in the workplace. "Do you dress up or play down your cultural mannerisms, intentional or unintentionally at work?"

Vignette on Gender: Masculinized Contexts—"It Is What It Is!"

When asked how gender influences leadership, a male CEO responded: "It is what it is" after describing how he is surrounded by all men in his leadership circle. Another male executive director surrounded by predominantly female managers commented: "I never thought about it." Both reflect the male privilege of how gender becomes invisible, one that most women do not have; their consciousness of gender is unavoidable.

A corporate female leader responded to the same question with: "It is always with me. [Despite my title and position as second in command in a large corporation], when I go in to negotiate, I always have to prove myself first. This is not true of my male colleagues. They never let me forget it."

Diversity leadership is incomplete without consideration of the contexts in which leadership is exercised. As Chapters 4 on Leader Identity and 5 on Leadership Style show, leaders both influence and are, in turn, influenced by contexts or the organizational cultures and societal cultures of which they are a part. This chapter examines organizational contexts by their cultures and to differences across different industry sectors, to organizational structures and compositions, and ends with the measurement of organizational cultures and assessment of organizational fit.

Yukl (2010) dichotomizes theorists who believe that the process of leadership is no different from the social influence processes of groups and therefore views leadership as a collective process shared among the members—shared leadership. This contrasts with the opposing view that all groups have role specialization; the leader is one of these roles, is usually held by one person, and usually has more influence than other roles. Yukl and Mahsud (2010) view leaders as influencing organizational culture; hence, leaders need to be flexible and adaptive in their leadership as the pace of change affecting organizations increases. These changes include increased globalization and international commerce, rapid technological change, changing cultural values, a more diverse workforce, more use of outsourcing, new forms of social networking, increased use of virtual interaction, more visibility of leader actions via the Internet, and concern for outcomes besides profits (e.g., ethical actions, social responsibility, environmental impact, and sustainability)—common to the 21st century. Yet, there is considerable ambiguity about what actually is the nature of flexible leadership. For example, flexibility is required within the same position as conditions change for a leader; flexibility is also required when moving from one type of leadership position to another. An indicator of flexibility is whether a leader's behavior can vary in ways appropriate for different tasks and subordinates and across different contexts and organizations. Leadership becomes a matter not of accepting things as they are but of changing organizational cultures to become what they ought to be; it is a matter of examining contexts in which leadership is embedded. While contexts generally were viewed to mean organizational contexts, the inclusion of societal contexts incorporates the lived experiences of leaders and the social zeitgeist in which leadership and organizations are embedded. This will be discussed further in Chapter 7.

Schein (2004, p. vii) argues that "culture and leadership are two sides of the same coin." He focused on how leaders create culture and how culture defines and creates leaders. At Digital Equipment Corporation, he "discovered" that an assumption shared by senior managers was that you cannot determine whether something was true or valid unless the idea or proposal was subject to intensive debate. At Cieba-Geigy, the shared assumption was that each manager's job was his or her private "turf" not to be infringed upon. At Amoco, the strong assumption was that "'good work should speak for itself' and that engineers should not have to go out and sell themselves." At Alpha Power, work units had strong norms and values of self-protection that often overrode requirements "imposed" on the company from the outside. Dealing with each of these different cultures effectively meant taking a cultural perspective—learning to see the world through cultural lenses.

According to Schein, any group with a stable membership and history of shared learning will have developed a culture. Leaders must first create cultures when they form groups and organizations. Once these organizational cultures exist, they determine the criteria for leadership and who will become a leader. A leader is successful when he or she can create an organizational culture responsive to the social contexts expected by its followers. Schein speaks to the assumptions held by the group that influence how the organizational culture will function. While Schein recognizes that subgroup cultures can exist within an organizational culture, these studies have primarily examined organizations created to mirror the power elite of White middle class Anglo values and an inattention to the cultural assumptions brought in by organizational members from the larger social and cultural contexts in which these organizations are situated.

This contrasts with Zweigenhaft and Domhoff's (2006) view of organizational cultures as static and how diverse leaders conform to the values and behaviors of the organizational culture and dominant group values. White, male, middle class, Anglo values are typical of the power elite in U.S. corporations with an inattention to the cultural assumptions brought in by other diverse members. As Chapters 4 and 5 demonstrate, leadership behaviors and member expectations are influenced by culturally implicit assumptions held by both leader and group members and reflect their social identities. Diverse leaders often must negotiate multiple contexts associated with their varying social identities; hence, these social identities may become invisible as they become embedded in an organization according to Zweigenhaft and Domhoff (2006).

How the social identities of leaders and members align with one another and with the organizational context is the rationale for using a diversity leadership paradigm. It means examining the subgroup cultures within an organization and the nature of their interaction in influencing leadership behavior. It is intentionally inclusive in examining how the leader-member-organization exchange influences the exercise of leadership. The point is reinforced in the concept of how leadership is "cocreated." Leaders are autonomous cutting edge individuals and, at another level, are mere actors in a drama co-constructed by the group or society. A leader is a member of a group(s) who receives, contains, and carries out the often unconscious intentions of the group in an ongoing dialogue—that is, the cocreation of leadership (Klein, Rice, & Schermer, 2009).

Organizational Culture

While an organization's mission, vision, and strategic plan often drive the direction of an organization, its underlying values and culture often shape its direction and focus irrespective of the leader. In more mature organizations, these values and culture often transcend the lives of individual leaders and members in the organization and remain stable and consistent over time. They may be reflected in unspoken rules and practices or the company motto or slogan. It becomes the "way of doing things around here." It drives how members interact and work but can also prevent progress and change because "we've always done it that way." There are multiple levels through which to view an organization's culture. One might view it through the cultural orientation values or the external environment (i.e., public policy, social norms), which drive leader and member behaviors. Or one might view it at the level of its operations and practices, which is driven by an organization's vision, mission, and strategic plan. One might view it through the relationships of members, leaders, and consumers to one another. While each organizational culture is unique, it typically reflects the "mainstream culture." Organizations may develop unit cultures within the organization; organizational cultures may also develop within industry sectors and share commonalities among its counterparts.

Organizational Culture: Academic Health Center

Academic health centers serve as an instructive example to illustrate the complex and multileveled dimensions of leadership and organizational culture within an industry sector. An academic health center has been defined as a higher education institution consisting of a medical school, one or more other health professions schools and an affiliated hospital (Wartman, n.d.). Hence, it is an organization with a single mainstream culture and many departmental (unit) cultures. Each departmental unit must respond to the mainstream culture; simultaneously, departmental cultures can vary dramatically from each other. Each unit often sees itself as in charge with its physicians providing care to patients. Most academic health centers have a tripartite mission of education, research, and service; this results in a diverse collection of departmental units often responding differently to varied demands of their constituencies and competitors. One anonymous insider described an academic health center as "a collection of fiefdoms connected by a common ventilation system." Faculty within the system includes physicians of dramatically different specialties (e.g., internal medicine, pediatrics, psychiatry, surgery). Faculty members may teach, conduct research, and/ or deliver patient care. Each operates in the context of his or her discipline and department and in the context of his or her particular function at the moment; that is, classroom, lab, and clinic are all different cultural contexts. They must lead successfully across these diverse cultural contexts. Also unique to the medical culture is that each physician is in charge when it involves the lives of patients—that is, a leader. A surgeon is considered "the captain of the ship" in the operating room; surgeons have been described as "seldom in error, but never in doubt" (Wartman, n.d.).

Changing Organizational Culture Toward Becoming Diverse

Augustus White, MD, PhD, a successful orthopedic surgeon, was the first African American to head a clinical department at Harvard Medical School; his memoir, *Seeing Patients: Unconscious Bias in Health Care*, White (2011, p. 259) describes how he had to learn to navigate the politics of his institutions and profession as well as the clinical needs of his patients amidst racial concerns. He felt, "My strongest ally on the diversity front was Henry Makin," a White physician who recognized that there was only so much political capital. "So he'd try to get me to lay back a bit. I'd be in the middle of making some point loud and clear, and Henry would lean over and whisper in my ear, 'Gus, no. Not now, okay?' Sometimes he wouldn't even say anything; he'd just kick me under the table." In so doing, he helped Dr. White succeed in creating organizational change by bringing more interns and residents of color into the predominantly White Harvard-affiliated hospitals. The collaboration of two experienced leaders with different social identities: an outsider and an insider, one Black and one White, mentor and protégé, with a shared commitment to increasing the diversity of their institutions and their profession helped create lasting change.

Multinational Organizational Cultures

Appropriately gauging the organizational culture was one of the problems for leaders as U.S. companies went global. The initial foray for many multinational corporations failed to take into consideration local cultures in the countries where satellite operations were established. The training of American managers imported to these countries was often superficial as to how "the locals" might behave. They are often considered "expatriates," maintaining a social class and social networks a cut above and isolated from that of "the locals." Culture and leadership was often not viewed as relevant to "good business practice" about which U.S. managers believed they knew and was universal (see Kao, Sinha, & Wilpert, 1999). Although theorists have increasingly incorporated national or ethnic culture into our understanding of leadership (Hofstede, 2001; House, Hanges, Javidan, Dorfman, & Gupta, 2004; Kao, Sinha, & Wilpert, 1999), many studies started from an ethnocentric vantage point of comparing management and the exercise of leadership in "foreign" countries with that of U.S.-based models of leadership (Bess, 1995) rather than starting from an indigenous view of management and leadership (Kao, Sinha, & Wilpert, 1999). As a result (see Chapter 2), multinational companies began to experience the frustration and failure of methods "that have always worked" [in the United States] assuming that social and cultural contexts and social identities had no bearing on management and leadership methods.

Power Distribution

Leader-Member Exchange theory conceptualizes leadership as a process centered on the interactions between leaders and followers (Graen & Uhl-Bien, 1995). In recognizing this relationship, the exercise of leadership must focus on teams, dynamics and processes of teams, and team member diversity (Rodrigues, 2001) to be effective. With influence comes power, an issue that is ambivalently addressed in the leadership literature. Power can also be concentrated in the leader or distributed throughout the organization as in shared power versus centralized command and control models. Many theorists have come to eschew McClelland's (1985) early emphasis on power in the exercise of leadership in command and control models of leadership, especially as the trend moved toward models of shared power.

Shared power is often a common aspiration in higher education institutions presumably in response to values of shared governance and academic freedom (e.g., American Federation of Teachers [AFT], 2013) as opposed to the hierarchical command and control style as found in the military. Community empowerment, often termed as advocacy or community, is a process to engage the community served by sharing power or distributing power to the community (Laverack, 2001). In the United States, it became salient during the 1960s Civil Rights Movement in response to the protest of the severely mentally ill not being served in the public system and who felt their voices were not heard. As one severely mentally ill client and community advocate aptly puts it, she demands that there should be "No [federal and public] services for us, without us" (severely mentally ill community advocate, personal communication, March, 2006).

This view of power in leadership unfortunately dichotomizes management versus members and the haves versus the have-nots. It poses the problem as an adversarial relationship between *we-they*. It does not address the distribution of power within organizations associated with ascriptions based on different social groups and identities. For example, the power and influence of a leader's role may be incongruent with the social identity group from which he or she comes. There may be tension between who holds the power in an organization as defined by its formal roles and what members ascribes to its leader based on social identities and affiliations. Often, informal power held by individuals or groups within an organization can drive or derail an organizational agenda. Social identities held by members of these groups may also serve to differentiate where power is distributed. Marginalized, minority groups may not be given power or view themselves as having power within the organization. What happens when diverse leaders from these marginalized social groups attain power from the leadership roles they attain? Do they change the status quo or do they conform as Zweigenhaft & Domhoff (2006) contend? Do they take vengeance or do they forge reconciliation as Nelson Mandela did in response to his jailors and apartheid fellowmen? Do they bring different perspectives and skills that can bring new potential for creative leadership? This will become increasingly common as more diverse leaders enter the ranks of leadership in mainstream organizations and demand attention.

Organizational Culture Across Industry Sectors

Organizational cultures often differ across industry sectors while they are often similar within an industry. Overarching similiarities within industry sectors often reflect the values and objectives deemed important to achieve the mission within industry sectors. As leaders enter different industry sectors, they usually need to adapt or conform to the organizational culture in order to be effective. These are often expressed in the language or mottoes of an organization. Within the health care sector, the emphasis is to cure illness, promote wellness and healthy lifestyle behaviors, and eliminate health disparities. Within higher education, the emphasis is to create knowledge and to train future citizens to live and work productively in society. Within corporate and business sectors, emphasis is on profit and the bottom line along with the production of goods and services. Within community and nonprofit sectors, emphasis is on community need, social responsibility, and community empowerment. The examples that follow reflect considerations when promoting diverse leaders and diverse work environments across industry sectors. Common values and objectives are inclusivity, valuing of differences, and achieving outcomes that link diversity with its central mission.

Health Care Sector

In the health care industry, health care reform is the current context and culture that is having a major effect not only in changing systems of care but also on the ways in which management and leadership are exercised. Health care spending in 2013 accounted for approximately 17% of the U.S. economy; 30 years earlier, the country was debating whether it could afford to spend 10% of GDP on health care. For years, the rate of increase in health care costs per year was significantly greater than the overall rate of inflation. The Affordable Care Act may shift this paradigm. Signed into law in 2010, the Affordable Care Act has as its goal to give more Americans access to affordable, quality health insurance and to reduce the growth in health care spending in the United States. It expands the affordability, quality, and availability of private and public health insurance through consumer protections, regulations, subsidies, taxes, insurance exchanges, and other reforms.

The Flexner report (Duffy, 2011) examines the history of health care in the United States, which has policy and practice implications for health care reform in the 21st century. Health care for most of the 18th and 19th century was provided by physicians in their patients' homes or in private offices. A new concentration of medical services emerged in medical schools and hospitals during the 20th century where hospitals were largely viewed as "doctors' workshops" managed as nonprofits; many had religious affiliations or were public institutions. Both physicians and hospitals were largely paid on a fee for service basis based on quantity; the more surgeries performed, the greater the payment; the more hospital beds filled, the greater the profit. Health care economists and policy makers identified the organizational mission of providing care as a health care "Iron Triangle, where the three elements of the health care system that are essential are: cost, quality, and access" (Carroll, 2011).

For much of the country's history, the emphasis was on access and volume of services; the health care culture viewed more care as better care. As services expanded dramatically, providers argued that increasing volume and efficiency would increase quality of care. This view changed as critics argued that this merely increased the economic health of organizations seeking healthier bottom lines. From the 1970s forward, as health care costs skyrocketed, managed care health insurance plans emerged and grew as a form of cost containment that included utilization review, prospective payment systems, and capitated care. Managed care plans were generally paid on a per member per month basis, regardless of services rendered. Providers kept the difference between the dollars received and the costs of services provided—infamously known as the "medical loss ratio." Highly rated plans, such as Kaiser Permanente and Harvard Community Health Plan, emphasized prevention, early detection, primary care, and a population-based approach in an effort to control costs and improve patient care quality while increasing the health status of their members and the broader community. Other organizations sought to "manage costs" by erecting barriers to care and selectively recruiting and retaining healthier members. Despite its early success in cost savings, costs continued to skyrocket under managed care shifting the power from providers to managed care organizations. This set the stage for the Affordable Care Act as the new context of health care.

The Affordable Care Act uses three major new approaches intended to shift the health care culture: (1) Coverage for previously uninsured Americans transforms health care from a privilege to a right. (2) Accountable Care Organizations (ACOs) to coordinate care delivery for specified populations, compensated based on the health outcomes of those populations; this is a cultural shift to value-based purchasing rather than volume-based reimbursement. (3) ACOs will then contract with Patient Centered Medical Homes (PCMHs) to deliver and coordinate care across the spectrum of patients' needs; for example, a child's sore throat, a mother's appendicitis, and a grandparent's dementia are all coordinated through a primary care practitioner as a single point of contact. The Affordable Care Act provides an opportunity to further reduce health care disparities through its emphasis on specified populations, value-based purchasing and care coordination—for example, women (see Chin, Yee, & Banks, 2014).

Unequal Treatment: Confronting Racial and Ethnic Disparities in Health Care (Smedley, Stith, & Nelson, 2003, p. 1) exhaustively demonstrated that "racial and ethnic minorities tend to receive a lower quality of health care than nonminorities, even when access related factors, such as patients' insurance status and income are controlled." The federal Agency for Healthcare Research and Quality now issues an annual National Healthcare Disparities Report, which details progress in some areas, holding in others, and retreat in still others. The Affordable Care Act provides an organizational framework in which patients, community residents, physicians, nurses, hospital executives, managed care executives, policy makers, and all stakeholders can develop and execute a shared vision that benefits all.

Stubblefield-Tave (personal communication, November, 2013) argues that successful implementation of the Affordable Care Act will require a shift in health care culture toward the Triple Aim (Institute of Health Care Quality Improvement, www.IHI.org) of (1) improving the patient care experience (including quality and satisfaction), (2) improving the health of populations (including eliminating health disparities), and (3) reducing the per capita cost of health care. To address health disparities and health equity, he argues for a major shift toward community empowerment reflected in the "Power to the Patient" campaign for consumer-driven health care envisaged by the Center for Culturally Fluent Leadership. The approach seeks to integrate the community and patients as constituents of the exchange that needs to take place in the delivery of health care services; its emphasis aligns with the goal of creating a diverse leader-member exchange organizational framework for health care delivery. It attempts to shift the base of power from the provider or managed care organizations to the patient or consumer. It is grounded in community-engaged research (Michener et al., 2012) to promote greater participation and empowerment of consumers in their care in this new context of health care reform. It offers a synergistic approach to the leader-member-organization exchange that needs to occur in order to change organizational cultures. Leadership commitment is essential to its success as leaders must synergistically balance cost, quality, access, and equity.

Corporate Sector

Organizational culture of the corporate and business sector focuses on the bottom line, good business practices, customer service, and productivity. Its focus on accountability and profitability influences the choice of leaders based on their ability to achieve these objectives. Many have questioned the value and role of diversity within the corporate and business sector by asking the question: But is it good for business? Over the past century, the growing diversity in the population and the emphasis on social responsibility in society has urged businesses to consider diversity as part of their business culture. This led to much soul searching with a growth in diversity initiatives. Many businesses emphasized diversity training and having a diversity plan to train its staff to be more culturally competent. Many businesses now have a Chief Diversity Officer. Digital Equipment's Valuing Differences Initiative was one of the early initiatives to engage teams of diverse racial and ethnic minority staff in dialogue and activities toward building a corporate culture that valued inclusion and difference. This was felt important to boost productivity and creativity, enhance the bottom line, and demonstrate its social responsibility (Walker & Henson, 1992).

While the above initiatives focused on organizational climate, other efforts focused on the recruitment of diverse leaders and staff to address composition. Women, Blacks, and Hispanics were often the target of these efforts. We now have metrics demonstrating the diversity of corporations and rankings of some of the best companies to work for in such magazines as

Forbes and *Fortune.* There are books speaking to the success and challenges of such efforts. For example, *Cracking the Corporate Code: The Revealing Success Stories of 32 African American Executives* (Cobbs & Turnock, 2003, p. xi) points out that advances by African Americans in the business sector have been impressive and well-documented. However, they are still few and far between. "Whether in the form of insensitivity, change-averse corporate cultures, socioeconomic factors, or outright racism, African Americans still face very real obstacles along the path to professional success." *Cracking the Corporate Code* delves deeply into the lives and careers of 32 such leaders in the highest echelons of corporate power and influence with interviews that recount career trajectories, motivations, discouragement, support, conflict, and strategies they developed for success. The common threads that emerged were

- Needing to reconcile the ambiguities inherent for Black professionals in corporate culture
- Trusting your own abilities and potential while managing the ever-present issue of race
- Overcoming isolation to establish not only your place in the organization but also a voice that will be heard and respected
- Reading the unwritten rules and developing the "sixth sense" necessary to play the game
- Cultivating and managing the relationships that will be crucial to securing more meaningful and influential positions
- Understanding what true power is, how to compete for and acquire it, and how to translate it into substantial leadership

While not addressing the challenges of other racial/ethnic group leaders, such as Asian Americans and Latino Americans, these themes can be generalized to the challenges faced by leaders coming from marginalized and minority group identities. Not addressed in most of these efforts is the need to go beyond promoting an inclusive and respectful organizational climate and recruitment and retention efforts to address composition of an organization's members. "Providing diversity leadership education is distinct from traditional forms of general diversity training. . . . This requires a fundamental shift in institutional thinking about diversity . . . and the personal and visible commitment of top leaders (Military Leadership Diversity Commission, 2011, p. 10)." It is inherent in the policies, goals, and commitment of leaders and the organization to diversity.

Higher Education Sector

The mission of many institutions of higher education embraces the values of service, scholarship, truth, freedom, justice, community, and democracy (Young, 1997). While academic freedom and shared governance are foundational values within institutions of higher education, they also operate within institutions that are fairly hierarchical. This tension and balance plays out in much of the organizational cultures of higher education institutions. The lines of reporting are often fairly hierarchical while faculty enjoy a fair amount of power in controlling the curriculum—the core of the enterprise. Tenure and promotion systems are also fairly hierarchical, while it presumably upholds the principle and value of peer review. Unlike the corporate sector, issues and policies often take inordinate amounts of time and effort to be vetted. While the organizational cultures of higher education institutions are to create knowledge and to train future citizens to live and work productively in society as the ultimate goal, the processes in place often appear focused on meeting degree requirements, responding to regulatory compliance, and accreditation standards. In institutions where there are unions, the rift between management and faculty often seems large. Ascriptions of leadership emerge out of both formal and informal means.

In these contexts, several overarching themes capture the issue of diversity leadership, which the senior author coined as *The 3 Cs of Diversity: Climate, Composition and Curriculum.* Student admissions, affirmative action, and faculty recruitment reflect composition goals to achieve a diverse student and faculty body. Failure to meet the composition goal is often explained as there being an insufficient pool of qualified candidates. It is followed by the criticism that the organization is lessening its standards to recruit a diverse pool when candidate interests do not align with those of traditional core faculty or students. Curriculum goals include curriculum transformation to reflect the full range of human experience, including the contributions of diverse individuals, a more inclusive history of different cultural groups and countries, and teaching methodology that addresses the diverse needs of different populations. This includes both crosscutting measures to infuse diversity across the curriculum and targeted courses on diversity within the curriculum. Last, climate goals include the campus environment for both student and faculty and the issue of retention once admitted. Research on the "chilly atmosphere" and "hostile environment" for feminist women or racial/ethnic minorities abound as reflections of how many higher education institutions fail to provide a welcoming and nurturing environment for diverse individuals. For the student, isolation and alienation by virtue of being different or not accepted can influence retention. The absence of academic supports and the existence of institutional bias can be confused with student inability. For faculty, similar concerns of isolation and alienation can occur when diverse faculty members stand out because of community and research interests or are pigeonholed by their social identities. This is complicated by tenure and promotion reviews that may carry inadvertent bias against diverse groups based on presumably "objective" standards of peer review and gold standards of empirical research. It is not uncommon to have racial/ethnic minority faculty interested in community-based research that draw on their lived experiences and use qualitative methods, given the paucity of literature in these areas, yet have these interests marginalized as "soft," less relevant, too personal, or unscholarly.

While the 3 Cs of Diversity are overarching, too often, the diversity focus of many higher education institutions remains limited to affirmative action goals or meeting quotas. According to Hurtado (2007), emerging work on the educational benefits of diversity is part of a long-term effort to transform undergraduate education, which will prepare the next generation of citizens for a multicultural society. Scholarship on inequality can play a similar role in helping shape the agenda for change. There are several reasons for advancing research and practice that will link diversity with the central educational and civic mission in higher education. One is practical, emerging from the needs of a society where economic, racial, and religious differences are both prevalent and inevitable. Another is to achieve greater coherence in undergraduate preparation. The Association of American Colleges and Universities (AAC&U) has "taken this charge to advance diversity and equity in higher education and promote the best educational practices for an increasingly diverse population as part of its broader responsibilities for higher education today. AAC&U understands diversity and equity as fundamental goals of higher education and as resources for learning that are valuable for all students, vital to democracy and a democratic workforce, and to the global position and wellbeing of the United States. AAC&U's commitment to make excellence inclusive—to bring the benefits of liberal education to all students—is rooted deeply in commitment to a diverse, informed, and civically active society. It has developed resources in the form of publications, toolkits, and seminars to advance this agenda through all aspects of higher education" (AAC&U, n.d.). Its goals reflect the intricate relationship between diversity and leadership we are to train our students to become the leaders in the future.

Changes in the 21st century have also impacted higher education in the responsibility to train citizens and leaders to live, work, and lead in a global and diverse society. Some of the changes that currently challenge higher education include "fiscal austerity, downsizing, heavy faculty workloads, underprepared students, a growing cohort of nomadic adjunct faculty, a tenure system under fire, [and] a demand for greater accountability and productivity from a disenchanted public" (Barton, 2006, p. 2). In response to changing demographics, the influx of new immigrants, international students, and students who are first in their families to attend college bring different races, cultural identities, and socioeconomic classes to share academic spaces and create hybrid identities and new academic cultures. Policies, institutional practices, teaching methods, methods of assessment, and leadership will all need to change to better serve constituents in these evolving academic communities.

The colleges and universities that will survive the rapid change ahead will be those that are focused on students (Zahorski & Cognard, 1999). Speaking from a feminist perspective, the primary defining trait of successful universities will be "a nurturing institutional culture." Therefore, we need "a more strongly proactive leadership model" (Barton, 2006, p. 9). If we hope to meet the challenges of the future, we need leaders who recognize the importance of student centeredness, social justice, and equity and who will work to transform our academic institutions into more inclusive, holistic, nurturing organizations.

Feminist leaders in academia are student centered, focused on equity, and work to build holistic environments in which all constituents can thrive (Barton, 2006). This includes attention to dimensions of diversity and being watchful for oppression and working to ensure that no one is treated unfairly. In articulating a transformative agenda, feminist leaders in higher education also focus on the big picture or a broad social justice agenda. They work toward change and transformation and to establish a diverse environment, and one that is inclusive. In arguing for the development of nurturing academic communities, Barton (2006) found an emphasis on themes of fairness, justice, equity, and community building in a qualitative study interviewing seven feminist higher education academic administrators.

To create a sense of community, according to hooks (1994), everyone's presence and participation must be valued. Barton (2006) conducted focus group interviews of feminist leaders and found community development to be a very strong theme. Participants shared numerous examples of how they build community in their academic environments. As one participant, Joni, explained, "I very much believe in relational leadership. You have to forge the connections with the people who work for and with you; you have to be willing to do a lot of vision creation that's collaborative, and I think the standard is the leader who has the vision and rallies everyone around the vision. I prefer to think of vision as something that's created by the group, and also that you get what primal leadership calls a tribal kind of feeling where people feel connected and they're motivated, they're excited, and they're enthusiastic, and your own passion is something that becomes everybody's passion." Instead of the ivy towers, which create knowledge for the elite, a new view of higher education institutions is for its leaders to create the environment and community conducive to collaboration, fairness, and knowledge for the masses.

Community Nonprofit Sector

Within the community and nonprofit sector, organization culture revolves around community need, service, social responsibility, and community empowerment. The organizational purpose is often dedicated to a targeted population or dimension of diversity (e.g., ethnic minority, women, LGBT) or to a cause (e.g., mentally ill, diabetes); this is the community served or constituents of the organization. Community empowerment often refers to the will and needs of the community as paramount in defining the organization's mission and activities. While all organizations must respond to the needs of its consumers (i.e., customers, students, patients), consumers are often the reason for the institution's mission in the community or nonprofit sector.

With changing demographics and a growing global society, these trends strike at the core of the mission in many community-based organizations. Does an agency remain true to its original mission, or does it change with the changing trends? If an organization started as an advocacy group for African Americans (e.g., NAACP), does it shift its focus from its population or goals with changing contexts and changing demographics? The difference between not-for profit and community organizations and for profit corporate and business organizations is the emphasis of the latter on the bottom line and returning surplus revenues as profit or dividends to shareholders while nonprofit organizations use their surplus revenues to achieve its goals and purpose.

Government/Military Sector

Historically within the government and military sector, organizational culture tends to show a greater emphasis on hierarchy, the chain of command, and rules and regulations. Government is often viewed as the authority with its laws and regulations reflective of how its power is exercised. State, county, and national legislatures as well as elected government leaders presumably represent the citizenry of its jurisdiction in democratic societies. These structures are often so well set that citizen groups and lobbyists often have formalized means for influencing policy and making change since the use of laws are the base of power which citizens must follow. Government will make use of advisory groups from its citizens to make and revise policy.

Within this organizational culture, men have prevailed as the leaders of countries, states, and other entities; thereby the norms within this sector are that of a masculinized culture. Conformity to masculine norms typically includes winning, risk-taking, emotional control, pursuit of status, violence, dominance, playboy, self-reliance, primacy of work, power over women, and disdain for homosexuals (Dunivin, 1997).

In the military sector, a subset of government, the organizational culture is further based on a hierarchy geared toward combat and war. Therefore, the need for command and control models of leadership is deemed important to survival and winning. Conformity and uniformity are deemed necessary for effective leadership. From a historical perspective, the military was typically male dominated. War and combat is the military's core activity and has been a male endeavor based on masculine concept of strength and power. Military culture valued "Duty, Honor, Country" (Dunivin, 1997). The military emphasis on discipline and hierarchy prioritizes the group over the individual and uses specific rituals and symbols to convey important meanings and transitions in the form of uniforms, protocols, and ceremonies.

In recent years, these policies have been challenged in the United States, as government and the military have been taken to task about policies such as women serving in combat roles and *Don't Ask, Don't Tell* regarding disclosure of sexual orientation in the military. The military's view of conformity and uniformity is a marked contrast to views of diversity. The struggle is now with promoting and advancing diversity while maintaining the core principles central to survival and winning in combat. Allowing women into the military and allowing them into combat further reflects this conformity to stereotypic gender norms. The controversy revolves around prevailing notions of "what is normal," the greater upper body strength of men, and social role of traditional gender roles of hunter-gatherer societies. Those who have challenged this position point to the availability of technology that diminishes reliance on physical strength. On the other hand, women in the military tend to take on noncombat service roles.

While both policies have been recently repealed, underlying biases remain but reflect a changing organizational culture. In its 2011 report to Congress, *From Representation to Inclusion: Diversity Leadership for the 21st Century Military* contends that "Providing diversity leadership education is distinct from traditional forms of general diversity training. . . . This requires a fundamental shift in institutional thinking about diversity . . . and the personal and visible commitment of top leaders" (Military Leadership Diversity Commission, 2011, p. 10). This reflects the new thinking of the U.S. military on diversity.

This military code and culture has led to reactive behaviors at both extremes. As one female military leader pointed out during the Diversity Leadership Summit in 2013, diverse leaders often need to prove that they are as good by being twice as good (Chin et al., in progress). She gave as an example how Japanese American fighters during WWII needed to prove their loyalty as American citizens with their lives by taking on the most risky military missions. At the other extreme, Private Danny Chen, a Chinese American, was victim of bullying and discrimination as a new

Army recruit, which led to taking his own life in 2011 (Rawlings, 2012). Military investigators found that Chen was the target of ethnic slurs and endured physical attacks at the hands of his fellow soldiers and his superiors who singled him out for being Chinese American. As the only Chinese American soldier in the unit, he was singled out, endured taunts, including racial slurs such as "gook," "chink," and "dragon lady," assigned excessive duties and exercises to the point of exhaustion, and forced into a "simulated sitting position" while kicked by other soldiers using their knees, among other abuses. Although the incident was reported to Chen's platoon sergeant and squad leader, it was not reported to superior officers. On the day he died, other soldiers forced him to crawl on gravel for over 330 feet while carrying equipment, as his comrades threw rocks at him. This miscarriage of the military code and culture of "being a man" intersects with race and ethnic discrimination. Sergeant Holcomb, his platoon leader, was sentenced to 30 days in jail. "The events leading to Chen's death reveal a failure in leadership up and down the chain of command in Chen's unit. Both of the large issues—the treatment of minority soldiers and the difficulty in dealing with an unprepared, inexperienced soldier in a combat zone—are challenges that units have faced, the latter especially during the past decade of war. The units that do well in combat are ones whose leaders are engaged, pay attention to how their subordinates are handling immense challenges and set left-and-right limits for what junior leaders can and cannot do" (Rawlings, 2012). Chen's treatment occurred in a platoon and a company filled with other noncommissioned officers and officers above them who should have seen what was going on and stopped it.

Multinational and Global Organizations

Organizational cultures are more difficult to gauge in multinational and global organizations. Multinational organizations inherently involve a mix of cultures with the potential of leaders coming from dominant cultures. Examining organizations on a global level raises different criteria about dominant versus minority groups within the cultures. While race and color is a dominant theme in the United States, religion is more prominent in countries such as Great Britain and Ireland. Not only do we view the impact of U.S.-based practices outside the United States but also we must examine the impact of practices indigenous to countries such as China, Japan, India, and Russia.

Women are now becoming leaders and gaining positions of power in large multinational corporations, foundations, and important political positions. Angela Merkel, Chancellor of Germany, topped the *Forbes* list of the 100 most powerful women in the world, Wu Yi of China in second place as Vice Premier of the People's Republic of China and nicknamed "the Iron

Lady," Ho Ching of Singapore third, and the Indian Sonia Gandhi in sixth position. American women dominated the top ten most powerful women in the world for 2006 with 7 out of 10 places but lost some of their dominance in 2007 with 5 out of 10 women being from the United States.

Organizational Structure

In addition to the differences in organizational culture by industry sector, the authors consider variation in organizational structure and forms of leadership as another factor of diversity leadership. Several dimensions important to diversity leadership are noteworthy. They are dichotomized, categorized for simplicity, recognizing that the dimensions are not mutually exclusive and other ways of categorization are possible. Diversity plays itself out differently along each of these dimensions.

Maturity of an organization: New organizations more often are mission driven and show a willingness to change as they grow; they may be willing to embrace diversity as a new way of being ahead of the curve while more mature organizations may become complacent in doing what they have always done. At times, their willingness to change is more superficial as in seeking a facelift; this may result in conforming to values and practices that serve to maintain the status quo.

Formal versus informal leadership: While those in formal positions of leadership hold the responsibility and authority for the leadership of the organization, leadership, influence, and power can also be informal. This could result from subgroups in the organization who may hold different values or perspectives or thought leaders in an organization whose voice may be influential among members. A union within an organization is one such example; while union representatives and the union head hold no formal position within the leadership ranks of the organization, they are a voice that cannot be ignored. Similarly, organizations with unofficial thought leaders, ones who members consult and respect, can have a strong voice in the direction of the organization.

Voluntary leadership positions: Membership organizations often have leaders who represent the constituents being served. Unlike leaders in formal paid positions (e.g., CEO, ED), these leaders may be unpaid or nominally paid with the CEO serving at the pleasure of the board. They are both responsible for the organization and provide direction and set policy for the CEO and organization. These include professional organizations, where the CEO may or may not be a member of the profession. Division 45, The Society for the Psychological Study of Race, Ethnicity, and Culture, is one such member organization operating as a division of the American

Psychological Association (APA). It is committed to diversity and the advancement of race, ethnicity, and culture amidst the broader focus of its parent group, the APA. In a focus group of its past presidents held in 2013, different views of leadership emerged among the leaders who came from diverse racial/ethnic minority groups. These leaders felt situated in the cultural values and cultural practices that they brought to their leadership.

Hierarchical versus egalitarian organizations: Hierarchical organizations tend to emphasize the chain of command while egalitarian organizations emphasize equality across its ranks. While there is a tendency to dichotomize these dimensions, it is possible for both to exist simultaneously in different parts of an organization. For example, both democratic and communist countries are associated with egalitarianism; while the former are associated with individualism, the latter are associated with collectivism. These types of leadership differ from oligarchies, which are associated with more autocratic styles.

While these structural dimensions will influence how an organization embraces diversity into its mission and goals, another dimension is when diversity is central to the mission and values of an organization versus organizations ignore diversity because they view themselves as "boutique businesses" filling a niche market. Still other organizations may promote diversity only as part of compliance and regulatory requirements. These structural dimensions of an organization dictate what leaders do in the allocation of resources, setting of priorities, and accountability to the goals and outcomes of diversity.

Inclusive Workplace Model

In a global economy, diversity moves to the top of the agenda as ethnically diverse work environments become the norm, but this can also lead to hostile relations and discrimination. Mor Barak (2011) suggests that "problems of managing today's diverse workforce come not from heterogeneity but from the inability of corporate managers to fully comprehend its dynamics, divest themselves of their personal prejudicial attitudes, and creatively unleash the potential embedded in a multicultural workforce" (p. 2). He poses the problem as one of social exclusion where social group divisions exclude group members from positions of power in the workplace and create barriers to job opportunities and promotion. He poses the "inclusive workplace model for managing diversity, which refers to a work organization that accepts and utilizes diversity of its workforce—while also active in the community, in state and federal programs that support immigrants, women, the working poor, and other disadvantaged groups—and that collaborates across cultural and national boundaries" (p. 8). Underlying values include being pluralistic and identifying global mutual interests. Diversity efforts are focused on managing and engaging the company's heterogeneous workforce in ways that give it a competitive advantage. It makes the case for diversity as good business and includes important dimensions of morality, ethics, fairness and human dignity. Mor Barak observes this inclusive workplace model as a "global trend where many countries are now enacting legislation against sexual orientation discrimination" (p. 32); countries are also "offering protections that support fairness and equal rights across dimensions of diversity" (p. 50). He notes that Russia, under Putin's leadership, is an extremely negative outlier. In 2013, legislation, prosecution, and harassment toward members of the LGBT community occurred with appalling frequency and apparent popular support. In the United States, only 7 states have legalized gay marriage; over 20 have defined marriage as between a man and a woman. While progress is occurring, it is uneven. An inclusive workplace model is allied with the view that organizations must be socially responsible in its policies toward all groups.

In-Group Versus Out-Groups

Social identity theory is based on the proposition that people desire to belong to groups that enjoy distinct and positive identities. At the same time, it explains exclusion based on the meanings attached to identity group membership (Tajfel, 1982). Using social comparisons between the in-group and out-group, in-group members seek to maintain or achieve superiority; they will accept and include people they consider to be like them and exclude those they perceive to be unlike them. They tend to give members of their own group the benefit of the doubt in ambiguous situations that they would not give to members of other groups (Tajfel & Turner, 1986). We see this play out in race relations in the United States. For example, Whites and Blacks differed in their attribution of guilt in the O. J. Simpson murder trial, given the ambiguity in the circumstances surrounding the murder of his wife; Blacks were more likely to defend O. J.'s innocence (Neuendorf, Atkin, & Jeffres, 2000).

Similarly, the categorization of President Barack Obama's identity illustrates the meaning attached to his racial identity. As the son of a U.S.-born White mother and African father from Kenya, and raised for some time in Asia with his mother and Indonesian stepfather, Obama's experiences were viewed as a strength by those highlighting his openness to different experiences and as a weakness by his opponents as detached from the common American experience. For the latter, he is viewed as part of the out-group and is less likely to be trusted in ambiguous siutations. Donald Trump, White entrepreneur, led the charge in questioning his loyalty and Americanness, demanding that he produce his birth certificate as proof. Some Blacks also asked, "Is Obama Black enough?" questioning his authenticity as a Black man in America (Coates, 2007). While individuals will seek to change their status through upward social mobility, those who do often become viewed as exceptions; for example, you are not like other Blacks, or you're not like a typical woman (too emotional), constraining them to the stereotypes associated with their social identities. Socially mobile racial minorities are sometimes viewed as "acting White." Among African Americans, the term "oreo" means the person is Black on the outside and White on the inside. Native American Indians use the term "apple;" Asian Americans use the terms "banana" or "twinkie," while South Asian Americans and Pacific Islander Americans use the term "coconut" to connote this false sense of identity. This creates tension because the very nature of intergroup relations is that people are motivated to seek inclusion and to avoid exclusion; hence, they often seek to belong to those groups associated with higher social status and prestige. Such choices have costs as well as benefits.

Intergroup Leadership

Pittinsky (2010) frames these issues of inclusion-exclusion associated with social identities into a two-dimensional model of intergroup leadership. He proposes bringing together not only individuals from diverse identity groups but also the subgroups or communities to which they belong with a goal of maintaining their subgroup identities while creating a superordinate group identity of "we." This will illustrate how power plays out within intergroup communication and relationships based on differences (e.g., race, ethnicity, religion). Dominant-minority status associated with these social identities will emerge as well as the historic struggle of power and conflict globally. In all instances, covert values of equity remain and have been played out in struggles between Shiite versus Muslim, Catholic versus Protestant, and White versus Black. For many, an inattention to diversity results in privileging dominant groups who often do not know they have it and keeping dimensions of diversity invisible to how they influence intergroup interactions. We see this in stereotypic perceptions and expectations that often operate outside consciousness; they are constraining because they are based on social identities irrespective of the unique identities and leadership roles an individual may hold. Often, they are reinforced through media images and public symbols of leadership.

Organizational Composition

While differences across industry sectors and organizational structures may influence how diversity and leadership interact, organizational composition is another dimension that deserves discussion. Three organizational compositions based on dimensions of diversity are discussed below with the challenges that each present.

Dominant Versus Minority Social Identity Status of the Leader

While it is clear the social identity status of the leader does influence the nature of the interaction with the members, there are challenges depending on whether the leader's social identity is from the dominant or minority group. Where the leader and group members are from the same dominant group is the prototypic scenario, how does a leader modify that communication with members of a minority group, or should he or she do that? Is the leader able to recognize and address his or her privilege when interacting and communicating with minority group members? On the other hand, when the leader is from a minority group, how does he or she adapt and conform to the dominant cultural mode of communication and still retain his or her social identity? If he or she is too conforming, will mistrust be aroused among minority group members? For dominant group leaders, it is a process of enlightenment; for the minority group leaders, it is a process of necessity and survival. Perceptions of competency and trust associated with his or her social identity status would not be uncommon.

The more homogeneous the organization is, the more prototypic mismatch there is. A leader can have less power and credibility if the members perceive this difference to be significant and attribute stereotypic perceptions and expectations associated with a social status to leadership as being less effective or less competent. The more heterogeneous an organization, the greater openness it will have to diverse leaders because the prototypic leader for that organization will be more diverse.

There is a transition point for an organization in its identity and culture. This is the direction of 21st century organizations. Richard Suinn and Melba Vasquez were pioneers as the first Asian American and female Latina presidents, respectively, of the APA, a 100-year-old professional organization led predominantly by White men. Adaptability was deciding when to conform and when to assert the status of their role. Melba Vasquez did this intentionally as a minority woman leader and role model for change. She reported how she gave her competitor, a White male, running for the same office, information to mirror her inclusiveness and cooperation as her feminist style and process of leadership (Moritsugu, Arellano, Boelk, Pfeninger, & Chin, in progress).

President Obama's position on race several times during his presidency is another good example. As the first biracial president of the United States, his stance on Professor Henry Louis Gates and the Trayvon Martin cases were noteworthy. His handling of these two instances involving the issue of race received widespread media coverage as well as bringing both personal and political risk as a leader. Trayvon Martin, a 15-year-old Black teen returning home from the grocery store, was followed because he looked suspicious and later shot and killed by a neighborhood watch, George Zimmerman, after a scuffle. In saying that "if I had a son, he could have been Trayvon Martin"(Condon, 2012), he called attention to the double standards held in society and the continued effects of racism. With Professor Henry Louis Gates Jr., a Harvard University professor who was arrested on July 9, 2009, at his home by a local police officer responding to a 9-1-1 caller's report of men breaking and entering the residence, Sergeant James Crowley, a White officer, charged him with disorderly conduct after a heated discussion between the two and after verifying that it was, in fact, Professor Gates's home. The arrest generated a national debate about whether or not it represented an example of racial profiling by police. President Obama called both men and invited them to the White House to discuss the situation over beers—later called the Beer Summit. It led to a peaceful resolution and deescalated a brewing national controversy on race.

Mainstream Versus Minority Group Status of the Organization

On the other hand, this dynamic changes depending on whether the organization is a "mainstream" organization or minority group organization. We presume that most minority organizations will be homogeneous, given that their mission and purpose are intentionally targeted toward a social group or population of interest. A prototypic match would have a minority leader with the social identity status associated with the organization. For such leaders, the challenge is to avoid the constraints of being pigeonholed (i.e., one's competence and interest are limited to that population) while "majority leaders" running minority organizations are viewed as bringing greater expertise and lauded for their ability to work with minority population.

The dominant group leader leading a minority group organization faces a different set of challenges. Although there is a prototypic mismatch here, he or she brings the social capital associated with privilege and power of his or her social identity status. A power dynamic often comes into play with possible perceptions of his or her "being a savior" to the mission or accorded greater recognition for his or her "commitment;" the reverse can also be true of greater mistrust or alienation from group members. For the minority group leader, a different set of challenges arises. While commitment to the organizational mission is less often questioned, a form of aversive racism is not uncommon. Group members may not perceive the leader as competent, or a "bunker mentality" may develop toward the mainstream society.

Heterogeneous Versus Homogeneous Composition of the Organization

A third factor of organizational composition is whether it is heterogeneous or homogeneous. For the latter, what was discussed for dominant versus minority group leaders holds true. In a heterogeneous organization, the mixed composition of social identities among group members is less likely to privilege one over the rest. Here the challenge is to the dominant group leader to recognize and address the diversity in the heterogeneous composition to address decision making, communication, negotiation, goal orientation, and planning. Unlike the homogeneous organization, there is less likely to be unspoken rules about how things should be done. Rather, the differences are likely to influence how the organizational culture develops. Minority group leaders may have a slight advantage based on their social identity status, which generally has required more flexibility and adaptability to difference.

Challenges of Intersection

The above three dimensions characterize the leader, members, and organizations along dimensions of diversity. The intersection of each of these dimensions makes for some important challenges. The greater the heterogeneity within organizations or between leaders and members, the more likely it is that cultural misunderstandings and tension might arise. In the studies where American leaders worked with non-American members, the leader-member aspect of the situation was greatly affected by greater heterogeneity (Ayman, 2002). Leaders who bring social identities different from what an organization is accustomed to will face greater challenges. For example, a minority leader entering an organization accustomed to leaders from the dominant group will face having to demonstrate his or her effectiveness and credibility first while a leader from a dominant group will have that readily accepted. While a minority leader may be more empathic within minority group organizations where these identities are shared, members may be more forgiving of leaders from dominant groups who are different from them. The opposite may be true in majority group or mainstream organizations where members are more forgiving of those more like themselves. These differential responses are influenced by social perceptions that shape attributions of competence and leadership based on social identities.

In addition, the match versus mismatch between leaders and members in their social status identities are also likely to influence the nature of the leader-member exchange. For dominant group leaders may have an advantage given the unconscious biases held by society of minority group status. For minority group leaders, they may have to prove themselves early in the game to gain the respect and credibility. In heterogeneous organizations, acceptance is less a challenge although unconscious bias about race and ethnicity may still exist.

For majority group leaders worldwide, leading a homogeneous organization was more typical during the 20th century given the homogeneity of organizations in most countries. Hence, this was a prototypic match. The privilege afforded these majority group leaders was often invisible and unspoken. Adaptation to differences among members was minimal. As organizations become increasingly heterogeneous in the 21st century, majority group leaders will need to develop greater sensitivity, competence, and fluency in leading diverse and heterogeneous organizations—development of "global leadership."

At the end of the 20th century, the growth of multinational organizations and the dominance of U.S. corporations internationally led to a dominant and privileged status for Western models of leadership. The failures in communication and management led to rethinking and reeducation of managers in preparing leaders for "overseas" assignments as expatriates from the United States. Today, non-U.S. multinational corporations are emerging as well as outsourcing of services from U.S. companies to countries globally has expanded given the advancement of digital technology and communication.

Now we have two scenarios; majority group leaders of U.S. multinational corporations previously had an advantage because their social identities imbued them with the perception as leaders with the knowledge and expertise of the West for the "indigenous workforce" in developing countries. This privilege and advantage was often limited to White leaders from the United States although that is now changing. With the growth of non-U.S. multinational corporations and the rise of non-Western countries in world leadership, new groups of international and global leaders are emerging. Global leaders will now need to conform and adapt to difference and diversity among its members within increasingly heterogeneous corporations. "Mainstream tactics" will no longer be dominated by White or western privilege.

Diverse Leader-Member-Organizational Exchange Organizational Paradigm

Given these considerations of subgroups and power within organization cultures, it would be useful to have tools for mapping dynamics of organizations and identifying organizational goals and outcomes. Returning to our Diverse Leader-Member-Organizational Exchange paradigm (DLMOX) introduced in Chapter 2, Figure 2.1 highlights the goals of diversity leadership while Figure 2.2 highlights the dynamic interaction of components integral to a DLMOX paradigm. It includes the diverse composition of leaders and participants (described in Chapters 4 and 5) and defines the organizational and external environment as both diverse and global (described in Chapters 6 and 7). The contexts of 21st century organizations are to be inclusive of the social identities and lived experiences of diverse leaders and members and the perceptions and social expectations that shape the leader-member exchange, and reflect how organizations implement their mission and adapt their structures to external changes. This paradigm goes from an individual/dyadic perspective to a group/social perspective, from an organizational to societal perspective, and from a situational to systemic leadership perspective.

Mapping Organizational Contexts

Kaschak (2010) describes the mattering map as a tool to map the exchange and relationships among components and could well be used to reflect the "realities" of leaders in context. This model organizes the principles of context in a manner that honors the complexity, multiplicity, and morphing of the energetic field of mattering, drawing from 21st century physics, neuroscience, and constructionist thought rather than from 19th and 20th century's reductionist and fragmenting epistemological models. In assessing context and cognitive schema used in combination with the mattering map, Kaschak (2010) questions the existence of boundaries as an invention of the human senses and neurological system. According to Kaschak (2010, p. 6), "each of us constructs a life, a worldview out of what is possible for us to see and names it reality when it is instead only possibility. This sort of myopia can also be significantly affected by the corrective lenses of diversity and complexity, which depend upon keeping as much as possible in view rather than as little." She suggests mapping organizational contexts based on the social constructions that matter. These include the social identities of leaders and members, which are informed by affiliation needs and lived experiences, and how they interact within organizations to achieve the mission and goals of an organization.

One of the signature aspects of this tool is that it acknowledges that contextual variables are not static and prior models do not provide for this (Kaschak, 2010). It enables people to see that these qualities change even as they interact with different people and in different contexts. In her organizational consultations, she has them all first map the organizational mattering map of relationships within the organization. At least two things flow from that. Each participant can see how well his or her own map fits with that of the organization as a whole, not just specific other individuals. It is really interesting to open the discussion with their matching perceptions of the organization and where and why they do not match.

Measuring Organizational Culture: Tools Versus Instinct

Shah (2013) discusses how to uncover a company's true culture. While all organizations have a culture, Shah looks not to measurement tools but suggests that the true nature of a company's culture is determined not by what is declared but by what members do. He feels that assertions are easy to make; mission statements are easy to create. A quick litmus test on culture is to ask: When folks on the team assert some of our values, are they putting mental "air quotes" around the value? For example, how do they answer: "At our company . . ." The true nature of a company, and its culture, is determined by how one *instinctively reacts*. If your culture code says, "We put customers first," are your words and actions, and instinctive reactions, congruent with that code? The following is an example.

> One day, someone on your team suggests adding a simple way for customers to send you feedback and ideas. If your first reaction is to think, "That's a great idea. If we make it easy for customers to give feedback, we'll likely get more of it—and it's hard to solve for the customer if we don't know what they want and how we're doing in terms of delighting them. Let's do it!" Then, your actions are matching the culture you think you have. Your initial reaction is "that makes complete sense—there's no such thing as too much customer feedback."

If your first reaction is to think, "We are already overloaded. This is just one more channel that we'll have to deal with, and it's one more way for customers to file complaints. Where will we find the time to react/respond to what customers tell us? It's just asking for trouble . . ." Then, chances are, you may not really think that customers should come first.

According to Shah, culture is a set of shared beliefs, values, and practices. When you believe something, you do not need a mission statement to remind you. When you value something, you do not need a checklist or policy to remind you. You simply respond and in time the people around you respond the same way—and that's how a company's true culture is built.

Performance Appraisals

Bersin (2013) calls to question the nature of current performance appraisal processes, which he argues is based on output rather than coaching and development. Much interest among human resource managers more recently has been to revamp or eliminate the performance appraisal process with his research showing that more than 70% of all organizations dislike the process. This differs from before when organizations were very excited about topics such as cascading goals, pay for performance, goal alignment, and automated performance management software. Appraisal forms were developed from the early 1900s when employees were "workers" and managers were "supervisors." The supervisor rated and ranked people based on output.

Bersin argues that in 21st century organizations, more than 70% of workers are "knowledge workers" or "service providers." These are people who become more productive and valuable over time; they are more likely to benefit from coaching and development and become more productive and happy workers in the end. Hence, there is a need to move the performance appraisal process away from "competitive evaluation" toward "coaching and development."

Bersin also argues that the second big change today is the flattened, team-oriented, networked nature of companies. Work is less often viewed by one's manager and more often viewed by teammates; hence, they should be evaluated and reviewed by all the people we work with. Feedback should come from multiple sources, not just the manager. Teams should evaluate each other during projects, not only once per year. This feedback should be "developmental"—not just positive.

Last, Bersin believes that why traditional appraisals are not working has to do with the dynamic nature of goals. While 60% of companies set goals annually, this is less effective than when organizations reset goals quarterly. Moreover, he endorses weekly review of goals to promote more "agile management."

Consequently, Bersin's research on employee recognition shows that companies with a "recognition rich culture" far outperform those that are more "punitive" or "evaluative" in nature. This is premised on the fact that when people feel recognized and valued, they are more willing to take more feedback and focus on improvement. If all they hear is criticism, they more likely stop listening and leave. Appraisal and rating forms essentially encourage managers to focus on the "appraisal" and not the feedback, recognition, and coaching. With the growing emphasis on teams, more research now show that "boss-less teams" outperform those with "bosses." Performance appraisal tools are often overly prescriptive and "top-down," and therefore, not empowering people. Bersin concludes that performance management must be more developmental, coaching-based, agile, and frequent in today's environment.

Organizational Diversity Leadership Skill Sets

Organizational Fit

Based on the challenges associated with organization structure and composition and differences in organizational cultures across industry sectors, we need to raise questions of organizational fit. Not only must we understand the consequences of a prototypic match or mismatch between the social identities of leaders and members, we must also consider the different contexts. For organizations, promoting awareness of how these variables influence performance appraisals, different views of the same evidence, and how these influence organizational goals and outcomes become important. What is the fit between leaders and the organizations that they lead? How is this influenced by stereotypic perceptions and expectations of the leader based not on the leader's actual skillset?

Adapt or Conform

For the leader, it is the question of change or be changed and to make the invisible visible. What is adaptive to be able to lead the organization, and how does a leader incorporate cultural worldviews into his or her leadership? For example, women often do better than men in adapting or conforming since men are more likely to claim a "know it all" position. Women and ethnic minorities often prefer a cooperative to a competitive approach.

Intercultural Competence

Moodian (2009) examines contemporary leadership in the form of intercultural competence as part of the dynamics within organizations. There is an emerging consensus that intercultural competence consists of a set of cognitive, affective, and behavioral skills and characteristics that supports effective interaction across a variety of cultural contexts. This starts with good skills and training. "The premier skill of an interculturalist is empathy—that capacity to take the perspective of the other culture, to shift frames of reference, and to act in the context of the other's perspective" (Bennett, 2009, p. 104). "This excess challenge might occur if the training began with powerful discussions of racism for a group of learners in ethnocentric stages of denial, defense or minimization of cultural differences. Tempting though it may be to confront ethnocentrism immediately, there is greater likelihood of transformation when the group has experienced a 'learning edge' or teachable moment. . . . In general, a large proportion of our learners are likely to be in ethnocentric stages and therefore prone to finding intercultural competence challenging at best and quite threatening at worst. Since cultural topics become less challenging only in the ethnorelative stages of acceptance, adaptation, and integration of cultural differences, training methods for difference avoiders are typically more supportive and low risk, leaving the more complicated and demanding activities until the later stages" (p. 99).

Those in ethnocentric stages are likely to say things as follows (Bennett, 2009, pp. 100–106). In the denial stage, "Since the world is a global village and the Internet brings us all together in a common language, why worry unnecessarily about culture differences? With my experience, I can be successful anywhere." The developmental task of training here is exposure to cultural differences and creating a stimulus for recognizing culture. In the defense stage, "Now that I've noticed the Indian culture is different, I recognize they're bad!" They might also take the "reversal" perspective, which involves denigrating their own culture. The developmental task of training here is to develop the ability to manage anxiety and help leaders recognize that those from the other culture are "just like me." In the minimization stage, "We are all the same despite surface differences," or "The best way to get along in any culture is just to be yourself." The developmental task of training here is to develop cultural awareness and comfort with the discussion of difference. This contrasts with the ethnorelative stages where the experience of difference and the development of intercultural sensitivity are more advanced. In the acceptance stage, we understand distinction as difference without being bad. The challenge here is around a fear of compromising their own values and beliefs as they respect others. Simulations, role-plays, and case studies are more useful at this stage. In the adaptation stage, we may wonder, "Do I have to give up being a feminist while I work in a male-dominated culture?" The developmental task of training here is to improve the capacity to shift frames of reference and continue to function effectively. Here the task is not simply to observe but to do. The integration stage follows in-depth intercultural adaptation with bicultural identity as a possible result that occurs for minority group members to a dominant culture. The developmental task of training here is to facilitate an individual's resolution of his or her multicultural identity through self-exploration; this includes developing a culturally sensitive sense of humor, role and identity flexibility, and the ability to recognize new cultural patterns.

Importance of a Reconciliation Process

Trompenaars and Woolliams (2009) recognize the cultural variation in behaviors and actions across the world and across corporations. Once aware of and respect for cultural difference, they suggest a reconciliation process to integrate seemingly opposing values as opposed to compromise solutions or ignoring these differences. They point out that all cultures and corporations share the same dilemmas but their approach to them is culturally determined. They propose an Intercultural Competence Profiler composed of four aspects:

1. Recognition: How competent is a person to recognize cultural difference around him or her?

2. Respect: How respectful is a person about those differences?

3. Reconciliation: How competent is a person to reconcile cultural differences?

4. Realization: How competent is a person to realize the actions needed to implement the reconciliation of cultural differences?

The reconciliation component draws on worldview orientations of human relationships, time, and nature, which show variation across cultures. Intercultural competence is the reconciliation of dilemmas of contrasting value systems; ability to do so differentiates successful from less successful leaders and performance of the organization. Dilemmas are value based; for example, if one group is more individualistic and another group is more teamwork oriented, how the leader manages these contrasting cultural styles to serve both groups become central to intercultural competence. Reconciling aspects of human relationships might include reconciling persons who are emotional and passionate with those who control the display of emotion or reconciling individual creativity with team spirit. Reconciling aspects of time may involve sequential and parallel notions of time.

Fischer (2009, see pp. 191–201) discusses various ways of measuring intercultural competence. There are commercially available leadership assessments that do not specifically measure cultural competence but are useful in revealing an individual's potential to function and lead in today's multicultural workplace. These include instruments such as the Fundamental Interpersonal Relations Orientation Behavior (FIRO-B), Myers-Brigg Type Indicator, Leadership Practices Inventory, Emotional Quotient, and the DISC Assessment. The latter is one that measures four key personality factors: Dominance, Influence, Steadiness, and Compliance, leading the sum of all a person's varying response styles; it has been used extensively across different national cultures. Whereas most leaders have high Dominance scores, these individuals are competitive and will seek success on their own merits without asking for help. Multiculturally competent leaders have high Influence scores; these individuals are communicative, socially confident, open, and interested in other people. Steadiness is relatively rare in Western cultures; individuals high on Steadiness show sympathy for and loyalty to those around them and are resistant to change. This is common in Japanese and Mediterranean cultures, which tend to prefer a heavier adherence to rules and structure and avoidance of uncertainty. Individuals with high Compliance scores tend to be rule oriented and appreciate structure and order.

The Intercultural Development Inventory (Hammer, 2009, see pp. 203–217) is more specifically intended to measure intercultural competence progressing from a less complex perception of culturally based patterns of difference to more complex experience around cultural diversity along a continuum. They identify ten "culture general" dimensions of cultural difference that influence cross-cultural interactions: (1) sense of self and space (2) communication and language, (3) dress and appearance, (4) food and feeding habits, (5) time and time consciousness, (6) relationships, (7) values and norms, (8) beliefs and attitudes, (9) learning, and (10) work habits and practices.

Summary

Leaders both influence and are, in turn, influenced by contexts or the organizational cultures and societal cultures of which they are a part. This chapter examines organizational cultures and their differences across different industry sectors. It dissects organizational structures and compositions and ends with consideration of measuring organizational cultures and assessing organizational fit between leaders and organizations. Whereas leaders create cultures when they form groups and organizations, the underlying values, unspoken rules and practices, or company motto often reflects an organization's culture that remains stable and consistent over time. The question is whether leaders must conform to the organizational culture or can they help shape and evolve that culture.

Different industry sectors such as health care, education, or corporate businesses will emphasize different priorities and consequently evolve different organizational cultures. Often, the values and beliefs of subcultures or minority groups within an organization will create tension within the organization. Effective leadership means developing the skill sets to manage this diversity for the organization to remain productive, or to offer training and coaching for members to promote diversity while sharing common organizational goals. This may mean developing strategies or introducing processes to map the organizational context to understand the relationships, measuring the organizational culture, or identifying indicators to guide performance appraisals in ways to foster and achieve organizational goals. Leaders will do well to understand organizational structures, which promote inclusion, in-group/out-group divisions, and intergroup leadership as well as organizational composition, which defines the heterogeneity of the organization as well as its status as a minority or dominant mainstream organization. These factors dictate what organizations and leaders do in the allocation of resources, the setting of priorities, and the holding of its members accountable to its goals and outcomes. Equality across the ranks of egalitarian organizations will foster results very different from hierarchal organizations that emphasize the chain of command. As the trend toward global and diverse environments grows, leaders must look to the social orientation and identities of organization members. Leadership does not occur in isolation; it is cocreated out of an interpersonal and group process in the exchange between leader and members. While leaders are autonomous cutting edge individuals, at another level, they are mere actors in a drama coconstructed by the group or society. A leader is a member of a group(s) who receives, contains, and carries out the often unconscious intentions of the group in an ongoing dialogue.

Discussion Questions: Promoting Organizational Change—Building Organizational Cultures

1. An organization is often composed of its core culture and many subcultures. What happens when organizational subcultures clash? How can a leader manage these clashes?

2. Discuss leadership styles across different industry sectors. Are there styles that are a better match with a particular industry sector? What are they and why?

3. How do we identify bias within an organization toward specific subcultures and groups? How does a leader manage this bias to achieve organizational outcomes?

4. What happens when there is a mismatch between the identities, worldviews of a leader, and that of the organizational culture? Is this irreparable such that a leader will have to leave that organization? How might this place role constraints or double binds on a leader that might influence their effective exercise of leadership?

5. How can team approaches be enhanced to be more productive and effective when its members are more diverse?

6. What leadership styles are more effective for what contexts with which followers? For example, when is a collectivist or collaborative style more effective?

7. Imagine a business organization whose employees are highly heterogeneous in the composition of their different ethnic origins. What psychosocial and cultural factors must a leader consider in directing and leading that organization?

7

Societal Contexts of Leadership

With Contributions by Beauregard Stubblefield-Tave

Notable Quote: *On Culture and Expressing Affect*—"It's a Different Experience"

"Sometimes people said that I was angry like this is a bad thing; I don't think a male in my position would be given that feedback." (White Female leader)

"The issue of being a Latina is a big influence on my expression of anger. If I become angry, it means something different than when a White male becomes angry. It is tolerated a lot more in the White man, and it has a more positive impact. If I get angry, people focus so much on the anger that they forget the issue." (Latina female leader)

"But I think, as a Chinese, particularly brought up in a very traditional Chinese family, I was always very conscious of face. I would never deliberately go out of my way to make somebody lose face . . . maybe it's in my upbringing. . . . I don't think I've ever lost my temper in front of my boss or in front of my subordinate officers." (Asian female leader)

Vignette on Social Responsibility

"It takes a village" and "Reach as you rise!" are the mottoes of a national ethnic minority organization, The Society for the Psychological Study of Race, Ethnicity, and Culture, Division 45 of the American Psychological Association. They reflect the underlying values of its collectivistic nature and sense of social justice responsibilities within the division.

As we redefine leadership to be inclusive of global and diverse perspectives, societal and organizational contexts matter. This chapter examines global and diverse contexts and the intersections of race, ethnicity, and gender within societal contexts. It ends with a consideration of the opportunities and dilemmas these contexts pose to leadership as in public policy. Societal contexts include public policy, cultural and social norms, and the social zeitgeist (i.e., the spirit of social change that marks the thought or feeling of a period; it is a force that influences events) of the time in which leadership is exercised. The lived experiences amalgamated from these societal contexts of leaders and members influence the exchange that occurs between them. The broader contexts of social, cultural, and environmental factors influence the organizational cultures in which leadership is exercised. They shape what researchers study, how theories are formed, leadership behavior, member expectations, and organizational vision and mission.

The distinction between global and diverse perspectives is important. Global implies variation between countries, between cultures, essentially between entities typically viewed as having official boundaries. In times past, this was limited to the United Nations, foreign policy, and the growth of multinational corporations during the 20th century. Today, it includes the awareness and skills taught by institutions of higher education to train global citizens. It includes the awareness of corporations to target the global marketplace for untapped consumers and sources of products and services. Diverse, on the other hand, implies differences within. It includes cultural subgroups within a country such as race, ethnicity, and gender. Historically, the United States has struggled with diversity because of continued immigration of new groups. Today, increased mobility globally has led to many other countries also having to grapple with the diversity of their populations. For some, this new global awareness poses challenges for individuals and organizations to balance this shift away from local issues while trying to find meaning and relevance of global events. The case that follows reflects all these tensions.

Hong Kong Versus China: A Case Example

The changing social and political contexts following the handover of Hong Kong had major implications on issues of leadership, social identities, and power influences. Hong Kong went from being a colony of the British government "back" to mainland China, its motherland, after 100 years. While under colonial rule, Hong Kong was "oppressed" by the dominance of the British culture as the power elite. Speaking English, becoming urbanized, and embracing Western culture was defining as a reflection of social status, influence, and power. Given its strategic geographic location and the confluence of social, economic, and political factors, Hong Kong evolved to become one of the most cosmopolitan cities in the world during this 100 year takeover. Advancement in business, trade, finance, and banking led to its prominence internationally. After the handover, this felt like the trading of one oppressive rule for another, according to many Hong Kong citizens. While intended as liberation, many felt they were now accountable to a government that was less advanced and less cosmopolitan than under British rule. Language differences compound this schism as many Hong Kong citizens coming from Cantonese origins under British rule speak English and the Cantonese dialect while the main dialect of China is Mandarin. Cultural customs and practices also diverged under an urban and British environment versus a rural and communist environment such that some have described the post-handover environment as "it's like we are two different cultures."

This context has significantly influenced the organizational cultures of many corporations in Hong Kong, which had become multinational under British rule. These mature Hong Kong multinational corporations are now faced with the challenge of being under the rule of China (its parent country), which is now rapidly becoming a world power vying with the West in GDP, currency, and economic trade. Hence, we have a model for world leadership that is based on economic, not military, power in contrast to past models of the conqueror mentality. We also have an example of tension and conflict as Hong Kong and China address the challenges of diversity, autonomy, and dominance. It offers the opportunity for creative partnering and a new model for global leadership.

Global Contexts: Cultural Orientation Value Dimensions

At a global level, we return to cultural orientation value dimensions identified in the GLOBE studies that often shape organizational and societal cultures. These dimensions derived from Hofstede's work have been criticized because they have as a central premise that the nature of cultures is uniform (Hofstede, 2001; Hofstede & Hofstede, 2004) and minimize difference and diversity. However, the dimensions do highlight central tendencies that may help explain mismatch and miscommunication between leader and members, failures of leadership, and the need for intercultural competence and cultural fluency. The dimensions that follow illustrate the multidimensional societal facets that shape leadership based on underlying cultural orientation value dimensions and reflect some of the dilemmas faced by organizations in the 21st century. As researchers and scholars urge for new models of leadership relevant to and competent in the 21st century, these dimensions presume skill sets needed to achieve intercultural competency and fluency.

Universality

Gentry, Patterson, Stawiski, Gilmore, and Sparks's (2013) global study attempts to understand whether specific managerial skill sets (taking action, making decisions, and following through; relationships; energy, drive, and ambition) are believed to be important to a manager's job across 30 countries. Using ratings from the bosses of 6,130 target managers from 30 countries, their findings suggest cultural convergence in that these managerial skill sets were universally similar and important across the countries examined and not driven by cultural difference (which would have supported a divergence perspective). However, these findings of universality reflect the macro level at which the skill sets are identified rather than the absence of cultural divergence. While leadership skills of decision making, communication, and negotiation may be common for all leaders, cultural variation is the result of the process, methods, emphasis, and so forth used. Cultural values and orientation will dictate process and outcomes, not whether they exist or not. At macro levels of analyses, phenomena can appear to be universal while at more micro levels, we begin to see cultural variation. These skill sets will be discussed in Chapter 8.

Power: Competition and Cooperation

Power is one of those dimensions that invoke both fear and admiration. Contemporary leadership theories have diminished the emphasis on power perhaps in response to the possibility of nuclear devastation following WWII with the launch of the atomic bomb. Following the peace movement and antiwar rallies of the 1960s, there was a shift toward empowerment models to avoid the abuses of power engendered by the dictatorships of Hitler and Mussolini during WWII. McClelland (1985) studied these models of power and achievement as they applied to masculinity and femininity and to leadership. These were incorporated in the GLOBE dimensions, in particular, power distance (degree to which members expect power to be distributed) and cultural orientation and value. Studies find that hierarchical systems in society are common in high power distance societies such Latin, Asian, and African countries. This translates into the workplace and organizational cultures and the relationships between supervisors and their subordinates, where the ideal leader is viewed as a benevolent paternal figure. This contrasts with low power distance societies such the United States, Canada, Great Britain, and Denmark where supervisors and subordinates are considered equal; in such cases, the ideal leader is viewed as resourceful and democratic (Mor Barak, 2011).

Following WWII, the United States and other world powers worked on moving away from military power toward world peace and nuclear disarmament in such initiatives as the United Nations. In the 21st century, many former developing countries have now gained economic power and become world leaders. China's engagement with the world market, the multilateral international economic organizations, and international and regional security institutions have caused a concern about the threat of China to the existing world leadership in the 21st century. Ye (2002) provides an analysis about whether China will be a threat to the security of East Asia as they gain in economic power. Given China's low per capita GDP, its comparatively low military budget, and the serious challenges in its domestic affairs, Ye argues that China's national power has not been increased such that it will threaten the security of the region or that of the world. Given the continued influence of Confucian peaceful tradition in China's foreign policy, this is even less likely. Using a neo-realist paradigm, Ye uses power structure transformation analysis to point to potential threat. Its premise is that as countries become wealthier and more powerful, they inevitably seek greater political influence worldwide. It presumes that "a rising power dissatisfied with its secondary status may try to enhance it by confronting the dominant but declining country" (p. 57), for example, through war as the opportunity to changing the status quo. However, Ye suggests that China as a rising power seems to be orienting itself much more than the established powers toward cooperation as opposed to competition. Offering another viewpoint, Ye suggests that the dominance of countries as the focus of political authority is declining with the impact of globalization. Any country today is not only unable to decide the exchange rate of its own currency (i.e., economic power) but also is unable to decide to go to war as easily as previously (i.e., political power). While Chinese economic power has been increasing, globalization has led to a shrinking of the world and the growing interdependence of all. Cooperation is the attitude in the 21st century. China's actions reflect this orientation toward cooperation in its becoming a member of the International Monetary Fund (IMF), the World Bank, and other international economic institutions.

Ye also sees this strategy as aligned with Confucian values for China not to prefer an assertiveness strategy as a threat to the region as some Western scholars have predicted. Rather, Ye views the long history and traditional Confucian ideology of "restraining oneself and restoring the ritual to the world (p. 62)" has led the Chinese not to impose its culture or worldview on others. Under the strong influence of Confucian tradition China has been modeled and cultivated to be reactive rather than aggressive. Historically Chinese military action has been defensive or punitive in nature and seldom imperialistic.

Research suggests high power-distant cultures gravitate toward autocratic leadership (Hofstede, 2001; Rawwas, 2003). However, this is somewhat paradoxical because studies (e.g., Ping Ping, Hau-siu Chow, & Yuli, 2001) show autocratic leadership is not preferred by followers (neither Chinese nor American), nor does it produce a high quality work motivation. While autocratic leadership demands a respect for authority and subordination to management, autocratic leaders may therefore resort to embarrassment tactics or power-based tactics to force worker compliance (Rawwas, 2003). Such embarrassment contributes to a low and ineffective form of motivation (Misumi & Seki, 1971). While autocratic techniques are assumed to exist only in high power distance countries like China, ironically the data (Rawwas, 2003) show autocratic forms of leadership also prevail in low power distance cultures such as the United States.

Interestingly, Ping Ping et al. (2001) found that consultative approaches to decision making are far more popular among Chinese workers; workers had more motivation when working under a participatory style of leadership, providing strong evidence for a people-oriented leadership correlating with high worker satisfaction. The best Chinese leaders seem to be high in both people and task orientation. At first glance, these leader-follower attributions sound quite Western. However, they are paradoxical given the results of a study by Wenquan, Chia, and Liluo (2000) representing the complexity of the collectivist environment. Subordinating to the collective greater good among Chinese is often a cause for misunderstanding and oversimplified labeling creating the false notion that Chinese leaders are only autocratic. When a need and a desire for the opportunity to participate coexists with the recognition that the needs of the group, community, or organization prevail over those of the individual, both authoritarian and participatory methods may coexist. In such environments, a leader may feel forced to be authoritative on behalf of the group, out of necessity to achieve balance and harmony; in other words, authoritarian behavior can be paradoxically viewed as a community duty and satisfying the needs of both people and organizations.

This example demonstrates the changing landscape of power globally and the social zeitgeist that may shape leadership. Corporations and institutions will change accordingly as higher education institutions decide whether and how to recruit and train international students, as corporations and businesses become increasingly global and multinational, as military power may defer to economic power, and as human rights and social justice goals prevail.

Collectivism and Individualism

Individualistic has been contrasted with collectivistic cultures. During the 20th century, countries with individualistic cultures were the world leaders, often a function of the military power they had. In collectivist societies (e.g., Latin American, Japan and other Asian, and Arabic-speaking countries), the extended family or other ingroups are expected to protect them in exchange for loyalty; relationships between employer-employee in organizations are seen as a family relationship with mutual obligations for employee loyalty in exchange for employer protection and security.

Bush (2011) contrasts an individual-centric model of leadership where the power and influence to exert and maintain control flows from the leader versus a collective-centric approach where leaders set the prevailing goal of achieving consensus on all decision-making activities. The goal is achieved through process-oriented communication where opinions and the voices of the group are valued above the individual. He makes a distinction between authority, which flows downward and is unidirectional; influence is multidirectional and can flow upward, downward, or horizontally. His study respondents indicated they were not interested in competing with their constituents for resources and resource allocations; rather, they were interested in promoting an agenda stemming from intrinsically motivated values and status mobility. Many collective-oriented leaders showed a high respect for humility, dignity, lack of vanity, deference to the group's welfare, and functioning from a self-effacing demeanor in a gracious, respectful, and polite manner. Those who expressed and endorsed collective-oriented styles did not see their styles as weaknesses or in any way influencing their persuasiveness, potency, and effectiveness. They perceived individual-centric leaders as more consumed with a high need for achievement, power, influence, and the domination of others. These factors were mirrored in Chin's study of diverse leaders who prioritized consensus and the voice of the group over individual-centric models of leadership (Chin, 2013).

Chinese leadership patterns align with a collectivist culture (Wong, 2001), which respects cooperation, affiliation, and subordination (Ping Ping et al., 2001; Rawwas, 2003). In fact, Chinese people ranked high in their willingness to subordinate personal objectives to a group purpose (Rawwas, 2003). Collectivism attributes included high power distance, divisions of wealth and power, limits to risk and uncertainty, low levels of individualism, and high degrees of loyalty to family, friends, and organization. Although Chinese managers aligned with collectivism, one cannot assume that collectivist approaches to organizational management simply equate to autocratic leadership. The relationships were far more complex. For example, Chinese managers were often far more engaged with relationship issues, such as conflict management, than their American counterparts (Rawwas, 2003). Chinese leaders were generally interested in the holistic development of those they lead and not simply focused on achieving a production target (Wenquan et al., 2000; Wong, 2001). While iron-hand rule is often associated with Chinese leadership, this is only true where it was needed to protect a community or organizational objective. In reality, a high degree of self-directed activity occurs within Chinese organizations (Ping Ping et al., 2001). Thus, from the lens of the Chinese culture, participatory relationships in organizational leadership are not at all unique. Perhaps it is rather the manner of how the interaction occurs that leads to misinterpretation by Western observers.

Native American Indian leadership also aligns with a collectivist cultural orientation, although there is some debate on the extent to which Natives and Indians were purely collectivistic (Rodriguez, Galbraith, & Stiles, 2006). Lori Arviso Alvord bridges two worlds of medicine—traditional Navajo healing and conventional Western medicine—to treat the whole patient. She provides culturally competent care to restore balance in her patients' lives and to speed their recovery (Alvord & Cohen Van Pelt, 2000). As a Stanford-trained surgeon, she developed her technical and clinical skills and was the first Navajo woman to be board certified in surgery. But when she returned to the New Mexico reservation to work in a Navajo community, she discovered, she says, that "although I was a good surgeon, I was not always a good healer. I went back to the healers of my tribe to learn what a surgical residency could not teach me. From them I have heard a resounding message: Everything in life is connected. Learn to understand the bonds between humans, spirit, and nature. Realize that our illness and our healing alike come from maintaining strong and healthy relationships in every aspect of our lives." Her approach to leadership is summarized as follows:

> My ideal operating room would have a team of people who worked together smoothly and easily, with respect for one another and their patients. Each member, no matter what their rank, would be considered important and invaluable. (Alvord & Cohen Van Pelt, 2000)

As surgeon, she remained "captain of the ship" while recognizing the worth of each crewmember as "important and invaluable." A scrub nurse who identifies a sponge left in a patient can save a life as readily as the surgeon who makes the appropriate incision. Alvord also recognized her patients as critical partners in her work as a surgeon and healer:

> I needed the patients' spirits to assist me in surgery; and their minds should be relaxed and in a state of trust before they went into the operating room. They should be prepared to let me enter the sacred chambers of their bodies. Their spirits and mind had to work together to allow the process of healing to occur. (Alvord & Cohen Van Pelt, 2000)

She attributed bringing the patients' spirits into the healing process as resulting in fewer medical complications and happier patients. This collectivist approach of leaders working in partnership demonstrates good clinical and satisfaction outcomes and reflects the family and community as integral to leadership.

Collectivism within Latin American communities play on in a more extended family manner through a paternalistic model (Rory, 2013). "Obligations for a Latino supervisor generally include being a mentor, a role model, a coach, a financial supporter and a friend. It is an unwritten part of the job description, something we naturally fall into, and something that may be as important as the job itself. For a Latino, being a supervisor implies having an attitude that most of us have in our personal relationships, that of *providing care for loved ones*." Central to the role of leader or manager is *personalismo* or *familismo*, equated to the relationship that they have with their families. It involves exerting power with a caring attitude, delivering results responsibly, and providing support for those that count on them (Chong & Baez, 2005).

An example is provided where a Latino supervisor's obligations may conform or conflict with his organizational culture. In an individualistic culture focused on bottom-line performance, laying off a well performing employee is part of the role. When recognizing the employee's family responsibilities as part of a cultural obligation *to exert power with a caring attitude and deliver results responsibly*, a Latino supervisor may seek other ways to reduce costs without laying off the employee. Although this may be felt among other cultures, the Latino supervisor's cultural identity and values may magnify the conflict.

Egalitarianism: Masculinity-Femininity

Historically, male dominance and values prevailed among institutions and societies as part of a masculinized context. The masculinity-feminity dimension refers to the extent to which dominant cultural values emphasize assertiveness, competition, and material achievements associated with masculine qualities compared with feminine qualities of relationships among people, caring for others, and care for quality of life. It was identified by Hofstede as a core dimension" (Mor Barak, 2011). Initial studies of femininity characterized these as dichotomous dimensions until Bem (1974) separated them as independent variables resulting in a third androgynous dimension combining both. While studies of masculinity-femininity led to goals for achieving equity between the sexes and egalitarianism within the culture and society, societies have been characterized as feminine (e.g., Sweden, Norway, Netherlands, Denmark) where there is a preference for solving work-related conflicts by compromise and negotiation; others have been characterized as masculine (Japan, Italy, Mexico, United States), where assertiveness, ambition, and competitiveness are expected, and where power struggles and direct confrontation are more common in conflict resolution (Mor Barak, 2011). Ghei and Nebel (1994) studied androgyny in hotel managers and found that effective managers or leaders use both forceful (masculine, authoritarian) and enabling (feminine, benevolent) methods depending on circumstances.

Yet there continues to be a tendency to dichotomize masculinity and femininity, which often results in favoring masculine dimensions as strong and marginalizing, feminine dimensions as weak and results in stereotyping gender roles. Furthermore, cultural values associated with dimensions of masculinity and femininity may value the characteristics differently. For example, definitions of assertiveness associated with masculinity and asserting one's position as found in Western cultures contrasts with remaining silent and using an indirect route to achieve the same ends while maintaining interpersonal harmony as found in Eastern cultures.

Humane and Social Responsibility

An emerging construct of leadership is the emphasis on integrity and virtuous leadership or social justice orientation in leadership theories. Organizationally, this translates into corporate social responsibility or performance. While having moral and ethical values is obvious, they have generally been associated with religious institutions and Eastern countries. Only recently do we see accumulating research showing that corporations and businesses draw tangible benefits from such activities. There is now a shift from organizational policies aimed at compliance and preventing lawsuits to one of creating good will, increasing employee loyalty, and improving corporate image. There is suggestion that increased corporate social performance is linked to financial performance (Mor Barak, 2011; Orlitzky, Schmidt, & Rynes, 2003).

The emphasis on human rights and social justice grows strong in the social consciousness worldwide with individuals and groups now demanding corporations and governments to sanction those who violate these norms.

Diverse Contexts: Influence of Lived Experiences

In viewing leadership as contextual, value driven, diversity inclusive, and collaborative, we look to transform models of leadership—to identify diverse leadership styles across diverse groups and to embrace core values that motivate those in leadership roles. Lived experiences of leaders and members include not only the social and cultural values, practices, and beliefs of their communities in which they receive support and caring but also the biases, stereotypes, challenges, and dilemmas they face as they negotiate their social roles in society. It is what they bring to the workplace as part of their social identities and core values. As discussed in Chapter 6, the match or mismatch between the social identities of the leader and group composition influences the nature of the leader-member exchange, often calling for different styles of leadership.

Social Zeitgeist

Sociopolitical contexts and the zeitgeist of the times have a major influence on how leadership is viewed, constructed, and studied. Post WWII led to studies of democratic versus autocratic versus laissez-faire styles of leadership that reflected the fear about abuses of power, while the Civil Rights era of the 1960s led to an emphasis on equity and social justice. Interest and concern over these abuses led to models of servant leadership and empowerment as themes for good leadership. As we have become cognizant of our potential for destructive power in the form of nuclear and chemical warfare, efforts worldwide are now geared toward our interdependence and sustainability of our environment. In all sectors, the emphasis is now on how to harness technology toward these ends and how to promote intercultural communication and competence.

In-Groups Versus Out-Groups

In-groups and out-groups commonly develop in society and social groups. Under certain conditions, people will show preference and have affinity for one's in-group over the out-group, or anyone viewed as outside the in-group. This *in-group favoritism* can result in negative evaluations of those outside the group or *out-group derogation*. The out-group is often perceived as threatening to members of the in-group, or as blocking the goals of the in-group, often resulting in discriminatory behavior or inequitable allocation of resources. *In-group favoritism* and *out-group derogation* in society are often mirrored in the workplace and are often justified based on privileged views and ethnocentric conceptions. It is not uncommon for both positive and negative beliefs toward out-groups to coexist although both may serve the purpose to deny conscious biases by an in-group while harboring unconscious mental associations that affirm stereotypes (i.e., aversive sexism or racism) and disqualify "outsider" groups (e.g., women and minorities) from leadership roles—reduced access and poorer appraisals (Heilman & Eagly, 2008; Leslie, King, Bradley, & Hebl, 2008; Pittinsky, 2010).

The tendency to like and associate with others like oneself (i.e., in-group preference) exacerbates the biases stemming from gender and cultural stereotypes and results in out-group suspicion (Byrne & Neuman, 1992). The in-group often becomes dominant in society although out-groups are often, but not always, based on minority status. As a result, women, racial, and ethnic minorities are likely to face entry barriers to important social networks because they are unlike those within the dominant in-group. It also reduces access to influential social networks that are essential to building the social capital that allows people to emerge as leaders and become effective in leader roles (Brass, 2001). Size is not always an indicator of in-group dominance, as demonstrated by colonized countries where minority groups ruled and the caste system in India that privileged the elite upper classes (Pittinsky, 2010).

When cultural values and orientations differ between a leader and members or a leader and the organization, or when differences exist because of dimensions of diversity, out-group members often feel oppressed in their voices not being heard, in the lack of mechanisms for input and inclusion, and in their inability to share in the benefits associated with being part of the privilege class, in-group, or dominant group. These may be material benefits (higher pay), social status (entry to country clubs and restaurants, recognition of competence), and freedom from discrimination (biased performance appraisals, restricted access). Out-group members also share the experience of stigma, exclusion, and discrimination based on group membership.

Credibility

As discussed in Chapter 6, the dynamic is different when the leader comes from a social group categorized as an out-group or minority group. Here the leader retains statuses that are incongruent. When perceptions and expectations of a typical leader are associated with the dominant in-group, or being White Anglo as it is in the United States, the credibility of a leader from a minority or out-group is typically questioned although it may have little to do with effective leadership. Moreover, out-group membership often constrains accepted leadership behaviors to stereotypic roles. The challenge is how to expand our notions of leadership to enable more enriched contributions from those belonging to out-group membership.

"Notably, what Blacks find frustrating in situations where these mistaken or unfair perceptions occur, and what often contributes to deteriorating trust between Blacks and their White colleagues, is the seeming lack of malignant intention behind White colleagues' behavior. Purposeful racism is easier to identify and therefore combat than race based conjecture . . . when Blacks work with Blacks in a White organization, their actions are scrutinized in a way seldom experienced by their White counterparts" (Livers & Caver, 2002, p. 150).

Privilege Versus Marginal Status

While credibility can often be proven after a leader has demonstrated his or her expertise, the privilege or marginal status of in-group or out-group membership often remains invisible and sustaining. In a diverse workforce where people from different cultural or social groups must constantly interact with one another, people's own cultural identities and perceptions of those from different social groups as well as in-group and out-group dynamics will impact the leadership experience (Ayman, 2004).

Racism

While racism and discrimination were sanctioned in U.S. laws such as through slavery and anti-Asian immigration, more recently, social media and corporations have increasingly taken strong positions and sanctions against public displays of racist behaviors. This has been fueled by the ability for such incidents to go viral creating strong public opinion against such behavior. For example, in May 2013, the Food Network fired Paula Deen, its TV celebrity cook of *Paula's Home Cooking* from Savannah, even after she posted two videotaped apologies online begging forgiveness from fans and critics who were troubled by her admission to having used racial slurs in the past. She had been swamped in controversy since court documents revealed that Deen had admitted under oath that she has used the N-word. Though her apology claimed that "inappropriate, hurtful language is totally, totally unacceptable," and she insisted that "Your color of your skin, your religion, your sexual preference does not matter to me," Deen was involved in a discrimination lawsuit filed by a former employee who managed a Savannah restaurant owned by Deen and her brother. The ex-employee, Lisa Jackson, claimed she was sexually harassed and worked in a hostile environment rife with innuendo and racial slurs. During the deposition, Deen's answers to questions about her racial attitudes were not received well. . . . Deen also acknowledged she briefly considered hiring all Black waiters [dressed to look like slaves] for her brother's 2007 wedding, an idea inspired by the staff at a restaurant she had visited with her husband. She insisted she quickly dismissed the idea (Bynum, 2013).

When societal contexts are homogenous, its members often show no awareness of the importance of diversity. These contexts often create a bias, which favors the dominant majority group, its values, and behaviors. While overt racism has diminished as evidenced by the sanction against Paula Deen for uttering racial slurs, their pernicious effects remain in the form of micro-aggressions, which are now common in the 21st century. Sue et al. (2007) describe microaggressions as, "brief and commonplace daily verbal, behavioral, or environmental indignities, whether intentional or unintentional, that communicate hostile, derogatory, or negative racial slights and insults toward people of color" (p. 271). Many leaders of color report being recipients of such microaggressions, which include such things as assuming that the leader or manager in charge must be the White person, expecting the leaders of color to remain subservient in a reversal of roles, overt acts of disrespect that would not be accorded to someone White. This leads to the common experience of "always having to prove oneself" or double bind situations of having to "assert one's authority" and then accused of being "too autocratic."

The emphasis on Affirmative Action has been legislated into policy for workplace compliance. It demands that institutions and corporations demonstrate in their policies that they are equal opportunity employers and do not discriminate on the basis of race, gender, ethnicity, and so forth. And yet there are criticisms of institutions complying with the letter of the law, not with the spirit of the law. A backlash effect also exists where ethnic minority leaders are often questioned in subtle and indirect ways about their competence or it is assumed that they got to where they were because of affirmative action, not because they could do the job.

Biculturalism: Acculturation and Immigration

Lived experiences associated with biculturalism in response to acculturation and immigration experiences are powerful aspects of societal contexts that influence leadership. When America was proclaimed as "God's Crucible, the great melting pot where all the races of Europe are melting and reforming" (Gerstle, 2001, p. 51), a phrase first coined in a play by Israel Zangwill in 1908 as the American dream, it failed to recognize that the melting pot was a myth, exclusive to those who were White. It was blind to the discriminatory laws and policies inherent in 1882 Exclusionary Acts against the Chinese, in slavery, and in treaties with Native American Indian tribes.

For early non-White immigrants to the United States, maintaining biculturalism was a way of restoring and enhancing self-esteem and self-identity amidst alien cultures and discrimination. The striving for a multicultural/multiracial America without distinction to cultures of origin is unrealistic given the tendency to draw differences for positive as well as negative reasons; these differences support in-group bonding needs as well as out-group rejection.

These myths and ideals form the social zeitgeist of the times. The immigration debate in the 21st century has shifted from a welcoming stance to a focus on "illegal immigrants," their rights to stay in the country, and to benefit from its resources. While some focus on "making things right" for the millions of undocumented immigrants who entered the United States without proper documents, including such things as giving children a right to education and creating a legal access to citizenship, others focus on deportation and other punitive measures to rid the country of these "undesirables." The latter ignores the fact that the no one verified or gave permission for the Pilgrims to enter the country or the fact that the historical focus has been limited to the "illegal" entry of non-White Mexicans, Asians, and Africans.

Masculinized Contexts

Societies clearly have gender role norms that shape how women behave. Women leaders more commonly lead in the context of a male advantage—that is, masculinized contexts (Fletcher, 2003); they are often evaluated and perceived differently from men based on current gender-related biases. Women leaders often manage within masculinized contexts and must adapt their leadership styles accordingly. These contexts often constrain women leaders with expectations to behave consistent with their gender roles. At the same time, these same behaviors may be defined as signs of ineffective leadership. In examining the lived experiences of women leaders and in transforming leadership, it is not that men cannot or should not be leaders. It is that women can and should be effective leaders without needing to change their essence or to adopt those values that are not syntonic with their gender or culture. It is about using feminist principles to promote pathways to leadership, recognizing the obstacles, and drawing on its strengths. It is about measuring and identifying effective leadership styles that are not simply based on identifying the characteristics of good male leaders. It is about how issues of power, privilege, and hierarchy that influence the contexts in which leadership occur.

The bias toward women leaders often result in double-bind situations when they feel compelled to conform to conflicting role expectations associated with gender and leadership. Are they to be feminine women and be perceived as weak, or to be strong leaders and be perceived as too domineering? Whereas current organizations typically conform to masculinized norms that are more congruent for men, women leaders can be at a disadvantage when exercising behaviors that contradict such expectations or when they are compelled to conform to these norms. In managing the organizational culture, it is not devoid of the societal norms about gender and gender roles.

The effect of these in-group and out-group biases is that leadership remains a different experience for women (Eagly & Carli, 2007, p. xviii) as they "navigate a labyrinth" to reach top leadership positions. As women, their lived experiences include growing up in male-dominant societies, facing social expectations associated with gender roles, and needing to negotiate work-family balance in their lives. As women, they are likely to hold leadership roles through community and service leadership positions as wives and mothers.

Their lived experiences challenge historic theories of leadership drawn primarily from the experiences of White men leading in contexts governed by male values and White middle class norms. Current definitions of leadership in the corporate world include full-time work and career tracks that do not factor in discontinuities related to childrearing, childbearing, or parental caretaking responsibilities. Women's time away from their careers are often viewed as reflecting their lesser commitment to the job and disinterest in career advancement. Leadership and leadership styles, as a result, are viewed from a masculine perspective and evaluated against masculine norms. It is increasingly clear that cultural worldviews, socialization of gender roles, and different life experiences do contribute to one's resulting philosophy and style of leadership. Women leaders also face challenges in eliciting more negative nonverbal affect responses from others for the same suggestions and arguments compared to men (Butler & Geis, 1990). There operates a social mechanism that causes devaluation of women's leadership. The implications are that repeated exposure to negative nonverbal affective responses when attempting to exercise leadership could result in women withdrawing from the opportunities when presented.

Alice Eagly concludes that

> the qualities women bring to leadership are also more conducive to a better life balance, since it is more participative and compassionate, less focused on immediate profit. The Norwegian quota is used as an example. Public companies in Norway are required to have a minimum of 40% women on their boards of directors. After introducing this mandate, there was found to be a small decline in profitability, apparently as a consequence of the change. When researchers looked closely at the data, they found that the reason for the decline appeared to be due to fewer staff layoffs during the economic downturn. This led to higher costs and lower profits in the short term. Researchers speculated that the women were considering other stakeholders—the workers themselves and the impact of losing their jobs on their families. The long-term impact could in fact be more favorable for both the companies and community at large because they do not have to find and train new employees when conditions improve. This example points to the fact that women face varied challenges, right from the beginning of their careers. (Quoted in Hayes, 2012)

The most difficult area is related to family issues. According to Eagly and Carli (2007), "Women still lose out on opportunities for higher executive positions when they become mothers, or take time out for family reasons. . . . There's a sense of being automatically discounted as potential fast-track candidates." She suggests new ways of doing business to ensure that companies do not lose the talent that they really need by presenting people with these dichotomous decisions: "stay at home or work part-time for a while and you can never have a fast-track career or move up in the company. . . . Some men might enjoy concentrating on their young child for a while if they knew it would not ruin their careers. There needs to be easier on-ramps for women returning to work after childbearing and easier off- and on-ramps for men too" (Hayes, 2012). These suggestions point to the importance of change in the societal and organizational contexts for the next generation of women in leadership (Hayes, 2012).

Intersections of Race, Ethnicity, and Gender in Masculinized Contexts

The book, *Women and Leadership: Transforming Visions and Diverse Voices* (Chin, Lott, Rice, & Sanchez-Hucles, 2007), which examined leadership among more than 100 feminist women leaders, found that the experience of difference was pronounced. These women also added stressors of being expected to behave according to stereotypic gender, race, and ethnic norms while managing a work-family balance. The case examples that follow suggest how different leadership styles are influenced by cultural differences. An African American woman might identify with the values of straightforwardness and assertiveness in her leadership style while an Asian American woman might identify with values of respectfulness and unobtrusiveness. However, others may perceive the direct confrontational style of an African American woman as intimidating and deem the use of an indirect teaching style of an Asian American woman as passive (Sanchez-Hucles & Sanchez, 2007). Black feminist leaders described themselves as "Black activists who, from the intersections of race and gender, develop paths, provide a direction, and give voice to Black women" (Hall, Garrett-Akinsanya, & Hucles, 2007, p. 283). Ann Yabusaki (2007, p. 55) suggests that Asian American women may use more indirect communication in their leadership styles. In Asian cultures, the balance of opposites and emphasis on the yin and the yang can bring out the best in leadership enriched by different perspectives. She identifies "how the emphasis on hierarchy influences ways in which leaders and authority figures communicate in Asian cultures (resulting in the expectation and tendency of Asian leaders) to teach or convey a moral message when communicating." When this communication operates within a context that values kinship bonds and elders, the concept of benevolent authority is ascribed to leaders in the Asian culture.

Native American Indian women, on the other hand, described their leadership as "stand[ing] beside, rather than behind, [their] men in their effort to preserve their tribes and treaty rights" (Kidwell, Willis, Jones-Saumty, & Bigfoot, 2007, p. 327); they will not distance themselves from their men as did White women during the Women's Movement because of the inherent threat posed by the broader society against their men if they were to do so.

Women leaders from these diverse racial/ethnic groups defined their leadership relative to their lived experiences and cultural values. Differences in their leadership styles were aligned with their worldviews and cultural perspectives and were not divorced from their gender and racial/ethnic identities. And yet the significance of these differences in lived experiences as they influence the exercise of leadership did not feel well understood. The women felt like an "out-group" relative to men compounded by negative views of their leadership.

A 1999 study of women leaders of color in corporate America led *Catalyst* to coin the term *concrete ceiling* "This metaphor stands in sharp contrast to the more common *glass ceiling* as more difficult to penetrate. Women of color said they cannot see through it to glimpse the corner office," said *Catalyst* President Sheila Wellington. The study also noted that Asian American, African American, and Latina leaders faced varied concrete ceilings and responded with varying strategies in response (Catalyst, 1999).

Role Constraints

In studying diverse women leaders, Chin et al. (2007) found that feminist women often embrace leadership styles that are value driven, ethics based, social change oriented, and transformational. They generally preferred using a collaborative process, empowering followers, and promoting inclusiveness. Their pursuit of an egalitarian model of leadership reflects a desire to level power dynamics inherent in the leader-follower relationship. At the same time, many of these diverse women leaders felt constrained by the masculinized contexts in which leadership was exercised where this is not sanctioned. As a result, they felt the need to use more hierarchical leadership styles to be effective and to be viewed as decisive rather than using a more preferred collaborative process.

Many feminist women often sought leadership positions to achieve social justice goals and gender equity, striving to be transformational in their vision, empowering in their actions, and upholding of ethical principles. These principles often were felt to be at odds with strivings for power and status, which they believed to be more commonly associated with men. Many of the women felt constrained to follow institutional rules defined by masculinized norms and needed to compromise feminist principles in their leadership styles to be effective.

The influence of these identities on leadership is reflected in a comment by Lorene Garrett-Browder (Chin et al., 2007, p. 57), who suggests that "African American women throughout history have been able to be effective leaders despite living in oppressive environment and dealing with power structures that do not always include our voice. . . . Consequently, African American women (leaders might tend to use more direct communication styles and) have used our anger as an ally to help us speak the truth . . . even though it may be unpopular." In a context of oppression and power, value is placed on trust and fairness to accept leadership from an African American perspective. This approach places an emphasis on parity and social justice.

The following case vignette exemplifies this dilemma. Vanessa Northington Gamble considered using a *very emotional, dynamic* speaking style inspired by her grandmother, a storefront minister, when addressing the status of minority faculty, residents, and students at a medical school dean's retreat. She describes how "on this day I altered my style. I gave what I thought was a clinical, dispassionate presentation. I reported my observations about some of the obstacles that minorities in medicine faced. I made my diagnosis: The medical school needed to create an environment that was more hospitable to people of color. . . . At my table sat the acting chair of one of the departments, who made the first comments on my presentation" (p. 166). He said: "I talk to a lot of minority students, and I've not heard what we've heard here today. I doubt if it is an accurate depiction of what goes on here. I have a woman resident who will tell you differently" (p. 166). This response was a total denial of Gamble's reality based on anecdotal observations, who then noted: "I was taken aback by the hostility of his comments. I had not expected such a response. His words hurt. He was dismissing out of hand my experiences and those of other minority physicians. He was calling me a liar. He was saying that my words could not be trusted but that those of a White woman resident who was under his supervision could. He also was disrespecting my status as a senior faculty member. I was the first and only Black woman tenured at the medical school, and I was very proud of that accomplishment. I wanted to cry, but I translated my hurt into anger. With my voice raised, I retorted, 'I will not be dismissed. Just because you have not heard the stories does not deny their existence'" (p. 166). Though other attendees gave Dr. Gamble private support, none rose to her defense publicly or questioned the comments of the acting department chair (Gamble, 2000).

These examples suggest that diverse women leaders may hold different views about assertiveness and express their leadership in different ways. Yet their competence and effectiveness as leaders may be defined by social role stereotypes and expectations. Asian American women may need to learn how to "toot one's horn" without losing one's modesty or to "speak up" despite the emphasis on listening in the Asian culture. Native American Indian women may need to learn how to "get a seat at the table," and not wait to be asked. The challenge for diverse women leaders is to learn that it is a different game governed by different rules while transforming the organizational culture in the process.

Racial and ethnic identities that represent people's psychological relationships and bonds to their social groups can also constrain their behavior (Frable, 1997, Phinney, 1990). For example, Cheung and Halpern (2010) explain how some women import mothering metaphors into their understanding of leadership. Fassinger, Shullman, and Stevenson (2010) discuss whether the assumptions that leaders and followers make about sexuality constrain or enhance the capacities that lesbian and gay leaders bring to leadership. Sanchez-Hucles & Davis (2010) suggest that identities pertaining to race and ethnicity affect the ways in which individuals lead.

Double Binds

Gender biases and attributions constrain women's leadership behaviors and create double-bind situations that may contribute to their feeling marginalized or weak if they behave in feminine ways and criticized if behave in masculine ways. All too often, "feminine" emotionality is rated negatively as a weakness with respect to leadership while "feminine" nurturing is viewed as lacking in substance. Conversely, women leaders adopting "masculine" behaviors are also viewed negatively as aggressive and overbearing while aggressive and direct male leaders are viewed as forthright and taking charge. Much research has shown that task-oriented competencies have come to be associated with leadership success, whereas expressive, person-oriented qualities are generally given low weight in the determination of leadership (Korabik, 1990). Female leaders are often expected to take charge and lead in the same ways as their male colleagues. At the same time, female leaders are expected to be warm and nurturing as culturally prescribed for women. Simultaneously impressing others as a good leader and a good woman is often challenging to achieve with common pitfalls of appearing "too masculine" or "too feminine."

Negotiating between masculine and feminine traits apparently seems to push women leaders toward a relatively androgynous style that incorporates both (Eagly, Karau, & Makhijani, 1995). Women also perceive a need to adapt their behavioral style so men do not feel intimidated (Ragins, Townsend, & Mattis 1998) and that a narrower range of behavior as acceptable behavior exists for female leaders than for male leaders (Eagly, Makhijani, & Klonsky, 1992).

Stressors

Iwasaki, MacKay, and Ristock (2004) explored the experiences of stress (e.g., negative and positive aspects of stress, different levels of stress, lack of sleep, pressure, financial stressors, being a manager) among both female and male managers. In addition to substantial similarities, a number of important gender differences emerged. Gender continues to be socially constructed in society; specifically, there are differing gender role expectations and responsibilities for women and men. Female managers experienced "emotional stress," primarily because of the pressure to meet expectations of being responsible and caring for people both inside and outside of their home. In contrast, male managers tended to focus on themselves and regard other things as beyond their control or responsibility. These stressors reflect the different experiences of women leaders and the different contexts in which they lead even when all conditions appear to be the same.

This is where scales of intercultural sensitivity matter, and promoting multicultural and diversity goals can be challenging. Some will say that color does not matter, "I treat a person as a person"; this often is a way to deny bias and discrimination and reflects denial. Often leaders of color find themselves not unlike the "lone ranger" as the only one speaking up to promote diversity; this can have its toll and result in feelings of marginalization or being pigeonholed as only interested in diversity.

Biased Performance Appraisals

In encountering negative appraisals and portrayals of their effectiveness as leaders, women and diverse leaders may seek to portray themselves from positions of strength, reactive to those who fail to see their potential benefits as leaders (e.g., Ayman & Korabik, 2010; Cheung & Halpern, 2010). In response to such doubts about and resistance to their leadership, many have focused on demonstrating a feminine advantage for women leaders compared with men based on women's tendencies toward greater connectedness, nurturing, and collaborative styles. For example, several female managerial writers have provided particularly laudatory descriptions of women's leadership styles as interactive and inclusive (e.g., Chin et al., 2007; Helgesen, 1990; Rosener, 1990). Related superiority claims have emerged concerning leadership by African American women (Parker, 2005; Parker & Ogilvie, 1996) and gay men (Snyder, 2006). Such claims of advantage can reflect instances of group pride noted by Pittinsky (2010).

These claims may also accurately reflect the superior performance that can emerge from having one's abilities challenged on the basis of membership in a social group that has usually been excluded from leadership or has been historically oppressed. For example, research has shown that women who are confident about their leadership ability are not deterred by statements that women have less leadership ability than men but instead react by exhibiting even more competence than they do in the absence of an explicit challenge (Hoyt & Blascovich, 2007). In addition, diverse leaders can potentially perform especially well to the extent that they have had to meet a higher standard to attain leadership roles in the first place. Many of the qualitative studies note the common belief among women and racial/ethnic minorities that they must meet higher standards to be accorded competence and agency (see reviews by Biernat, 2005; Foschi, 2000; Thomas & Gabarro, 1999).

Yet another rationale for thinking that diverse individuals are often good leaders is that the differences in their lived experiences do confer special qualities. Individuals from racial and ethnic minority groups, in particular, generally have more multicultural experiences because of having to negotiate both minority and majority cultures. Multicultural competence can foster flexibility and openness to change (Musteen, Barker, & Baeten, 2006), an ability to shift one's thinking between contexts (Molinsky, 2007), and promote creative cognitive processes and problem solving (Leung, Maddux, Galinsky, & Chiu, 2008), dimensions that can translate into more effective leadership.

Despite these possible advantages of diverse leaders, the good performance of diverse leaders is not necessarily recognized as outstanding (Eagly & Carli, 2007; Eagly & Chin, 2010). For example, studies of female and male managers show that, despite generally good managerial skills, women tend to be judged as less effective than men in male-dominated roles and masculine settings. Moreover, female leaders whose qualifications and skills are made equivalent to male leaders in controlled lab experiments still receive somewhat lower evaluations, especially if they behave in culturally masculine ways and are portrayed in male-dominated roles (Eagly, Makhijani, & Klonsky, 1992). Such findings demonstrate that leader behavior is only one determinant of their effectiveness. Effective leadership is also related to the exchange between leaders and members as well as member expectations and prejudices, or the contexts in which leadership is exercised.

While Vecchio (2003) believes this feminine advantage is overstated, Eagly and Carli (2007) demonstrates the association of female communal style with gains in leader effectiveness but acknowledges that women also suffer some disadvantages from prejudicial evaluations of their competence as leaders, especially in masculine organizational contexts. Their findings suggest that once women break through the glass ceiling, they may experience a leadership advantage relative to men. Specifically, when women succeed in top-level positions, they are more likely to be viewed as highly agentic, and their communal characteristics are more likely to be considered beneficial because of the changing construction of what it means to be a good leader. Effective women leaders not only need to be achievement oriented, competitive, decisive, and independent but also must recognize the importance of building strong relationships, collaborating with others, and taking care of their employees through coaching and development. In other words, when women reach top leadership roles, their very success conveys information that may augment their evaluation. These enhanced evaluations seem to occur because women were perceived to face higher standards than men and were expected to engage in increasingly valued feminized management tactics (Rosette & Tost, 2010).

Public Policy

In recognizing the societal contexts in which leadership is exercised, public policy initiatives reflect opportunities for social change and innovative forms of leadership. The following two examples illustrate how public policy is part of the societal context to which communities respond in creating social change and to which institutions and corporations respond in promoting organizational change and achieving social benefits. It illustrates how public policy can demonstrate effective leadership.

Community Benefits

Former Massachusetts Attorney General, Scott Harshbarger, demonstrated powerful leadership and produced substantive social change when he called on hospitals to report on their voluntary community benefits in 1994. Responding to an ongoing trend of community hospital closures, Harshbarger issued voluntary guidelines that encouraged hospitals to establish community benefit programs and publicly report on those programs on an annual basis. In a state "well known for its efforts to maintain the dominance of not-for-profit health care organizations" (p. 84) and with a longstanding commitment to universal health care access (Katz & Thompson, 1996), this act of leadership was monumental in using public policy to urge hospitals to integrate social responsibility into their business practices for the benefit of underserved racial and ethnic communities.

Although the guidelines were voluntary, Harshbarger gave them added force when he used them to evaluate Columbia/HCA's acquisition of a metropolitan Boston medical center. Not-for-profit organizations were already aware that their tax-exempt status was subject to scrutiny based on their contributions to their communities. When he obtained a commitment from Harvard Pilgrim Health Care managed care organization, during its merger, to spend $3.25 million for education on AIDS, health care for the homeless, and violence prevention, he further expanded its impact, leading to voluntary guidelines for HMOs comparable to those for hospitals in 1996 to address diversity and cultural competence directly; he stated that "The HMO should develop and market products which would attract all segments of the population, and that the HMO should take steps to reduce cultural, linguistic, and physical barriers to accessible health care at key points of patient contact" (Kasprak, 1997, p. 10). No legislative action was required to create these guidelines. Harshbarger's leadership, in a favorable social context, enabled their voluntary implementation in collaboration with hospital and managed care leaders.

Chinese Exclusion Acts

The passing of the Chinese Exclusion Laws by Congress in 1882 reflects a failure of U.S. leadership to guarantee the basic civil rights of Chinese Americans and to discriminate against persons of Chinese descent based solely on their race. Chinese labor immigration to the United States was barred in repeated laws up to 1904, each time imposing increasingly severe restrictions on immigration and naturalization. Although they were repealed in 1943 after more than 60 years, as a war measure after China became a World War II ally of the United States, Congress never expressly acknowledged that the laws singling out and ostracizing Chinese persons violated fundamental civil rights. This anti-Chinese legislation contradicted the Declaration of Independence's basic founding principle that all persons are created equal and the guarantees of the 14th and 15th amendments. Moreover, the Congressional debates accompanying the laws condoned anti-Chinese attitudes by frequently portraying Chinese immigrants as *aliens, not to be trusted with political rights* and not able to assimilate in America. It reflected and reinforced the social zeitgeist against the Chinese, legitimized the political alienation and persecution of Chinese laborers and settlers, affected the ability of Chinese persons to pursue life in America without fear, and impaired the establishment of Chinese family life in America. More than 120 years later, the 1882 Project in 2010 began a campaign to work with Congress to pass resolutions expressing regret for the passage of the Chinese Exclusion Laws, to increase public awareness of the impact of the laws, and for Congress to reaffirm its commitment to protect the civil rights of all people in the United States.

Why is this important to leadership? For almost a century, it shaped the occupations to which Asians could aspire and enter. Few Asians entered the law profession between post WWII to the Civil Rights era of the 1960s because it was viewed as fruitless when you could not win as an Asian in the legal system. The laws served to reinforce social perceptions about Asians and behaviors that deterred their entry to positions of leadership because they were considered a threat to national security. Their status as forever "foreigners" and permanent "aliens" has shaped the perceptions and expectations of their performance.

Golden Dilemmas: Ordinary People Can Become Great Diversity Leaders

Lived experiences amidst the social zeitgeist and one's social status as an out-group member highlight the dilemmas and challenges faced by diverse leaders in exercising leadership. They grapple with dimensions of social identities, which both constrain behavior and create double binds. Not only does this place additional stressors on them but also this leads to biased appraisals of their effectiveness. How to change this dynamic of lived experiences shared among diverse leaders is one of the Big Questions of the day. Leadership is creating one small change that can have a ripple effect to make a difference. As the Baby Boomers retire and age out of the workforce, a new generation of leaders for an increasingly global and diverse society will emerge. Will these new leaders show greater compassion given their lived experiences? Will they strive for social justice goals given the successes of the Civil Rights Movement of the 1960s? Or will they fall hostage to the more "selfish" goals of the Me Generation[1] of the 1980s or the tech savvy Generation X[2] facing change?

Membership in social groups defined by race, ethnicity, sexual orientation, and gender is generally not by choice; nor is deciding that

---

[1] The 1980s was known to many as the Me! generation of status seekers with an emphasis on the self. During the 1980s, hostile takeovers, leveraged buyouts, and mega-mergers spawned a new breed of billionaire—Donald Trump and Leona Helmsley as two examples. The watchwords were: *"If you've got it, flaunt it," "You can have it all!"* The decade began with double-digit inflation, and was known as the spendthrift 80s, fostering binge buying and credit as a way of life. Retrieved from http://kclibrary.lonestar.edu/decade80.html

[2] **Generation X** is the generation born after the Western post-World War II baby boom from the early 1960s to the early 1980s. They experienced the introduction of the personal computer, the start of the video game era, cable television, and the Internet. Their cultural perspectives and political experiences were shaped by: post-assassination of John F. Kennedy, the controversial Vietnam War, Watergate scandal of Nixon's presidency, the Space Shuttle Challenger disaster, the Chernobyl nuclear disaster, the fall of the Berlin Wall and the end of the Cold War, the launch of the Hubble Telescope, the savings and loan crisis, the 1990s economic boom, and the longest recorded expansion of GDP in the history of the United States. It was summarized as "a generation whose worldview is based on change, on the need to combat corruption, dictatorships, abuse, AIDS, a generation in search of human dignity and individual freedom, the need for stability, love, tolerance, and human rights for all."

one's group is the out-group. Privilege associated with membership in the in-group is often invisible. *White privilege* is a term coined to refer to the invisible systems that confer dominance on Whites through being socialized in a racist society, even though none has chosen to be racist or prejudiced (McIntosh, 1989). In the 21st century, there is growing diversity in the social groups of work, family, and leisure. Training in diversity leadership needs to address these issues of privilege and status and how they interact with the exercise of leadership. Moodian (2009) calls this intercultural competence in reconciling dilemmas. He and his colleagues have found a recurring series of *Golden Dilemmas* that provide a basis for diagnosing organizational challenges that owe their origin to cultural differences. Achieving this intercultural competence includes the following: (1) Recognition: How competent is a person to recognize cultural differences around him or her? (2) Respect: How respectful is a person about those differences? (3) Reconciliation: How competent is a person to reconcile cultural differences; and (4) Realization: How competent is a person to realize the actions needed to implement the reconciliation of cultural differences? This reconciliation could involve dealing with different notions of time, which influence scheduling and synchronization in management. It could involve reconciling different views of one's inner and outer worlds or of definitions of self versus other. Only by making these Golden Dilemmas explicit through a reconciliation process does it result in successful leadership. Moodian (2009) views these Golden Dilemmas as universal, but their interpretation and approach are culturally determined. For example, the need for a technology push (what a company can make from its own intellectual capital) versus what the different markets want (what the organization can sell) is one such dilemma. An analysis within a corporation of the time, resources, sales, and so forth takes into consideration the cultural context as an important aspect of the effectiveness of leadership.

Summary

As we redefine leadership, we emphasize that societal and organizational contexts matter. Variations in global and diverse perspectives can be seen in the challenges facing Hong Kong and China today as an example. The handover of Hong Kong back to mainland China, after a century as a British colony, did not erase the influence of British culture, in notable contrast with the rural and communist culture of its motherland, China. The effects of this cultural clash force both Hong Kong and China to address the challenges of diversity, autonomy, and dominance—creating a potential for new models of global leadership.

Variation in cultural orientation value dimensions can help explain miscommunications that can occur between leader and members, failures of leadership, and the need for intercultural competence and fluency. Five cultural orientation value dimensions are important to this process: *universality* of managerial skillsets, use of *power, collectivism* and *individualism, egalitarianism* of masculine and feminine dimensions, and *humane and social responsibility.* In viewing leadership as contextual, we acknowledge how it is shaped by lived experiences along with core values of leaders. This includes the current social zeitgeist with its focus on harnessing technology and promoting intercultural communication. It includes the intersection of race, ethnicity, and gender. It includes the lived experiences of racism, biculturalism, marginalization of nondominant groups, or leading in masculinized contexts; these experiences can force leaders to conform rather than to use their preferred styles, remain as perennial "outsiders," or experience double binds. Given the tendency to form in-groups and out-groups, these societal contexts may pose access barriers to women and racial/ethnic minorities, raise credibility concerns about leaders whose social identities are associated with being members of out-groups, and afford "unearned" privileges to in-group members.

In considering societal contexts, Harshbarger's initiative on community benefits in health care and the 1882 Project against the Chinese Exclusion Act demonstrate the important use of public policy to promote change. Leadership is creating one small change that can have a ripple effect to make a difference. As a new generation of leaders emerge, their challenge will be to formulate the Big Questions and solve the Golden Dilemmas that are universal, but whose interpretation and approach are culturally determined, if they are to be effective leaders in an increasingly global and diverse society.

Discussion Questions: Golden Dilemmas—Social Zeitgeist and Global Contexts

1. Globally, cultures have been characterized as collectivistic versus individualistic with a corresponding emphasis on the group and interpersonal relationships versus on the individual and his or her achievement. Discuss how these orientations might influence the goals and outcomes of leadership.

2. Using the Hong Kong versus China example, think about a situation in which a new racial, ethnic, or cultural group has moved into your neighborhood or community. What are the feelings and reactions you may have? How might it threaten your security, sense of belongingness, identity? Discuss mechanisms for responding to the interactions between groups that might occur.

3. There is an emphasis on transformational and collaborative styles of leadership today. Discuss how the social zeitgeist and the influence of social factors and contexts might have contributed to this.

4. The Masculinity-Femininity dimension has been associated with the gender. Discuss the dilemmas created by the intersections of race, ethnicity, and gender. What might happen when dimensions across identities are incongruent?

5. What leadership styles might be needed during times of crisis? For example, do we need a leader who is confrontational and aggressive? Is this to address concerns of safety by the members, or is it needed to address effectiveness to achieve successful outcomes?

6. Identify a current public policy issue (e.g., gay marriage, violence against women, rights of undocumented immigrants). Discuss some effective leadership strategies to address the issue.

7. Identify what you consider to be a Big Question or Golden Dilemma of leadership today. How would you go about addressing this as a leader?

8. Bicultural or multicultural individuals are often said to be living in two or three different cultural environments. They are often said to have to constantly balance their cultural preferences across different contexts and problematic situations. Identify some problematic situations that might occur for a multicultural or bicultural person. What coping strategies might such a person need to effectively deal with such situations?

9. The term "race" has been eliminated as a means to describe people in many of the sciences because the category is said to be meaningless and restrictive. Identify some reasons why there has been a trend to eliminate use of the term. Are there other ways to describe and differentiate culturally distinct people from one another other than race? Would eliminating use of the term race eliminate "racism"?

10. Homophilous, or tightly knit, homogenous, groups, are often known to restrict their openness to new ideas; that is, they all tend to think the same way. Identify and describe some techniques, procedures, and strategies that you might use to create ideological and behavioral changes in such groups.

8

Applications—Training Culturally Competent and Diverse Leaders

With Contributions From Roger Husbands and
Beauregard Stubblefield-Tave

Notable Quotes on Minority Leadership

Mentorship: "In my mind and in my experience, mentorship for minority leaders is one of the most critical aspects for developing leadership muscles in the Western world." (Black American female leader)

Leadership training: "Our training is intentional for minority leaders. It is about relationships and building a leadership pipeline. It is about mobilizing change and social responsibility. . . . It is not about filling a quota but is about blazing a trail." (Alvin Alvarez, Founder of the Leader Development Institute of the Council of National Psychological Associations for the Advancement of Ethnic Minority Interests)

Vignette on Cultural Competence Awareness Training

"Well, you know all homosexuals are going straight to Hell, right? It says so right in the Bible." When a workshop participant made this comment, I was stunned into silence. After a pause, I replied, "Well, you know there are Christians who don't read the Bible the same way you do. Would you like to share your thoughts with your colleagues?" The participant looked at me as if I'd asked "Would you like to take a trip to Mars?" We were at a break, and it was clear he did not feel safe sharing his views with his colleagues. Was it in response to my listing sexual orientation as a core identity issue rather than a sin (along with age, race/ethnicity, and sex/gender)? Was it that his colleagues had nodded in acknowledgment? I felt as though I had failed in my training objectives; however, it reminded me of two key points: (1) You can only take an individual, or a group, so far during any training session; (2) it would be difficult for others to be safe if he had shared his true feelings; and (3) he did feel safe enough with me to share his views when he knew I would disagree with them. This difficult dialogue is a type of experiential, "Aha!" learning, which is at the heart of cultural competence awareness training. (Beau Stubblefield-Tave, Cultural Imperative Trainer)

In identifying new paradigms and reframing existing theories toward a DLMOX paradigm for diversity leadership, we can look not only at the creation of new knowledge and research about an inclusive and culturally competent leadership framework as discussed in Chapter 3 but also to consider its application for leaders and organizations. Potential and existing leaders can become multiculturally or interculturally competent and culturally fluent regardless of their social identities; however, each group may have some different training needs as well as different lived experiences that they bring to their leadership. The application of principles in this book in promoting a DLMOX paradigm toward the development and training of diverse leaders is discussed in this chapter.

Purpose of Diversity Leadership Training

"Diversity leadership must become a core competency at all levels. . . . An effective leader promotes fairness and equity in the organization . . . and knows how to focus a broadly diverse group to use its members' difference on ways to benefit the mission. . . . It is a learned skill. . . . Providing diversity leadership education is distinct from traditional forms of general diversity training. . . . This requires a fundamental shift in institutional thinking about diversity . . . and the personal and visible commitment of top leaders" (Military Leadership Diversity Commission, 2011). To have the United States support this position is profound within a culture known for its emphasis on conformity and command and control. It supports the implications of this book for developing leadership training that aligns with the principles of diversity. The underlying assumptions, goals and objectives, and training structure of a Diverse Leader-Member-Organizational Exchange Paradigm (DLMOX) proposed in this book are to train leaders to lead in a diverse and global environment. For this to happen, a focus on leadership development and leader self-awareness is first and foremost. Because leaders from minority, marginalized, and underrepresented groups have a different experience, targeted training may be useful for these groups. Because organization cultures vary in their heterogeneity and as to whether or not their missions incorporate diversity as a goal, training needs for organizations may also be different.

We see training as an application of the principles discussed in this book to enable organizations to promote an inclusive, culturally competent culture and environment for all individuals to have access to and be effective in positions of leadership irrespective of the social groups from which they come and for all leaders to incorporate diversity objectives in their exercise of leadership.

Using a diversity leadership or DLMOX paradigm can be applied in very practical ways to build culturally sensitive workplace climates, design new employee orientation programs, conduct programs in relocation training, improve global team effectiveness, and facilitate multinational merger implementation. More inclusive and diverse leadership not only is responsive to growing diversity in the workplace but also promotes innovation and flexibility among work teams.

Understanding issues about diversity, difference, and culture are useful in several ways. First, it can help leaders understand their own cultural biases and preferences as the first step toward understanding that other people in other cultures have different preferences. Second, different cultures have different worldviews, perceptions, and expectations about what they want from their leaders and what it means to be a good leader. Understanding these differences can help leaders adapt their style to be more effective across different cultural settings or to manage the discrepancies that hinder them from being effective. Third, understanding different cultural orientation dimensions can promote more effective communication among diverse leaders across cultural and geographic boundaries. By understanding cultural differences, leaders can become more empathic and accurate in their communication with others.

Training for Culturally Competent Leaders: KSA Model

Global leadership often focuses on cross-cultural relationships where the acknowledgment of difference between equal partners is presumed—that is, between countries, corporations, and businesses. Here, the differences between leaders based on their social identities are explicit. The term *global leadership* is often used when multinational companies send their managers to another country to manage its indigenous workforce. This use and perception of leadership is quite ethnocentric with the term indigenous reserved for the less privileged and "underdeveloped" countries to which managers are sent. As a result, countless examples of cultural miscommunications under these circumstances illuminate the need to be aware that differences do matter and the influence of culture is real. Diversity training of managers under these circumstances has often emphasized learning the basic and more superficial rules and values of the culture.

The term *diverse,* on the other hand, differs from global in its focus on differences within a country, corporation, or group, which may or may not be acknowledged. Inequality between social identity subgroups within the organization also may or may not be acknowledged or may be invisible. When management strategies, viewed as "typical" or universal, are ineffective across these different subgroups, it is easily blamed on "the other" as incompetent, lazy, or unmotivated rather than on the method or process of leadership.

Research has shown consistent and significant differences between Western and Eastern points of view, both in the United States and globally. Many examples of culturally blind business practices lead to miscommunication when leaders impose a structure from their ethnocentric but differing view in cross-cultural and diverse settings. For example, Westerners often misunderstand the spontaneous behavior in Eastern cultures of one taking full responsibility for paying the bill in a restaurant. Easterners nurture the relationship and operate on the principle of unequal exchange as a demonstration of generosity and reciprocity, which evens out in the long term. Westerners, who operate on the principle of equal exchange in the short term, are often unable to understand this concept and end up viewing Easterners as foolish. Easterners, on the other hand, view Westerners who fail to reciprocate as callous and rude. If we contend that culture matters and provides the context for leadership, this could have important ramifications in business negotiations and management practices. In a business negotiation, this could lead to an inability to reach agreement or termination of the relationship. In managing a diverse workforce, this could result in lower productivity because workers feel unappreciated and exploited.

As cultural practices get transplanted through immigration or globalization, it is not uncommon for hybrid cultures to emerge. For example, shifting views of the McDonald's chain restaurant have occurred as it expanded globally. While viewed as "fast food and cheap" in the United States, it is often viewed as "international and modern" in other countries. The reverse occurs in immigrant communities. As immigrants strive to retain their culture post migration, many retain and develop bicultural identities linking their cultures of origin with their acculturation to the new host culture. This dynamic often results in many immigrants viewing conformity to mainstream practices as "selling out" one's identity. This idea of selling out or "acting White" in the United States by persons of color has been described graphically using nicknames such as "apple" for those who are Native American Indian on the outside and White on the inside, "banana" or "Twinkie" for Asian Americans, "coconut" for Pacific Islander Americans, and "Oreo" for African Americans.

Toward this end, the training for culturally competent leaders would address challenges faced by leaders in dealing with a diverse workforce as well as training diverse leaders for the unique challenges faced as a result of their marginalized social identities. Sue, Arredondo, and McDavis (1992) offer a Cross-Cultural Competencies model. Using multidimensional objectives to develop cultural competence based on a Knowledge, Skills, and Awareness model (KSA model) for the training of clinicians, this can be applied to the training of diverse leaders (Moodian, 2009; Connerley & Pedersen, 2005). *Knowledge* is the body of information needed to perform a task—that is, about cultural differences. It includes specific knowledge about racial and cultural heritage, and about how lived experiences affect leaders personally and as leaders. It is the acknowledgment of racist attitudes, beliefs, and feelings as well as the privileges one may have benefited from because of one's social identities. *Skills* are the proficiencies to perform a certain task—that is, skills for cross-cultural communication. It includes seeking out training, development, and consultation experiences to improve understanding and effectiveness cross-culturally. *Awareness* is the sensitivity, affect, and attitudes toward difference and diversity. It includes valuing these differences and being aware of how they influence interaction and communication. It is the ability to recognize the limits of one's competence.

Connerley and Pedersen (2005) expand this model to the training of leaders in a diverse and global multicultural environment. They use training exercises to address stages of intercultural sensitivity going from awareness to knowledge and skills to different challenges faced by diverse leaders.

Developing Culturally Fluent Leaders: Training Applications

Culturally Fluent Leadership is an emerging concept that builds on Cross, Bazron, Dennis, and Isaacs's (1989) continuum of cultural competence, which is defined as "a set of congruent behaviors, attitudes, and policies that come together in a system, agency or among professionals and enables that system, agency, or those professionals to work effectively in cross-cultural situations" (p. iv). Stubblefield-Tave (personal communication, 2013) offers the following working definition: "Culturally fluent leaders use their awareness, skills and knowledge to earn the trust and loyalty of diverse followers in pursuing a shared vision, mission or goal." "Cultural fluency is the ability to move comfortably among cultures from the family culture of home and the ethnic culture of one's community to the educational culture of school and the corporate culture of one's workplace" (Center for Cultural Fluency, n.d.).

The concept is based, in part, on the work of Josefina Campinha-Bacote (2003), who developed the ASK model (Awareness, Skills, Knowledge) to describe a culturally competent clinician and to train clinicians' cultural competence. While the ASK model involves the same terms as the KSA model described above, its varying emphases are different. *Awareness* includes cultural and self-awareness and the in-depth exploration of one's own cultural background as well as that of others. *Skills* includes the cultural skills to perform a task, including cross-cultural communication and the skills to lead cross-cultural teams. *Knowledge* includes not only the acquisition of cultural knowledge but also a process of seeking and obtaining a sound educational foundation about diverse cultural groups.

The ASK model recognizes that no leader can have encyclopedic knowledge of all the cultural groups with whom they interact. The cultural knowledge process may involve "learning just enough of a culture . . . and being able to effectively put this knowledge to work through honed skills specific to the business tasks at hand" (Foster, 2010). Leadership involves the leader working with team members. The Center for Culturally Fluent Leadership (CCFL) (B. Stubblefield-Tave, personal communication, 2013) adds Behaviors to this model to become the BASK model and emphasizes the exchange of behaviors that takes place between leaders and members; it is consistent with the DLMOX paradigm proposed in this book. The concepts of culturally fluent leadership also reflect earlier leadership concepts of Drucker (2013), who emphasizes effective leadership as including (1) thinking through the organization's mission, defining it, and establishing it clearly and visibly—that is, the goals; (2) seeing leadership as a responsibility rather than rank and privilege; and (3) earning the trust of members.

An example from sports illustrates the BASK model. Bill Russell, whose Boston Celtics teams won 11 National Basketball Championships in 13 years, identified 11 Russell Rules as skills-based behaviors of effective leaders (Russell & Falkner, 2001):

1. Commitment Begins with Curiosity

2. Ego = MC^2 (Team Ego Only)

3. Listening is Never Casual

4. Toughness or Tenderness: Creating Your Leadership Style

5. Invisible Man

6. Craftsmanship

7. Personal Integrity

8. Rebounding, or How to Change the Flow of the Game

9. Imagination, or Seeing the Unseeable

10. Discipline, Delegation, and Decision Making

11. Everyone Can Win

These rules became the foundation of CCFL's leadership training program *Leading More Effective Teams: Leveraging the Power of Culturally Fluent Leadership* (B. Stubblefield-Tave, personal communication, 2013). The training asserts that a culturally fluent leader uses feedback loops in order to recognize and respond to cultural differences and shifts—illustrating the rule that *Listening is Never Casual.* According to Russell and Falkner (2001), "when a team is functioning on all cylinders, listening is an essential component of success. . . . Red (Auerbach)'s greatest talent was that he was a listener who translated what he heard into effective action. . . . The key to Red's method was that when he asked a question or wanted to know if you could do something, he did it in such a way that you knew you had room to answer him without feeling threatened" (p. 63–64). In listening, Auerbach (Russell's coach, mentor, and friend) got quality information and understood how to speak with each player to result in decisions and actions that would advance the team's goals: winning games and NBA titles. Auerbach developed the ability to lead individuals from diverse cultural backgrounds and with widely varied personalities, reflecting his ability to live and communicate amidst diversity; he did not need to travel globally; the Celtics brought diversity to him. Accordingly, he used BASK type training exercises to address stages of intercultural competence among team members, including that of managing constructive conflict.

A very different example of culturally fluent leadership in the field of medicine involves the leadership of Lori Arviso Alvord, MD, the first Navajo woman surgeon (Alvord & Cohen Van Pelt, 2000). She describes her ideal operating room as follows:

> My ideal operating room would have a team of people who worked together smoothly and easily, with respect for one another and their patients. Each member, no matter what their rank, would be considered important and invaluable. (p. 128)

Dr. Alvord describes an Awareness of the value each member brings to the team. She brings her technical surgical skills and combines leadership Skills to listen and respond to changes in the patient and her team members. She acquires Knowledge of the cultural backgrounds of her patients and staff on an ongoing basis in the context of completing successful surgery. Dr. Alvord's Behaviors in the operating room leads her team toward a common goal of improving the patient's health. Lisa Arviso Alvord's quote is often used in the CCFL training as an early step in developing culturally fluent leaders to exhibit *cultural humility* (Tervalon & Murray Garcia, 1998) and become lifelong learners. It emphasizes that leaders learn from their team members, from diverse written sources, from customers/patients, peers, mentors, coaches, and others. Culturally fluent leaders may exist in all types of organizations; what defines culturally fluent leaders, however, is their behavior in the context of the teams they lead.

Training Diverse Leaders

Leader Self-Awareness: Self-Assessment

Leader self-assessment is training at the Awareness level using the KSA model and is directed toward awareness of how one's own cultural influences, social identities, and personal lived experiences interact with access to, exercise of, and effective leadership. While awareness of cultural differences and its implications for leadership is an initial step, it is unfortunate that most leadership training stop here as well. There are many components to leader self-awareness. They include the following:

- Assessing one's strengths and weaknesses enables one to harness them to one's advantage. This includes those weaknesses attributed to you based on stereotyped perceptions as well as real ones based on one's core self or one's cultural values, which may be disjunctive with the environment that you lead. How do you harness your strengths and compensate for your weaknesses? Do you recruit others to assist?
- Exploring one's cultural and personal identity structures is vital. Taylor Cox (1993) developed a cultural identity exercise that enables participants to visually identify important elements of their cultural identity and the relative strength of those identity elements. Using a pie chart, individuals divide the elements of their cultural identity into slices according to their relative importance. Based on dozens of focus group discussions and hundreds of interviews with workshop participants, Cox concluded that most individuals have a relatively high awareness of the identity that most distinguishes them from the majority group in a particular setting, and considerably less awareness of their other identities. For example, of 50 one-on-one interviews at a large international company (B. Stubblefield-Tave, personal communication, 2013), 89% of White women focused exclusively on gender, 88% of expatriates focused on nationality, and 78% of non-White men focused on racial/ethnicity of their cultural identities as affecting workplace interactions.

- It is not uncommon for race to account for a larger slice among African Americans while gender often accounts for a larger slice among European American women. Asian American women are likely to have both ethnicity and gender slices as large. Fifty percent of the non-White women in the above example addressed both racial/ethnic and gender issues in their identities speaking to the dominance of White males as the norm. Which of your identities do you bring to your leadership?
- Cultural identity also includes many elements beyond race, ethnicity, and gender, of course. These include employer, nationality, occupation, and religion and may vary with the context. How does your cultural identity structure affect your leadership? Is your pie chart—that is, how you see yourself—significantly different from how others see you?
- Racial/ethnic minorities often acquire a "victim culture" as part of their identities—a stance that often communicates that success is impossible because others are privileged. Stubblefield-Tave (2013) used Cox's Identity Structure exercise to have leaders answer the question: "Who am I?" This is also translated as "What cultural groups do you identify with?" Participants can also be asked to elaborate the question "Who am I?" with personal as well as cultural characteristics: for example, "I am a leader," "I am a father," "I am an optimist," or "I am a victim." Hence, training in leader self-awareness with minority leaders might promote their ability to identify and counter "victim culture" in their organization and community.
- Awareness of opportunities and pitfalls—Identifying what one can or cannot do means taking the environment into consideration. This might include assessing sociocultural trends and the zeitgeist of the external environment. As one leader said, "It was being there at the right time!" It means continually taking stock of the organizational need and organizational culture. Who you are leading? What values and identities do they hold? What is the purpose of the organization is and what is its typical means for getting there? How have individuals who share your cultural background fared within the organization? What can you learn from these experiences, directly or indirectly?
- Making a workable career trajectory plan—This means shaping one's journey and having a plan. What are your leadership goals? How do you establish a plan, develop and monitor shared goals? This plan should align with interests and passion since commitment, motivation, and success follows. This may reflect a particular Western form of leadership development as Chin (2013) has noted that diverse leaders often tend to "fall into the role" or follow the urging of their community, role models, and mentors. For diverse leaders, the task may be how and when to consult with trusted leaders and mentors in the community, as well as how to instill the confidence of having someone believe in you.
- Learning from one's lived experiences—Too often, the personal and relationship aspects of leadership development are overlooked in the interest of "objective" skills needed to become a leader. As emphasized throughout this book, diverse leaders often have different experiences and frequently need to grapple with stereotypic perceptions and expectations from others, which may be biased or unrealistic. It is important that self-awareness includes an assessment of these lived experiences of oppression, marginalized status, immigration, or invisibility.

Leader Skills: Developing Cultural Fluency

Cultural proficiency, the highest level of Terry Cross's continuum of cultural competence, can be defined as the ability to work with, and navigate between and across, diverse cultures fluidly, responsively, and organically. This emphasis on fluidity suggests an interactive and dynamic process. The development of skills and the emphasis on proficiency are consistent with the goals identified in the BASK model described above A leader needs to understand and measure the organization's ability and its members to work effectively in cross-cultural situations, and then to develop the skills to do so. These could include role-playing workplace scenarios involving individuals coming from diverse backgrounds and perspectives. It could involve identifying challenging dilemmas that occur when different perspectives come into play in decision-making situations, or when diverse work teams need to arrive at a common solution.

Leader Knowledge: Dimensions of Cultural Difference

The acquisition of knowledge of cultural difference is both a process and skill. Often the measurement of leadership style or personality style helps a leader know how to lead in different situations. There are a number of psychometric measures that examine personality style or interpersonal or communication styles, often along a two dimensional axis, that are then correlated with how leaders should lead (see Fischer, 2009, pp. 191–201). Key questions that arise for diversity leadership are:

- Do you adapt your style to the expectation of the organization and its members or do you be yourself when there is a mismatch between the two?
- Through what lens do you assess the environmental or organizational context, yours or that of the organizational culture?
- What competencies are developed by virtue of belonging to a socially marginalized group (e.g., racial, ethnicity, women, LGBT, religion)?

Dimensions of Cultural Difference: Leader Skill Sets

Based on the concepts and perspectives presented in this book, especially in Chapter 2, a set of 14 cultural dimensions are identified that have shown cross-cultural cross-group variation and have been shown to influence patterns of leadership behavior. They are presented in no particular order and draw on the extensive cross-cultural literature (Hofstede, 2001; House, Hanges, Javidan, Dorfman, & Gupta, 2004; Trompenaars & Hampden-Turner, 1998). Hofstede (2001), in particular, has developed a set of national profiles characterizing different countries on a number of these dimensions. The GLOBE studies (House et al., 2004) have also identified leadership profiles across 62 different countries. These profiles and dimensions have not been applied to individual or subgroup analysis and can be valuable here for training in self-awareness and skills associated with each of the dimensions. However, one must caution against a simplistic use that might result in stereotypic characterizations of groups and countries. These dimensions overlap with one another and are not dichotomous; they often intersect with one another in complexity. Some are unidimensional while others are bipolar. Individuals, groups, or countries that are high on one end of a bipolar continuum do not imply nonexistence of its polar opposite. The dimensions are also relative in comparing one group to another, and manifestations will vary across different contexts.

The dimensions are useful here to focus on how leadership training can focus on awareness, skills, and knowledge of these dimensions; the dilemmas that arise when leaders with varying styles must interact within teams needing to solve a problem or make a decision; or when leader styles are disparate with member styles or expectations or how they influence the communication process. The dimensions highlight the importance of understanding alternative and multiple perspectives and how diversity leadership training can be important to avoid miscommunication, address power dynamics, and minimize pejorative or biased judgments of behavior.

Power Distance

Power distance (Hofstede, 2001; House et al., 2004) refers to whether individuals accept inequality in power. Low power distance individuals expect equality in power and do not accept a leader's authority based on position. Malaysia, Spain, Japan, and Mexico are high power distance countries while the United States and Denmark are low power distance countries.

Hence, high power distance countries are more respectful based on age, education, and seniority. They use titles, follow protocol, avoid open disagreement with supervisors, and often use silence or not making eye contact to signal disapproval. They often view informality as disrespectful. Low power distance countries are more egalitarian; individuals will speak their mind or will interrupt one another. They often view those acting with formality as having nothing to contribute and unable to lead who are then passed over for leadership roles. This often plays out in the communication.

Uncertainty Avoidance

Uncertainty avoidance (Hofstede, 2001; House et al., 2004) refers to the feeling of comfort or discomfort associated with levels of ambiguity and uncertainty. Low uncertainty avoidance individuals easily tolerate unstructured and unpredictable situations. The fundamental issue here is how a society deals with the fact that the future can never be known: Should we try to control the future or just let it happen? Countries exhibiting strong uncertainty avoidance maintain rigid codes of belief and behavior and are intolerant of unorthodox behavior and ideas. Weak uncertainty avoidance societies maintain a more relaxed attitude in which practice counts more than principles. In leadership situations where problem solving or decision making is needed, tension may arise among team members when there is variation in individual styles on this dimension.

Individualism and Collectivism

Individualism and collectivism (Hofstede, 2001; House et al., 2004) refer to the social frameworks in which individuals prioritize needs. Individualistic societies expect individuals to take care of themselves, while collectivistic societies expect individuals to look out for one another and organizations to protect their employees' interests. Individualism is high in many Western countries, while collectivism is high in many Eastern countries and among ethnic minorities in the United States.

Social interactions in individualistic cultures use a principle of equal exchange—that is, "do your own thing"—whereas social interactions in collectivistic cultures are marked by unequal exchange over a long period; there is a tendency to pursue group goals and pay attention to context and nonverbal cues.

Gender Differentiation

Also known as the masculinity and femininity dimension (Hofstede, 2001; House et al., 2004), this dimension refers to the emphasis of a culture on emotional and social roles and work goals. The masculinity side of this dimension represents a preference in society for achievement, heroism, assertiveness, and material reward for success. Society at large is more competitive. Its opposite, femininity, stands for a preference for cooperation, modesty, caring for the weak, and quality of life. Society at large is more consensus oriented.

This dimension has distinguished Western from Eastern cultures. Perceptions have historically favored the masculine dimension although there is an increasing sense that the feminine dimension is more necessary for 21st century leadership. As discussed earlier, definitions for assertiveness may vary cross-culturally. A feminine culture values relationships, cooperation, and quality of life and may incorporate this into its definition of assertive behavior differently from masculine conceptualizations. Japan, the United States, and Mexico are masculine cultures, while Sweden, Norway, Netherlands, and Denmark are characterized by feminine cultures. This dimension is important to negotiation skills in leadership.

Universalism and Particularism

In universalistic cultures, rules are more important than relationships. Legal contracts are seen as trustworthy and to be honored. Much of business practice in Western countries operates on these principles in negotiations and making business deals. In particularistic cultures, whether a rule applies "depends" on the situation and relationships involved as is true in China and Islamic countries (Trompenaars & Hampden-Turner, 1998). In China, principles of *Ren-Qing* and *Quanxi* make for fluid rules and are often prevailed upon in negotiating a business deal.

Neutral Versus Affective

Individuals in neutral cultures hide their thoughts and feeling while maintaining a cool self-control, as in Asian countries, Germany, and England; individuals in affective cultures express their thoughts openly while using gestures and dramatic expression, often with much passion and touching, as in Latin American countries (Trompenaars & Hampden-Turner, 1998). Without an awareness of these different styles, miscommunication of intent or affect is likely to occur. An Asian or British individual may be viewed as unemotional while a Latino(a) may be viewed as too emotional.

Specific Versus Diffuse

Individuals are direct, clear, blunt, and to the point while examining the facts in specific cultures as in the United States. Individuals are more indirect and tactful in diffuse cultures; they are more able to tolerate ambiguity as in Asian countries (Trompenaars & Hampden-Turner, 1998). Americans, Germans, and Israelis tend to send clear messages; for example, "You can take my words to the bank." Asians and Middle Easterners tend to send messages that include both verbal and nonverbal and direct and indirect components. This is considered more polite and enables someone to save face especially when the message is harsh or negative. They view direct messages as rude while Americans, Germans, and Israelis view indirect messages as evasive, dishonest, and misleading.

Achievement Versus Ascription

In achievement-oriented societies, there is little focus on titles unless they reflect competencies (e.g., Dr., Professor, or Professor Doctor). Leaders are judged on what they do and know. In ascribed status societies, titles are important; leaders with authority are usually older males; the boss is "the boss" (Trompenaars & Hampden-Turner, 1998). When this overlaps with a humane orientation, achievement may not always be considered in individualistic and egoistic terms, as it is in most Western cultures, but constitutes a strong social concern rather than a matter of individual striving and competition (Agarwal & Misra, 1986). The misunderstanding that may occur is when an individual from an achievement-oriented society denigrates a leader while an individual from an ascribed status society will accord the same leader respect by virtue of his or her status even when both may hold the same view of the leader's competence.

Attitudes Toward Time Control

Whether one perceives his or her ability to control time is related to one's time orientation about the past, present, or future (Kluckhohn & Strodtbeck, 1961; Trompenaars & Hampden-Turner, 1998). It affects how a culture values time and believes it can control it. Americans are oriented toward the future. This is the result of many things, including the relatively short time the United States has been in existence and immigration patterns, which have made for short histories of different groups in the country. Indians are oriented toward the past. This causes India to be focused on traditions and long-term commitments. In business practices, Indians are less understanding of the Americans' emphasis of being on time; they are likely to miss deadlines and be late for meetings. This affects the emphasis on speed in business whereby most large U.S. organizations maintain an absolute focus on quarterly profits. Most decisions are based on results rather than relationships. In cultures like India where relationships matter, longer term orientation abounds. Life is viewed as an ongoing cycle where influences from the past explain the current situation and the present is only a result of past action and cannot be controlled (Moore, 2006).

In cultures where time is fixed, time and structure are precise; schedules are maintained; meetings start and end on time. Those who are late are considered disrespectful, rude, and unprofessional. This is noted in American and German cultures. In cultures where time is fluid, time is loosely organized. People simply wait; they are willing to let a meeting run longer if business is not completed. They are more concerned about the relationship. They open meetings by getting to know people before starting business.

This is noted in Native American Indian and Latin cultures. They believe that those who have fixed time should relax.

Internal Versus External Control

Internal versus external control (Kluckhohn & Strodtbeck, 1961; Trompenaars & Hampden-Turner, 1998) involves subjugation and domination in the sense of one being able to control what happens in the environment and whether one sees that control as coming from within oneself or external in the environment. It is also viewed as people's relationship to nature. The Japanese culture's relationship with nature is that of harmony with nature. The Japanese people respect nature and don't attempt to manage or control nature. Instead, they feel a spiritual bond with nature evident in practices such as Japanese gardening and the simplicity of rock gardens, which date back to the beliefs of the ancient Shinto religion in Japan. This harmony with nature and the environment is similarly found in Native Hawaiian and Native American Indian cultures.

In contrast, the American culture does not live in harmony with nature but rather attempts to master nature. This is evident in how it responds to natural phenomena such as hurricanes; people try to manage and protect themselves and their belongings by boarding up their houses, taping windows, moving furniture, and evacuating. It is also reflected in its architectural planning of changing the landscape to accommodate man-made structures. This orientation leads to differences in how different groups accept certain projects in business planning and development.

Assertiveness

Assertiveness (House et al., 2004) refers to the extent a society encourages individuals to be tough, confrontational, assertive, and competitive compared to low assertive societies, which encourage individuals to be modest and tender. Germany and Austria are high assertive countries that value competition compared to New Zealand and Sweden, which value warm and cooperative relations and harmony. As discussed earlier, Asian American groups, often defined as low assertive, may maintain different rationale and definitions of assertiveness related to purpose and outcomes intended by their behaviors—that is, using indirect methods to maintain a relationship while achieving an assertive outcome. This dimension also leads to much miscommunication because of pejorative attributions to low assertive behaviors and negative appraisals of behaviors that do not fit in with characteristics of being confrontational and competitive. Cultures that value warm and cooperative relations and harmony often perceive this form of assertiveness as rude and ruthless. Whereas women have been viewed to be less assertive than men, early assertiveness training focused on teaching them to behave like men; today's assertiveness training would focus on how to make one's point or achieve one's goal without sacrificing the relationship or forcing one's opponent to "lose face."

Future Orientation

Future orientation (House et al., 2004) refers to the level of importance a society attaches to future-oriented behaviors such as planning, investing, and delaying gratification. A future orientation according to GLOBE findings is "the extent to which members of a society or an organization believe that their current actions will influence their future, focus on investment in their future, believe that they will have a future that matters, believe in planning for developing their future, and look far into the future for assessing the effects of their current actions" (Ashkanasy, Gupta, Mayfield, & Trevor-Roberts, 2004, p. 285). Singapore and Switzerland are high on future orientation signified by their propensity to save for the future and longer time horizon for decision making. Russia and Argentina have shorter time horizons for decisions and place more emphasis on immediate gratification. This is an important aspect of strategic planning for a leader or organization.

The long-term orientation dimension can also be interpreted as dealing with society's search for virtue. Societies with a short-term orientation generally have a strong concern with establishing the absolute Truth. They are normative in their thinking. They exhibit great respect for traditions, a relatively small propensity to save for the future, and a focus on achieving quick results. In societies with a long-term orientation, people believe that truth depends very much on situation, context, and time. They show an ability to adapt traditions to changed conditions, a strong propensity to save and invest, thriftiness, and perseverance in achieving results (Hofstede, 2001).

Performance Orientation

Performance orientation (House et al., 2004) measures the degree to which a society encourages and rewards individuals for performance improvement and excellence. Singapore, Hong Kong, and the United States score high, reflecting the value of training, development, and initiative taking compared with Russia, Italy, and Argentina who score low, reflecting an emphasis on loyalty and belonging. In the latter, family background is more important than performance.

Humane Orientation

Humane orientation (House et al., 2004) measures the extent to which a society encourages and rewards people for being fair, caring, generous, altruistic, and kind. The Philippines, Ireland, Malaysia, and Egypt scored highest on this dimension reflecting a focus on sympathy and support for the weak. Spain, France, and former West Germany scored lowest on this dimension reflecting the importance given to power, material possessions, and self-enhancement. This orientation, in particular, contrasts with charismatic and transformational orientations in which a leader draws on the prominence of his or her personality to influence and motivate people to change. A humane orientation aligns with social justice goals, self-sacrificing behavior, and role modeling as ways to motivate members to change. Increasingly, this orientation is important to 21st century leadership. A question might be whether this is a skill that can be learned, or is it an orientation one must have?

Targeted Training Models

The specific challenges and needs of subgroups, minority groups, or outgroups that have historically faced biases or disadvantages in accessing leadership roles may call for targeted training. Several examples below demonstrate how an emphasis on the challenges faced by women, racial/ethnic minorities, and Asian Americans can be empowering in developing pipelines to leadership and enabling leaders to become more effective. They arose out of the felt need for targeted training, and that existing leadership training institutes omitted a dimension central to their experience. The process and structure of these training institutes enable specific groups to address challenges that arise out of microaggressions, bias, ignorance, or a lack of commitment to diversity, and to negotiate their leadership from a position of strength, to avoid miscommunications, to develop awareness of stereotyped perceptions and expectations, and to learn leadership skills in a safe and trusted environment.

Leadership Institute for Women in Psychology (LIWP): Training Women Leaders

"When the baby boomer exodus does ramp up, more female executives will necessarily have to backfill those positions. Proper experience and training must be ensured, but thus far many programs are focused on fixing women to play the man's game," as stated in "Taking Gender Into Account: Theory and Design for Women's Leadership Development Program" (Cooke, 2013). The article noted research that found, among graduates of top business schools, women's career trajectory was not on par with the men's, and females' advancement in their careers has even slowed in recent years. Rather than jamming a round peg in a square hole, the article suggests "providing tools for leaders to do what the author called the 'identity work' to become leaders by internalizing that identity and developing an elevated sense of purpose. . . . Twice as many women than men launch startups. They're looking to carve out their own destiny and want to be in charge. Korn/Ferry International surveyed women who left careers to strike out on their own and found that 40% cited lack of advancement and 43% stated lack of recognition were key factors. Another 48% said they were turned off by the corporate politicking" (Cooke, 2013).

The Leadership Institute for Women in Psychology (LIWP) sponsored by the American Psychological Association's Women's Office has as its mission to prepare, support, and empower women psychologists as leaders to promote positive changes in institutional, organizational, and practice settings as well as APA and SPTA (State, Provincial and Territorial Psychological Associations) governance, and increase the diversity, number, and effectiveness of women psychologists as leaders. A major focus of the Institute is to ensure that leadership training opportunities are available for mid-career and senior women psychologists in all their diversities. Institute objectives include (1) ensuring that mid-career and senior women in psychology have the knowledge and skills necessary to compete for leadership/senior management positions, (2) enhancing the number and effectiveness of women psychologists holding leadership positions, (3) increasing the diversity of women psychologists in leadership positions, (4) creating networks of women psychologists in leadership/senior management positions, and (5) documenting the career movement, professional advancement of LIWP participants (APA, n.d.).

The education and training component of LIWP is represented by highly interactive case-based workshops held twice a year and by the Webinars held bimonthly on leadership development topics. A research component includes surveying the leadership training needs of LIWP participants. Specific topics include strategic planning, negotiation skills and strategies, leadership goal setting, mentoring, and self-care. Activities that make the institute unique and relevant to women leaders are: self-assessment using the FIRO-B with opportunities for networking, small group discussion drawing on the lived experiences of the faculty of women leaders, and developing an elevator speech.

CNPAAEMI Leadership Development Institute: Training Racial and Ethnic Minority Leaders

The Council of National Psychology Associations for the Advancement of Ethnic Minority (CNPAAEMI) Leadership Development Institute (LDI) developed out of a coalition of national professional psychological associations for Asian Americans, Black Americans, Latino Americans, and Native American Indians who saw the need for targeted leadership training for psychologists of color. Few existing theories of leadership delve meaningfully into the effects of culture, worldview, out-group perspectives, or other such factors important to leaders of color. The LDI, therefore, aims to identify and attract racially and ethnically diverse psychologists and mental health professionals to foster and support culturally grounded leadership skills that are transferable to multiple settings (e.g., families, work settings, professional organizations, neighborhoods, communities) and to establish networking and sustainable coaching and mentoring opportunities to nurture ongoing leadership development.

Begun in 2012, a cohort of eight Fellows was identified to be matched with a primary mentor for a yearlong training experience. This included two hours of mentoring per month for one year, working with a primary mentor from one's home CNPAAEMI's organization and a secondary mentor from another CNPAAEMI organization, bimonthly facilitated discussions with other Fellows throughout the year led by one of the mentors, and monthly conversations among the Fellows on their leadership project. Fellow responsibilities include developing a personal leadership plan for a project, addressing a current leadership issue in the host organization, peer mentoring, and producing a final report.

Training topics include the following:

- Strategies for Using Mentoring Successfully
- Defining the Role of a Mentor Cross-Culturally
- Establishing Professional Goals
- Making a Workable Career Trajectory Plan
- Early Career Development
- Negotiating Institutional/Political Systems
- Self-care for Healthcare Professionals
- Successful Bids for Leadership Positions
- Upward Mobility Time Management Strategies
- Developing Your Leadership Niche in the Field
- Networking and Developing Collaborative Partnerships
- Paying it Forward: Mentoring Others

These topics and the initial orientation focused on models of leadership competencies relevant to leaders of color. A central feature of the LDI rests on the relationship between Fellows and their Mentors. Their monthly meetings were critical in exposing the Fellow to a leader within the field and the process of leadership as a person of color as well as exposing the Fellow to organizational cultures and leadership opportunities within the field. The Leadership project is intended to develop a culturally grounded model of leadership competencies. One project involved interviewing leaders to provide grounded research and case studies about diversity leadership. Another important objective of the LDI is to foster coalition building across ethnic minority psychological associations and to provide Fellows with insights into various models of organizational leadership. For this purpose, Fellows met with a secondary mentor outside of their home organization on a regular basis.

LEAP: Training Asian American Leaders

In 1982, Leadership Education for Asian Pacifics, Inc. (LEAP) was established to address the lack of API leadership representation across the private, public, and nonprofit sectors. Through LEAP, its founders hoped to create an environment where APIs could develop leadership skills, realize their full leadership potential, and assume visible leadership roles that would impact the larger society. LEAP embarked on a plan both to increase the number of API leaders as well as to train those leaders to be more effective in their work (Atsutakawa, 2013).

LEAP's original programming began with awareness and skills building workshops and symposia featuring prominent API civic and community leaders. While the initial intent of LEAP's founders was to expand the pool of community leaders, they were surprised to find that their leadership training was attracting not only API nonprofit staff and community volunteers but also large numbers of APIs in corporate, government, and higher education jobs who were frustrated with the lack of advancement and leadership opportunities. Repeated stories and experiences of the "glass ceiling" or "bamboo ceiling" effect led LEAP to expand its training and definition of "community" when it realized that the model minority myth, combined with cultural misunderstanding, racism, and ignorance severely hobbled Asian Americans in the mainstream and prevented them from fuller economic, social, and political participation (U.S. Department of Labor, 1991). The "bamboo ceiling" refers to the barriers that serve to exclude Asians and Asian Americans from executive positions based on biased and stereotypic perceptions of "lack of leadership potential" and "lack of communication skills" that cannot actually be explained by job performance or qualifications. It is a derivative of the term "glass ceiling," which refers to the more gendered metaphor used to describe invisible barriers through which women and minorities can see managerial positions but cannot reach them. By the mid-1980s, LEAP had expanded its focus to encompass API advancement in all sectors—public, private, nonprofit—and across interest areas such as education, civic and government, youth and students, first in Southern California and, by the end of the 1980s, had expanded across the country.

Through the creation of culturally relevant workshops and programs, more than 125,000 people from colleges and universities, community and student organizations, federal and state government agencies, and Fortune 1000 companies across North America and Asia have participated in over 2,500 leadership development programs, organizational development workshops, career management, and diversity trainings. LEAP found it essential to create programming in which Asian American participants can speak freely without fear of being judged, where they can build self-awareness and confidence, while learning new skills. LEAP strives to create an atmosphere that allows participants to feel confident about asking honest questions, sharing experiences, and giving opinions without feeling like they must constantly be explaining, defending, or justifying themselves. In other words, effective Asian American leadership development demands that we release participants from the burden of constantly having to perform cultural translation. With the leadership philosophy "Keep your values. Develop new skills™.", LEAP focuses on trying to show Asian American would-be leaders that they can retain their culture, identity, and values while, at the same time, developing skills necessary to become effective leaders within their organizations, communities, and broader society.

Multicultural and Global Leader Dilemmas

Using the cultural dimensions identified above, we might examine how they influence common leadership competencies and dilemmas. Training leaders to lead in a diverse multicultural and global environment is aligned with broad social goals of valuing diversity as not only good for business but also promoting a harmonious diverse and global society. Is is aligned with diversity principles of inclusion, including both in-group and out-group members, privileged and oppressed groups, majority and minority groups to ensure that leaders are interculturally fluent. Targeted training for diverse leaders and historical "out-groups" has as an additional goal the ability to address the challenges of incongruities between one's lived experiences and that of their members' identities, or the incongruities between one's social identities and "typical" leader prototypes.

Self-Awareness: Identity

The dilemma of deciding "Who am I?" or one's self-identity can be challenging when leaders need to decide when and how to conform to organizational and member perceptions and expectations. Exercises and activities asking leaders to define: "Who are you?" address this dimension. They are intended to promote awareness of social identities and how they influence leader behaviors and member perceptions. Leaders need to decide in what situations and contexts must they adapt or conform to organizational and member values to be effective, and at what cost. This raises the added dilemma of how leaders use a moral compass to ensure that they maintain their authenticity and conduct themselves ethically as leaders. It is a process of continuous development.

Image Management

While managing one's image can appear superficial and disingenuous, it is a dilemma to decide when and if one needs to do so. Competency at this level starts with an awareness of how social identities can constrain leadership behavior or bias appraisals of leader effectiveness and competence. Leaders need to decide when to align the image one communicates with what members expect. Contrary to popular belief, these are specific skills that can be taught by identifying concrete ways of dress and self presentation. Often, this is more important for first impressions when one's competence is usually unknown. It is also important to recognize how and what physical presentations (within one's control) align with attributions of leader power, influence, status, and legitimacy held by members. Image management intersects with social identities, which can be a distraction in communicating one's leadership. How a leader manages the benefits of using one's privilege or disadvantage to overcome stereotypic expectations can be useful.

Proper attire, tone of voice, and pitch of voice are important conveyers of image. While seemingly superficial, these visible images often convey the first impressions of a leader's credibility and competence. Attention to one's image enables one to make a choice about when to display one's ethnic and cultural ways. For example, should one wear ethnic garb and ornaments? Is it "to make a statement" or is it simply "who I am"? Will it "distract from one's competence as a leader" by invoking stereotypic perceptions and expectations or will it convey a distinct sense of self?

Business etiquette is generally governed by social rules of decorum that differ cross-culturally. These include such rituals as greetings on meeting one another, which range from a bow to a handshake. Religious sensitivities may also dictate different rituals for addressing women. The exchange of business cards is another ritual that is much more formal in Asian countries; proper decorum and respect is accorded in presenting cards with both hands and having the words facing the receiver; the receiver is expected to do this in return and to read the card before putting it away. The accepting or refusing of refreshments also follows cultural rules of etiquette that include initial refusal by a guest and insistence by the host as a form of politeness in Asian and Middle Eastern cultures. Hostess gifts, which may involve food, is considered a necessity and often expected in Asian cultures. In learning and observing these rules of etiquette, the biggest challenge is how to present an authentic self while managing one's image in a way to project a leaderful image.

Negotiation

Negotiation is one of the necessary tasks of leadership and helps people achieve goals and resolve problems. It is a process involving two parties or groups to resolve matters of dispute by holding discussions and coming to a mutual agreement between the parties. This can involve a course of action, a bargaining position, or a desired outcome. Often, negotiation involves winning and losing, competition and cooperation, aggressive and passive behavior, direct and indirect behaviors (both verbal and nonverbal). Every negotiation takes places within the context of a relationship, in which each party has something of value to offer.

Two common negotiation styles are cooperation and competition; the latter is more common in Western cultures while the former is more common in Eastern cultures. While legal contracts are often the outcome of negotiation in Western cultures to represent what is mutually agreed to, leaders from Eastern cultures often approach negotiation and international trading based not on legal contracts but on trust and family ties. This dynamic also plays out in the employer-employee relationships in the workplace, where employees from Eastern cultures often expect their bosses and leaders to have their interests in hand and may be less likely to ask for accommodations, promotions, and raises.

Women are found to negotiate less often based on their tendency toward cooperation. They are more likely to ask for less particularly on salary and promotion, to set lower targets, and to settle for less than what they want. Women find negotiation more appealing when it becomes more collaborative. They need to capitalize on this as strengths of their emotional intelligence, listening skills, and tendency toward cooperation. They need to aim higher and be more specific in what they want. Men, on the other hand, tend to assert their needs more often, are more oriented toward affirming their status, and are more comfortable negotiating such issues as salary and promotion.

Several key negotiation strategies include the following: Avoidance, Compromise, Accommodate, Competing to win, and Collaborating to problem solve. Successful negotiation involves being clear about: What do you really want to get out of the negotiation? It involves a focus on the goals versus the bottom line and an assessment of what you think the other party wants out of the negotiation. Westerners and Easterners often differ in their response to these questions. In negotiation, Westerners often view that "It's not personal; it's business" while Easterners often view that "The relationship is what matters." Hence, there is value in exploring diverse perspectives and cultural dimensions when negotiating to solve complex problems. A keen awareness of cultural differences will avoid potential misunderstandings.

Communication

Leadership is a process of influence and communication. There are both formal and informal ways in which communication occurs. British rely mostly on formal communication while Chinese rely on face to face or are more relationship oriented. Japanese styles are also noted to be formal and follow more strict protocols. Often, underlying cultural value dimensions dictate these modes of communication and can result in misunderstanding. Communication has three goals: instrumental goals (performing tasks), relational goals (negotiating conflict), and identity management (self-image). Whereas different cultures may place varying emphasis on each of these dimensions, cross-cultural communication and miscommunication can be challenging when original intent of a person is different from the meaning received by another person. Nonverbal communication, including the use of facial expression and posture, is known to communicate meaning and to vary cross-culturally. The use of physical structure has been used to communicate power and status in different cultures. For example, King Arthur and the knights of the round table were designed to signal equality while the Chinese Temple of Heaven and Imperial palace in Beijing used concentric circles of importance with the highest ranking leader seated facing the main entrance in a round table with descending order on his or her right or left.

Decision Making

The main finding of decision-making style in eight countries with widely differing orientations as to level of subordinate participation in decision making was that 75% of managers used "consultative-participative" means to reach their decisions—that is, in consultation or jointly with their subordinates. While differences existed, they were not statistically different except for the extremes; Swedish managers were low while Israeli managers were high on centralized, authoritarian decision making. When the context was competitive within a similar worldwide task environment where organizational characteristics (of size and technology) and sociocultural backgrounds of industrial countries were relatively similar, there tended to be more homogeneity and convergence of leadership styles on decision making (Kao, Sinha, & Wilpert, 1999). Hence, decision making is dependent on an optimal fit between managerial style and organizational and sociocultural environments.

In the United States, women leaders are found to use a more collaborative style of decision making in line with their emphasis on relationships and consensus building. However, within masculinized contexts, this decision-making style has been viewed as weak and indecisive. Hence, it may explain why many women tend toward more androgynous styles of leadership.

Problem Solving and Managing Conflict

Conflict is any situation where incompatible goals, attitudes, emotions, or behaviors lead to disagreement or opposition between two members. In multicultural organizations, cultural differences add to the potential for conflict. While conflict can lead to innovation, stimulate creativity, and solutions to problems, conflict can also divert energy from work, waste resources, create a negative climate, affect productivity, and lead to hostility and aggressive behavior (Nelson & Campbell Quick, 2003). Thomas (1976) uses five conflict-handling orientations according to an individual's desire to satisfy his or her own or other's concerns; he orders these along a continuum of assertiveness and intersecting continuum of cooperation. Competing styles are characterized by assertive and uncooperative behavior and collaborating strategies as win-win for both assertive and cooperative behavior. Avoiding and accommodating styles are both unassertive but uncooperative and cooperative, respectively. Compromising is in between.

It was noteworthy that Asians preferred the avoiding and accommodating styles while expatriates from the United States and Canada preferred the competing, collaborating, and compromising styles (McKenna, 1995). A qualitative follow up suggested that Asian participants felt Americans would often "shout first and ask questions later," which they saw as arrogant; Americans, on the other hand, felt Asians were timid and unassertive while their goal was to "get things out in the open." The example points to the bias inherent in Thomas's model, which is based on a view from individualistic cultures. Individuals from collectivistic cultures such as China also value preserving the relationship and are more likely to avoid conflicts; or they may be more inclined to compromise and accommodate as a way of showing concern for the outcome of others in their problem solving styles. Hence, they view the American respondents as selfish and only interested in their own outcomes (Connerley & Pedersen, 2005, pp. 131–132). This example calls for complexity in evaluating responses in the context of culture.

Work Culture

Japanese management styles were notable after the rapid rise of Japan to become one of the most industrially advanced countries in the world post WWII. Without abandoning its traditional social values and cultural characteristics, work attitudes and values rooted in Confucian social philosophy became embedded in Japanese management styles and work culture (Kao, Sinha, & Wilpert, 1999). This included a synergistic blend of traditional indigenous roots and modern techniques as Japan sought to catch up with the rest of the world. The emphasis on groupism and on "li" or propriety of the social rules and obligations that bound the relationships between worker and manager or leader and follower characterized the work culture as important offshoots of Confucian philosophy.

Japanese *bushido,* or spirit, defined as refinement toward enlightenment, included Zen principles of realizing one's own potential, and Buddhist principles emphasizing self-reliance, self-discipline, and self-perfection leading to a calm trust in fate, submission to the inevitable, and stoic endurance and composure in the face of danger—a concept embodied in the Samurai warrior. It is shaped by feudal values of group loyalty, commitment to duty, honor, and group harmony. Japanese employees have to be loyal to their companies and bosses for the sake of the business and to safeguard their jobs. In return, they expect their employers to be paternalistic in protecting them and offer a sense of belonging, guaranteeing lifelong employment.

This contrasts with the American emphasis on *rugged individualism,* first coined by President Herbert Hoover in 1928. It is the practice of individualism in social and economic relations emphasizing personal liberty and independence free from government intervention, self-reliance, resourcefulness, self-direction of the individual, and free competition in enterprise.

While both concepts focus on the individual, Japanese *bushido* has, as its goal, reaching enlightenment and group harmony while American *rugged individualism* has, as its goal, free competition with others. The concepts capture the different work culture characteristics, respectively. In the United States, people typically work from 9:00 to 5:00 for a total of 8 hours. This is not true in Japan and other countries where a typical workday might be 9:00 to 9:00 for a total of 12 hours, although this is beginning to change as the social factors contributing to their existence change. While Japanese *bushido* led to a work ethic in Japan that was once praised for digging Japan out of the post WWII rubble to a world superpower, it is now blamed for destroying employees' lives.

The examples provide a context for how work cultures may be shaped by the cultural values held by members within the organization, the organization's values and mission, or the sociopolitical trends shaping the organizational context. Hence in the 21st century, emphasis on work-family balance is now prominent, especially as more women enter the workforce. The overworked males of the past working long hours striving for career advancement and leadership positions are replaced by dual couple careers who share the burden of child care, homemaking, and caretaker as well as bringing in the family income. Hence, the emphasis on work cultures is now toward family friendly environments with flexible work schedule options, work-sponsored day care, and more generous family life benefits. Emphasis is now greater on self-care.

Team Building: Leading Global Teams

Diversity brings innovation to a team. Diverse thinkers help a team think out of the box and bring in different perspectives for more creative solutions. At the same time, diversity can create conflict as teams negotiate their differences. Team building is a process and goes through stages involving group dynamics. With diverse teams, the leader or facilitator might often have to address underlying hostilities and prejudices associated with different social identities, orientations, and styles; these often are unconscious or taboo.

In leading or building global teams, self-awareness and cultural competence becomes paramount. When organizations focus on expanding market and opportunities globally, they need focus on how to incorporate culture and customs when trying to market to a local population that is not their own. Leaders must learn about communication styles, attitudes toward meetings and deadlines, even the very notion of what makes a good leader in a given culture before entering into business negotiations cross culturally or within minority communities.

Summary

In identifying new paradigms and reframing existing theories toward a DLMOX paradigm for diversity leadership, we can consider its application for training leaders. Using a KSA model to train leaders, we emphasize diversity, difference, and culture. It is a process for leaders to understand their own cultural biases, to adapt their leadership styles to be more effective across different contexts, and to learn more effective means of communicating across cultures and subgroups—that is, to train culturally fluent leaders. Central features of diversity training include *Awareness*—for leaders and organizations to understand the influences of culture, social identities, and lived experiences on leadership, and to recognize opportunities and pitfalls; *Skills*—for leaders to develop cultural fluency to navigate between and across cultures fluidly and responsively; and *Knowledge,* which might include psychometric measures to examine and identify personality styles and strengths and weaknesses for effective leadership. The fourteen cultural orientation value dimensions identified can be useful as the content of leadership training as leaders need to negotiate with those holding different cultural orientation values. Potential incongruities between a leaders' social identities and leader identities raise additional dilemmas. Targeted training, such as those focused on women or minorities, to address specific challenges and needs of these subgroups, or designing training to address the eight multicultural and global dilemmas that are identified addresses this. Racial minority leaders may face greater challenges with image management given how social identities can constrain leadership behavior or bias appraisal of leader effectiveness and competence. Leaders with differing cultural values regarding cooperation and competition may face greater challenges with negotiation processes and conflict management. Gender differences in preferred modes of communication may create misunderstanding and conflict.

Discussion Questions: Applications to Training Diverse Leaders and Practicing DLMOX Leadership

1. Using the 14 dimensions of cultural difference, identify some scenarios where you and someone else are approaching a problem or decision from opposite perspectives. How might you reconcile this?

2. Should a leader adapt his or her leadership style to conform to the organizational context? Is this possible or should a leader leave the organization?

3. Identify some of the differences and similarities between training targeting all leaders and those targeting racial/ethnic minority leaders. Develop a list of skills that you would include in a targeted training.

4. Using the multicultural and global dilemmas, identify a dilemma you may have faced in your organization. Have a group discussion on developing some solutions to managing these dilemmas.

5. Identify several characteristics of vertical and horizontal collectivism. Then identify some culturally based values that might be aligned with one or the other dimensions. Can the same discussion be applied to vertical and horizontal aspects of individualism, and if so how?

6. Discuss the *national character* concept. Is it useful to capture common characteristics of a group or does it simply result in stereotypes? Does it have at least some practical validity?

7. U.S. culture is commonly associated with individualism. What percentage of the population would fit this description? In deriving your estimate, factor the following considerations: Most people in the United States enjoy individual freedom; there are more individualist than collectivist features in the U.S. culture; individualists influence the level of power distance; and individualists influence the level of uncertainty avoidance. Provide brief descriptions for each factor and provide a rationale for your description and response.

8. Consider the following list of considerations. In most traditional cultures social roles are prescribed individuals, there is a clear distinction between good and evil in behavior, individuals' choices are restricted to the boundaries of social perceptions, and truth is revealed through the competition of ideas. Is it possible that all or some of these considerations are truly applicable to traditional societies? Justify your answer and in so doing provide examples based on your knowledge of such cultures.

9. Discuss why some people in nondemocratic countries believe that authoritarian leaders are "good" for these countries?

10. As discussed in this chapter, considerable attention has been given to describing cultures on the basis of a collective-individual continuum. In considering the extreme poles of the continuum, is it possible that there are cultures that truly fit the extremes? In your reply, provide illustrations of how that might be possible and what the characteristics might be.

9

Applications—Training Culturally Competent Organizations

**With Contributions From Roger Husbands and
Beauregard Stubblefield-Tave**

Vignette: On Making Change

"There had been a heavy snowstorm. I was cold getting to work. As my women colleagues huddled together to discuss the weather, I announced that I was going to wear pants in the next day. There was awe and shock that I would violate the skirt dress code and social norm for women in the 1970s where the leadership was all men. When I arrived in pants the next day, all the women stood around observing in silence, expecting me to be disciplined or sent home. Well, nothing happened! This small act of defiance led the women to begin to wear pants to work, at their choice, from that day on within the organization." (Jean Lau Chin)

In identifying new paradigms and reframing existing theories toward a DLMOX paradigm for diversity leadership, the creation of new knowledge and research about an inclusive and culturally competent leadership framework as discussed in Chapter 3 can also be applied toward training organizations to be culturally competent. This assumes organizational change as well as the developing and transforming of organizational cultures to become diverse and multiculturally competent. This generally requires buy-in at the top by an organization's leaders and the creation of an organization's climate receptive to the goal of diversity in order to be successful.

Training for Culturally Competent Organizations: SWOT Analysis

Culturally competent leadership training and development requires a shift in one's ethnocentric perspective; one that begins with an awareness of cultural differences but is not judgmental. Moodian (2009) describes this as an envisioning process for both leaders and organizations and identifies a paradigm for how organizations address diversity. Several paradigms currently in use are problematic. A *Discrimination and Fairness paradigm* emphasizes recruitment, retention, advancement, and mentoring of ethnic minority staff toward compliance with Affirmation Action goals. It is problematic because its focus is on achieving number targets and does not consider what ethnic minority members bring to the organization. The *Access and Legitimacy paradigm* has, as its goal, matching organizational demographics to those of constituent groups. This generally involves the strategy of hiring ethnic minority staff to target the constituent group as a market niche. It is problematic because it can be exploitive such as when cigarette companies began targeting ethnic communities, when their markets in White communities began to shrink. The *Learning and Effectiveness paradigm* values the personal and cultural experiences of their members and what they bring to the core institutional culture. It does not necessarily promote changes to the core business of the organizational culture.

Moodian (2009) proposes an *Envisioning and Transcending paradigm,* which commits to the envisioning process of diversity as a potential strength, a culturally inclusive climate, equity, and cultural accommodation as organizational goals. There are four levels of organizational engagement. These include (1) stages of compliance (doing something because you have to), (2) normalization (accepting it as normal), (3) utilization (using it positively in the workplace), and (4) maximization (harnessing the value that it brings).

Applying an organization to a Strengths, Weaknesses, Opportunities, and Threats (SWOT) analysis is commonly used to identify and establish a plan with goals, objectives, and action steps. Using Moodian's *Envisioning and Transcending paradigm* as a framework, organizations can assess the different levels or different developmental stages it is at with regard to diversity. Additionally, an organization can assess its composition, as defined in Chapter 6, as to its degree of homogeneity or heterogeneity or its mission as to whom its business is targeted or reaches.

Managing Diversity as Organizational Change

In addition to training diverse leaders or training leaders to be more diverse, it is also important to address as a goal, managing diversity as organizational change. It means training for organizational change—to promote a diverse multicultural and global environment with broad social goals aligned with valuing diversity as good for business and promoting a harmonious diverse and global society. It means having a diverse workforce, diverse clientele and business. It means an awareness of the bias and ethnocentrism that shape attitudes and create barriers to doing business, offering quality products and services, or marginalize and disadvantage outgroups and minority groups based on dimensions of diversity.

The Three Cs of Managing Diversity: Composition-Core-Climate

Managing organizational diversity starts with developing an organization's strategic planning to be inclusive of diversity and directed toward organizational and systemic change. It presumes a commitment to goals of diversity leadership. It makes the business case for training to move leaders and members toward a goal where diversity means good business; it brings in customers, expands the customer base, promotes a climate where all voices are included, and strives toward a workforce composition that is diverse and delivers its products or services in a culturally competent manner. The senior author has defined this to mean addressing the *Three Cs of Diversity*: recruiting and retaining a diverse Composition of the workforce and clientele, developing the Core of business products and services to be delivered in a culturally competent manner, and promoting a welcoming and inclusive workplace Climate within the organization.

Moodian (2009) views contemporary leadership and leadership success as attainable through intercultural competence and stresses the importance of moving away from ethnocentric leadership philosophies given the growing dominance of diverse workforces and greater racial/ethnic heterogeneity of populations in countries throughout the world today. He suggests a strategic planning process or business plan that is inclusive of diversity and offers seven steps toward managing diversity for organizational change. "The business case is about capturing talent, understanding markets, utilizing diverse perspectives for innovation, knowing how and how not to pitch products, and ultimately, how to generate employee commitment" (Moodian, 2009, p. 39). The seven steps include the following:

1. Generating Executive Commitment—Nothing happens in an organization without buy-in from the top. Diversity needs to be a goal embraced by leaders within an organization and starts with a visioning process.

2. Assessment—This process helps the organization understand its current state regarding diversity. This essentially means doing a SWOT analysis of the Three Cs; this might include assessing composition of the workforce and its

clientele, assessing policies and procedures that might pose internal barriers for hiring and promotion, assessing climate of the organization for inclusion and respect for all dimensions of diversity, and marketing strategies and business goals that are inclusive of diversity. This helps identify needs, set priorities, and to define goals and objectives for a strategic plan that is inclusive of diversity and provides data to serve as benchmarks.

3. Diversity Council—The establishment of such councils provides a formal mechanism within the organization that serves the purpose of getting feedback to and from employees and explaining diversity and any initiatives that are created to employees.

4. Systems Change—The executive leadership needs to align organizational systems and operational practices with diversity goals. These include pay equity reviews, revamping promotional processes to ensure fairness and equal access, setting performance objectives for hiring, establishing affinity groups or mentoring for employees, or establishing performance objectives for managers and employees in their performance reviews.

5. Training—This should NOT be designed to change an organization. Training is effectively and appropriately used to create awareness and help people develop knowledge and skills, which could result in behavior change. Training is too often used as an isolated tool to promote organizational change with limited or even negative results. At best, using training in this way is like using a screwdriver to drive a nail.

6. Measurement and Evaluation—"What gets measured gets done" is a common phrase supporting the importance of measuring the effects of change processes and evaluating the results of targets and goals that are; this includes both process and outcomes of the strategic plan.

7. Integration—Creating a feedback mechanism for continuous improvement is always important to ensure that short-term changes have long-term impact.

A strategic planning process is different from diversity training as a tool for organizational change. It is when an organization or its leaders attempt to envision the future, conduct a SWOT analysis, and develop a plan for organizational success and direction that it can have lasting impact on promoting a diverse and global workplace culture. Organizational change will flow from its policies, procedures, and strategies.

Evaluation of Outcomes

- Managing diversity as part of organizational change is best done when systems audit for organizational diversity are in place to measure outcomes. This includes measures for the Composition of the workforce, Core products of the business, and Climate of the organization. A systems audit for organizations on its level of diversity might include whether or not the organization does the following:

- Promote access for all populations
- Is relevant for today's leadership contexts
- Empowers the clients and workforce
- Is applicable to solving contemporary problems
- Establishes diverse work group teams
- Addresses the dynamics of organizational composition based on heterogeneity of its workforce and organizational culture

A set of criteria to evaluate the inputs (plan and commitment) and outputs (activities, services, and products) with feedback mechanisms to answer the core question of: How do you know when the organization is doing well? What data are available to indicate how to stop, adjust, or improve less effective actions? On screening and appraisal of leaders, what are the criteria for identifying potential leaders? Do they unintentionally exclude some groups based on their social identities that are immaterial to their effectiveness as leaders? Do criteria for performance appraisals lead to bias because of unconscious beliefs and values about leader behaviors? How is it objectively measured?

Measuring Organizational Cultural Competence

Measuring organizational cultural competence has proven to be very challenging. As discussed in Chapter 2 and 8, cultural competence is represented by the acceptance and respect for differences, continuing self-assessment regarding culture, careful attention to the dynamics of differences, continuous expansion of cultural knowledge and resources, and a variety of adaptations to belief systems, policies, and practices. However, organizational cultural competence needs to be evaluated at the same level as other organizational indicators such as measuring profitability, market share, and customer satisfaction.

Cross, Bazron, Dennis, and Isaacs (1989) first coined the term *cultural competence* as part of six developmental levels along a continuum from cultural destructiveness to cultural proficiency to describe where a mental health service delivery system might be situated in its responsiveness to the culture of its patients. Over the years, cultural competence developed its own language, values, principles, norms, and expected behaviors; by its own definition, it became a culture and a movement.

While *cultural competence* has been used extensively in health and mental health systems of care, it has only recently come into the leadership literature as a way to promote diversity within corporations and organizations. Although it has become well accepted that focusing on the cultural identities of patients and staff is essential to deliver quality culturally competent care for all patients, the cultural competence movement was challenged from the beginning to develop definitions and standards for organizations that could be more specific than "I know it when I see it." The development of the measurement of organizational cultural competence saw three milestones:

1. Cross's Cultural Competency Continuum—is a framework of the developmental process of cultural competence (Cross et al., 1989) that was a major contribution to understanding how cultural competence could develop within an organization or in individuals. The six stages are identified on Table 9.1. However, by defining these developmental stages based on values, beliefs, feelings, and behaviors, the continuum is more a description of "cultural good" than a standard for measurement. This continuum contains a cultural bias with categories such as "destructiveness" or "blindness" that tend to demonize the early stages of the development of cultural competence. Consequently, it cannot provide the basis against which the cultural competence of disparate organizations can be measured. Since the early stage categories, as defined by Cross, can also exist in a culturally competent organization, a problem arises when one culture is measured with another. Values, beliefs, and feelings of the continuum are also the primary elements of culture. As Albert Einstein (n.d.) demonstrated, "problems cannot be solved at the same level of awareness that created them."

2. Culturally and Linguistically Appropriate Services (CLAS) Standards—Based on Cross's continuum, 14 federal standards/norms were developed to improve healthcare organizations' ability to deliver "effective, understandable and respectful" care to all patients/consumers (U.S. DHHS, 2001). It was a contribution to

Table 9.1   Cross-Cultural Competence Continuum

Stage	Definition
Proficiency	Hold culture in high esteem and value positive role of culture in health and well-being
Competency	Accept and respect differences. Continuously self-assess and expand cultural knowledge resources
Pre-competency	Desire to deliver high quality services and committed to civil rights. May feel one change in system is adequate
Blindness	Provide services with philosophy of no bias. Believe if system works that all people will be served with equal effectiveness
Incapacity	Make biased decisions with clients from other cultures and perpetuate stereotypes
Destructiveness	Devalue cultures and individuals within them through attitudes, policies, practices

Adapted from Cross, T., Bazron, B., Dennis, K., & Isaacs, M. (1989). *Towards a culturally competent system of care.* Washington, DC: Georgetown University Child Development Center, CASSP Technical Center.

establishing standards against which cultural competence could be measured in organizations. Standard 1, for example, states that: "Health care organizations should ensure that patients/consumers receive, from all staff members, effective, understandable, and respectful care that is provided in a manner compatible with their cultural health beliefs and practices and preferred language" (p. 7). While regulators could hold healthcare organizations accountable to quality care by measuring compliance, the standards were not directly measurable.

3. Lewin Framework—The first "analytic or organizing framework and set of specific indicators for assessing cultural competence in direct service health-care delivery organizations." (U.S. DHHS, 2004). It provided the concrete tools of indicators to operationalize cultural competence.

Cultural Imperative Measure of Cultural Competence

The Cultural Imperative (CI) was commissioned by an academic health center to build a cultural competence self-assessment tool that could be used directly by health center staff members to measure the organization's cultural competence. In developing this self-assessment tool, the Cultural Imperative built on the research of the cultural competence movement but created a novel measurement approach that modified Cross's cultural competence continuum. This approach was first described in *Measuring Cultural Competence* (Husbands & Stubblefield-Tave, 2008) and is discussed below. While the tool was developed for healthcare organizations, it has implications for measuring cultural competence in other types of organizations as well.

The CI (Husbands & Stubblefield-Tave, 2008) first suggested that organizations are often complex rather than implicit in Cross's model; many have both a primary culture (the organization) and subcultures (departments, units, locations, functions, etc.). Each culture has a unique level of cultural competence. Assessing these diverse levels with respect to the CLAS Standards or any attempt to measure an organization's cultural competence requires three components:

1. An objective cultural competence developmental framework and measurement scale

2. An organizing framework for health care organizations that addresses the multiple and diverse functions of the organization

3. A developmental cultural framework that identifies cultural characteristics and identities of an organization independent of cultural competence

Level 1: CI Cultural Competency Scale

The CI Cultural Competency Scale has five levels and was built on the definition of cultural competence used by Cross et al. (1989) from

Incapacity to *Proficiency* (see Table 9.2). However, the levels of this scale are all defined differently than those used in the Cross Continuum. Each level includes the capabilities of the previous level in addition to new criteria providing a clear differentiation between levels.

The new cultural competence scale addresses overt manifestations in an organization such as its structures, behaviors, and processes and procedures. Structural capacity includes such things as an assessment of physical structures (e.g., signs, printed resources), training programs, and availability of interpreters. Competency skills and behaviors include the identification of essential skills, ability, and the level of execution of these skills. Proficiency includes whether or not cultural competency skills are integrated across the institution and community and reflected in the policies and procedures of an organization.

Level 2: Organizing Framework of Diverse Functions Within an Organization

Healthcare organizations are complex and carry out many different functions simultaneously. It is critical that each function be measured with respect to its own unique culture. The cultures of the operating room, emergency department, front desk, and billing are dramatically different from one another with different values, priorities, and belief systems. How a department addresses cultural competence will vary depending on the medical subculture of the department. In an emergency room, for example, focusing attention on cultural identity issues important to a culturally competent intake in a routine visit can distract from urgent and critical patient

Table 9.2   Cultural Imperative Cultural Competency Scale

Title	Definition
Incapacity	Where an organization has no awareness of, capacity for, or structures in place to support cultural competence
Pre-competency	Organization shows awareness of, and is in the process of, creating culturally competent capacity
Competency	Organization is fully aware of and demonstrates culturally competent behaviors
Pre-Proficiency	Organization shows awareness of, and is in the process of, creating culturally fluent capacity
Proficiency	Organization actively integrates the patient, family, staff, and the community into daily performance of organizational activities (e.g., patient care, teaching)

triage. If a triage nurse were to focus on an in-depth assessment of patients' ethnicity, race, or religion in adherence to CLAS standards and recommendations, patients' health outcomes could be at risk.

The Lewin framework is used as an organizing framework to group these functions into seven domains and to identify indicators of cultural competence for each domain.

1. Organizational Values: An organization's perspective and attitudes regarding the worth and importance of cultural competence, and its commitment to providing culturally competent care

2. Governance: Goal setting, policy making, and other oversight vehicles an organization uses to help ensure the delivery of culturally competent care

3. Planning and Monitoring/Evaluation: Mechanisms and processes used for: (a) long- and short-term policy, programmatic, and operational cultural competence planning that is informed by external and internal consumers and (b) the systems and activities needed to proactively track and assess an organization's level of cultural competence.

4. Communication: Exchange of information between the organization/providers and the clients/population and among staff in ways that promote cultural competence

5. Staff Development: An organization's efforts to ensure that staff and other service providers have the requisite attitudes, knowledge, and skills for delivering culturally competent services

6. Organizational Infrastructure: The organizational resources required to deliver or facilitate delivery of culturally competent services

7. Services/Interventions: An organization's delivery or facilitation of clinical, public health, and health-related services in a culturally competent manner

While the Lewin framework itself is not essential to organizational cultural competence assessment, using a framework that comprehensively organizes and accounts for the diverse activities of the organization is. At this time, it may be preferable to use the Joint Commission hospital accreditation standards addressing cultural competence and patient-centered care (http://www.jointcommission.org/accreditation/hospitals.aspx).

Level 3: Framework to Identify Organizational Culture
Independent of Cultural Competence

While cultural competence can be measured by identifying behaviors and the structures that support these behaviors, measuring a level of cultural competence is more complex. It is both developmental and dependent on both the departmental unit culture as well as the organizational culture. For example, the cultures of community health centers and teaching hospitals have diverse organizational and departmental cultures. Understanding and assessing organizational and departmental unit cultures is a necessary first step before measuring their level of cultural competence. A high level of cultural competence in one organization or department may look totally different from that of another simply because of differing core values and priorities.

Given the diversity of cultures in and within organizations based on their different functions, a developmental model is required to assess the impact of diverse values and how they are expressed in the organization. Cultures are dynamic systems with characteristics of any living system such as the tendency to both propagate beliefs and resist change. Hence, CI selected the development model of Spiral Dynamics (SD) as the tool for cultural assessment. SD was initially conceived by psychology professor Clare W. Graves and later developed by Don Beck and Chris Cowan (2006) along with other developmental models to account for cultural development. Advantages of SD include that it (1) starts with the premise that human nature is not fixed, (2) provides tools to assess cultural development and awareness, (3) is based on 40 years of extensive research, and (4) offers a tool kit for organizational development.

The SD framework postulates that individuals and societies evolve over time through definable stages as they respond to changing life conditions. As cultures move through these stages, they transcend and include their previous stage. Just as a healthy child emerges from the 'terrible twos' with a sense of boundaries, cultures always include the experience and knowledge developed in the previous stage. Each stage "manifests the core intelligences that form systems and impact human behavior: [the stage] contains the basic thought, motives and instructions that determine how [organizations] make decisions. . . . Each stage "has core values" (Beck & Cowan, 2006, p. 40) and "contains its own framework for . . . education, mental health, work and management, social order and law" (p. 41) that inform all aspects of life at that particular stage. Locating a department in a given stage by its corresponding core values, framework, and behaviors allows the evaluation tool to assess the cultural competence independently.

SD identifies six historical stages of human (cultural) development. Locating both the departmental and organizational cultures on these stages helps determine their mutual impact and whether or not an assessment of cultural competence is viable. The stages are color coded as

1. Survival (Beige)—is fear driven, and a focus on staying alive, meeting physical needs, and reproduction; individuals have little understanding of *future*, planning, or the *self*.

2. Safety (Purple)—is security driven for one's own kind, trusting blood relationships and believing in magical powers; individuals honor ancestors' ways and seek to live in harmony with nature.

3. Power (Red)—is power driven and attempts to take charge of people; individuals tend to bend nature to the organization's will and demand respect; they will do anything, without guilt, to avoid being shamed.

4. Truth (Blue)—is order driven and operates on the belief in one right way and obedience to authority.

5. Prosperity (Orange)—is success driven and operates on the belief in win-lose competition, pragmatic solutions, and exploration.

6. Communitarian (Green)—is people driven, operates on the belief that the hearts and minds of people are core; truths are relative not absolute.

Determining that the current departmental stage is appropriate is a serious matter. If the team finds that the departmental culture is inconsistent with the organization's culture, senior leadership needs to be informed. If the team believes that either the department or the organizational culture is inappropriate for assessment and training, the team must also raise that finding to organizational leadership. Senior leadership can then consider other interventions, for example, changes in departmental leadership and/ or organizational structure.

The Cultural Imperative Tool in Action

Implementing a cultural assessment of an organization requires six steps:

1. Assembling an assessment team

2. Identifying the departmental culture within the SD stages

3. Assessing cultural competence capacity

4. Quantitatively measuring departmental skills and behaviors

5. Combining the assessment components

6. Preparing the report and recommendations for management (Husbands & Stubblefield-Tave, 2008)

Assembling the Assessment Team

Both the organizational and departmental assessments are designed as team based efforts. An assessment team can be as small as 3–4 members for a small clinic or hospital or as large as 30–40 for a large urban health center. The assessment team should reflect the diversity of an organization's workforce and its service area. Each major function needs to be represented with involvement and support of the departmental leadership if the findings and recommendations are to be respected. The departmental assessment team should have 3–4 members made up of departmental staff and one from outside the department, who could be from Human Resources or Organizational Development. Using the department of surgery within an academic health center as an example, the Chief of Surgery may appoint a diverse five-member assessment team to include an attending physician, a chief medical resident, a surgical technician, a nurse anesthetist, and a human resources staff member. The assessment team will then need to establish its operating rules, including its decision-making process. CI recommends that decisions be made through consensus, defined as: The majority of team members agree with the decision, and no team member objects to the decision.

Identify the Departmental Culture Using the Spiral Dynamics Stages

Because organizational and departmental cultures will influence the nature and outcome of a cultural competence assessment, it is important to first identify what that culture is. The assessment team compares the department's values, beliefs, and practices with the culture templates provided by Spiral Dynamics (SD) and decides which stage(s) best fit the organization and the department being reviewed. A department or organization may fit more than one SD stage, especially if it is in transition. This is an important first step because an assessment team could decide that the organizational or departmental culture is inappropriate for cultural competence assessment or training; this would warrant the assessment team reporting back to senior leadership for further discussion and resolution.

Continuing with the example, the assessment team discusses the diverse experiences among the members and within the department in order to identify departmental values, beliefs, and practices. In this example, the team reviews the SD stages and identifies Power (Red) and Truth (Blue) as possible stages in which the surgery department is situated. The team finds that individual surgeons operate in the Power (Red) stage; these surgeons are tough, powerful, and highly ambitious *haves* as defined in the SD stages. They behave as though "Respect and reputation matter more than life itself." Overall, the team identifies that the department operates in the Truth (Blue) stage; most of the surgeons and other department staff members find meaning in their collective ability to save lives and improve patients' health through surgical practice, education, and research. The surgeon is recognized as "captain of the ship," and other staff members always subject themselves to the directives of proper authority.

The team determines that both the Red and Blue stages of their organizational culture are amenable to cultural competence assessment and training. Both departmental and organizational leadership endorse the process. The Red surgeons will respect this power although some surgeons may offer resistance. Blue departmental members will recognize the potential for the assessment and training efforts to improve patient care, education, and research.

Overall, the academic health center or hospital is viewed as operating in the Prosperity (Orange) stage although its stated mission of patient care, research, and education is Prosperity (Orange) and Communitarian (Green). The hospital is highly successful programmatically, responsive to the community, and financially sound. It is nationally recognized for its excellence and financially successful in highly competitive local, national, and global markets. The team determines that both the Orange and Green stages are amenable to cultural competence assessment and training. The hospital supports the *business* case for cultural competence in health care to gain market share and prestige through effective assessment and training. It also supports the *social justice, quality,* and *health equity* cases for cultural competence to promote community and unity within the department, with patients and family members, and with the broader service area. The assessment and training effort is viewed as helping advance the hospital's mission.

Finally, the team determines that the department's Red/Blue culture is compatible with the hospital's Orange/Green culture. The department operates with respect for the overall mission of the hospital. It is highly regarded within the hospital for its technical excellence and for bringing in substantial patient care, education, and research dollars to support the hospital's operations.

Assessing Cultural Competence Capacity

Measuring the department's capacity to deliver culturally and linguistically competent care and services is the next task. This requires developing a number of Yes or No questions (less than 30) to identify the presence or absence of cultural competence capacity based on indicators within the Lewin framework; there are literally hundreds of generic cultural competence indicators available in the public domain. It is essential that these indicators be tailored to the culture and language of the department and organization being assessed. This becomes the Cultural Competence Scale.

The team then does an internal audit of organizational and departmental published resources, procedures, and policies to answer the questions on the scale and comes to agreement about the answers. These answers can be ranked on a 5-point Likert scale yielding a cultural competence level for each question. The team combines the results to create an overall assessment of the department's structural capacity—that is, physical structures, signage, consumer brochures, training programs, availability of interpreters for clients being served, and so forth.

Quantitatively Measuring Departmental Skills and Behaviors

The team's next task is to describe department members' attitudes, experiences, and behaviors regarding cultural competence. Here, the goal is to survey as many members of the department or organization as possible. The team identifies its areas of interest in cultural competence and develops a cultural survey of 40 or fewer questions that can be completed anonymously online with such tools as Survey Monkey. While demographic data, including dimensions, should be included, the survey should be designed so that the team cannot identify any one individual. These results can be summarized by race, ethnicity, gender, and other dimensions of diversity to identify disparate patterns of experience, skills, attitudes, and behaviors. They can be interpreted in the context of the departmental culture.

Combining Assessment Components

The team's next task is to combine the findings of the three assessments to prepare an overview of organization's or department's cultural competence capacity, its culture, and employee attitudes, knowledge, skills, and behaviors. The team then discusses and develops its recommendations and identifies action steps that are feasible.

Preparing the Report and Recommendations for Management

The team's final task is to prepare and submit its report to the departmental and/or organizational leadership. The report will include both the team's consensus of findings and recommendations for feasible action steps for improving an organization's or department's cultural competence based on an awareness of organizational and departmental cultures. The findings, recommendations, and final report are all reviewed and approved by the full assessment team.

Multiple Perspectives in Examining Departmental Cultural Competence

The CI Measure of Cultural Competence is an approach that uses four different lenses to examine departmental and organizational cultural competence. Each lens offers powerful insights and a comprehensive assessment of the department's and organization's culture. The process minimizes subjective bias by utilizing diverse sources of data. Culturally proficient departments integrate the perspectives of patients, families, and community members.

1. Diverse Assessment Team—The process for forming the assessment team ensures diversity in its members. This brings diverse viewpoints to acquiring, analyzing, and interpreting data and minimizes the potential of a singular viewpoint being forced on the assessment process.

2. Cultural Stage—Determining the departmental cultural stage is one of identifying the context in which attitudes, skills, knowledge, and behavior interact. This lens uses both qualitative and quantitative tools to enable the assessment team to self-identify the appropriate stage(s) in which it is situated.

3. Cultural Competence Capacity—In determining the capacity of the department, the team identifies the presence or absence of programs and the policies and structures necessary for delivering culturally and linguistically competent services.

4. Department Members' Attitudes, Skills, Knowledge, and Behaviors—Survey data reveal the department's performance in delivering culturally and linguistically competent services as experienced by departmental employees. This includes overall experiences and those of cultural subgroups. An earlier survey developed by the CI (Husbands & Stubblefield-Tave, 2004) in its cultural proficiency assessment of the UT College of Pharmacy was modified to be a self-assessment tool for the CI measure.

The primary domain of this tool is to first provide an objective assessment of the organizational culture. Then, the level of cultural competence within a complex organization and its disparate departments is assessed by examining their actions, behaviors, and structures. The tool does not directly measure disparities, health outcomes, or the quality of care, although it may identify the disparate treatment of patients, staff, or faculty. The organization itself is the context and metric by which to compare the cultural competence of departmental units within the organization; this enables the organization to develop benchmarks to differentially identify units that would benefit from improving their cultural competence through diversity training or other interventions such as rewarding preferred behaviors. It could also identify best practices that can be emulated.

Patient-Centered Care

Health disparities can be diminished through greater patient involvement, which often means involving the patient/consumer and the community in his or her health care. Recent studies indicate that patients who have a sustaining health care relationship, or *medical home,* report that health disparities are minimized and in some cases nonexistent (Beal, Doty,

Hernandez, Shea, & Davis, 2007). In the Commonwealth Fund report, "Patient-Centered Care: What Does It Take?," Dale Shaller (2007) presents case studies of two innovative health systems that have successfully implemented patient-centered care programs. In addition to engaged leadership and a clearly communicated vision, Shaller found that a high degree of patient and family involvement, a supportive work environment, systematic measurement and feedback, and deployment of information technology all played critical roles in reducing health disparities.

Greater consumer involvement supports the notion of culturally competent communication as a partnership between provider and patient. It is a joint responsibility of the patient and provider or organization where the organization might facilitate the process by providing adequate information, understandable forms, and assuming that the patient is capable of gathering and utilizing this information. This is analogous to concepts of shared governance and shared leadership developed in arenas outside of health care. In assessing organizational cultural competence of a health care system, a key question becomes: How are patients permitted and/or encouraged to actively participate in the delivery of their health care? Specific questions include the following:

- Can patients understand the need to communicate their health beliefs? How can this be facilitated?
- How does the health care organization communicate its culture and the level of participation available to its patients?
- How can patients become aware of the need to inform their clinician of their use of home remedies?
- Are patients encouraged to request a comfortable level of participation with their clinician?
- What *formal* resources does the health care organization develop and provide patients?
- How does the organization use *informal* resource networks to inform its patients?

For organizations in general, these questions can be modified accordingly to emphasize the partnership between the organization and the customers it serves—to provide appropriate information, to encourage participation, to recognize cultural beliefs and worldviews, and to promote access, availability, and quality of its services.

Cultural Fluency of Organizations

Cultural fluency requires the highest level of both structural capacity and organizational performance. In a health care context, this requires that a department "actively integrates the patient, family, staff and the community into daily performance." The specifics of these definitions will change based on an organization's mission and culture. Departments will integrate feedback loops from key stakeholders—customers, staff members, others—to allow continuous adjustments in daily performance.

Harvard Pilgrim Health Care (HPHC), a major New England health plan, provides an example of cultural fluency. Using the BASK model, it realized (Awareness) that members of differing cultural and linguistic groups could have systematically different experiences in its clinical operations. Using its patient satisfaction survey tools (Skills), HPHC confirmed that Hispanic and Asian patients were less satisfied with its health centers' services than Black or White patients (Knowledge). After medical interpreting was introduced within the health centers to our Limited English Proficient (LEP) members (Behaviors), patient satisfaction of LEP patient with the total health care experienced improved from 59% to 66% (Harvard Pilgrim Health Care, 1997). HPHC cited this action as an example of the success of its "Commitment 4: Changing the organizational culture through leadership, policies and practices." This represents cultural fluency at the organizational and leadership levels.

Leaders need the skills to negotiate cross-cultural and diverse differences. With ongoing globalization, leaders need to become competent across cultural settings. Adler and Bartholomew (1992) contend that global leaders need to develop five cross-cultural competencies. First, leaders need to understand business, political, and cultural environments worldwide. Second, they need to learn the perspectives, tastes, trends, and technologies of many other cultures. Third, they need to be able to work simultaneously with people from many cultures. Fourth, leaders must be able to adapt to living and communicating in other cultures. Fifth, they need to learn to relate to people from other cultures from a position of equality rather than cultural superiority. This awareness and practice is developing the cultural fluency to navigate between and across cultures fluently and responsively.

Summary

In identifying new paradigms and reframing existing theories toward a DLMOX paradigm for diversity leadership, we can consider its application for training organizations to be relevant and effective in the 21st century. For training organizations, we use a SWOT analysis model to understand organizational culture, conduct organizational self-assessment, and develop a plan for organizational change. Managing organizational diversity requires addressing the Three Cs of Diversity: Composition of workforce and clientele, Core of business products and services, and workplace Climate. This can best be done through a systems audit for organizational diversity, setting goals and targets, and measuring outcomes. Cultural competence has proven difficult to measure since our instruments and methods must minimize cultural bias. The Cultural Imperative has developed a cultural competency scale to measure the cultural capacity, competency, and fluency of an organization using a process of organizational self-assessment. For the 21st century, the reshaping of *work cultures* will become more salient as organizational values and sociopolitical trends change.

Discussion Questions

1. If your organization were to train leaders and members to be culturally competent, using the KSA model, identify some specific domains of knowledge, skills, and attitudes that you think important to address within the organizational context.

2. Pick a specific organization for this exercise. Using the *3 Cs of Managing Diversity*, identify the components of the 3 Cs that you would use to construct a plan to advance diversity within the organization and achieve its business goals.

3. Imagine an organization with many people from diverse cultural backgrounds where there is mistrust between different groups. As a leader, identify and discuss some culturally competent strategies to forge positive relationships amidst differences. How would you go about motivating the different groups toward a shared goal?

4. Identify and describe a situation where you have been asked to influence someone to accept an idea contrary to his or her cultural values. Relying on the tools of measuring cultural competence, how you would explain your idea, outline its objectives, share the information to support it, and promote its benefits to the organization. Identify the potential obstacles to getting someone to accept your idea and the techniques you would use to overcome them.

5. Briefly describe and explain microaggressions. Provide some examples of microaggressions that you have experienced. What did you do to deal with the underlying hostility of the experiences? Were they effective in heightening awareness of the person making the microaggression?

10

Developing a Paradigm of
Diversity Leadership

Vignette: On a Paradigm for Diversity Leadership

"There is a difference. When people ask, isn't what you are saying true of all human beings? [I say No! A paradigm for Diversity Leadership is about] the inattention to social status and negative attributions made about differences in social identities. It is about dominant and subordinate groups, majority and minority status, having privilege or not, being in the in-group or out-group, and all that shape the different [lived] experiences of leaders. . . . It is also about training potential leaders to effect change in their institutions and communities." (Ethnic minority leader about targeted training for ethnic minority leaders)

In reviewing the theories and literature on leadership, the need for a more global and diverse model of leadership is evident. Today, the face of diversity is changing. Diversity in the 1960s meant a seat at the table; it meant dealing with underrepresented ethnic minorities of Blacks, Hispanics, Asian Americans, and Native American Indian groups in the United States. Today, there are many more racial/ethnic groups, including Arabic and Middle Eastern countries and many more dimensions of cultural diversity, including religion, disability, sexual orientation, age, and social class. Our contexts are also changing. World leadership is no longer the Big Four (consisting of the allied powers of the United States, Britain, Italy, and France after WWI). China, once a third world country, now vies as a new world power. Our vision for the future must link to the past. What does diversity mean today?

Whereas emphasis in the 20th century was on underrepresentation, on people of color as minorities, and on the adverse consequences of racism, we now grapple with diversity in a global village. A global perspective of population diversity, not only within the United States but also in many countries throughout the world, coupled with the vast intercultural exchange through technology and the Internet changes how we must now view diversity.

Whereas leadership theory for the 21st century is still in its nascent stages, conducting grounded theory research and collecting qualitative data as methods of inquiry are important to build a foundation of knowledge to minimize inherent bias from ethnocentric views in current theories of leadership. We see a paradigm for diversity leadership as both evolving and dynamic. Crosscutting themes emerging in this book are only the beginning. Further research is needed to confirm and expand the important questions about what we now know about diversity and leadership.

However, several things are clear. Single dimensions of leadership are no longer viable to capture the complex, multiple, and intersecting dimensions influencing how leadership is exercised among diverse leaders in a culturally diverse and global society. Any paradigm must evolve continuously as societal trends and new contexts shape how leadership is exercised and raise new challenges for contemporary leaders. A paradigm for diversity leadership must be inclusive of all voices and of varying leadership styles that intersect with the social identities and cultural value orientations across diverse groups. We should not resort to the dichotomous views (e.g., of task vs. relationship oriented styles) to reflect the styles of specific groups. Rather, we need to view each dimension as existing along a continuum in all groups and leaders; it is a matter of relative emphasis as to which are more salient consistent with individual and cultural values and orientations across varying contexts. Chapters 8 and 9 on Applications summarize some of the multiple cultural dimensions that contribute to leadership effectiveness.

In emphasizing culture and leadership, we return to Northouse's (2004, p. 3) definition of leadership as "a process whereby an individual influences a group of individuals to achieve a common goal." In addition to the notion of *influence,* we add that leadership is all about *relationships,* a process that will vary across cultural contexts. For example, respect and trust is often viewed as important to relationships but may mean different things in different cultures. In Japan, for example, the concept of *enrio* governs behavior in the workplace such that one may not accept promotion if you know the person who you will replace; rather than bring dishonor onto that person, you might quit in disgrace. While such a notion may be "foreign" to Western thinking, the relationship exists within the context of respect and honor; such cultural values often influence leadership behaviors. A collective orientation context, where the welfare of the group is foremost is common among Eastern countries, stands in contrast to an individualistic orientation, common among Western countries where the emphasis is on individual achievement. These examples, also discussed throughout the book, underscore the need to shift from current cultural dimensions that underlie many contemporary leadership models today to allow for the development of models that are more inclusive of or start from the premises of other cultural orientations—to be less ethnocentric.

Common among leadership models today is the assumption that there is a presumed ideal leader prototype. From a diversity leadership perspective, we need to expand the range of leader prototypes beyond those to which we unconsciously subscribe based on cultural orientation values; we need to go beyond the social and cultural constraints that limit our leadership. We offer a process to change the "traditional" prototype to one that is diverse. This means an awareness of how stereotypic images may bias judgments against those who do not look or behave in a "leaderful" manner when, in fact, they are behaving in accordance with their social roles. We need to move from the development of fixed leadership profiles toward ones that recognize leader competencies and adaptability to be responsive to cultural contexts within both society and organizations. Our tendency to contrast Eastern versus Western styles or industrialized versus underdeveloped third world countries polarizes our thoughts and opinions about leadership.

A 21st century conceptualization of leadership means a noncolonial, nonindustrial notion of leadership that does not equate dominance and power of the leader with a conqueror mentality. An emphasis on context is central to a contemporary diversity leadership paradigm. Increased use of technology and social media and instant communication via the Internet is causing rapid change and innovation. Twenty-first century leadership will shift from measuring outcomes based not on military power and the conqueror mentality but on economic power and interdependence associated with the production of services and the ability to manage continuous change in a digital age. The diversity of leader teams can facilitate creativity and innovation as it brings in diverse perspectives and urges flexibility. Social groups experiencing a history of oppression are more likely to focus on shared power and empowerment. However, instead of eschewing the acknowledgement of power as was done in the 20th century, it is distinguishing bad, destructive, and abusive use of power from good, creative, and benevolent use of power. Hence, we include these parameters within a Diverse Leader-Member-Organization Exchange Paradigm (DLMOX).

Changing the Prototype: Evolving and Emergent

Leadership theories and the popular media have put forth leadership prototypes that are viewed as universal and ideal, when in fact, they reflect both an ethnocentric, culturally specific, and value-laden prototype of a White, middle class, heterosexual Eurocentric male. It is time to offer different, more diverse, and inclusive leader prototypes. How do we develop a prototype that challenges the narrow ones that exist? How do we develop ones that are inclusive, dynamic, and flexible and representative of unique, culturally diverse lifeways and thoughtways?

Bass's *Stogdill's Handbook of Leadership: A Survey of Theory and Research* revised edition first mentioned the importance of culture and ethnicity in leadership (Bass, 1990) with Chapter 32 on women and leadership and Chapters 33 and 34 on leadership characteristics among Blacks, Hispanics, other ethnic minorities, and on cross-cultural leadership styles. Although the chapters were based on little empirical evidence, the chapters forged a new direction for research in leadership that is active and vital in the 21st century.

Several seminal culturally driven leadership studies since 1981 helped shape our understanding of cultural variations in management and leadership styles. Peter Dorfman and Jon Howell (1988) examined culturally contingent leadership patterns, preferences, and styles in non-Western countries. Using Gert Hofstede's four culture dimensions (i.e., individualism-collectivism, masculinity-femininity, uncertainty avoidance, and power distance), the researchers found that paternalism was a major influence on one's leadership style. Respondents tended to prefer egalitarian styles when the power distance was low (i.e., the extent to which a society accepts the fact that power in institutions and organizations is distributed unequally). When power distance was high, leadership styles were more authoritative and directive.

Peter Dorfman and his colleagues published the results of an extensive and ambitious cross-national study of leadership styles and characteristics (Dorfman et al., 1997) with the intent of finding a synthetic universal or etic-based prototype drawn from cross-cultural samples in Japan, South Korea, Taiwan, Mexico, and the United States. While they did not find a universal characteristic that transcended cultural lifeways and thoughts, they found partial support for leaders' supportiveness, contingent reward, and charismatic leadership. In the U.S. sample, they found support for a form of contingent punishment style, which was viewed as undesirable in the other countries speaking to contrasting styles that have been consistent between Eastern and Western countries.

Colin Silverthorne (2001) also found support for a relationship between culture and leadership styles. He found variations in neuroticism and extroversion among participants from the United States, Taiwan, and Thailand that could be attributed to their respective collective and individualistic orientations. An extensive review of theory and methodology on the emerging interests in culture and leadership by Dickson, Den Hartog, and Michelson (2003) led to the cautionary note that one should not ignore significant [within-group and between-group differences] within a country or culture. They conclude that "technological advances, larger multicultural samples, clarification of cultural dimensions, and better measurement of cognitive processes across cultures will allow us to better understand the role societal culture plays in the enactment and interpretation of leadership" (p. 761).

As indicated throughout this book, leadership concepts are culturally endorsed; the GLOBE studies (House, Hanges, Javidan, Dorfman, & Gupta, 2004) supported how cultural orientation values influence leadership and demonstrated cultural variation in leadership profiles across 62 countries. Ethnographic data from the late 1800s, for example, clearly demonstrate consideration variation in leadership styles from one culturally diverse group to another. These data show how leadership styles are often tradition bound, showing little variation over time within many culturally diverse communities. However, in communities where colonization and immigration generated contact with other different culturally diverse groups, leadership styles of the indigenous population often had to change to accommodate and even challenge the styles brought in by outsiders.

In many of the studies, researchers hoped to find universal leadership patterns that transcended unique culturally diverse lifeways and thoughts of specific groups. For example, studies by Gertsner and Day (1994), House, Wright, and Aditya (1997), Hanges and Dixon (2004), House et al. (1999), and Brodbeck et al. (2000) anticipated finding this seemingly elusive universal pattern. However, several research methodological and procedural concerns about the *cultural equivalence of meanings* of the constructs continue to be the most problematic (Trimble & Vaughn, 2013). Dimensions are difficult to measure and observe in equivalent semantic terms and to demonstrate ethnocultural comparability.

Brodbeck et al. (2000) concluded that leadership concepts differ as a function of cultural differences in Europe and identified cultural variation of leadership prototypes. With a sample size of 6,052 representing 22 European countries using a 112-item questionnaire, the study developed and validated a set of dimensions representing core differences in leadership prototypes. Among many compelling findings and aspects of the study, the research team attempted to identify a leadership prototype of a greater magnitude than some of the attempts that had been undertaken before (Gertsner & Day, 1994; Kenney, Blasovich, & Shaver, 1994).

If leadership theorists and researchers truly acknowledge that culture matters, then different culturally styled leadership approaches or prototypes deserve more serious scholarly attention. While these early efforts were useful in identifying cultural variation across countries, how do we take this down to an individual level to identify a set of leadership dimensions that can be used to identify leadership styles and profiles used by diverse leaders and social identity groups under varying contexts? Formulating, conceptualizing, and identifying leadership concepts and styles inclusive of multiple ethnocultural perspectives and reflective of leadership behaviors across diverse groups and cultures is a challenge at best. Whereas the attempts to identify a universal set of leader traits have been unsuccessful, our goal is not to identify a single leadership prototype. Rather, it is to offer a process to identify and evolve diverse leadership prototypes based on ethnocultural differences that can be used to characterize the leadership styles that become salient across varying contexts, cultures, and social identity groups. In doing so, we can identify what diverse leaders bring to their exercise of leadership and which behaviors are effective under what circumstances.

Culturally Diverse Leadership Prototypes

The coauthors of this book have independently engaged in developing such a process. Two sets of leadership concepts and descriptors emerged. Jean Lau Chin with her colleagues took on this challenge and compiled a set of leadership dimensions culled from a review of the research on leadership. Dimensions that were measured and identified as important to the exercise of leadership such as collaborative and transformational leadership were included. Adding to this list were dimensions identified from leadership studies of non-Western cultures and from qualitative interviews and focus groups with diverse racial and ethnic leaders. Sixty-four dimensions were identified. Instead of starting from single or dual dimensions derived from existing theories, this compilation of multiple dimensions brings in both "traditional" and nontraditional dimensions of leadership with the goal of identifying their importance and meaning to a diverse group of leaders. In having leaders from different social identity groups and cultures rank these dimensions, we might identify whether or not clusters will emerge that might lead to different leader profiles or leader prototypes. For example, the ranked ordered profile of these dimensions that emerged from the Diversity Leadership Summit discussed next is shown in Table 10.1.

What this table shows is that dimensions involving virtue or integrity, authenticity, collaboration and relationships, humane and altruistic characteristics were ranked most highly with ratings of 4.13 and above. It is noteworthy that these characteristics are affirming ones and consistent with cultural values endorsed within the group of diverse leaders. Those dimensions that identified individual characteristics with negative overtones of self-denigration or self-promoting were ranked lowest with ratings of 1.87 and below. It is noteworthy that these "value" judgments are influenced by different cultural views or meaning associated with the same behavior.

Table 10.1   Rank Order of Leadership Characteristics Important to Leadership

Leadership Characteristics Important to Your Leadership	Rating Average
Integrity	4.93
Authentic	4.80
Honest	4.73
Resourceful	4.73
Communicator	4.67
Adaptability	4.60
Collaborative	4.60
Resilient	4.53
Culturally sensitive	4.47
Flexibility	4.47
Visionary	4.47
Empowering	4.40
Transparency	4.40
Cooperative	4.33
Open minded	4.33
Team builder	4.33
Value based	4.33
Conviction	4.27
Humane	4.20
Compassionate	4.13
Decisive	4.13
Diplomatic	4.13
Optimistic	4.13
Passionate	4.13
Humility	4.07
Persuasive	4.07
Being direct	4.00
Direct	4.00
Motivating	4.00
Participative	4.00
Self-knowledge	3.93
Caring	3.87
Intuitive	3.87
Organized	3.87
Inspirational	3.80
Warmth	3.80
Assertive	3.73

(Continued)

Table 10.1   (Continued)

Leadership Characteristics Important to Your Leadership	Rating Average
Emotionally tough	3.67
Expressive	3.53
Kind	3.47
Democratic	3.40
Independent	3.40
Stability	3.40
Benevolent	3.27
Adventurous	3.20
Modest	3.20
Ambitious	3.07
Powerful	3.00
Unique	3.00
Gentle	2.93
Charismatic	2.87
Affectionate	2.80
Forceful	2.73
Self-sacrificing	2.73
Competitive	2.67
Individualistic	2.13
Indirect	2.00
Dominant	1.87
Conflict inducer	1.80
Aggressive	1.73
Celebrity	1.67
Status conscious	1.53
Submissive	1.33
Self-centered	1.20

Implications are to identify a set of concepts and descriptors that are affirmative of diverse cultural values and facilitative of the relational aspects of leading diverse members. These may vary across contexts, groups, and time.

Joseph Trimble with the assistance of three research assistants reviewed the culture and leadership literature to identify various concepts and descriptors of leadership. Forty-eight concepts and descriptors emerged from the leadership literature with the selection criterion that culture or ethnicity was present as a variable in the studies. The 48 items were reviewed

Table 10.2   Dimensions for Culturally Diverse Leadership Prototypes

Imagination	Synergy	Constructive	Principled	Virtuous
Farsighted	Encouraging	Established	Loyal	Benevolent
Intuitive	Collaborative	Informed	Diplomatic	Compassionate
Visionary	Communicative	Intellectually-stimulating	Just	Respectful
Unique	Coordinator	Logical	Humble	Trustworthy
	Worldly	Convincing	Charismatic	Patient
	Democratic	Grounded		Culturally-sensitive
	Open-minded	Ambitious		Humane
	Optimistic	Assertive		Integrity
		Competitive		
		Forceful		
		Value-based		
		Inspirational		
		Self-knowledge		
		Decisive		

for similarities and differences in concept meaning through use of a Q-sort methodology; that is, concepts were sorted into various unstructured open-ended categories according to their implicit meaning. Each member of the small research team sorted the items independently of the others. Five general categories were identified from this process based on the criterion that the common dimensions of the items were synonyms—that is, words that have the same or nearly the same meaning as another word(s). The five *meaning dimensions* that emerged are: *constructive, imaginative, principled, synergy,* and *virtuous*. Following this sorting step, the research team sorted the items once again with the intent of winnowing the list down to a more manageable number by removing redundant items. To assist them in the item reduction process, the original list was graphed using a social network program called GEPHI and analyzed with TROPES and NVivo10, both of which are content analysis analytic programs. Results from the analysis were analyzed for patterns and *meaning dimensions*.

Items list generated by Jean Lau Chin's research were combined with those developed by Joseph Trimble's research team. The stepwise process described above was repeated and generated 39 concepts and items that fell into one of five categories. There are 4 items in the *Imagination* category, 8 in the *Synergy* category, 14 in the *Constructive* category, 5 in the *Principled* one, and 8 in the *Virtuous* one.

As the reader can see from the characteristics listed in Table 10.1, most of them are adjectives and a few are nouns. In looking over the 39 characteristics, one quickly notices the absence of any with harsh or negative connotations; all convey a positive orientation. These were characteristics generated from focus group discussions and interviews discussed in the next section of this chapter; all were provided by individuals who came from distinct and diverse cultural and ethnic backgrounds. As pointed out above, some of the characteristics were extracted from the literature. Is it possible that the respondents reflected deeply held cultural beliefs about leadership? Were they idealizing their descriptions? Or were the descriptions grounded in the reality of their own experiences as leaders?

It is important to acknowledge that many of the characteristics listed in Table 10.2 are similar to those identified by Brodbeck et al. (2000) in their study of leadership prototypes across 22 European countries. The consistency of these findings suggests that these 39 items form a beginning for further investigation of characteristics and features of culturally diverse leadership prototypes, styles, and practices. The research, however, is complicated by the research methods available to probe deeply into the lifeways and thoughtways of diverse cultural populations; most existing methods are grounded in Western-based methods of the social and behavioral sciences, that for the most part have to be modified extensively to be effective in culturally unique settings. The bias toward using less diverse samples limits any findings as to whether they can be generalizable. In an article titled "The Weirdest People in the World?" psychologists Joseph Henrich, Steven Heine, and Ara Norenzayan suggest "that members of WEIRD societies, including young children, are among the least representative populations one could find for generalizing about humans. These empirical patterns suggest that we need to be less cavalier in addressing questions of human nature on the basis of data drawn from this particularly thin, and rather unusual, slice of humanity" (2010, p. 61). To capture the essence of our culturally diverse prototype, the researcher must heed the advice of these University of British Columbia psychologists.

While there are other numerous culturally distinct research considerations, the one that poses the most serious challenge has to do with cultural measurement equivalence; the concept was presented earlier in this book (Trimble & Vaughn, 2013). Central to the concerns of equivalence is the fundamental precept that comparisons between culturally diverse groups require that common, if not identical, measurement and assessment processes exist; a universal process must be developed to demonstrate and assess ethnocultural group comparability. In constructing and using leadership instruments and assessment tools in cultural comparative or cultural-sensitive research, the investigator must give serious attention to matters of equivalence. The instrument's content, format, and metric style must be congruent with and comparable across the cultural groups selected for study. Researchers must provide hard evidence that the components of the measurement process meet the standards of functional, conceptual, metric, linguistic, and stimulus equivalence. To further understand the implications of the approach, consider the meaning of each of the 39 descriptors in Table 10.1 and decide whether or not they would be the same or meet the rigid criteria for equivalence in different languages and cultures. Consider the characteristic of *trustworthy;* how would the concept be defined and understood in different languages and what implication might that have across a variety of settings? The meaning and implications of the 39 culturally diverse characteristics are described in the next section.

Redefining Leadership: Difference and Context

A Diversity Leadership Summit held in January 2013[1] (Chin et al., in progress) exemplifies a process toward developing new paradigms using a DLMOX framework that is attentive to difference and contexts. It enables us to deliberate how our leadership models can be inclusive and relevant as we recruit and train our next generation of leaders. Just as early models of leadership drew on the experiences of Anglo, North American men, we now need a cadre of case examples of diverse leaders to expand our foundations for more diverse and global paradigms of leadership.

Fifteen diverse leaders representing corporate, higher education, government, military, and community nonprofit industry sectors were invited to deliberate in a process to define their view of leadership informed by their social identity dimensions of race, ethnicity, gender, sexual orientation, and their lived experiences. Prior to the Summit, they were asked to rank a list of 64 leadership dimensions (identified in the process above) in order of importance to their leadership (see Table 10.1). They participated in three focus group discussions addressing (1) How do you view leadership? (2) How do race, ethnicity, gender, and sexual orientation influence their exercise of leadership? (3) How do we project the kind of leadership needed for the future given the rapid change, growing diversity, and increased

---

[1] These qualitative findings are the result of a Diversity Leadership Summit in Houston, TX, in January 2013, which was cofacilitated by Jean Lau Chin and Lyne Desormeaux with contributions from Pam Remer, Katina Sawyer, Kizzy Parks, Vanessa Li, Edith Arrington, Chris Liang, and Connie Matthews. We also acknowledge the participation of the Summit leaders who contributed to this grounded research process.

globalization in society? Observers to the process provided feedback to identify common themes. This grounded theory process to develop leadership theory was inspiring to all participants. "Transformative, innovative, cutting edge, inspiring, and one of the best conferences in my career" were some descriptions of that experience. Following the summit, observer comments and analysis of the focus group transcripts identified a set of themes central to the views and lived experiences of diverse leaders. The themes are described below and are important because they illustrate and offer confirmation of the concepts discussed in this book about diversity leadership.

Rank Order of Leadership Characteristics

As shown in Table 10.1, this group of diverse leaders ranked as high in importance to their leadership many of the leadership characteristics discussed in this book. In particular, *integrity, authenticity, communicator, adaptability, collaborative, resilient,* and *culturally sensitive* were among the highest while *self-centered, status conscious, aggressive, dominant, competitive,* and *individualistic* were ranked lowest. These findings are suggestive of how some characteristics might carry different value or semantic meaning across leaders from different groups or with different lived experiences. In addition, further research would be useful to see how the influence of context and lived experiences might change these rankings and priorities in how leaders choose to lead.

Shared Lived Experiences

While the leaders represented different industry sectors, and their lived experiences were an intersection of social identities, including race, ethnicity, gender, and sexual orientation, the process did not attempt to differentiate these different demands and characteristics. Rather, all leaders shared the experience of social identities coming from less privileged, oppressed, marginalized, or nondominant social groups. All felt their lived experiences included both benefits and challenges to their leadership. The benefits included their being more adept at reading the cultural contexts of their workplaces, being able to build relationships with a variety of constituents, and being able to take another's perspective. All felt their lived experiences of oppression based on a dimension of diversity helped build resiliency, adaptability, and flexibility, and to adjust their leadership style to the organizational contexts in which they led.

The leaders viewed context and culture as important when talking about diversity leadership. They felt they were attuned to the voices that were represented as well as those that were missing. The leaders found it important to mesh their diversity goals with variations in the organizational cultures that they faced. They also noted how they drew on the importance of family upbringing, family life, and lived experiences to their exercise of leadership. In doing so, they underscored how dimensions of their diversity and social identities always made them a symbol in the organization whether they wanted it or not.

However, challenges to their competence and sense of belonging were not uncommon. For some, their experience of tokenism based on being perceived as having been chosen to meet a quota were further assaults to their self-esteem. Many felt a challenge to their authenticity as they strived to conform to expectations while remaining true to themselves; many emphasized the importance of being comfortable with themselves, which was defined as being able to translate cultural values without losing yourself. Others felt the challenge of being alienated and isolated and emphasized the need to build an external network to compensate. They felt this required great resoluteness and self-awareness, confidence and courage to be open and honest, a willingness to change and question one's assumptions, integrity and having a moral compass to do the right thing for the right reason, being compassionate, and taking risks to effect change.

Their experiences reinforced earlier findings that their "differences made a difference." How does one transcend these challenges? To do so often meant being able to find common ground, maintaining a passion to promote equity and social justice, and being able to self-promote balanced with humility. It was recognized that self-promotion can be important and necessary in some contexts in order to rise to leadership ranks; at the same time, this behavior may clash with cultural and gender values and expectations. This meant valuing humility and maintaining a genuine respect for differences.

Importance of Social Identities to Leadership

The lived experiences shared by the leaders became central to the values forming their social identities and were central to their professional lives as leaders. Their shared experiences of oppression and marginalization were used as a guide to decrease oppression for others through their leadership. They trusted their own lived experiences as a source of knowledge because they instilled a sense of purpose. The theme of trusting one's diversity lens as an important reality was central to empowering these leaders to accomplish change. Leaders found themselves attempting to reconcile the intersectionality of their multiple social identities with their identities as leaders and deciding when which identities should be salient depending on the context. It was felt that these dilemmas were unique and typically not faced by leaders whose social identities are syntonic with that of a dominant organizational culture.

These insights are consistent with findings from earlier studies and support our proposition for moving from trait theory to social identity theory as a paradigm for diversity leadership. The emphasis on contexts also supports our proposition to move from contingency theories to social and organizational contexts as a paradigm for diversity leadership. From an LMX theory perspective, we might well consider the influence of diversity in both leaders and members as influencing the preferred in-groups embraced by leaders in their exercise of leadership. As these findings demonstrate, case studies of successful diverse leaders should be incorporated not as exceptions but as dimensions of successful leadership.

Leadership Styles

Balance and collaboration appeared to be central to how these leaders perceived their leadership style. While contemporary views of leadership often emphasize the importance of transformational leadership styles, the diverse leaders here underscored the importance of collaboration as a process and style. This included balancing empowerment and consensus building with the need to exert authority; they all recognized the fine balance between a laissez-faire approach and an authoritative approach. While cooperation was valued, they also recognized the importance of using competition as a tool to promote diversity goals. An emphasis on building networks and community was central to this process over the focus on a task orientation. These perceptions are consistent with the notion of relationships in addition to influence as central to diversity leadership. They also balance the common emphasis on competition with the importance of cooperation as a style of leadership.

Managing and promoting change was also central to these leaders as they emphasized the need to change the organizational culture if one is to push for diversity as a goal. Strategies to do this included activating a vision for change and making the business case for diversity. The leaders underscored that diversity needs to be compelling to all within the organization; therefore, viewing diversity as a competitive advantage and as driving the bottom line are important concepts for an organization to define its goals. For a leader to get buy-in for promoting a more diverse organization, they felt a leader must understand what motivates people and how these motivations are often driven by cultural values. This included developing measures of accountability directed toward diversity and balancing the power and influence of a leader with a servant leadership perspective—hence, using power and influence wisely. They emphasized the need to be aware and proactive in working with different and diverse groups within an organization to reach a common direction. Last, they felt "giving back" and "empowering others" were responsibilities of diversity leadership.

These findings demonstrate the centrality of a humane and social justice orientation in their leadership styles and how lived experiences of oppression promote this orientation to equity and diversity. There appears to be a heightened awareness of power and how to use that power wisely. It does not preclude the absence of its polar opposites but the importance of balance. While the notion of promoting change is also central, the minimizing of a transformational orientation is noteworthy. While change, vision, and charismatic influence are common characteristics associated with transformational leadership, are there semantic meanings associated with transformational leadership that are viewed as less desirable?

Maintaining Authenticity and Integrity

Diverse leaders are often pioneers as "firsts" and need courage to initiate and pursue social change. This can sometimes take a personal toll in being alone, the token, or the model for one's group, or in experiencing the tension of being the "trailblazer." Many of the leaders believed that they "Have had to work twice as hard to get half as far" or "Are always having to prove their competence." As one leader said, "As a woman and as a minority, you have to be extraordinary to be a leader; White men only need to be ordinary," meaning your uniqueness takes you to an extraordinary level (Chin et al., in progress).

The challenge to one's authenticity comes about in having to decide to "conform to the power elite" as Zweigenhaft & Domhoff (2006) contend or to "blaze new trails." Often the very presence of a leader from a non-dominant social group challenges existing cultural scripts. For many of the leaders, it was also not uncommon to feel as if they were living in two worlds, an experience that creates role conflicts. Clashes between one's own cultural values with that of the organization were not uncommon such that leaders felt that sometimes "they do not bring all of themselves to work." This was especially true of gay and lesbian leaders who could not decide whether or not to disclose their sexual orientation. The push and pull between contrasting cultural, community, and family values and those required of being a leader could be stressful. For example, needing to self-promote was contrary to cultural values for many but viewed as essential in a context that is likely to denigrate one's competence based on stereotypic expectations. Some leaders made this challenge easier by distinguishing between self-promotion and promotion of the organization and its mission.

Diverse leaders felt they often faced challenges of bias, oppression, and marginalization even in their role as leaders. Many felt that double bind situations were common in being expected to perform according to stereotypic social roles and simultaneously criticized for not being an effective leader when they do. Many felt they could never lose their outsider status. To cope, many felt it important to build greater and more extensive networks outside the workplace.

Self-Protection and Safety

The importance of both personal and professional lives in the exercise of leadership was remarkable given the fact that one's personal life was also perceived as a buffer and source of self-care for diverse leaders. Unlike traditional leadership models that separate professional and personal lives, these diverse leaders assert the unhealthiness of this bifurcation and emphasize the dynamic interplay between the two.

While many resort to their personal networks and lives as mechanisms for self-protection and safety, most were initially reluctant to own this as characteristic of their leadership. This is consistent with findings on the GLOBE studies (House et al., 2004) where most leaders tend to rank this dimension low as instrumental to effective leadership. While initially viewing this dimension as self-serving, the diverse leaders ultimately came to consensus that self-protection was necessary amidst the frequent challenges to their competence and effectiveness as a leader as individuals with marginalized or less privileged social identities. They felt that they frequently needed to remind themselves not to take things personally and concentrated on creating safe havens for themselves. This took various forms of developing a protective shield to ward off continued invalid criticism, deciding to pick and choose one's fights when promoting diversity principles especially in homogenous organizational cultures or when organizational cultures were aligned with values of the more privileged groups in society.

The omission of women and racial/ethnic minorities from senior ranks of leadership is not uncommon. Therefore, these leaders were acutely conscious that their self-presentations could be jarring because they do not fit the prototype of the typical leader. As the gay and lesbian leaders asserted, the process of *coming out* is tough because of the stigma associated with same-sex orientations. Hence, they emphasized the need to be proud of who you are to counter the frequent communications that they are "not OK."

Mentoring and Building Pipelines

The leaders emphasized how crucial mentors were to their success. Receiving mentoring was viewed as extremely important for the support and affirmation needed to face the challenges of leadership especially when one's social identities are marginalized or less privileged. Mentors can model risk-taking strategies for remaining consistent with one's own values and identities (i.e., authenticity and integrity). Good mentorships often seem to last across time and geographical space. As a result, mentoring others was viewed as a vital part of being a diverse leader to build a pipeline of potential leaders who are diverse and committed to promoting a diverse workplace.

Mentorship, however, was not without its challenges. Diversity leaders often feel a greater obligation to mentor as a way of "giving back." There is also the tendency to pair mentors only with mentees who share the same social identity. While this provides important opportunities for an affinity bond between mentor and mentee, it needs to be balanced with the importance of expanding one's experience with different and multiple perspectives.

Paradigm for Diversity Leadership

In attempting to develop a paradigm for diversity leadership (Chin et al., in progress), the leaders spoke compellingly about the importance of recognizing where we stand in history and acknowledging the work of those who came before us. As one leader said, it is important to "be grounded by the ancestors and looking forward . . . looking to history and bringing it into today's reality." Another leader described the process of creating a sense of community as important in helping one become an effective leader. She had asked herself, "What is it that I need when I felt alone?" She realized that she "needed friends and a like-minded community for her to grow and thrive as a leader." Personal and lived experiences are anchored amidst a social and historical context and are part of one's identity development as a leader.

One observer's comment was provocative in stimulating discussion about the correlation between leader identity and authenticity; she asked: "In developing leaders, is there value in mentoring toward identity development? [It seems that] leaders able to make the greatest contribution are further along in their identity development." Some leaders felt they used their heritage to learn about good and bad leadership. Others detailed how embracing your complete identity as a leader can be liberating. An example was given about how LGBT stigma can be invisible and the privilege of that invisibility can create a different experience of one's identity. A leader attested to the need to constantly remind herself "not to subordinate dimensions of myself and not to tell less than full truths."

Acknowledging how one's identity as a leader evolves from a social and historical context and maintaining one's authenticity amidst the challenges faced by diverse leaders are two overarching principles of a diversity leadership paradigm. Managing change and the adaptive change skills that effective leaders need to have is a third overarching principle. One leader described the importance of cultural fluency as a skill to enable leaders to lead across different organizational contexts and cultures. Building on that point, observer feedback was instructive in bringing attention to generational differences as yet another dimension of cultural fluency. An observer talked about how leaders of a younger generation struggle with their comfort level about "who they are" and noted: "It appears to me that you [leaders] are settled with 'who you are' and are conscious of how other people view you and what impacts your role as a leader. [You've made it clear that] knowing yourself is important; to be a leader takes being aware of your surroundings, where you're at and what people think of you." Younger leaders may not be as far along in that process.

Many participants felt that often people assert that they "cannot see race," to which one leader spoke about how to reconcile the discomfort with discussions of race that exists when such statements are made. He asked; "At what point do you take the leadership, and decide that I am going to go there? That is the burden of awareness, [having to bring up difficult conversations]." Having to live in two different worlds, one of "privilege" as a leader and another of "oppression" as a racial or ethnic minority is a major challenge of leadership faced by diverse leaders.

Some observers spoke about the personal-professional identity dynamic since leaders are often counseled to leave their personal identities behind. This highlights many of the unspoken issues that arise when raising an awareness of diversity in leadership. Discussion ensued that centered on gender, sexual orientation, and other dimensions of diversity that appear to challenge the status quo and to recognize that there are costs to breaking the rules just by being present. A diversity leadership paradigm brings these personal dimensions together as part of a personal-professional leadership balance. As one leader said, there is "pain that comes with [challenging these notions] and courage that comes with doing that." Raising an awareness of diversity often leads to difficult conversations. This led to a discussion of the role of spirituality in leadership. A number of leaders considered spirituality analogous with integrity and spoke to their beliefs about the need for leaders to have a moral compass and purpose. Although they recognized that spirituality is not equivalent to a moral compass, "how to be in this world," and the importance of being "robust, vibrant and healthy in all dimensions of [one's] life" was underscored. In bringing forth any dimension of one's identities, leaders must not impose one's beliefs on others. How does one bring all oneself to his or her leadership and maintain a commitment to diversity and change without imposing one's beliefs and core values onto others; this is one of the major challenges of diversity leadership.

As a final take-away message, leaders responded to an observer's question: "What guidance would [these diverse] leaders offer about how to navigate future leadership issues?" Leaders responded with the following:

- Speak the business case of diversity first to get buy in from those in power;
- Focus on global issues and bring all generations and [voices] in to the conversation;
- Be technologically literate in today's environment of rapid change;
- Nurture relationship and consensus building as important vehicles of communication;
- Play a role in change by pushing social justice issues locally to achieve an eventual global impact;
- "Be a mentor; be a protégé; speak your truth." Mentoring is an obligation for all leaders in an organization;
- Know your purpose and find a network from which you can give and get support;
- Don't lose who you are in the process or eliminate the things that make you unique. Discern your own values and maintain your authenticity; no job is worth violating your own values.

These themes from the Diversity Leadership Summit reflect consensus that the experience of leadership is different when dimensions of diversity are highlighted. It provides not an end process but a beginning one to capture the lived experiences and social realities of diverse leaders. A synthesizing principle is the need for leadership models to evolve and transform what the nature of leadership is. Another principle is the fluidity, relationality, and intersectionality of dimensions of diversity for a dynamic model of leadership. Diversity and inclusion were viewed as core competencies that include Resilience, Excellence, Strength, Passion, Empathy, Courage, and Tenacity, or RESPECT (cited by Beauregard Stubblefield-Tave and credited to Dr. Rizza Lavizzo-Mourrey, President and CEO of the Robert Wood Johnson Foundation). The Diversity Leadership Summit ended with the work needing to be done. Developing a diversity leadership paradigm is an ongoing and dynamic process to be validated with ongoing empirical research. The Summit was a beginning rather than an end. Leaders viewed their experiences as different, and ones not captured in the existing leadership literature.

DLMOX Paradigm: Crosscutting Themes

We end with an overview of six crosscutting themes identified in this book as key ingredients for a diversity leadership paradigm; they were introduced as goals of diversity leadership in Figure 2.1 as progressive and evolving. They are to be researched, examined, and applied to reach a DLMOX model of leadership that is inclusive of all perspectives and respectful of differences, can be a model for leaders to embrace to lead effectively, and be adaptive and culturally fluent in their leadership styles for 21st century leadership. A diagram of a DLMOX paradigm of leadership was introduced in Figure 2.2 of how these six dimensions are interactive and dynamic.

Global

Society and its organizations are becoming increasingly global. How do we factor this into the examination of leadership?

- Cultural value orientations vary across cultures and groups.
- These values and assumptions underlie cross-cultural, cross-group, and interpersonal communication and relationships.
- Leadership is influenced by these value orientations and changing societal contexts and global perspectives.

Diverse

Growing diversity of populations within the United States and countries globally shape a mandate for inclusion and responsiveness to their needs in the exercise of leadership. What factors need attention to enable this process to occur?

- Growing diversity and changing population demographics shape the nature of the leader-member exchange.
- Valuing differences is important to effective leadership.
- Inclusion of all voices is necessary for leadership to be relevant to diverse groups.
- Acculturation and immigration experience add to the complexity of group member composition.

Leader Identity

What does a leader bring to his or her leadership? How does this influence the exercise of leadership?

- Multiple and intersecting social and individual identities shape leader identity.
- Maintaining one's authenticity is important to leader integrity but presents a challenge when diverse member groups demand total loyalty in response to the social identities of a leader.

- Role conflicts can arise for diverse leaders when demands from their social identities compete with that of their leader identity.
- Leaders need to maintain an ethical sense of self and avoid abusive use of power.
- Justice and fairness of purpose must remain a priority with a goal to eliminate inequity.
- Exercise virtuous leadership that includes supporting cultural values and a position of caring for others.

Leadership Style Dimensions

The following leadership style dimensions need further investigation as to their strengths and weaknesses under varying leadership situations and cultural contexts. Others can be identified from the diversity leadership prototype described in Chapter 8 as dimensions to be expanded without favoring one end of the continuum. Or they can be investigated for variation in semantic meaning across cultures and subgroups.

- Interpersonal versus task oriented
- Democratic versus oligarchic style
- Assertiveness: Direct versus indirect mechanisms
- Charisma: Influential versus self-sacrificing characteristics
- Collective versus individual cultural orientations
- Achievement: Cooperation versus competition
- Collaborative process
- Transformational style
- Authority: Egalitarian versus hierarchical

Lived Experiences

These are personal and cultural experiences that may pose opportunities and challenges for the exercise of leadership. Cultural variation will influence what is brought to the exercise of leadership and the values that drive mission and purpose of leadership.

- Sociocultural experiences: Influences of race, ethnicity, gender, and culture
- Adaptability versus conformity to the dominant culture
- Empowerment/shared power versus abusive/dictatorial power
- Oppression versus privilege

Contexts

Social contexts of public policy, social zeitgeists, and world events together with organizational contexts of mission, purpose, and organizational culture will drive the exercise of leadership. These include structures, policies, and processes within a society or organization:

- Organizational culture
- Affirmative paradigm
- Social justice orientation
- Multicultural society versus homogeneous society
- Social perceptions and expectations
- Bias and discrimination
- Family friendly versus masculinized contexts

New Paradigms

The crosscutting themes identified above offer avenues for new paradigms of diversity leadership. While 20th century views of leadership appeared to diminish the importance of power in leaders through empowerment models of leadership, the salience of power inherent in the social identities of members of out-groups and in-groups in society and their contribution to group and organizational dynamics is central to a new paradigm of diversity leadership. The lived experiences of subordinate groups within a culture or country share an experience of being marginalized or oppressed. New paradigms of diversity leadership are needed as a 21st century view of power in world leadership shifts from a country's military strength to its economic power.

Second, underlying cultural orientation values of implicit leader theories as identified in the GLOBE studies are central to understanding cultural variation in societies that influences perceptions of leadership effectiveness. From the multicultural literature, we cannot ignore the intersectionality of social, racial, ethnic, and gender identities along with one's identity as a leader in shaping leadership behavior. Lived experiences associated with racism, biculturalism, and privilege all shape the perception, expectation, and exercise of leadership. Moreover, differences in these cultural orientation values can contribute to miscommunication and conflict in the leader-member-organization relationship.

Last, the introduction of non-Western perspectives as described by Thomas (2008) is important in shifting contemporary views to a more inclusive and less ethnocentric model of leadership that is both diverse and global. Western models of leadership that currently dominate much of the leadership literature should be examined against Asian or Eastern models of leadership that emphasize collectivism, benevolence, and familial affiliations. The Daoist view of leadership, developed by Lee, Haught, Chen, and Chan (2013), as soft and malleable contrasts with Western views of leadership as strong and authoritative offers a different metaphor for effective leadership. The self-construal models of interdependent versus independent selves by Markus and Kitayama (1991) offer yet another opportunity for conceptualizing leadership behavior amidst a global world that is increasingly interdependent.

The emphasis on virtue and ethics and the salience of philosophy over empirical validation of leadership models (e.g., Kilburg, 2012; Li, 2013) offered by Eastern philosophies has received little attention in the leadership literature. There is a growing emphasis on virtue and ethics in 21st century leadership that involves leadership as caring for others and benevolence. It includes moral discourse on making a positive contribution to society and having open communication and honesty in relationships. This humane cultural orientation is related to the concept of benevolence, which has greater significance for leadership in Eastern cultures but is aligned with social justice notions of leadership. The motivation to lead based on altruism reflected in the "power to guide" as opposed to the "power to dominate" is growing in importance with this attention to a humane cultural orientation in leadership. While democracies have prevailed as ideal leadership structures, 21st century models might consider alternative structures of leadership such as oligarchies and benevolent paternalism, which have been effective and favorably accepted in different countries throughout the world. While masculinized contexts of leadership have prevailed, 21st century models might also consider feminist and humane orientations to leadership.

Summary

In redefining leadership to be global and diverse, we recognize that the face of diversity is changing and offer a new DLMOX paradigm. It is a framework that should be both evolving and dynamic. We first offer a process to change the "traditional" leader prototype to a "diverse leader" prototype. We then identify themes within the paradigm, including global and diverse perspectives, leader identity, leader style dimensions, lived experiences, and contexts. These themes will need further research, examination, and application to develop an inclusive model of leadership. While leadership is generally viewed an influence relationship, we emphasize the importance of relationships and the influence of cultural and social contexts. In the 21st century, the role and status of leaders have changed as the digital age has shifted the dominance and bases of power shift toward outcomes based on economic power and interdependence rather than military power.

The Diversity Leadership Summit provides an example of a process to examine diverse leadership and the lived experiences of diverse leaders.

The participants identified a set of common themes consistent with the findings about how leader identity, leadership style, and lived experiences intersect with dimensions of race, ethnicity, gender, and sexual orientation in the exercise of leadership. The findings reinforced the importance of collaboration and consensus, a social justice and humane orientation, authenticity, and integrity to diversity leadership. More importantly, the shared experience of marginality was a constant that shaped shared goals of promoting diversity and equity as well as the importance of self-protection, an affirmative paradigm, supportive networks, and mentoring as dimensions of diverse leadership. These diverse leaders also were often among the "firsts" to achieve such positions and were challenged with decisions to "conform to the power elite" versus "blaze new trails" as well as coping with cultural clashes between personal cultural and organizational values. Overall, it was clear that "difference makes a difference" as leaders grappled with dilemmas of maintaining authenticity, establishing credibility, and proving one's competence in ways not experienced by those leaders from dominant in-groups.

Discussion Questions: Future Directions—Evolving a DLMOX Paradigm

1. Pick one of the themes under Redefining Leadership. Discuss its relevance to your lived experiences and role in your exercise of leadership.

2. Using the DLMOX paradigm, discuss how your leadership might be influenced by each of the six themes. How would you manage these issues in your leadership? What dilemmas might arise? Discuss why and how they might arise, and what can be done to reach a resolution.

3. Can you identify any additional themes that would be important to develop and advance a paradigm for diversity leadership?

4. Redefining leadership is said to be shaped by social identities, cultural values, diverse lived experiences and global contexts that leaders bring to their leadership. Discuss some ways in which we can identify these factors without stereotyping an individual or his or her group.

5. Pick one of more of the characteristics listed in Table 10.1. How would a leader expressing these characteristics deal with a problem employee or disruptive organizational member? Would there be specific punishment and reward characterizing that ethnocultural leadership prototype? Justify your response with relevant examples.

6. Charisma and influential versus self-sacrificing characteristics are often posed as characteristics of an effective leader. Identify those characteristics in Table 10.1 that might closely fit with charisma and influential versus self-sacrificing characteristics. Can you provide an example of a leader who might best fit your description?

7. Describe how you would conceptualize and carry out a research project that would identify the endorsement (or lack of) of the 39 characteristics in Table 10.1 by leaders across a variety of samples. Which groups would be most likely to endorse which characteristics with what degree of intensity? Which groups would be unlikely to endorse them?

References

AAC&U (n.d.). *AAC&U diversity and inclusive excellence resources*. Retrieved from http://www.aacu.org/resources/diversity/index.cfm

Adler, N. J., & Bartholomew, S. (1992). Managing globally competent people. *Academy of Management Executive*, 6, 52–65.

AFT. (2013). Shared governance in colleges and universities: A statement by the Higher Educational Program and Policy Council (Item No.: 36–0696). Washington, DC: American Federation of Teachers Higher Education Council. Retrieved from http://facultysenate.tamu.edu/Quick_Links/Shared_Governance_in_Colleges_and_Universities.pdf

Agarwal, R., & Misra, G. (1986). Factor analytic study of achievement goals and means. *International Journal of Psychology*, 21, 217–231.

Ah Chong, L. M., & Thomas, D. C. (1997). Leadership perceptions in cross-cultural context: Pacific Islanders and Pakeha in New Zealand. *Leadership Quarterly*, 8(3), 275–293.

Albert Einstein Site Online. (n.d.). *Albert Einstein Quotes*. Retrieved from http://www.alberteinsteinsite.com/quotes/einsteinquotes.html

Ali, A. J. (1990). Management theory in a transitional society: The Arab's experience. *International Studies of Management and Organization*, 20, 7–35.

Al-Kubaisy, A. (1985). A model in the administrative development of Arab Gulf countries. *The Arab Gulf*, 17(2), 29–48.

Allen, K. E., Bordas, J., Hickman, G. R. Matusak, L. R., Sorenson, G. J., & Whitmire, K. J. (2010). Leadership in the 21st century. In G. R. Hickman (Ed.), *Leading organizations: Perspective for a new era* (2nd ed.). Thousand Oaks, CA: Sage.

Alvord, L. A., & Cohen Van Pelt, E. (2000). *The scalpel and the silver bear: The first Navajo woman surgeon combines Western medicine and traditional healing*. New York: Random House.

American Anthropological Association (AAA). (1998). *American Anthropological Association statement on "race."* Retrieved from http://www.aaanet.org/stmts/racepp.htm

American Indian Research and Policy Institute. (2005). *Traditional American Indian leadership. A report for the American Indian Research and Policy Institute*. St. Paul, MN: Author.

APA. (n.d.). Leadership Institute for Women in Psychology. Retrieved from http://www.apa.org/women/programs/leadership/index.aspx

Arnett, J. J. (2002). The psychology of globalization. *American Psychologist,* *57*(10), 774–783.

Ashkanasy, N., Gupta, V., Mayfield, M., & Trevor-Roberts, E. (2004). Future orientation. In R. House, P. Hanges, M. Javidan, P. Dorfman, & W. Gupta (Eds.), *Culture, leadership, and organizations: The GLOBE study of 62 societies* (pp. 282–342). Thousand Oaks, CA: Sage.

Atsutakawa, L. (2013). Breaking stereotypes: An Asian American's view of leadership development. *Asian American Journal of Psychology, 4*(4), 277–284. doi:10.1037/a0035390

Avolio, B. J. (2007). Promoting more integrative strategies for leadership theory-building. *American Psychologist, 62,* 25–33.

Avolio, B. J., Gardner, W. L., Walumbwa, F. O., Luthans, F., & May, D. R. (2004). Unlocking the mask: A look at the process by which authentic leaders impact follower attitudes and behaviors. *Leadership Quarterly, 15*(6), 801–823.

Ayman, R. (1993). Leadership perception: The role of gender and culture. In M. M. Chemers, & R. Ayman (Eds.), *Leadership theory and research: Perspectives and directions* (pp. 137–166). New York: Academic Press.

Ayman, R. (2002). Contingency model of leadership effectiveness: Challenges and achievements. In L. L. Neider & C. A. Schriesheim (Eds.), *Research in management: Vol. 2. Leadership* (pp. 197–228). Greenwich, CT: Information Age.

Ayman, R. (2004). Culture and leadership. In C. Spielberger (Ed.), *Encyclopedia of applied psychology* (Vol. 2, pp. 507–519). San Diego, CA: Elsevier.

Ayman, R., & Chemers, M. M. (1983). Relationship of supervisory behavior rating to work group effectiveness and subordinate satisfaction. *Journal of Applied Psychology, 68,* 338–341.

Ayman, R., & Korabik, K. (2010). Leadership: Why gender and culture matter. *American Psychologist,* 157–170.

Aycan, Z. (2006). Paternalism: Towards conceptual refinement and operationalization. In K. S. Yang, K. K. Hwang, & U. Kim (Eds.), *Scientific advances in indigenous psychologies: Empirical, philosophical, and cultural contributions* (pp. 445–466). London: Sage.

Aycan, Z., Kanungo, R. N., Mendonca, M., Yu, K., Deller, J., Stahl, G., & Kurshid, A. (2000). Impact of culture on human resource management practices: A 10-country comparison. *Applied Psychology: An International Review, 49,* 192–221.

Bacharach, S. B., & Lawler, E. J. (1980). *Power and politics in organizations.* San Francisco: Jossey-Bass.

Badwound, E., & Tierney, W. G. (1988). Leadership and American Indian values: The tribal college dilemma, *Journal of American Indian Education, 28*(1), 9–15.

Bandura, A. (1977). Self-efficacy: Toward a unifying theory of behavioral change. *Psychological Review, 84,* 191–215.

Barton, T. R. (2006, Fall). Feminist leadership: Building nurturing academic communities. *Advancing Women in Leadership, 21.* Retrieved from http://www.advancingwomen.com/awl/fa112006/barton.htm

Bass, B. M. (Ed.). (1990). *Stogdill's handbook of leadership: A survey of theory and research* (3rd ed.). New York: Free Press.

Bass, B. M., & Avolio, B. J. (1994). *Improving organizational effectiveness through transformational leadership.* Thousand Oaks, CA: Sage.

Beal, A. C., Doty, M. M., Hernandez, S. E., Shea, K. K., & Davis, K. (2007, June). *Closing the divide: How medical homes promote equity in health care*—Results from the Commonwealth fund 2006 health care quality survey. *The Commonwealth Fund.* Retrieved from http://www.commonwealthfund .org/Publications/Fund-Reports/2007/Jun/Closing-the-Divide-How-Medical-Homes-Promote-Equity-in-Health-Care-Results-From-The-Commonwealth-F.aspx

Beck, D. E., & Cowan, C. C. (2006). *Spiral dynamics: Mastering values, leadership, and change.* Malden, MA: Blackwell Publishing.

Becker, T. (1997). *Traditional American Indian leadership: A comparison with U.S. governance.* A report prepared for the American Indian Research and Policy Institute. St. Paul, MN.

Bem, S. L. (1974). The measurement of psychological androgyny. *Journal of Consulting and Clinical Psychology, 42,* 155–62.

Bengsten, V., Grigsby, E., Corry, E., & Hruby, M. (1977). Relating academic research to community concerns: A case in collaborative effort. *Journal of Social Issues, 33*(4), 75–92.

Bennett, J. (2009). Designing programs for cultural learning. In M. A. Moodian (Ed.), *Contemporary leadership and intercultural competence: Exploring the cross-cultural dynamics within organizations* (pp. 95–124). Thousand Oaks, CA: Sage.

Bennett, M. J. (1998). Intercultural communication: A current perspective. In M. J. Bennett (Ed.), *Basic concept of intercultural communications: Selected readings* (pp. 1–34). Yarmouth, ME: Intercultural Press.

Bennett, M. (1977). Testing management theories cross-culturally. *Journal of Applied Psychology, 62*(5), 578–581.

Berry, J. (1980). Introduction to methodology. In H. Triandis & J. Berry (Eds.), *Handbook of cross-cultural psychology* (Vol. 2, pp. 1–28). Boston: Allyn & Bacon.

Bersin, J. (2013, June 6). Time to scrap performance appraisals? *Forbes.* Retrieved from http://www.forbes.com/sites/joshbersin/2013/05/06/time-to-scrap-performance-appraisals/

Bess, J. L. (1995). *Creative R & D leadership: Insights from Japan.* Westport, CT: Quorum Books.

Bhindi, N., & Duignan, P. (1997). Leadership for a new century: Authenticity, intentionality, spirituality and sensibility. *Educational Management Administration & Leadership, 25*(2), 117–132.

Biernat, M. (2005). *Standards and expectancies: Contrast and assimilation in judgments of self and others.* New York: Psychology Press.

Boerner, S., Eisenbeiss, S. A., & Griesser, D. (2007). Follower behavior and organizational performance: The impact of transformational leaders. *Journal of Leadership and Organizational Studies, 13*(3), 15.

Bond, M. (2013). The pan-culturality of well-being: But how does culture fit into the equation? *Asian Journal of Social Psychology, 16,* 158–162.

Brass, D. J. (2001). Social capital and organizational leadership. In S. J. Zaccaro & R. J. Klimoski (Eds.), *The nature of organizational leadership: Understanding the performance imperatives confronting today's leaders* (pp. 132–152). San Francisco, CA: Jossey-Bass.

Brodbeck, F. C., Michael Frese, M., Akerblom, S.V., Audia, G., Bakacsi, G., Bendova, H., . . . & Wunderer, R. (2000). Cultural variation of leadership prototypes across 22 European countries. *Journal of Occupational and Organizational Psychology, 73,* 1–29.

Broyard, B. (2007). *One drop: My father's hidden life—A story of race and family secrets.* New York: Little Brown and Company.

Burhansstipanov, L., Christopher, S., & Schumacher, A. (2005, November). Lessons learned from community-based participatory research in Indian Country. *Cancer Control: Cancer, Culture, and Literacy Supplement* (pp. 70–76).

Burns, J. M. (1978). *Leadership.* New York: Harper & Row.

Bush, T. (2011). *Theories of educational leadership and management* (4th ed.). London: Sage.

Butler, D., & Geis, F. L. (1990). Nonverbal affect responses to male and female leaders: Implications for leadership evaluations. *Journal of Personality and Social Psychology, 58,* 48–59.

Bynum, R. (2013, June 21). Paula Deen fired: Food Network cancels show after racism scandal. *Huff Post Live.* Retrieved from http://www.huffingtonpost .com/2013/06/21/paula-deen-fired-food-network-cancels-show-after-racism-scandal_n_3480517.html

Byrne, D., & Neuman, J. (1992). The implications of attraction research for organizational issues. In K. Kelly (Ed.), *Issues, theory, and research in industrial/ organizational psychology* (pp. 29–70). Amsterdam, the Netherlands: Elsevier Science.

Campinha-Bacote, J. (2003). The process of cultural competency in the delivery of healthcare services: A model of care. *Journal of Transcultural Nursing, 13*(3), 181–184.

Carroll, A. (2011. January 21). The realities of health care reform. *The Incidental Economist.* Retrieved from http://theincidentaleconomist.com/wordpress/the-realities-of-health-care-reform/

Cassell, J., & Jacobs, S. (Eds.). (1987). *Handbook on ethical issues in anthropology* (Special publication No. 23). Washington, DC: American Anthropological Association.

Catalyst. (1999). *Women of color in corporate management: Opportunities and barriers* [Report]. New York: Author.

Center for Cultural Fluency (n.d.). *Philosophy and assumptions.* Los Angeles: Mount Saint Mary's College, Center for Cultural Fluency. Retrieved from http://www .msmc.la.edu/campus-resources/center-for-cultural-fluency/philosophy-and-assumptions.asp

Chávez, H. (n.d.). *Inspirational and famous quotes.* Retrieved from http://www .brainyquote.com

Cheng, B. S., Chou, L. F., Wu, T. Y., Huang, M. P., & Farh, J. L. (2004). Paternalistic leadership and subordinate response: Establishing a leadership model in Chinese organizations. *Asian Journal of Social Psychology, 7*, 89–117.

Cheung, F. M., & Halpern, D. F. (2010). Women at the top: Powerful leaders define success as work + family in a culture of gender. *American Psychologist, 65*, 182–193. doi:10.1037/a0017309

Cheung, F. M., Leung, K., Zhang, J.-K., Sun, H.-A, Gan, Y.-Q, Song, W.-Z, & Xie, D. (2001). Indigenous Chinese personality constructs: Is the five-factor model complete? *Journal of Cross-Cultural Psychology, 32*, 407–433. doi:10.1177/0022022110032004003

Cheung, F., Van de Vijver, F., & Leong, F. (2011, Oct). Toward a new approach to the study of personality. *American Psychologist, 66*(7), 593–603.

Cheung, Y.W. (1991). Overview: Sharpening the focus on ethnicity. *International Journal of Addictions, 25*(5A & 6A), 573–579.

Cheung, Y. W. (1993). Approaches to ethnicity: Clearing roadblocks in the study of ethnicity and substance abuse. *International Journal of Addictions, 28*(12), 1209–1226.

Chin, J. L. (2009). *Diversity in mind and in action*. Santa Barbara, CA: Praeger, ABC-CLIO.

Chin, J. L. (Ed.). (2010). Diversity and leadership [Special issue]. *American Psychologist, 65*(3), 149–225.

Chin, J. L. (2013). Diversity leadership: Influence of ethnicity, gender, and minority status. *Open Journal of Leadership, 2*(1), 1–10. Retrieved from http://www.scirp.org/journal/ojl

Chin, J. L., Desormeaux, L., Sawyer, K., Remer, P., Parks, K., Liang, C., Li, V., & Arrington, E. (2014). *Diversity leadership: Developing a paradigm*. Manuscript submitted for publication.

Chin, J. L., Lott, B., Rice, J. K., & Sanchez-Hucles, J. (2007). *Women and leadership: Transforming visions and diverse voices*. Malden, MA: Blackwell.

Chin, J. L., & Sanchez-Hucles, J. (2007, January). *Diversity and leadership* [Commentary on the "Special Issue: Leadership"]. *American Psychologist, 62*(6), 608–609.

Chin, J. L., Yee, B., & Banks, M. E. (2014). Women health and behavior health issues in health care reform. In F. Kuramoto (Ed.), Special issue on Affordable Care Act: Meeting the health and behavioral health needs of a diverse society. *Journal of Social Work in Rehabilitation and Disability*, March, 2(1 and 2). doi:10.1080/1536710X.2013.870509

Chong, N., & Baez, F. (2005). *Latino culture: A dynamic force in the changing American workplace*. Boston, MA: Intercultural Press.

Chopra, D. (2013, October 9). How to become a great leader [Web blog post]. Retrieved from https://www.deepakchopra.com/blog/view/1322/how_to_become_a_great_leader

Churchill, W. (1940). *We shall fight on the beaches*. The Churchill Centre. Retrieved from https://www.winstonchurchill.org/learn/speeches/speeches-of-winston-churchill/1940-finest-hour/128-we-shall-fight-on-the-beaches

Cirese, S. (1985). *Quest: A search for self*. New York: HOH, Rurehard, & Winston.

Coates, T.-N. P. (2007, February 1). Is Obama black enough? *Time.*

Cobbs, P. M., & Turnock, J. L. (2003). *Cracking the corporate code: The revealing success stories of 32 African-American executives.* NY: Amacom.

Cohen, D. A., Taylor, S. L., Zonta, M., & Vestal, K. D. (2007). Availability of high school extracurricular sports programs and high-risk behaviors. *Journal of School Health, 77*(2), 80.

Comas-Diaz, L., & Greene, B. (Eds.). (1994). *Women of color and mental health.* NY: Guilford Press.

Condon, S. (2012, March 23). Obama: "If I had a son, he'd look like Trayvon Martin." *CBS News.* Retrieved from http://www.cbsnews.com/news/obama-if-i-had-a-son-hed-look-like-trayvon/

Connerley, M. L., & Pedersen, P. B. (2005). *Leadership in a diverse and multicultural environment: Developing awareness, knowledge, and skills.* Thousand Oaks, CA: Sage.

Constantine, M., & Ladany, N. (2001). New visions for defining and assessing multicultural counseling competence. In J. M. J. Ponterotto (Ed.), *Handbook of multicultural counseling* (2nd ed., pp. 482–498). Thousand Oaks, CA: Sage.

Cooke, S.S. (2013, March 20). Demographic turnover provides opportunities. *Credit Union Times Magazine.* Retrieved from http://www.cutimes.com/2013/03/20/demographic-turnover-presents-opportunities

Corbin, J., & Strauss, A. (2007). *Basics of qualitative research: Techniques and procedures for developing grounded theory* (3rd ed.). Thousand Oaks, CA: Sage.

Cox, T. (1993). *Cultural diversity in organizations: Theory, research and practice.* San Francisco: Berrett-Koehler Publishers.

Creswell, J. W. (2013). Five qualitative approaches to inquiry. In J. W. Creswell (Ed.), *Qualitative inquiry and research design: Choosing among five approaches* (3rd ed., pp. 69–110). Thousand Oaks, CA: Sage.

Cross, T. L., Bazron, B., Dennis, K., & Isaacs, M. (1989). *Towards a culturally competent system of care.* Washington, DC: Georgetown University Child Development Center, CASSP Technical Assistance Center.

Cross, W. E. (1991). *Shades of Black: Diversity in African-American identity.* Philadelphia, PA: Temple University Press.

Davies, P. G., Spencer, S. J., & Steele, C. M. (2005). Clearing the air: Identity safety moderates the effects of stereotype threat on women's leadership aspirations. *Journal of Personality and Social Psychology, 88,* 276–287. doi:10.1037/0022-3514.88.2.276

De Cremer, D., & van Knippenberg, D. (2002). How do leaders promote cooperation? The effects of charisma and procedural fairness. *Journal of Applied Psychology, 87,* 858–866.

Den Hartog, D. N., & Dickson, W. (2004). Leadership and culture. In J. Antonakis, A. T. Cianciolo, & R. J. Sternberg (Eds.), *The nature of leadership* (pp. 249–278). Thousand Oaks, CA: Sage.

Den Hartog, D. N., Van Muijen, J. J., & Koopman, P. L. (1997). Transactional versus transformational leadership: An analysis of the MLQ. *Journal of Occupational and Organizational Psychology, 70,* 19–34.

Dent, E. B., Higgins, M. E., & Wharff, D. M. (2005). Spirituality and leadership: An empirical review of definitions, distinctions, and embedded assumptions. *The Leadership Quarterly, 16*(5), 625–653.

Dickson, M. W., Den Hartog, D. N., & Mitchelson, J. K. (2003). Research on leadership in a cross-cultural context: Making progress, and raising new questions. *The Leadership Quarterly, 14*, 729–768.

Dorfman, P. (1996). International and cross-cultural leadership research. In B. J. Punnett, & O. Shenkar (Eds.), *Handbook for international management research* (pp. 267–349). Oxford, UK: Blackwell.

Dorfman, P. W., & Howell, J. P. (1988). Dimensions of national culture and effective leadership patterns. *Advances in International Comparative Management, 3*, 127–150.

Dorfman, P. W., Howell, J. P., Hibino, S., Lee, J. K., Tate, U., & Bautista, A. (1997). Leadership in Western and Asian countries: Commonalities and differences in effective leadership processes across cultures. *The Leadership Quarterly, 8*(30), 233–274.

Dovidio, J. F., & Gaertner, S. L. (2004). Aversive racism. *Advances in Experimental Social Psychology, 36*, 1–52.

Drucker, P. (2013). *Managing for the future: The 1990s and beyond.* New York: Routledge.

Duffy, T. P. (2011). The Flexner Report—100 years later. *Yale Journal of Biological Medicine, 84*(3), 269–276.

Dunivin, K. O. (1997). *Military culture: A paradigm shift? (Maxwell Paper No. 10).* Air War College, Maxwell Airforce Base, Alabama.

Eagly, A. H., & Carli, L. (2007). *Through the labyrinth: The truth about how women become leaders.* Boston, MA: Harvard Business School Press.

Eagly, A. H., & Chin, J. L. (2010). Diversity and leadership in a changing world. *American Psychologist, 65*(3), 216–225.

Eagly, A. H., Johannesen-Schmidt, M. C., & van Engen, M. L. (2003). Transformational, transactional, and laissez-faire leadership styles: A meta-analysis comparing women and men. *Psychological Bulletin, 129*, 569–591. doi:10.1037/0033–2909.129.4.569

Eagly, A. H., & Johnson, B. T. (1990). Gender and leadership style: A meta-analysis. *Psychological Bulletin, 108*, 233–256. doi:10.1037/0033–2909.108.233

Eagly, A. H., Karau, S. J., & Makhijani, M. G. (1995). Gender and the effectiveness of leaders: A meta-analysis. *Psychological Bulletin, 117*, 125–145. doi:10.1037/0033–909.117.1.125

Eagly, A. H., Makhijani, M. G., & Klonsky, B. G. (1992). Gender and the evaluation of leaders: A meta-analysis. *Psychological Bulletin, 111*, 3–22. doi:10.1037/0033–2909.111.1.3

Ellis, F. (2013, August 15). Girl shot by Taliban to get Peace Award. *Independent. ie.* Retrieved from http://www.independent.ie/irish-news/girl-shot-by-taliban-to-get-peace-award-29500780.html

Erkut, S. (2001). *Inside women's power: Learning from leaders.* Wellesley, MA: Wellesley Centers for Women.

Erkut, S., Alarcon, O., Coll, C. G., Tropp, L. R., & Garcia, H. A. (1999). The dual-focus approach to creating bilingual measures. *Journal of Cross-Cultural Psychology, 30*(2), 206–218.

Farh, J. L., & Cheng, B. S. (2000). A cultural analysis of paternalistic leadership in Chinese organizations. In J. T. Li., A. S. Tsui, & E. Weldon (Eds.), *Management and organizations in the Chinese context* (pp. 84–127). London: Macmillan.

Fassinger, R. E., Shullman, S. L., & Stevenson, M. R. (2010). Toward an affirmative lesbian, gay, bisexual, and transgender leadership paradigm. *American Psychologist*, 201–215.

Fearon, J. D. (2003). Ethnic and cultural diversity by country. *Journal of Economic Growth, 8*, 195–222.

Fei, W.-Z. (1984). *Investigating and editing Laozi's Dao De Jing*. Taiwan, Taibei: Meizhi Library Press.

Ferrara, A. (1998). *Reflective authenticity: Rethinking the project of modernity*. London, New York: Routledge.

Fiedler, F. (1993). The leadership situation and the black box in contingency theories. In M. M. Chemers (Ed.), *Leadership, theory, and research: Perspectives and directions* (pp. 1–28). New York: Academic Press.

Fischer, C. M. (2009). Assessing leadership behavior as it relates to intercultural competence. In M. A. Moodian (Ed.), *Contemporary leadership and intercultural competence: Exploring the cross-cultural dynamics within organizations*. Thousand Oaks, CA: Sage.

Fisher, C., Hoagwood, K., Duster, T., Frank, D., Grisso, T., Levine, R., . . . & Zayas, L. (2002). Research ethics for mental health science involving ethnic minority children and youths. *American Psychologist, 57*, 1024–1040.

Fisher, P. A., & Ball, T. J. (2002). The Indian family wellness project: An application of the tribal participatory research model. *Prevention Science, 3*, 235–240.

Fitzgerald, T. K. (1993). *Metaphors of identity: A culture-communication dialogue*. Albany, NY: State University of New York Press.

Fletcher, J. (2003). *The greatly exaggerated demise of heroic leadership: Gender, power, and the myth of the female advantage*. Boston: Simmons School of Management, Center for Gender in Organizations. Retrieved from http://www.simmons.edu/gsm/cgo/insights13.pdf

Foschi, M. (2000). Double standards for competence: Theory and research. *Annual Review of Sociology, 26*, 21–42. doi:10.1146/annurev.soc.26.1.21

Foster, D. (2010, May 6). "Cultural fluency" or "language fluency"? What's more important when working globally? *The Cultural Prophecy*.

Frable, D. (1997). Gender, racial, sexual and class identities. *Annual Review of Psychology, 48*, 139–162.

Gamble, V. (2000). Subcutaneous scars: A black physician shares what it feels like to be on the receiving end of racial prejudice, despite a successful career. *Health Affairs, 19*(1), 164–169.

Gandhi, M. (n.d.). *The quotations page*. Retrieved from http://www.quotationspage.com/quote/2988.html

Gans, H. (1979). Symbolic ethnicity: The future of ethnic groups and cultures in America. In H. J. Gans, C. Jencks, N. Glazer, & J. R. Gusfield (Eds.), *On the making of Americans: Essays in honor of David Riesman* (pp. 193–220). Philadelphia: University of Pennsylvania.

Gans, H. (2003, March 7). Identity. *The Chronicle of Higher Education*, p. B4.

Gardner, W., & Avolio, B. J. (1998, January). The charismatic relationship: A dramaturgical perspective. *The Academy of Management Review, 23*(1), 32–58.

Gauthier, A. (2011, April 28). *The inner dance of collective leadership* [Webinar]. Retrieved from http://www.slideshare.net/leadershipera/webinar-collective-leadership-alain-gauthier

Geertz, C. (2000). *Available light: Anthropological reflections on philosophical topics*. New Jersey: Princeton University Press.

Geisinger, K. F. (1994). Cross-cultural normative assessment: Translation and adaptation issues influencing the normative interpretation of assessment instruments. *Psychological Assessment, 6*, 304–312.

Gentry, W. A., Patterson, A., Stawiski, S. A., Gilmore, D. C., & Sparks, T. E. (2013, March). A 30-country multilevel test of cultural convergence or divergence of three managerial skillsets. *Consulting Psychology Journal: Practice and Research, 65*(1), 17–39. doi:10.1037/a0032617

Gerstle, G. (2001). *American crucible: Race and nation in the twentieth century*. Princeton, NJ: Princeton University Press.

Gertsner, C. R., & Day, D. V. (1994). Cross-cultural comparison of leadership prototypes. *Leadership Quarterly, 5*(2), 121–134.

Ghei, A., & Nebel, III, E. C. (1994). The successful manager and psychological androgyny: A conceptual and empirical investigation of hotel executives. *International Journal of Hospitality Management, 13*(3), 247–264.

Ghosh, P. (2013, March 5). Hugo Chavez dies: His greatest quotes. *International Business Times*.

Gleason, P. (1983). Identifying identity: A semantic history. *Journal of American History, 69*(4), 910–931.

Goffee, R., & Jones, G. (2000). Why should anyone be led by you? *Harvard Business Review, 78*(5), 62–70.

Goldsmith, M. (2003). The changing role of leadership: Building partnerships inside and outside the organization. In L. Segil, M. Goldsmith, & J. Belasco (Eds.), *Partnering: The new face of leadership* (pp. 3–8). New York: Amacon.

Graen, G. B. (2007). Asking the wrong questions about leadership. *American Psychologist*, 604–605.

Graen, G. B., & Uhl-Bien, M. (1995). Relationship-based approach to leadership: Development of leader-member exchange (LMX) theory of leadership over 25 years: Applying a multi-level, multi-domain perspective. *Leadership Quarterly, 6*(2), 219–247.

Greene, B. (2010). Intersectionality and the complexity of identities: How the personal shapes the professional psychotherapist. *Women & Therapy, 33*(3–4), 452–471.

Greenleaf, R. K. (1977). *Servant leadership: A journey into the nature of legitimate power and greatness.* New York: Paulist Press.

Hackman, R., &. Wageman, R. (2007). Asking the right questions about leadership: Discussion and conclusions. *American Psychologist, 62*(1), 43–47.

Hall, R. L., Garrett-Akinsanya, B., & Hucles, M. (2007). Voices of black feminist leaders: Making spaces for ourselves. In J. L. Chin, B. Lott, J. K. Rice, & J. Sanchez-Hucles (Eds.), *Women and leadership: Transforming visions and diverse voices* (pp. 281–296). Malden, MA: Blackwell.

Hamady, S. (1960). *Temperament and character of the Arabs.* New York: Twayne Publishers.

Hammer, M. R. (2009). The intercultural development inventory. In M. A. Moodian (Ed.), *Contemporary leadership and intercultural competence: Exploring the cross-cultural dynamics within organizations.* Thousand Oaks, CA: Sage.

Hanges, P. J., & Dickson, M. W. (2004). The development and validation of the GLOBE culture and leadership scales. In R. J. House, P. J. Hanges, M. Javidan, P. W. Dorfman, & V. Gupta (Eds.), Leadership, culture, and organizations: The GLOBE study of 62 societies, vol. 1 (pp. 122–151). Thousand Oaks, CA: Sage.

Hart, J. G. (2006). Exploring tribal leadership: Understanding and working with tribal people. *Journal of Extension, 44*(4). Retrieved from http://www.joe.org/joe/2006august/a3.php

Harvard Pilgrim Health Care. (1997). *1997 diversity journal, our third checkup: Cultural competency.* Boston: Harvard Pilgrim Health Care.

Harvey, M. G., & Buckley, M. R. (2002). Assessing the "conventional wisdoms" of management for the 21st century organization. *Organizational Dynamics, 33,* 368–378.

Harzing, A. (2006). Response styles in cross-national survey research: A 26-country study. *International Journal of Cross Cultural Management, 6,* 243–266. doi:10.1177/147059580606632

Hayes, C. (2012, Winter). Alice Eagly on Breaking out of the Labyrinth. In R. S. Management (Ed.), *Women Mean Business,* pp. 24–25.

Health Resources and Services Administration, U. S. Department of Health and Human Services. (2002). *Indicators of cultural competence in health care delivery organizations: An organizational cultural competence assessment profile.* Retrieved from http://www.hrsa.gov/culturalcompetence/indicators

Heames, J. T., & Harvey, M. (2006). The evolution of the concept of the "executive" from the 20th century manager to the 21st century global leader. *Journal of Leadership & Organizational Studies, 13*(2), 29–40.

Heath, D. B. (1990–1991). Uses and misuses of the concept of ethnicity in alcohol studies: An essay on deconstruction. *International Journal of the Addictions, 25*(5A–6A), 607–627.

Heilman, M. E. (2001). Description and prescription: How gender stereotypes prevent women's ascent up the organizational ladder. *Journal of Social Issues, 57,* 657–674. doi:10.1111/0022–4537.00234

Heilman, M. E., Block, C. J., Martell, R. F., & Simon, M. C. (1989). Has anything changed? Current characteristics of men, women, and managers. *Journal of Applied Psychology, 74,* 935–942.

Heilman, M. E., & Eagly, A. H. (2008). Gender stereotypes are alive, well, and busy producing workplace discrimination. *Industrial and Organizational Psychology: Perspectives on Science and Practice, 1,* 393–398. doi:10.1111/j.1754-9434.2008.00072.x

Helgesen, S. (1990). *The female advantage: Women's ways of leadership.* New York: Currency/Doubleday.

Helland, M. R., & Winston, B. E. (2005). Towards a deeper understanding of hope and leadership. *Journal of Leadership & Organizational Studies, 12*(2), 42–54.

Helms, J. (1993). *Black and White racial identity: Theory, research and practice.* Westport, CT: Praeger.

Henrich, J., Heine, S. J., & Norenzayan, A. (2010). The weirdest people in the world? *Behavioral and Brain Sciences, 33*(2–3), 61–135.

Hickman, G. R. (2010). *Leading Organizations: Perspective for a new era* (2nd ed.). Thousand Oaks, CA: Sage.

Hodson, G. D. (2004). The adverse form of racism. In J. L. Chin (Ed.), *The psychology of prejudice and discrimination: Racism in America* (pp. 119–138). Westport, CN: Praeger.

Hofstede, G. (1980). Motivation, leadership, and organization: Do American theories apply abroad? *Organizational Dynamics, 9*(1), 42–63.

Hofstede, G. (2001). *Culture's consequences: International differences in work-related values* (2nd ed.). Thousand Oaks, CA: Sage.

Hofstede, G., & Hofstede, G. (2004). *Cultures and organizations: Software of the mind* (2nd ed.). New York: McGraw-Hill.

Hogg, M. A. (2001). A social identity theory of leadership. *Personality and Social Psychology Review, 5,* 184–200.

Hogg, M. A., Martin, R., & Weeden, K. (2003). Leader-member relations and social identity. In D. V. Kinippenberg & M. A. Hogg (Eds.), *Leadership and power: Identity processes in groups and organizations* (pp. 18–33). Thousand Oaks, CA: Sage.

Homan, A. C., & Greer, L. L. (2013). Considering diversity: The positive effects of considerate leadership in diverse teams. *Group Processes & Intergroup Relations, 16*(1), 105–125.

hooks, b. (1994). *Teaching to transgress: Education as the practice of freedom.* New York: Routledge.

House, R. (1977). A 1976 theory of charismatic leadership. In J. Hunt & L. Larson (Eds), *Leadership: The cutting edge* (pp. 189–207). Carbondale, IL: Southern Illnois University Press.

House, R. J., Hanges, P. J., Javidan, M., Dorfman, P. W., & Gupta, V. (Eds.). (2004). *Culture, leadership, and organizations: The GLOBE study of 62 societies.* Thousand Oaks, CA: Sage.

House, R. J., Hanges, P. J., Ruiz-Quintanilla, S. A., Dorfman, P. W., Javidan, M., Dickson, M., & 170 co-authors (1999). Cultural influences on leadership and organizations: Project GLOBE. In W. F. Mobley, M. J. Gessner, & V. Arnold (Eds.), *Advances in global leadership* (Vol. *1*, pp. 171–233). Stamford, CT: JAI Press.

House, R, J., Javidan, M., Hanges, P. J., & Dorfman, P. (2002). Understanding cultures and implicit leadership theories: An introduction to project GLOBE. *Journal of World Business, 37*(1), 3–10.

House, R. J., Wright, N. S., & Aditya, R. N. (1997). Cross-cultural research on organizational leadership: A critical analysis and a proposed theory. In P. C. Earley & M. Erez (Eds.), *New perspectives in international industrial organizational psychology* (pp. 535–625). San Francisco: New Lexington.

Hoyt, C. L., & Blascovich, J. (2007). Leadership efficacy and women leaders' responses to stereotype activation. *Group Processes and Intergroup Relations, 10,* 595–616. doi:10.1177/1368430207084718

Hugo, G. (2005). *Migrants in society: Diversity and cohesion.* A paper prepared for the Policy Analysis and Research Programme of the Global Commission on International Migration. Geneva, Switzerland.

Hurtado, S. (2007). Linking diversity with the educational and civic missions of higher education. *The Review of Higher Education, 30*(2), 185–196. doi:10.1353/rhe.2006.0070

Husbands, R., & Stubblefield-Tave, B. (2004). University of Texas College of Pharmacy Cultural Proficiency Assessment, 2004 [Unpublished].

Husbands, R., & Stubblefield-Tave, B. (2008). *Measuring cultural competence.* Dallas, TX: University of Texas, MD Anderson Cancer Center.

Israel, M., & Hay, I. (2006). *Research ethics for social scientists: Between ethical conduct and regulatory compliance.* Thousand Oaks, CA: Sage.

Iwasaki, Y., MacKay, K. J., & Ristock, J. (2004, Feb.). Gender-based analyses of stress among professional managers: An exploratory qualitative study. *International Journal of Stress Management, 11*(1), 56–79.

Jasim, A. S. (1987). *Mohammad: Al-Haqiqaha al-kubra* [Mohammed: The greatest truth]. Beinit: Dar al-Andalus.

Jason, L., Keys, C., Suarez-Balcazar, Y., & Davis, M. (Eds.). (2004). *Participatory community research: Theories and methods in action.* Washington, DC: American Psychological Association.

Jensen, S. M., & Luthans, F. (2006). Relationship between entrepreneurs' psychological capital and their authentic leadership. *Journal of Managerial Issues, 18*(2), 254–273.

Johnson, T. P. (1998). Approaches to equivalence in cross-cultural and cross-national research. In J. A. Harkness (Ed.), *Zuma-nachrichten spezial* (pp. 1–40). Mannheim, Germany: ZUMA.

Judge, T. A., & Piccolo, R. F. (2004). Transformational and transactional leadership: A meta-analytic test of their relative validity. *Journal of Applied Psychology, 89,* 901–910. doi:10.1037/0021–9010.89.5.755

Judge, T. A., Piccolo, R. F., & Ilies, R. (2004). The forgotten ones? The validity of consideration and initiating structure in leadership research. *Journal of Applied Psychology, 89,* 36–51.

Misumi, J., & Peterson, M. F. (1985). The Performance-Maintenance (PM) Theory of leadership: Review of a Japanese research program. *Administrative Science Quarterly, 30*(2), 198–223.

Kao, H. S., Sinha, D., & Wilpert, B. (1999). *Management and cultural values: The indigenization of organizations in Asia.* Thousand Oaks, CA: Sage.

Kaschak, E. (2010). The mattering map: Confluence and influence. *Women and Therapy, 34*(1–2).

Kasprak, J. (1997, April 14). Community Benefits—HMOs in Massachusetts, Connecticut Office of Legislative Research Report, #97-R-0591.

Katz, A., & Thompson, J. (1996). The role of public policy in health care market change. *Health Affairs, 15*(2), 77–91.

Katz, J. P., & Seifer, D. M. (1996). It's a different world out there: Planning for expatriate success through selection, pre-departure training and on-site social-ization. *Human Resource Planning, 19*(2), 32–47.

Kellerman, B. (2004). *Bad leadership: What it is, how it happens, why it matters.* Boston, MA: Harvard Business School Press.

Kenney, R. A., Blasovich, J., & Shaver, P. R. (1994). Implicit leadership theories: Prototypes for new leaders. *Basic and Applied Social Psychology, 15,* 409–437.

Khadra, B. (1990). The Prophetic-Caliphal model of leadership: An empirical study. *International Studies of Management & Organization, 20*(3), 37–51.

Kidwell, C. S., Willis, D. J., Jones-Saumty, D., & Bigfoot, D. S. (2007). In J. L. Chin, B. Lott, J. K. Rice, & J. Sanchez-Hucles. (Eds.). *Women and leadership: Transforming visions and diverse voices* (pp. 314–329). Malden, MA: Blackwell.

Kilburg, R. R. (2012). *Virtuous leaders: Strategy, character, and influence in the 21st century.* Washington, DC: American Psychological Association.

Kite, M. E., Deaux, K., & Haines, E. L. (2008). Gender stereotypes. In F. L. Denmark & M. A. Paludi (Eds.), *Psychology of women: A handbook of issues and theories* (2nd ed., pp. 205–236). Westport, CT: Praeger.

Kivisto, P., & Nefzger, B. (1993). Symbolic ethnicity and American Jews: The relationship of ethnic identity to behavior and group affiliation. *Social Science Journal, 30,* 1–12.

Klein, R. H., Rice, C. A., & Schermer, V. L. (2009). *Leadership in a changing world: Dynamic perspectives on groups and their leaders.* Lanham, MD: Lexington Books.

Kluckhohn, F., & Strodtbeck, F. K. (1961). *Variations in value orientation.* Evanston, IL: Row, Petersen.

Kobben, A. (1970). Comparativists and non-comparativists in anthropology. In R. Naroll & R. Cohen (Eds.), *A handbook of method in cultural anthropology* (pp. 1282–1289). New York: Natural History Press.

Koenig, A. M., Eagly, A. H., Mitchell, A. A., & Ristikari, T. (2011). Are leader ste-reotypes masculine? *A meta-analysis of three research paradigms. Psychological Bulletin, 137*(4), 616–642. doi:10.1037/a0023557

Kolb, D., & Williams, J. (2000). *Shadow negotiation: How women can master the hidden agendas that determine bargaining success.* New York: Simon & Schuster.

Korabik, K. (1990). Androgyny and leadership style. *Journal of Business Ethics, 9*, 9–18.

Kouzes, J. M., & Posner, B. Z. (2002). *The leadership challenge* (3rd ed.). San Francisco: Jossey-Bass.

LaFromboise, T., Coleman, H. L. K., & Gorton, J. (1993). Psychological impact of acculturation: Evidence and theory. *Psychological Bulletin, 114*, 395–412.

Lama, D. (n.d.). *Three Main Commitments*. Retrieved from http://www.dalailama .com/biography/three-main-committments

Lama, D., XIV. (n.d.). *Good reads*. Retrieved from http://www.goodreads.com/ quotes/246286-the-topic-of-compassion-is-not-at-all-religious-business

Laverack, G. (2001). An identification and interpretation of the organizational aspects of community empowerment. *Oxford University Press and Community Development Journal, 36*(2), 134–145.

Lee, J.-K. (2001). Confucian thought affecting leadership and organizational culture of Korean higher education. *Radical Pedagogy, 3*(3), 1–12.

Lee, Y.-T. (2004). What can chairs learn from Daoistic/Taoistic leadership? An Eastern perspective. *The Department Chair, 14*(4), 25–32.

Lee, Y.-T., Haught, H. Chen, K., & Chan, S. (2013). Examining Daoist big-five leadership in cross-cultural and gender perspectives. *Asian American Journal of Psychology, 4*(3), 267–276.

Leslie, L. M., King, E. B., Bradley, J. C., & Hebl, M. R. (2008). Triangulation across methodologies: All signs point to persistent stereotyping and discrimination in organizations. *Industrial and Organizational Psychology: Perspectives on Science and Practice, 1*, 399–404. doi:10.1111/J.1754–9434.2008.00073.x

Lester, S. (1999). *An introduction to phenomenological research*. Taunton, UK: Stan Lester Developments. Retrieved from: www.sld.demon.co.uk/resmethy.pdf

Leung, A. K., Maddux, W. W., Galinsky, A. D., & Chiu, C. (2008). Multicultural experience enhances creativity: The when and how. *American Psychologist, 63*, 169–181. doi:10.1037/0003–066X.63.3.169

Li, E. (2013). *Zhang Zai on becoming a sage: An interpretation based on virtue ethics, philosophical psychology and moral cognitive development* (Unpublished doctoral dissertation). Peking University, Beijing, China.

Li, J. (2012). *Cultural foundations of learning: East and West*. New York: Cambridge University Press.

Liu, Y. (2013, February). Exploring the impact of organizational culture on paternalistic leadership in Chinese SMEs. Proceedings of 3rd Asia-Pacific Business Research Conference, Kuala Lumpur, Malaysia. Retrieved from http://www .wbiworldconpro.com/uploads/malaysia-conference-2013/finance/341-Zahiruddin.pdf

Livers, A., & Caver, K. (2002). *Leading in Black and White: Working across the racial divide in corporate America* (p. 150). San Francisco: Jossey-Bass.

Lord, R. G. (1986). A meta-analysis of the relation between personality traits and leadership perceptions: An application of validity generalization procedures. *Journal of Applied Psychology, 71*, 402–410.

Lord, R. G., Brown, D. J., & Freiberg, S. J. (1999). Understanding the dynamics of leadership: The role of follower self-concepts in the leader/follower relationship. *Organizational Behavior and Human Decision Process*, 78, 1–37.

Lord, R. G., Foti, R. J., & DeVader, C. L. (1984). A test of leadership categorization theory: Internal structure, information processing, and leadership perceptions. *Organizational Behavior and Human Performance*, 34, 343–378.

Lord, R. G., & Hall, R. (2007). Identity, leadership categorization, and leadership schema. In D. van Knippenberg & M. A. Hogg (Eds.), *Leadership and power: Identity processes in groups and organizations*. Thousand Oaks, CA: Sage.

Lord, R. G., & Maher, K. J. (1991). *Leadership and information processing*. London: Routledge.

Lovegrow, N. & Thomas, M. (2013). Why the world needs Tri-Sector Leaders. *Harvard Business Review, HBR Blog Network*, February-13 -2013. Retrieved from http://blogs.hbr.org/cs/2013/02/why_the_world_needs_tri-sector.html October 13, 2013.

Mandela, N. (n.d.). Brainy quote. Retrieved from http://www.brainyquote.com/quotes/n/nelsonmand393048.html

Marin, G., & Marin, B. (1991). *Research with Hispanic populations*. Newbury Park, CA: Sage.

Markus, H., & Kitayama, S. (1991). Culture and the self: Implications for cognition, emotion, and motivation. *Psychological Review*, 98(2), 224–253.

Mattis, J. S., & Jagers, R. J. (2001). A relational framework for the study of religiosity and spirituality in the lives of African Americans. *Journal of Community Psychology*, 29(5), 519–539.

McAdams, D. P., & Pals, J. L. (2006). A new big five: Fundamental principles for an integrative science of personality. *American Psychologist*, 6, 204–217. doi:10.1037/0003–066X.3.204

McCall, M. W., & Hollenbeck, G. P. (2002). *Developing global executives: The lessons of international experience*. Boston, MA: Harvard Business School Press.

McClelland, D. C. (1985). *Human motivation*. Glenview, IL: Scott, Foresman.

McGorry, S.Y. (2000). Measurement in a cross-cultural environment: Survey translation issues. *Qualitative Market Research: An International Journal*, 3(2), 74–81.

McGregor, D. (1985). *The human side of enterprise*. New York: McGraw-Hill.

McGrory, M. (2002, November 16). Pelosi's a salve for a wounded party. *The Boston Globe*.

McIntosh, P. (1989, July/August). White privilege: Unpacking the invisible knapsack. *Peace and Freedom*, pp. 8–10.

McKenna, S. (1995). The business impact of management attitudes towards dealing with conflict: A cross-cultural assessment. *Journal of Managerial Psychology*, 10(7), 22–27.

Michener, L., Cook, J., Ahmed, S. M., Yonas, M. A., Coyne-Beasley, T., & Aguliar-Gaxiola, S. (2012). Aligning the goals of community-engaged research: Why and how academic health centers can successfully engage with communities to improve health. *Academic Medicine*, 87(3), 285–291.

Military Leadership DiversityCommission. (2011). *From representation to inclusion: Diversity leadership for the 21st century military, executive summary.* Arlington, VA: Military Leadership Diversity Commission.

Misumi, J., & Peterson, M. F. (1985). The Performance-Maintenance (PM) Theory of leadership: Review of a Japanese research program. *Administrative Science Quarterly, 30*(2), 198–223.

Misumi, J., & Seki, F. (1971). Effects of achievement motivation on the effectiveness of leadership patterns. *Administrative Science Quarterly, 16*(1), 51.

Mohatt, G. V. (1989). The community as informant or collaborator? *American Indian and Alaska Mental Health Research, 2,* 64–70.

Molinsky, A. (2007). Cross-cultural code switching: The psychological challenges of adapting behavior in foreign cultural interactions. *Academy of Management Review, 32,* 622–640.

Moodian, M. A. (2009). *Contemporary leadership and intercultural competence: Exploring the cross-cultural dynamics within organizations.* Thousand Oaks, CA: Sage.

Moore, B. (2006, October 31). What is time orientation? *India Think.* Retrieved from http://indiathink.com/what-is-time-orientation-updated/

Moore, M. R. (1989). Native American water rights: Efficiency and fairness. *Natural Resources Journal, 29,* 763–791.

Mor Barak, M. E. (2011). *Managing diversity: Toward a globally inclusive workplace.* Thousand Oaks, CA: Sage.

Moritsugu, J. (1999). Cultural competence. In J. Mio, J. Trimble, P. Arredondo, H. Cheatham, & D. Sue (Eds.), *Keywords in multicultural interventions: A dictionary* (pp. 62–63). Westport, CT: Greenwood.

Moritsugu, J., Arellano, Y. Boelk, K., Pfeninger, G. R., & Chin, J. L. (in progress). Diversity leadership: A qualitative study of a synergistic phenomenon.

Mother Teresa. (n.d.). Mother Teresa of Calcutta Center. Retrieved from http://www.motherteresa.org/layout.html

Moynihan, D. P. (1993). *Pandaemonium: Ethnicity in international politics.* New York: Oxford University Press.

Musteen, M., Barker, V. L., III, & Baeten, V. L. (2006). CEO attributes associated with attitude toward change: The direct and moderating effects of CEO tenure. *Journal of Business Research, 59,* 604–612. doi:10.1016/j.busres.2005.10.008

Nelson, D. L., & Campbell Quick, J. (2003). *Organizational behavior: Foundations, realities, and challenges* (4th ed.). Mason, OH: Thomson South-Western.

Neuendorf, K. A., Atkin, D., & Jeffres, L. W. (2000). Explorations of the Simpson Trial "Racial Divide". *The Howard Journal of Communications, 11,* 247–266.

Nisbett, R. E., & Masuda, T. (2003). Culture and point of view. *Proceedings of the National Academy of Sciences of the USA, 100*(19), 11163–11170. doi:10.1073/pnas.1934527100

Northouse, P. G. (2004). *Leadership: Theory and practice* (3rd ed.). Thousand Oaks, CA: Sage.

Orlandi, M. (Ed.). (1992). *Cultural competence for evaluators working with ethnic minority communities: A guide for alcohol and other drug abuse prevention practitioners*. Rockville, MD: Office for Substance Abuse Prevention, Cultural Competence Series 1.

Orlitzky, M., Schmidt, F., & Rynes, S. I. (2003). Corporate social and financial performance: A meta-analysis. *Organization Studies, 24*(3), 403–431.

Ospina, S., & Foldy, E. (2009). A critical review of race and ethnicity in the leadership literature: Surfacing context, power and the collective dimensions of leadership. *The Leadership Quarterly, 20,* 876–896.

Ouchi, W. (1981). *Theory Z.* Reading, MA: Addison-Wesley.

Parker, P. S. (2005). *Race, gender, and leadership: Re-envisioning organizational leadership from the perspectives of African American women executives.* Mahwah, NJ: Lawrence Erlbaum.

Parker, P. S., & Ogilvie, D. T. (1996). Gender, culture, and leadership: Toward a culturally distinct model of African-American women executives' leadership strategies. *Leadership Quarterly, 7,* 189–214. doi:10.1016/S1048-9843(96)90040-5

Patton, G. (n.d.). Patton quote. Retrieved from http://en.wikiquote.org/George_S._Patton

Paz, S. (2003). Cultural competency. *The School Administrator, 65*(10), 1–5.

Pedersen, P. (Ed.). (1999). *Multiculturalism as a fourth force.* Philadelphia: Brunner/Mazel.

Pellegrini, E. K., & Scandura, T. A. (2008). Paternalistic leadership: A review and agenda for future research. *Journal of Management, 34*(3), 566–593.

Pellegrini, E. K., Scandura, T. A., & Jayaraman, V. (2007). *Generalizability of the paternalistic leadership concept: A cross-cultural investigation* (working paper). University of Missouri–St. Louis.

Pellegrini, E. K., Scandura, T. A., & Jayaraman, V. (2010). Cross-cultural generalizability of paternalistic leadership: An expansion of leader-member exchange theory. *Group & Organization Management, 35*(4), 391–420.

Perlmann, J., & Waters, M. (Eds.). (2002). *The new race question: How the census counts multiracial individuals* (pp. 354–360). New York: Russell Sage Foundation.

Pew Research Center. (2011). *Muslim Americans: No signs of growth in alienation or support for extremism.* Washington, DC: Author.

Phinney, J. S. (1990). Ethnic identity in adolescents and adults: Review of research. *Psychological Bulletin, 108,* 499–514.

Phinney, J. (2000). Ethnic identity. In A. E. Kazdin (Ed.), *Encyclopedia of psychology* (Vol. 3, pp. 254–259). New York: Oxford University Press.

Phinney, J. (2003). Ethnic identity and acculturation. In K. Chun, P. B. Organista, & G. Marin (Eds.), *Acculturation: Advances in theory, measurement, and applied research* (pp. 63–81). Washington, DC: American Psychological Association.

Ping Ping, F., Hau-siu Chow, I., & Yuli, Z. (2001). Leadership approaches and perceived leadership effectiveness in Chinese township and village. *Journal of Asian Business, 17*(1), 1–15.

Pittinsky, T. L. (2010). A two-dimensional model of intergroup leadership: The case of national diversity. *American Psychologist, 65*(3), 194–200.

Pixton, P. (n.d.). Collaborative leadership: An overview. Retrieved from: http://www
.leadit.us/it-business-management/Collaborative-Leadership-An-Overview

Polzer, J. T., Milton, L. P., & Swann, W. B., Jr. (2002). Capitalizing on diversity: Interpersonal congruence in small work groups. *Administrative Science Quarterly, 47,* 296–324.

Poortinga, Y. (1975). Some implications of three different approaches to intercultural comparison. In J. Berry & W. Lonner (Eds.), *Applied cross-cultural psychology* (pp. 237–257). Amsterdam: Swets & Zeitlinger.

Poortinga, Y. (1983). Psychometric approaches to intergroup comparison: The problem of equivalence. In S. Irvine & J. Berry (Eds.), *Human assessment and cultural factors* (pp. 237–257). New York: Plenum.

Pope-Davis, D., & Coleman, H. (Eds.). (1997). *Multicultural counseling competencies: Assessment, education and training, and supervision.* Thousand Oaks, CA: Sage.

Prewitt, K. (2002). Race in the 2000 census: A turning point. In J. Perlmann & M. C. Waters (Eds.), *The new race question: How the census counts multiracial persons* (pp. 354–362). New York: Taylor & Francis.

Ragins, B., Townsend, B., & Mattis, M. (1998). Gender gap in the executive suite: CEOs and female executives report on breaking the glass ceiling. *Academy of Management Executive, 12*(1), 28–42.

Randolph, S. M., & Banks, D. H. (1993). Making a way out of no way: The promise of Africentric approaches to HIV prevention. *Journal of Black Psychology, 19*(2), 204–214.

Rawlings, N. (2012, August 2). Danny Chen suicide reflects Army's failure of leadership. *TIME.com.* Retrieved from http://nation.time.com/2012/08/02/a-young-privates-suicide-reflects-a-massive-failure-of-leadership/#ixzz2q8wjQ2pm

Rawwas, M. Y. A. (2003). The influence of leadership styles, conflict management, and individual characteristics on motivation: A cross cultural study of business supervisors. *Journal of Asian Business, 19*(1), 37–65.

Ridgeway, C. (2007). Status characteristics and leadership. In D. van Knippenberg & M. A. Hogg (Eds.). *Leadership and power: Identity processes in groups and organizations.* Thousand Oaks, CA: Sage.

Rikabi, F. (1964). *Al-Thawarah at-Arabiyyah al-Ishtirakiyyah Wai Tanzim* [Arab socialist revolution and organization]. Cairo, Egypt: Dar al-Kitab al Arabi.

Rodrigues, C. A. (2001). Fayol's 14 principles of management then and now: A framework for managing today's organizations effectively. *Management Decision, 39,* 880–889.

Rodriguez, C. L., Galbraith, C. S., & Stiles, C. H. (2006). American Indian collectivism: Past myth, present reality. *PERC Report, 24*(2).

Rodríguez, E., Allen, J. A., Frongillo, E. A., & Chandra, P. (1999). Unemployment, depression, health: A look at the African-American community. *Journal of Epidemiology Community Health, 53*(6), 335–342.

Root, M. P. (1992). Back to the drawing board: Methodological issues in research on multiracial people. In M. P. Root (Ed.), *Racially mixed people in America* (pp. 181–189). London: Sage.

Rory (June 26, 2013). Working with Latinos: Paternalism. *Common Ground International*. http://commongroundinternational.com/bilingual_workplace/paternalism-in-the-workplace/ Retrieved December 20, 2013.

Rosener, J. B. (1990). Ways women lead. *Harvard Business Review*, 68(6), 119–125.

Rosette, A. S., & Tost, L. P. (2010). Agentic women and communal leadership: How role prescriptions confer advantage to top women leaders. *Journal of Applied Psychology*, 95(2), 221–235.

Rost, J. C. (1991). *Leadership for the twenty first century*. Westport, CN: Praeger Publishers.

Rubin, H. (2009). *Collaborative leadership: Developing effective partnerships for communities and schools*. Thousand Oaks, CA: Corwin.

Rudman, L. A., & Glick, P. (2001). Prescriptive gender stereotypes and backlash toward agentic women. *Journal of Social Issues*, 57(4), 743–762.

Russell, R., & Falkner, D. (2001). *Russell rules: 11 lessons on leadership from the twentieth century's greatest winner*. New York: Penguin Putnam.

Sanchez-Hucles, J. V., & Davis, D. D. (2010). Women and women of color in leadership: Complexity, identity, and intersectionality. *American Psychologist*, 65, 171–181. doi:10.1037/a0017459

Sanchez-Hucles, J., & Sanchez, P. (2007). In J. L. Chin, B. Lott, J. K. Rice, & J. Sanchez-Hucles, *Women and leadership: Transforming visions and diverse voices* (pp. 211–227). Malden, MA: Blackwell.

Sayegh, A. (1965). *Fi Mc^houm al-Za'ama al-Siyassiyyah inda al-Arab* [On the concept of Arab political leadership]. Beirut: Al-Maktabah al Assriyyah.

Schein, E. H. (2004). *Organizational culture and leadership* (3rd ed.). San Francisco: Jossey-Bass.

Schwartz, P. (2010). Inevitable strategies. In G. R. Hickman (Ed.), *Leading organizations: Perspectives for a new era* (pp. 4–13). Thousand Oaks, CA: Sage.

Shah, D. (2013, October 16). How to uncover your company's true culture. Diversity Executive Magazine. Retrieved from http://www.linkedin.com/today/post/article/20131016164310-658789-how-to-uncover-your-company-s-true-culture?utm_content=bufferf1963&utm_source=buffer&utm_medium=linkedin&utm_campaign=Buffer#%21

Shaller, D. (2007, October). Patient-centered care: What does it take? *The Commonwealth Fund*, 74.

Shirey, M. R. (2006). Authentic leaders creating health work environments for nursing practice. *American Journal of Critical Care*, 15, 256–267.

Silverthorne, C. (2001). Leadership effectiveness and personality: A cross cultural evaluation. *Personality and Individual Differences*, 30(2), 303–309.

Smedley, B., Stith, A., & Nelson, A. (2003). *Unequal treatment: Confronting racial and ethnic disparities in health care* (p. 1). Washington, DC: The National Academies Press, Institute of Medicine.

Smith, L. T. (1999). *Decolonizing methodologies: Research and indigenous peoples*. New York: St. Martin's Press.

Snyder, K. (2006). *The G quotient: Why gay executives are excelling as leaders . . . and what every manager needs to know*. San Francisco: Jossey-Bass.

Sowell, T. (1994). *Race and culture.* New York: Basic Books.

Spillane, J. P. (2006). *Distributed leadership.* San Francisco: Jossey-Bass.

Spreier, S. W., Fontaine, M. H., & Malloy, R. L. (2006). Leadership run amok. *Harvard Business Review, 84*(6), 72–82.

Starratt, R. J. (2007). Leading a community of learners. *Educational Management Administration & Leadership, 35*(2), 165–183.

Steele, C. M. (1995). Stereotype threat and the intellectual test performance of African Americans. *Journal of Personality and Social Psychology, 69,* 797–811.

Sternberg, R. (2007). Special Issue: Leadership. *American Psychologist, 62*(1), 1–47.

Stubblefield-Tave, B. (2013). Leveraging the power of culturally fluent leadership: Leading more effective teams [Unpublished report].

Sue, D. W. (1978). World views and counseling. *Personnel and Guidance Journal, 56,* 458–462.

Sue, D. W., Arredondo, P., & McDavis, R. J. (1992). Multicultural competencies and standards: A call to the profession. *Journal of Counseling & Development, 70,* 477–486.

Sue, D. W., Capodilupo, C. M., Torino, G. C., Bucceri, J. M., Holder, A. M. B., Nadal, K. L., & Esquilin, M. (2007). Racial microaggressions in everyday life: Implications for clinical practice. *American Psychologist, 62*(4), 271–286.

Sue, D., Carter, R., Casas, J. M., Fouad, N., Ivey, A., Jensen, M., . . . & Vazquez,-Nutall, E. (1998). *Multicultural counseling competencies: Individual and organizational development.* Thousand Oaks, CA: Sage.

Tajfel, H. (1982). *Social identity and intergroup relations.* New York: Cambridge University Press.

Tajfel, H., & Turner, J. (1986). The social identity theory of intergroup behavior. In S. Worchel & W. G. Austin (Eds.), *Psychology of intergroup relations* (pp. 7–24). Chicago, IL: Nelson-Hall.

Tervalon, M., & Murray Garcia, J. (1998). Cultural humility versus cultural competence: A critical distinction in defining physician training outcomes in multicultural education. *Journal of Health Care for the Poor and Underserved, 9*(2), 117–25.

Thomas, D. A., & Gabarro, J. J. (1999). *Breaking through: The making of minority executives in corporate America.* Cambridge, MA: Harvard Business School Press.

Thomas, D. C. (2008). *Cross cultural management.* Thousand Oaks, CA: Sage.

Thomas, D. C., & Ravlin, E. C. (1995). Responses of employees to cultural adaptation by a foreign manager. *Journal of Applied Psychology, 80,* 133–146.

Thomas, K. W. (1976). A survey of managerial interests with respect to conflict. *Academy of Management Journal, 19,* 315–318.

Triandis, H. (1993). The contingency model in cross-cultural leadership. In M. M. Chemers & R. Ayman (Eds.), *Leadership theory and research: Perspectives and directions* (pp. 167–188). San Diego, CA: Academic Press.

Triandis, H. C. (1995). *Individualism and collectivism.* Boulder, CO: Westview Press.

Trickett, E. J., & Espino, S. L. R. (2004). Collaboration and social inquiry: Multiple meanings of a construct and its role in creating useful and valid knowledge. *American Journal of Community Psychology, 34*(1–2), 1–69.

Trickett, E. J., Kelly, J. G., & Vincent, T. A. (1985). The spirit of ecological inquiry in community research. In E. Susskind & D. Klein (Eds.), *Community research: Methods, paradigms, and applications* (pp. 331–406). New York: Praeger.

Trimble, J. E. (1991). Ethnic specification, validation prospects, and the future of drug use research. *International Journal of the Addictions, 25*(2A), 149–170.

Trimble, J. E. (1995). Toward an understanding of ethnicity and ethnic identity, and their relationship with drug use research. In G. Botvin, S. Schinke, & M. Orlandi (Eds.), *Drug abuse prevention with multiethnic youth* (pp. 3–27). Thousand Oaks, CA: Sage.

Trimble, J. E. (2005). An inquiry into the measurement of racial and ethnic identity. In R. Carter (Ed.), *Handbook of racial-cultural psychology and counseling: Theory and research* (Vol. *1*, pp. 320–359). New York: Wiley.

Trimble, J. E. (2010). Cultural measurement equivalence. In C. S. Clauss-Ehlers (Ed.), *Encyclopedia of cross-cultural school psychology* (pp. 316–318). New York: Springer.

Trimble, J. E. (2013). Advancing understanding of cultural competence, cultural sensitivity, and the effects of cultural incompetence. In M. Prinstein & M. Patterson (Eds.), *The portable mentor: Expert guide to a successful career in psychology, second edition.* NY: Kluwer Academic/Plenum.

Trimble, J. E., & Bhadra, M. (2013). Ethnic gloss. In K. Keith (Ed.), *Encyclopedia of cross-cultural psychology* (pp. 500–504). New York: Wiley.

Trimble, J. E., & Dickson, R. (2005). Ethnic identity. In C. B. Fisher & Lerner, R. M. (Eds.), *Applied developmental science: An encyclopedia of research, policies, and programs.* Thousand Oaks, CA: Sage.

Trimble, J. E., & Fisher, C. B. (Eds.). (2005). *Handbook of ethical considerations in conducting research with ethnocultural populations and communities.* Thousand Oaks, CA: Sage.

Trimble, J. E., Lonner, W., & Boucher, J. (1984). Stalking the wily emic: Alternatives to cross-cultural measurement. In S. Irvine & J. Berry (Eds.), *Human assessment and cultural factors* (pp. 259–273). New York: Plenum.

Trimble, J. E., & Mohatt, G. V. (2005). Coda: The virtuous and responsible researcher in another culture. In J. E. Trimble & C. B. Fisher (Eds.), *The handbook of ethical research with ethnocultural populations and communities.* Thousand Oaks, CA: Sage.

Trimble, J. E., & Vaughn, L. (2013). Cultural measurement equivalence. In K. Keith (Ed.), *Encyclopedia of Cross-Cultural Psychology* (pp. 313–319). New York: Wiley.

Trinidad, C., & Normore, A. H. (2005). Leadership and gender: A dangerous liaison? *Leadership & Organization Development Journal, 26*(7), 574–590.

Trompenaars, F., & Hampden-Turner, C. (1998). *Riding the waves of culture: Understanding cultural diversity in global business* (2nd ed.). New York: McGraw-Hill.

Trompenaars, F., & Woolliams, P. (2009). Getting the measure of intercultural leadership. In M. A. Moodian (Ed.). (2009). *Contemporary leadership and intercultural competence: Exploring the cross-cultural dynamics within organizations* (pp. 161–174). Thousand Oaks, CA: Sage.

Tsui, A. S., Wang, H., Xin, C., Zhang, L., & Fu, P. P. (2004). "Let a thousand flowers bloom": Variation of leadership styles among Chinese CEOs. *Organizational Dynamics, 33*(1), 5–20.

Tyler, T. R. (1997). The psychology of legitimacy: A relational perspective on voluntary deference to authorities. *Personality and Social Psychology Review, 1,* 323–345.

U. S. Census Bureau. (2013, March). *Overview of race and Hispanic Origin: 2010.* Washington, DC: Government Printing Office.

U. S. Department of Health and Human Services, Office of Minority Health. (2001). *National Standards for Culturally and Linguistically Appropriate Services in Health Care.* Washington, DC: Government Printing Office.

U.S. Department of Labor. (1991). Foreword. *A Report on the Glass Ceiling Initiative.* Washington, DC: Government Printing Office

Van de Vijver, F. (2000). The nature of bias. In R. H. Dana (Ed.), *Handbook of cross-cultural and multicultural personality assessment* (pp. 87–106). Mahwah, NJ: Lawrence Erlbaum.

van Knippenberg, D., & Hogg, M. A. (2007). *Leadership and power: Identity processes in groups and organizations.* Thousand Oaks, CA: Sage.

van Knippenberg, D., & Schippers, M. C. (2007). Work group diversity. *Annual Review of Psychology, 58,* 515–541.

Vecchio, R. P. (2003). In search of gender advantage. *Leadership Quarterly, 14*(6), 835–850.

Walker, B., & Henson, W. (1992). Valuing differences at Digital Equipment Corporation. In S. E. Jackson (Ed.), *Diversity in the workplace: Human resources initiatives* (pp. 119–137). New York: Guilford Press.

Walumbwa, F. O., Avolio, B. J., Gardner, W. L., Wernsing, T. A., & Peterson, S. J. (2008). Authentic leadership: Development and validation of a theory-based measure. *Journal of Management, 34*(1), 89–126.

Warner, L. S., & Grint, K. (2006). American Indian ways of leading and knowing. *Leadership, 2*(2), 225–244.

Wartman, S. A. (n.d.). *The Academic Health Center: Evolving organizational models.* Retrieved from http://www.aahcdc.org/Portals/0/pdf/AAHC_Evolving_ Organizational_Models.pdf

Weinreich, P., & Saunderson, W. (Eds.). (2003). *Analysing identity: Cross-cultural, societal, and clinical contexts.* New York: Routledge.

Wenquan, L., Chia, R. C., & Liluo, F. (2000). Chinese implicit leadership theory. *Journal of Social Psychology, 140*(6), 729–739

Westwood, R. (1997). Harmony and patriarchy: The cultural basis for "paternalistic headship" among the overseas Chinese. *Organization Studies, 18,* 445–480.

Westwood, R., & Chan, A. (1992). Headship and leadership. In R. Westwood (Ed.), *Organisational behaviour: Southeast Asian perspectives* (pp. 118–143). Hong Kong: Longman.

White, A. A. (2011). *Seeing patients: Unconscious bias in health care.* Cambridge, MA: Harvard University Press.

Whitehead, G. E., & Brown, M. (2011). Authenticity in Chinese leadership: A quantitative study comparing Western notions of authentic constructs with Chinese responses to an authenticity instrument. *International Journal of Leadership Studies, 6*(2), 162–188.

Wielkiewicz, R. M. (2007). Special issue on leadership falls behind. *American Psychologist,* 605–606.

Wong, K.-C. (2001). Chinese culture and leadership. *International Journal of Leadership in Education, 4*(4), 309–319.

Woods, P. A. (2007). Authenticity in the bureau-enterprise culture. *Educational Management Administration & Leadership, 35*(2), 295–320.

Yabusaki, A. (2007). Diverse feminist communication styles: Challenges to women and leadership. In J. L. Chin, B. Lott, J. K. Rice, & J. Sanchez-Hucles (Eds.), *Women and leadership: Transforming visions and diverse voices* (pp. 55–68). Malden, MA: Blackwell.

Yan, Y. (1996). *The flow of gifts: Reciprocity and social networks in a Chinese village.* Stanford, CA: Stanford University Press.

Yang, K. S. (2006). Indigenous personality research. The Chinese case. In U. Kim & K.-K. Hwang (Eds.), *Indigenous and cultural psychology: Understanding people in context* (pp. 285–314). New York: Springer. doi:10.1007/0-37-28662-4_13

Ye, J. (2002). Will China be a "threat" to its neighbors and the world in the twenty first century? *Ritsumeikan Annual Review of International Studies, 1,* 55–68.

Young, R. B. (1997). *No neutral ground: Standing by the values we prize in higher education.* San Francisco: Jossey-Bass.

Yukl, G. (2010). *Leadership in organizations* (7th ed.). Upper Saddle River, NJ: Prentice Hall.

Yukl, G., & Mahsud, R., (2010). Why flexible and adaptive leadership is essential. *Consulting Psychology Journal: Practice and Research, 62*(2), 81–93.

Zahorski, K. J., & Cognard, R. (1999). Reconsidering faculty roles and rewards: Promising practices for institutional transformation and enhanced learning. *A report on CAPHE's faculty roles, faculty rewards, and institutional priorities grant program.* Washington, DC: Council of Independent Colleges.

Zimbardo, P. (2007). *The Lucifer effect: Understanding how good people turn evil.* New York: Random House.

Zweigenhaft, R. L., & Domhoff, G. W. (2006). *Diversity in the power elite: How it happened, why it matters.* New York: Rowman & Littlefield.

Index

Tables are indicated by a t following the page number.

About the Authors

Jean Lau Chin, EdD, ABPP, is Professor at Adelphi University in New York. She has held senior management positions as Dean at Alliant International University, and at Adelphi University, and as Executive Director of South Cove Community Health Center, and the Thom mental health clinic. Currently, her work on leadership, diversity, and women's issues has included being an Oxford Roundtable speaker, a senior Fulbright Specialist, author of 15 books, 21 book chapters, 25 peer reviewed journal publications, and over 180 professional talks. As past President of The Society for the Psychological Study of Race, Ethnicity, and Culture (Division 45) and The Society for the Psychology of Women (Division 35) within the American Psychological Association, her presidential initiatives on leadership promoted the integration of diversity into our models of leadership and helped advance leadership training for women and ethnic minorities. She has served in many leadership positions on national, state, and local boards in which she has promoted grassroots advocacy to impact national policy on mental health and substance abuse issues related to access, cultural competence, women's issues, and eliminating disparities among low-income Asian American communities. She was the first Asian American to be licensed as a psychologist in Massachusetts and to be in a number of her leadership roles. She has received many awards for her leadership and her work on diversity and women; her most recent award includes the Diversity Award by the New York State Psychological Association, and her honoring as a Distinguished Elder at the National Multicultural Conference and Summit.

Joseph E. Trimble, PhD, is a Distinguished University Professor and Professor of Psychology at Western Washington University. He is a President's Professor at the Center for Alaska Native Health Research at the University of Alaska Fairbanks. He has generated over 140 publications on multicultural topics in psychology, including 20 books. He has received numerous excellence in teaching and research awards for his work in the field of multicultural psychology, including the Janet E. Helms Award for Mentoring and Scholarship in Professional Psychology; the Distinguished Elder Award from the National Multicultural Conference and Summit; the Henry Tomes Award for Distinguished Contributions to the Advancement of Ethnic Minority Psychology, the International Lifetime Achievement Award for Multicultural and Diversity Counseling awarded by the University of Toronto's Ontario Institute for Studies in Education; the 2013 Francis J. Bonner, MD Award from the Department of Psychiatry at Massachusetts General Hospital; and the 2013 Elizabeth Hurlock Beckman Award based in Winston-Salem, NC.